# FEAR

# FEAR
## The History of a Political Idea

COREY ROBIN

UNIVERSITY PRESS

2004

# OXFORD
UNIVERSITY PRESS

Oxford   New York
Auckland  Bangkok  Buenos Aires  Cape Town  Chennai
Dar es Salaam  Delhi  Hong Kong  Istanbul  Karachi  Kolkata
Kuala Lumpur  Madrid  Melbourne  Mexico City  Mumbai  Nairobi
São Paulo  Shanghai  Taipei  Tokyo  Toronto

Published by Oxford University Press, Inc., 2004
198 Madison Avenue, New York, New York 10016

www.oup.com

Oxford is a registered trademark of Oxford University Press

Library of Congress Cataloging-in-Publication Data
Robin, Corey, 1967–
Fear: the history of a political idea / by Corey Robin.
    p. cm.
ISBN 0-19-515702-8
1. Political theory.
2. Fear—Political aspects.
I. Title.
JA74.5R48 2004
320'.01'9—dc22    2004006813

Design and composition by Susan Day

9 8 7 6 5 4 3 2 1
Printed in the United States of America
on acid-free paper

TO MY PARENTS

# CONTENTS

# ACKNOWLEDGMENTS

I would like to thank the following friends, colleagues, teachers, and editors, who read and commented upon this manuscript, whether in draft, paper, or article form: Bruce Ackerman, Moustafa Bayoumi, Roger Boesche, Shelley Burtt, Josh Cohen, Peter Cole, Michael Denning, Jack Diggins, Tom Dumm, Sam Farber, Steve Fraser, Josh Freeman, Paul Frymer, Emily Gordon, Greg Grandin, Nancy Grey, Michael Hardt, Adina Hoffman, David Hughes, Judy Hughes, Allen Hunter, Victoria Kahn, Ariel Kaminer, Rebecca Karl, Scott James, David Johnston, Gordon Lafer, Jackson Lears, Chris Lehmann, Mark Levinson, Penny Lewis, Arien Mack, Ian Malcolm, Arno Mayer, David Mayhew, Kirstie McClure, John McCormick, John Medeiras, Laurie Muchnick, Sankar Muthu, Molly Nolan, Karen Orren, Christian Parenti, Kim Phillips-Fein, Francis Fox Piven, Robert Potts, Mel Richter, Jessica Robin, Andy Sabl, Scott Saul, Jim Scott, Ellen Schrecker, Jenny Schuessler, Alex Star, Michelle Stephens, Laura Tanenbaum, Rob Tempio, Peter Terzian, Jeanne Theoharis, Roy Tsao, Michael Walzer, Kathi Weeks, Eve Weinbaum, Keith Whittington, Daniel Wilkinson, Richard Wolin, Brian Young, and Marilyn Young. Special thanks to Rogers Smith, my dissertation advisor, to Tim Bartlett, my editor at Oxford University Press, and to Barbara Fillon, Peter Harper, and Catherine Humphries at Oxford University Press. Generous funding for the completion of this project was provided by the International Center for Advanced Studies of New York University; the Wolfe Institute for the Humanities at Brooklyn College; the Professional Staff Congress of the City University of New York; and the Center for Place, Culture, and Politics at the Graduate

Center of the City University of New York. Finally, a word of thanks to the students, faculty, and staff of Brooklyn College and the Graduate Center of the City University of New York; to Jonathan Stein, who long ago asked me what was so great about Hobbes since "everything with him is fear"; to John Dunn, who first suggested that I shouldn't read Hobbes as if he were Tocqueville; and to my family, for everything.

Portions of this book have appeared elsewhere. Many thanks to the relevant publisher for allowing me to use material from the following:

"Remembrance of Empires Past: 9/11 and the End of the Cold War." In *Cold War Triumphalism: The Misuse of History After the Fall of Communism*, ed. Ellen Schrecker (New York: The New Press, 2004), pp. 274–97.

"Fear, American Style: Civil Liberty After 9/11." In *Implicating Empire: Globalization & Resistance in the 21st Century World Order*, ed. Stanley Aronowitz and Heather Gautney (New York: Basic Books, 2003), pp. 47–64.

"Lavatory and Liberty: The Secret History of the Bathroom Break." *Boston Globe* (September 29, 2002), p. D1.

"Closet-Case Studies." *New York Times Magazine* (December 16, 2001), pp. 23–24.

"Denied the Fruits of Their Labors." *Dissent* (Fall 2001), pp. 131–35.

"Fear: A Genealogy of Morals." *Social Research* 67 (Winter 2000), pp. 1085–1115.

"Reflections on Fear: Montesquieu in Retrieval." *American Political Science Review* 94 (June 2000), pp. 347–60.

"Why Do Opposites Attract? Fear and Freedom in the Modern Political Imagination." In *Fear Itself: Enemies Real and Imagined*, ed. Nancy L. Schultz (West Lafayette, IN: Purdue University Press, 1999).

# FEAR

# Introduction

It is seldom noted, but fear is the first emotion experienced by a character in the Bible. Not desire, not shame, but fear. Adam eats from the tree, discovers he is naked, and hides from God, confessing, "I was afraid, because I was naked." Before this admission, God creates and sees that his creations are good. He sees that Adam is without a mate, which is not good. Eve sees that the tree of knowledge is "pleasant to the eyes, and a tree to be desired to make one wise." But these are reports of antiseptic perception, with no warming murmur of appreciation or aversion. Everyone looks, everyone sees. Does anyone feel? Not until they eat the forbidden fruit do we hear of felt experience. And when we do, it is fear. Why fear? Perhaps it is because, for the authors of the Bible, fear is the most electric of emotions. Prior to being afraid, Adam and Eve exist and act in the world, but without any palpable experience of it. Afraid, they are awash in experience, with God promising even more—for Eve the pain of childbirth, for Adam the duress of work, for both the dread knowledge of death. Unafraid, Adam and Eve have only the laziest appreciation of the good and haziest apprehension of the bad. Their dim cognizance of evil makes them spectators to their own lives, semiconscious actors at best. Adam names, Eve succumbs, but neither really knows what it is that they do. Afraid, they know. Shallow temptation gives way to dramatic choice, inertial motion to elected action. Their story—our story—is ready to begin.[1]

After September 11, 2001, writers tell us, an altogether different kind of fear drove a similar passage from passivity to feeling and action. Before 9/11, Americans were supposed to be in Eden, idling in a warm bath of social autism. According to David Brooks, the ethos of the day was to cultivate our "private paradises," to bask, in the words of Don DeLillo, in "the utopian glow of cyber-capital." At the time bliss seemed the glorious flower of peace and prosperity. In fact, many claim, it was the rotting fruit of decadence and decay. Suffering no difficulties, feeling no loss, we let our sense of the world go dim, our muscles atrophy. Holding up a mirror to our impoverished appetite for experience, Brooks notes that the most celebrated sitcom of the age was *Seinfeld*, "a show about nothing." But 9/11, writes Frank Rich, was a "nightmare," awakening us from a "frivolous if not decadent decadelong dream." The fear it provoked, adds Brooks, was a morning "cleanser, washing away a lot of the self-indulgence" of the nineties. According to George Packer, it brought us "alertness, grief, resolve, even love"—experience itself. Packer cites, approvingly, the comments of an investment banker fleeing the World Trade Center on the day of the attack: "I'm not in shock. I like this state. I've never been more cognizant in my life." Fear restored to us the clarifying knowledge that evil exists, making moral, deliberate action possible once again. What was to be dreaded was not a repeat of 9/11 but, according to Packer, a "return to the normality" that preceded it, for that would mean "instead of public memorials, private consumption; instead of lines to give blood, restaurant lines," instead of civic attention, personal dissolution. 9/11 was not the end of the story. Like the saving fear of Adam and Eve, it was just the beginning.[2]

This book is about fear, particularly as it pertains to modern politics. By political fear, I mean a people's felt apprehension of some harm to their collective well-being—the fear of terrorism, panic over crime, anxiety about moral decay—or the intimidation wielded over men and women by governments or groups. What makes both types of fears political rather than personal is that they emanate from society or have consequences for society. Private fears like my fear of flying or your fear of spiders are artifacts of our own psychologies and experiences, and have little impact beyond ourselves. Political fear, by contrast, arises from conflicts within and between societies. An American's fear of terrorism, for example, is a response to the attacks of 9/11 and the struggle between the United States and radical Islam. The fear among black Americans of the police—or, once upon a time, among Soviet dissidents of their government and among South African anti-apartheid activists of theirs—is sparked by friction in the civic world. Political fear can also have widespread repercussions. It may dictate public policy, bring new groups to power and keep others out, create laws and overturn them. The fear of communism during the early years of the Cold War, for example, helped roll back the New Deal. Black fears of white rule and white fears of black revolt underwrote a century of legal segregation. Political fear is often associated with government acts, but it need not be, at least not overtly. Take the fear a woman has of her abusive husband, or the worker of her unkind employer. To the casual observer, these fears are personal, the product of an unfortunate but entirely private derangement of power. In actual fact, they are political. They spring from pervasive social inequities, and help sustain long traditions of rule over women and workers. These inequities and traditions are often reinforced, however indirectly, and created, however remotely, by government policies. Behind the husband's abuse of his wife lie centuries of laws and doctrines awarding him authority over her; behind the employer's cruelty are statutes, past and present, granting him coercive power over his employees.

I make here three claims about political fear. The first concerns how we think of it; the second, how and why we have come to think of it in this way; the third, how we might think of it instead. What these arguments add up to is this: Though fear has a politics, we often ignore or misconstrue it, making it difficult to understand how and why fear is used. Convinced that we lack moral or political principles to bind us together, we savor the experience of being afraid, as many writers did after 9/11, for only fear, we believe, can turn us from isolated men and women into a united people. Looking to political fear as the ground of our public life, we refuse to see the grievances and controversies that underlie it. We blind ourselves to the real-world conflicts that make fear an instrument of political rule and advance, deny ourselves the tools that might mitigate those conflicts, and ultimately ensure that we stay in thrall to fear. Perhaps that is what some in our society seek: to be in thrall, perpetually, to fear. But since fear seldom yields, over the long term, the unity and energy so many hope to obtain from it, we should probably look for those goods elsewhere, and approach fear for what it is—a symptom of pervasive conflict and political unhappiness—rather than for what it is not.

## How We Think About Political Fear

It was the French essayist Michel de Montaigne who first declared, "The thing I fear most is fear." Since then, philosophers and politicians, scholars and pundits, have taken his lead, deeming fear the great evil of civilization, the most lethal impediment to freedom, to be fought at all costs.[3] But something within us resists this antipathy. We—or those who write on our behalf—seem to like the idea of being afraid. Not because fear alerts us to real danger or propels us to take action against it, but because fear is supposed to arouse a heightened state of experience. It quickens our perceptions as no other emotion can, forcing us to see and to act in the world in new and more interesting ways, with greater moral discrimination and a more acute consciousness of our surroundings and ourselves. According to John Locke, one of the guiding spirits of modern liberalism, fear is "an uneasiness of the mind," and "the chief, if not only spur to human industry and action is *uneasiness*." Though we might think that men and women act on behalf of desire, Locke insisted that "a little burning felt"—like fear—"pushes us more powerfully than great pleasures in prospect draw or allure." Locke's conservative counterpart Edmund Burke had equally low regard for pleasure. It induces a grotesque implosion of self, he wrote, a "soft tranquility" approximating an advanced state of decay if not death itself. But when we imagine the prospect of "pain and terror," we experience a "delightful horror." Without fear, we are passive; with it, we are roused to "the strongest emotion which the mind is capable of feeling."[4]

Likewise in politics. Though most modern writers and politicians oppose political fear as the enemy of liberty, reason, and other Enlightenment values, they often embrace it, in spite of themselves, as a source of political vitality. Whether condemning Jacobin terror, Soviet despotism, Balkan genocide, or September 11 terrorism, they see opportunities for collective renewal in the fear of these evils. Not for the victims, but for us, who look upon these evils from without. Political fear is supposed to teach us the worth of specific political values. The fear of civil war, for instance, is supposed to breed a respect for the rule of law, the fear of totalitarianism an appreciation for liberal democracy, the fear of fundamentalism support for toleration and pluralism. Afraid of contracting these ills, we are persuaded to take appropriate measures to ward them off. Once persuaded, we appreciate and cherish, as we did not before, the value of antidotes like the rule of law, liberal democracy, and so on. Political fear is also supposed to prompt a more general spiritual awakening. Without danger and consequent fear, we not only lack passionate conviction about political values, we lack all conviction. We feel dead. Only in the face of fear will we be roused to action and believe that there is something in the world justifying our efforts to stay in it.

For political fear to arouse us, the object of fear must belong to the realm of politics and yet somehow, in the minds of the fearful, stand apart from it. If fear is to commit us to political values like the rule of law or liberal democracy, we must confront a political threat to those values. After all, a coastal city threatened by a tidal wave may be incited to public action, but natural disaster seldom provokes citizens to embrace or enact specific political principles. Political dangers like war or insurrection, however, require a society to define or affirm its beliefs, to mobilize against the threat on behalf of its political values. Unlike natural disaster, political disaster forces a society to discover and pursue the political ideals that under less threatening circumstances might simply bore it.

At the start of his career, for example, a young Abraham Lincoln remarked upon the indifference and lethargy of his countrymen. Comfortable and complacent, they did not cherish the values that once inspired their fathers to take up arms on behalf of liberty. The men who created the republic, Lincoln lamented, "*were* a fortress of strength; but, what invading foemen could *never do*, the silent artillery of time *has done*; the leveling of its walls. They are gone." At the same time, with anarchic spirits of mob rule stalking the land, Lincoln's America was threatened by a restless mood of lawlessness and popular violence. What might help recommit the republic to its original values and spark a robust spirit of civic engagement? The very knowledge of this violence, the awareness that "there is, even now, something of ill-omen among us." The notion that savagery was afoot would produce a fresh appreciation of what the country's founders had achieved and inspire a new "*political religion*"—a religion of law, consecrated by the memory of blood once spilled and now threatened. The fear of political disaster, in other words, would awaken a generation whose only task had been to pass on that which it had inherited.[5]

At the same time that many writers and leaders see opportunity in the fear of political dangers, they insist upon viewing those dangers as not political, as having little to do with the issues and controversies that animate political discussion and action. Consider again the response of American commentators to 9/11. While many embraced the day's politically galvanizing fear, they argued that the terrorism that aroused it did not arise from political concerns. It was not the hijackers' hostility to U.S. power, for instance, that piloted three planes into the Pentagon and the World Trade Center. Nor was it anger at America's patronage of Israel or sponsorship of despotic regimes in the Middle East. The 9/11 terrorists, many claimed, were simply not interested in politics. "Their grievance," explained Thomas Friedman, "is rooted in psychology, not politics."[6] For some commentators, terrorism was fueled by an anxiety over modernity, by the march of secularism and other Western values, which threatened the Muslim world's fragile sense of identity. This anxiety had nothing to do with power, resources, or policy. It had everything to do with cultural uneasiness. People in the grip of such anxiety, the argument goes, are ripe for the totalizing thinking of Islamic radicalism, where Allah serves as a substitute for a lost sense of authority, the terrorist cell a replacement for a ruined solidarity.[7] For other observers, the psychology of terrorism was less cultural than personal. To understand what drove Mohamed Atta, the Egyptian-born ringleader of the 9/11 attacks, analysts recommended that we look to "the raw ingredients of his personality."[8] Much was made of the fact that Atta sat on his mother's lap until well after he had begun college. Atta's father complained that his wife raised their only son as a girl, and frequently told young Mohamed, "Toughen up, boy." Atta stayed away from women—right unto his death. (His will left strict instructions that none should attend his funeral.) He lived in a pink house. Though Atta's friends claimed he was incensed by U.S. support for Egypt's repressive government, the Gulf War, and the Oslo peace accords, the implication of these press reports was clear: Atta and his co-conspirators suffered from a troubled masculinity; 9/11 was the action of sexually ambiguous boys trying to prove that they were men.[9]

There seems to be a contradiction in our approach to fear. On the one hand, we see political fear as an opportunity for renewal, as the moment to swallow the political medicines that keep fear at bay. On the other hand, we look upon the objects of fear as politically empty. We probably cannot resolve this contradiction solely through logic; for though it arises, as we shall see, from abstract thought, it is buttressed by political need. Understanding the objects of our fear as less than political allows us to treat them as intractable foes. Nothing can be done to accommodate them: they can only be killed or contained. Understanding the objects of our fear as not political also renews us as a collective. Afraid, we are like the audience in a crowded theater confronting a man falsely shouting fire: united, not because we share similar beliefs or aspirations, but because we are equally threatened. Were we to understand the objects of our fear as truly political, we might argue about them, as we do about other political things. We might find ourselves less united than we thought. Some of us might sympathize with the grievances of our foes; others might not see them as so implacable or dangerous. By removing these objects from the controversies of politics, however, we achieve the political unity—and renewal—so many writers crave.

## Why We Think of Political Fear as We Do

We did not always think of political fear in this way. Genesis notwithstanding, most writers prior to the modern era viewed fear as an artifact of our moral beliefs, which were the product of political education, laws, and institutions. For these writers, fear could not be an instrument of civic renewal and its objects could not be nonpolitical because fear depended upon a preceding apprehension of good and evil. Only if we knew what was good could we know evil and be afraid of it. What made something fearful, in other words, was morality, and behind morality, politics. Aristotle, for example, believed that an individual's fear was the concluding sentence of a dialogue between his passions and beliefs. Ethical reflection helped determine the objects of a person's fear. A man who appreciated the difference between virtue and vice would realize that disgrace on the battlefield—but not poverty—was a vice. As a result, he would fear the first, but not the second. Ethical reflection also informed his response to fear. Depending on his degree of virtue, a fearful person confronting death in battle would flee, stand and fight, or take simple precautionary measures. The good person was one, in that famous Aristotelian formulation, who feared "the right things, for the right motive, in the right manner, and at the right time."[10] Augustine believed that "the most important factor" in any emotion, including fear, was "the character of a man's will." A good will made for a man whose "emotions will be not only blameworthy, but praiseworthy," a bad will for a man whose "emotions will be wrong." Genuine Christians, Augustine explained, "live by God's standards" and as a result "feel fear and desire, pain and gladness in conformity with the holy Scriptures and sound doctrine." For both Aristotle and Augustine, fear was intimately related to each person's rational judgments of good and evil, virtue and vice.[11]

Fear in the Old Testament also requires a prior acquisition of moral knowledge. Even in the opening pages of Genesis, what awakens Adam's fear is the awareness, somewhere between premoral and moral, that he is naked, an awareness he obtains only after he has eaten from the tree of knowledge. Throughout Deuteronomy, Moses bids the Jews, "Thou shalt fear the Lord thy God." But fearing God, Moses discovers, is an ethical injunction his followers must be commanded to perform, again and again—in the same way they must be told, and reminded, not to steal, kill, or covet their neighbors' wives. The Israelites must also be given reasons to be afraid. Moses is compelled to explain, "And the Lord commanded us to do all these statutes, to fear the Lord our God, for our good always, that he might preserve us alive, as it is at this day." Like Aristotle recommending that the virtuous man forgo his fear of poverty and embrace his fear of dishonor, Moses encourages the Jews to abandon their fear of their enemies and to fear God instead. The former fear, he intimates, suggests an inadequate appreciation of God's stature, a failure of the moral imagination that gets in the way of fearing God: "Thou shalt not be afraid of them: but shalt well remember what the Lord thy god did unto Pharoah, and unto all Egypt."[12]

Whether religious or secular, premodern thinkers argued that fear had to be deliberately cultivated and sustained by a serious moral understanding of who men and women are and how they should conduct themselves as ethical beings. Developing such morally appropriate fears also required a nexus of political institutions. Hobbes, often taken as a harbinger of modernity, was in this respect decidedly premodern. He claimed that it was the state's primary responsibility to teach people to fear certain items, and to act upon only those fears they were morally entitled to act upon. Hobbes believed in an absolute state, with power concentrated in the hands of a single sovereign agent. But that sovereign would have to rely on more than a monopoly of arms to instill fear in the population. The sovereign would have to work through a combination of laws, elites, and institutions like churches and schools to transmit a doctrine of fearful obedience. The cultivation of fear thus arose from a collaboration between the individual, society, and the state. Political fear was not simply a top-down affair, a violent imposition from above, but a complex negotiation of passion and intellect, among all the various ranks of society and politics.

Even Plato, who had so little esteem for fear that he tried to banish it from his imagined republic, believed that its exile could be wrought only by a reorientation of belief and institution. Plato's guardians, the protectors of the republic, had to be courageous, particularly when confronting death. But no man, Plato believed, could be courageous in the face of a danger he truly feared. "Do you believe that anyone who has this terror [of death] in him would ever become courageous?" Plato has Socrates ask Adeimantus. "By Zeus, I don't," Adeimantus replies. "Do you suppose," Socrates presses, "anyone who believes Hades' domain exists and is full of terror will be fearless in the face of death and choose death in battles above defeat and slavery?" "Not at all," says Adeimantus. Could the guardians learn not to fear death? Yes, but only through a comprehensive reeducation. "Concerning these tales" of death, Socrates says, "we must supervise those who undertake to tell them and ask them not simply to disparage Hades' domain in this way but rather to praise it, because what they say is neither true nor beneficial for men who are fighters."[13] Socrates goes on to itemize all those instances of poetic excess—from Homer's account of the unhappiness of the dead to his recounting of the lamentations of Achilles and Priam over the loss of their loved ones—that must be expunged from the republic's literary imagination. For only then will they disappear from the individual's moral imagination.

Fear, in other words, was a product of belief, belief a product of poets and teachers, poets and teachers a product of the republic.

Today, we tend not to think of political fear as an ally of our beliefs and judgments, moral or political. Nor is it an item of deliberation or choice.[14] "Fear needs no definition," writes Raymond Aron. "It is a primal, and so to speak, subpolitical emotion."[15] Political fear is thought to be a species of terror or anxiety. Terror is a "physiological reaction" to overweening physical danger; it is an automatic response, "involuntary and far too impervious to be controlled," to arbitrary, lawless violence—the terror, for instance, felt by so many just after 9/11 or experienced by Soviet citizens during the Stalin years.[16] Anxiety is the free-floating insecurity a people experience in the face of moral anarchy and social breakdown. These are "anxious times," writes Michael Sandel, when we suffer from "the sense that, from family to neighborhood to nation, the moral fabric of the community is unraveling around us." Among our most "paralyzing collective fears," continues Jean Bethke Elshtain, is the anxiety that "communities will continue to disintegrate; families will continue to collapse; the center simply will not hold."[17] As individual political experiences, terror and anxiety do not take their bearings from morality and ideology, but from violence and anomie. Neither are terror and anxiety thought to be generated and sustained by the conventional instruments of politics. Instead, they arise from nonpolitical sources. In the case of terror, writers urge us to look to lawlessness and unsanctioned violence, which have their roots in psychology and culture; in the case of anxiety, to the absence of morality and loss of customary modes of civil and political life.

Because we separate fear from morals and politics, we believe it can be the ground of both, particularly at moments of moral doubt and political sluggishness. Writing after the French Revolution, for example, Alexis de Tocqueville noted the anxieties that seemed to haunt his generation: despair over the loss of the Old Regime, uneasiness about democracy, worries about the future and disquiet about the past. Lacking confidence in the traditional truths of God and king, Tocqueville hoped his contemporaries might find a renewed confidence in the experience of fear, which could activate and ground a commitment to freedom. "Fear," he wrote in a note to himself, "must be put to work on behalf of liberty," or, as he argued in *Democracy in America*, "Let us, then, look forward to the future with that salutary fear which makes men keep watch and ward for freedom, and not with that flabby, idle terror which makes men's hearts sink and enervates them."[18] More than a century later, Hannah Arendt surveyed the moral wasteland created by Europe's second Thirty Years War. Auschwitz and the gulag, she observed, had shredded the nineteenth-century assumptions of right and left; the verities of the past were no longer useful, the axioms of universal progress inoperable. All that remained was the fear these horrors had generated, but in that fear lay the instrument of a new moral and political consensus: "The fear of concentration camps and the resulting insight into the nature of total domination might serve to invalidate all obsolete political differentiations from right to left and to introduce beside and above them the politically most important yardstick for judging events in our time, namely: whether they serve totalitarian domination or not."[19] Fifty years after Arendt, her successors discovered the galvanizing energy of political fear yet again. In the wake of the cold war, writers and journalists were no longer certain about the basis of liberal principles like individual rights and equality. So they turned to the memory of cruelties past and the threat of cruelties present as the justification, albeit negative, for liberal norms. This new "liberalism of fear," as Harvard scholar Judith Shklar called it, "does not, to be sure, offer a *summum bonum* toward which all political agents should strive, but it certainly does begin with a *summum malum*, which all of us know and would avoid if only we could. That evil is cruelty and the fear it inspires, and the very fear of fear itself."[20] Or, in the words of journalist Michael Ignatieff:

> In the twentieth century, the idea of human universality rests less on hope than on fear, less on optimism about the human capacity for good than on dread of human capacity for evil, less on a vision of man as maker of his history than of man the wolf toward his own kind. The way stations on the road to this new internationalism were Armenia, Verdun, the Russian front, Auschwitz, Hiroshima, Vietnam, Cambodia, Lebanon, Rwanda, and Bosnia. A century of total war has made victims of us all, civilians and military, men, women, and children alike.[21]

We may not know who we are, the argument goes, we may not know what is truly good or just, but we do know what it is to be afraid. That simple, almost instinctive knowledge can structure our public life and animates its exertions. It is the dissonant energy of our civic faith, the necessary irritant of common purpose.

How did we come to this view? Because of larger changes in how we think about the self, morality, and political order, and because of a specifically liberal conception of political rule. Prior to the modern era, writers like Aristotle and Augustine presumed a natural order to the universe, from which morals and politics, society itself, were supposed to emanate.[22] Human beings, in this view, were born into a preexisting structure of permanent standing, and they derived their identity from their place in that structure. The self as we know it—that creature of intense interiority and creativity, generating her identity and beliefs against the force of tradition and society, what Irving Howe once called "a tacit polemic, in opposition to the ages"—simply did not exist.[23] Even Augustine and Luther, those great poets of the inner life, believed that the task of each person was to reconcile himself to God's eternal order, to find his place within the grand work of a provident creator. But with the rise of modern science and philosophy, particularly the work of Galileo and Descartes, that natural order and all that went with it—identity, morality, and political order—could no longer be taken for granted. Writers now required proof of its existence, furnished not by observation or experience, but by a relentless inspection of the thinking process itself. Only by beginning with incontestable first principles, and by pursuing their implications through deductive reasoning, could the individual produce—produce, not discover—a vision of order. Able to orchestrate his morals and politics in this way, the individual also fashioned his own identity—without reference to God, the cosmos, tradition, or his station in life. Removed from society, surrounded by the perimeter of his reason, the self looked upon the world not as a welcoming ground or familiar home but as an alien landscape to be mastered and tamed.

But if morals and politics, as well as the self, were made, they could be unmade. And so they were: beginning in the early modern era through our own time, in battle after battle of civil and international war—sometimes about religion, other times about politics and economics, usually about all three. Unlike their predecessors in the ancient world, these wars seemed to hurl men and women into an empty universe, lacking any foundation for the truths of morality and politics, for even presuming that those truths existed. With civil order now understood to be life's precious and precarious achievement, it necessarily followed that civil war, in the words of Hobbes—in this respect a modern—was "*Death*."[24] Philosophers and writers also began to wonder whether the self was not something of a fiction. The self did not appear to them the vital maker of his own meanings. Instead, he seemed a being of intense frailty and lackluster ambition, with an easily crushed, perhaps non-existent, will. The self did not naturally seek to create morals, the polity, or much of anything; it could barely support the weight of its own independent existence. For Locke, the self was lured to near dissolution by the pleasures of contentment. "When a man is perfectly content with the state he is in . . . what industry, what action, what will is there left, but to continue in it?" Weakened by contentment, the self lost the will to act creatively, to set about establishing the truths of the world. For Burke, the natural state of the self was not even contentment, which at least implied some pleasure in the self's ongoing activities. "The human mind," wrote Burke, "is often, and I think it is for the most part, in . . . a state of indifference." This indifference threatened to produce "a state of rest and inaction," in which "all the parts of our bodies . . . fall into a relaxation, that not only disables the members from performing their functions, but takes away the vigorous tone of fibre which is requisite for carrying on the natural and necessary secretions." The result was "melancholy, dejection, despair, and often self-murder."[25] The self, in short, could quickly become no self at all—entirely through its own doing. Long before Foucault predicted the end of man, writers like Burke were performing his autopsy.

These new ideas of order, morality, and the self—and their corollaries, the specter of nothingness and the self's disappearance—made the world, whatever its actual state of conflict or violence, seem an inherently insecure and precarious place, and the self, whatever its physical liabilities and limitations, seem naturally vulnerable to external manipulation and control, to collapse in the face of the pressing demands of others. Self and society were now thought to be eternally besieged by the threat of destruction, sowing a natural breeding ground for fear: a fear of loss, of anarchy, of personal and political "non-being."[26] According to Tocqueville: "Such a state inevitably enervates the soul, and relaxing the springs of the will, prepares a people for bondage. Then not only will they let their freedom be taken from them, but often they actually hand it over themselves. When there is no authority in religion or in politics, men are soon frightened by the limitless independence with which they are faced. They are worried and worn out by the constant restlessness of everything."[27] Something was required to brace self and society against these threats of annihilation. And that something was fear. Not the fear of nothingness, which was so disabling—"that flabby, idle terror," as Tocqueville wrote, "which makes men's hearts sink and enervates them"—but the fear of that fear, the "salutary fear which makes men keep watch and ward for freedom."[28] As Franklin Roosevelt, cribbing from Thoreau who got it from Montaigne, would put it, "The only thing we have to fear is fear itself—nameless, unreasoning, unjustified terror which paralyzes needed efforts to convert retreat into advance."[29] Fear itself was disabling, the fear of fear itself restorative and revivifying. Only the second possessed the requisite energy to press the self and society forward. Armed with fear, the self—and society—was fortified against not only external and domestic enemies but also the inner tendency, the almost native desire, to dissolve into the soupy indifference of which Burke spoke.

Such ideas have not been confined to the rarified province of the philosopher. Eventually, they permeated the work of popular writers and influential journalists. At the height of the Cold War, for instance, Arthur Schlesinger wrote *The Vital Center*. Ostensibly a liberal call to arms against the Soviet Union and American communism, *The Vital Center* was really a diagnosis of despair and anxiety, similar to that voiced by Tocqueville in *Democracy in America*. "Western man in the middle of the twentieth century," wrote Schlesinger, "is tense, uncertain, adrift. We look upon our epoch as a time of troubles, an age of anxiety. The grounds of our civilization, of our certitude, are breaking up under our feet, and familiar ideas and institutions vanish as we reach for them, like shadows in the failing dusk." Even though the year was 1949, the Soviet Union was just about to explode the atom bomb, and the United States was on the verge of the Korean War, Schlesinger was emphatic that the greatest threat to the United States was not external but internal, not political but spiritual and psychological. "The crisis of free society has assumed the form of international collision between democracies and totalitarian powers; but this fact should not blind us to the fact that in its essence this crisis is internal." The solution? Turn the conflict between the Soviet Union and the United States into a proving ground of self and society. By confronting an external enemy, the Soviet Union, Americans could thereby transform their existential anxiety into focused, galvanizing fear. Let us "strike at the dilemma of history," urged Schlesinger, referring to the anxieties of meaninglessness and despair, "in terms of the problem" between the United States and the Soviet Union.[30]

In talking about political fear, then, modern writers have seldom been simply talking about the dangers any person or society may confront. Instead, they have approached danger with these images of personal loss and political nothingness in mind. Though many writers reject fear in the name of freedom, reason, or the Enlightenment, these specters of personal destruction and political nothingness have also impelled them to embrace fear, often in the name of those very values. But if fear is to serve as the agent of personal and collective salvation, its objects must approximate or resemble the nothingness writers believe haunts the modern self and society. For only if fear lies beyond the constraints of politics and politesse of civilization can it contain the titanic force necessary to restore to the self and society their rightful and requisite energy.

But there is a second reason that writers and politicians have embraced political fear and understood its objects as not political. And this has less to do with these assumptions of modern thought than with the imperatives of political liberalism, which are especially potent in the United States. Modern liberalism is a complex teaching that is not easily reducible to slogans or sound bites but that nevertheless coheres around a skepticism of strong, centralized government. For it is such governments, in the liberal imagination, "with their overwhelming power to kill, maim, indoctrinate, and make war," that are uniquely positioned to raise fear among men and women. "While the sources of social oppression are indeed numerous," Shklar insists, "none has the deadly effect of those who, as the agents of the modern state, have unique resources of physical might and persuasion at their disposal."[31] To counter governments that arouse such fear—not all governments, only those that make fear a deadly condition of everyday life—liberals recommend an array of prescriptions: the rule of law, toleration, a government of fragmented power, and a pluralistic civil society. In other words, many of those elements of our liberal democracy that citizens, leaders, and intellectuals cherish as keystones of American freedom.

This teaching has posed a problem, particularly in the United States. For all the limitations our Constitution places upon strong, centralized government, no one can deny that we have witnessed the periodic flourishing of political fear. From the Alien and Sedition Acts of the late 1790s to the repression of abolitionists in the early nineteenth century to the anti-immigrant and antilabor panics of the late nineteenth century to the various red scares of the twentieth, the United States has hardly been immune to the use of fear as a form of intimidation. Influential analysts of these episodes have had difficulty reconciling their occurrence with our liberal political institutions. How have they done so? By identifying the origins of political fear outside the political sphere, in the psychic insecurities and cultural anxieties of a restless populace.

Take the case of McCarthyism. McCarthyism was a multidimensional movement of political repression, but one of its critical energies derived from the combined efforts of big business, the Republican Party, and the FBI to clamp down on the stirrings of organized labor and the progressive Left during the late 1940s. Contrary to popular belief, McCarthyism worked through the very contrivances of state and society that the liberal imagination prizes and recommends as an antidote to fear. Individual legislators like Senator Joseph McCarthy thrived on the fragmented nature of congressional power championed by the Framers. The separation of legislative from executive power, the ambition of and competition between individual politicians—praised throughout *The Federalist Papers* as a check upon repressive government—led Harry Truman, Hubert Humphrey, and a good many other liberal Democrats to sponsor, often against their better judgment, some of the most draconian pieces of legislation in twentieth-century America. And where the state couldn't act, a pluralist society stepped in. Literally thousands of employers and employees, business groups and labor unions, churches and synagogues, local organizations and civic associations—that dense, teeming infrastructure of civil society celebrated by intellectuals from Tocqueville to Robert Putnam—helped generate and sustain political fear, often with the stealthy support of the FBI. Neighbors spied and informed on neighbors, preachers on parishioners, teachers on students. Employers fired or refused to hire workers, labor leaders purged union locals, private groups expelled individual members.

But for many intellectuals at the time—luminaries of Cold War social thought like Richard Hofstadter, Daniel Bell, Talcott Parsons, Seymour Martin Lipset, Nathan Glazer, and David Riesman—McCarthyism was little more than a psychopathology, the cultural curio of a democratic society. The fear of communism, they argued, rose from the status anxieties of an egalitarian society, which were foisted upon the state in the form of repressive legislation. McCarthyism, in other words, was not an instrument of elite or institutional power, nor was it the product of liberal government. It was a symptom of what Hofstadter called "the paranoid style of American politics."[32] With fear described as a style rather than a reality, the issue of an overheated imagination rather than a response to policies and practices, intellectuals were freed from worry about its repressive tendencies. Confident that McCarthyite fear had no political meaning, cultural critic Leslie Fiedler breezily dismissed its actuality: "From one end of the country to another rings the cry, 'I am cowed! I am afraid to speak out!' and the even louder response, 'Look, he is cowed! He is afraid to speak out.'"[33] This, at precisely the moment when one to two of every five American workers was subject to some kind of political investigation or loyalty oath.[34] Though intellectuals had multiple reasons for downplaying the political origins and consequences of McCarthyism, one of them was their commitment to liberalism and its analysis of political fear. For if the only kind of polity that gives rise to fear is a lawless, violent state crushing an independent civil society, it stands to reason that fear in America arises from other, nonpolitical sources, in the culture and psyche of the masses. And so it has, in the minds of many intellectuals.

## How We Might Think of Political Fear Instead

But political fear, I would like to suggest, is not the saving agent of self and society. Nor does it reside beyond the domain of politics, liberal or otherwise. It is instead a political tool, an instrument of elite rule or insurgent advance, created and sustained by political leaders or activists who stand to gain something from it, either because fear helps them pursue a specific political goal, or because it reflects or lends support to their moral and political beliefs—or both. To think of political fear as we do only distracts attention from what political fear does. By recommending that we embrace our fear, by obscuring the political conflicts that give rise to it, by seeing liberalism as solely a solution and not also a problem, the writers who proffer these notions of fear lend support, wittingly or unwittingly, to the forces in society that have much to gain from fear. So do they deny support, again wittingly or unwittingly, to the forces in society that have much to lose from fear.

Political fear can work in one of two ways. First, leaders or militants can define what is or ought to be the public's chief object of fear. Political fear of this sort almost always preys upon some real threat—it seldom, if ever, is created out of nothing—but since the harms of life are as various as its pleasures, politicians and other leaders have much leeway in deciding which threats are worthy of political attention and which are not. It is they who identify a threat to the population's well being, who interpret the nature and origins of that threat, and who propose a method for meeting that threat. It is they who make particular fears items of civic discussion and public mobilization. This does not mean that each member of the public actually fears the chosen object: not every American citizen, for instance, is actively afraid today of terrorism. It merely means that the object dominates the political agenda, crowding out other possible objects of fear and concern. In choosing, interpreting, and responding to these objects of fear, leaders are influenced by their ideological assumptions and strategic goals. They view danger through a prism of ideas, which shapes whether they see a particular danger as threatening or not, and a lens of political opportunity, which shapes whether they see that danger as helpful or not.

Consider, for instance, the fate of the anthrax scare in the wake of 9/11. Between October 5, 2001, when the story broke, and the end of November, five people were killed by anthrax, and eighteen others were infected with it. Government officials immediately hunted for signs that the attack originated in the Middle East, particularly Iraq. As a top government scientist associated with the investigation later revealed, "I know there are a number of people" in the Bush administration "who would love an excuse to get after Iraq." As a result, according to a high-level intelligence official, the U.S. government "looked for any shred of evidence that would bear on this [the Iraq connection], or any foreign source." But, he added, "it's just not there." So long as anthrax had a whiff of the Middle East about it, officials aggressively pursued the threat, and the media lavished attention upon it. In October, following the outbreak, the *New York Times* and the *Washington Post* ran 1,192 stories mentioning anthrax, and in November, 886 stories. In December, however, that number plummeted to 400; by February, anthrax tallied a mere 140 mentions. What happened? Partially, the outbreak subsided, with the last case of infection reported in late November. Partially, the investigation stalled, with few leads turning up, though not as few as the government would later claim. Also important, though, was the government's growing acknowledgment throughout November and December that the perpetrator of the attack was probably an American citizen, with likely connections to the U.S. military. At that point, the government simply lost interest in the case—perhaps because the idea of anthrax's domestic origins did not fit with the Bush administration's foreign policy goals, or because domestic terrorism did not register as a threat to officials viewing danger solely through the lens of the Middle East. So did the media lose interest. Whatever the reason, when the *New York Times* ran a piece the following July headlined "Anthrax? The FBI Yawns," everyone else yawned too. Even though the perpetrator of the attack had still not been found and the damage to various government offices was still not repaired, even though the article accused the FBI of refusing to put a leading suspect in the biochemical industry under surveillance or to compare his handwriting with that of the anthrax letters, hardly a single newspaper or television network picked up the story. No one in these circles seemed to care, and anthrax disappeared from the public agenda.[35]

Or consider how the government and media inflate the danger of dissenting individuals accused of supporting terrorism while minimizing that of corporations accused of similar crimes. On February 20, 2003, the Justice Department filed charges against Sami Al-Arian, a Kuwaiti-born Palestinian professor of engineering at the University of South Florida, accusing him of financing and supporting Islamic Jihad. Hoping to seize upon the indictment as a showcase for the newly passed Patriot Act, the Justice Department announced Al-Arian's arrest to much fanfare, and found a receptive audience in the American media. The *New York Times* and the *Washington Post* ran front-page stories about the indictment, and in the week following, 318 stories appeared in other outlets.[36] By contrast, when the federal government revealed two months later that it had fined fifty-seven companies and organizations for doing business with rogue states and terrorist groups, hardly anyone in the government or the media raised an eyebrow—even though the companies included Chevron-Texaco, Wal-Mart, Citigroup, the New York Yankees, and Amazon.com, and even though their partners ranged from Iraq to Iran to an undisclosed terrorist organization. The government levied minimal fines, totaling a mere $1.35 million, and posted notice of these crimes on a lonely Treasury Department web site—and that only after a watchdog group filed a lawsuit to force the government to make the records public. The government disclosure merely cited the offending corporations, their trading partners, and the fines, and then made oblique reference to the sections of the Trading With the Enemy Act the companies had violated (for example, "E013121 FT"). Not a single major U.S. newspaper or television network picked up the story; it only appeared in twelve media outlets, several of them in foreign countries.[37] In neither case did the alleged crimes involve anyone participating in or plotting actual violence—Al-Arian and the corporations were only accused of involvement with or support of terrorist groups or rogue states, and in Al-Arian's case, the terrorist threat was to Israeli, not American, citizens—but only in the first case did it serve government interests to make so much of the danger threatened and now averted.

Thus far, I have been talking about one mode of political fear: the definition and interpretation by political leaders of public objects of apprehension and concern. This mode usually presumes that the leaders and people to which they are appealing share a common identity, and that both groups are equally threatened by virtue of that identity. It is no accident that this mode of fear is most common during wartime, for its primary constituency is the nation or some other presumably cohesive community, and its primary object a foreign enemy or some other approximation of the alien, like drugs, criminals, or immigrants. But there is a second mode of political fear, which has little to do with political leaders' defining a common object of apprehension on behalf of a single people. This second kind of fear arises from the social, political, and economic hierarchies that divide a people. Though this fear is also created, wielded, or manipulated by political leaders, its specific purpose or function is internal intimidation, to use sanctions or the threat of sanctions to ensure that one group retains or augments its power at the expense of another. Where the first mode of fear involves a collective's fear of faraway dangers or of objects, like a foreign enemy, separate from the collective, this second mode of political fear is more intimate and less fabulist, arising from the vertical conflicts and cleavages endemic to a society. These are the inequities of wealth, status, and power. This second kind of political fear grows out of and helps perpetuate these inequities, which are so helpful to their beneficiaries and so detrimental to their victims. While it would be too much to claim that this second fear is the foundation of social and political order, it is so closely linked to society's various hierarchies—and to the rule and submission such hierarchies entail—that it qualifies as a basic mode of social and political control.

This kind of fear may be aroused by dramatic acts of violence, but it need not be. As Martin Luther King remarked in his "Letter from Birmingham City Jail," whites in Jim Crow America possessed a rather large inventory of fears by which they ruled over blacks: "When you have seen vicious mobs lynch your mothers and fathers at will and drown your sisters and brothers at whim; when you have seen hate-filled policemen curse, kick, brutalize and even kill your black brothers and sisters with impunity; . . . when you are humiliated day in and day out by nagging signs reading 'white' and 'colored'; when your first name becomes 'nigger' and your middle name becomes 'boy' (however old you are) and your last name becomes 'John,' and when your wife and mother are never given the respected title 'Mrs.' . . ."[38] During the McCarthy years, officials inspired a fear of their power among liberals and leftists via loyalty investigations, mass firings, and blacklists. With the exception of the execution of the Rosenbergs—probably not intended as an instrument of fear, the Rosenberg trial and execution aroused it nonetheless[39]—none of the instruments of McCarthyite fear entailed physical violence. Because fear is an apprehension of harm, and because harm is the deprivation of some good to the individual, wielders of power can arouse fear merely by threatening the individual's enjoyment of that good. That may entail lethal violence, but often it does not, as in the case of McCarthyism, where what is threatened is the loss of a career or steady employment.

As King also made clear, it is not necessary to make active or express threats in order to arouse fear; instead, fear can, and usually does, hover quietly about the relationships between the powerful and the powerless, subtly influencing everyday conduct without requiring much in the way of active intimidation. In fact, what makes this unspoken fear so influential, especially in a liberal democracy, is that it does not, as a rule, require overt acts of coercion. As the Supreme Court has written, "the threat of sanctions may deter" the exercise of freedom "almost as potently as the actual application of sanctions."[40] This is particularly true when the victims of this threat are powerless or somehow dependent for their well-being upon the good wishes of the powerful. Because of this dependence, the victims are already inclined to obey their superiors for fear of losing their patronage, so fear does not require much additional coercion. This unspectacular, quotidian fear is the American way of repression.

It is not only the powerful who wield fear and the powerless who are afraid. People with power are themselves often seized by a fear of those without it, either the fear aroused by guilt for having committed injustice, or, more commonly, the fear that the powerless will one day rise up and dispossess them. Again, King understood this elite fear all too well. Jim Crow, he wrote, was "buttressed by such irrational fears as loss of preferred economic privilege, altered social status, intermarriage, and adjustment to new situations." The "guilt-ridden white minority" feared that "if the Negro attains power, he will without restraint or pity act to revenge the accumulated injustices and brutality of the years." Whites, King added, were like the proverbial parent "who has continually mistreated his son" and "suddenly realizes that he is now taller than the parent. Will the son use his new physical power to repay for all of the blows of the past?"[41]

Nevertheless, the most salient political fear, the one that most pervasively structures our lives and limits our possibilities, is the fear among the less powerful of the more powerful, whether public officials or private employers, far-off agents of state or local, familiar elites. And here we come to the crux of the argument. For all our talk today of the fear of terrorism, or, before that, of communism, the most important form of fear is that which ordinary Americans have of their superiors, who sponsor and benefit from the inequities of everyday life. This kind of fear is repressive, constraining the actions of the less powerful, enabling the actions of the more powerful. It ensures that the less powerful abide by the express or implied wishes of their supervisors, or merely do nothing to challenge or undermine the existing distribution of power. Such fears are critical to power holders, enabling them to pursue their agendas with a freer hand, ensuring that they will enjoy their position for some time to come.

A good place to begin an investigation of intimidating fear in contemporary America is the workplace, for it is there—in the underregulated practices of hiring and firing, promotion and demotion; in the coerced and coercive intimacies between employer and employed, supervisor and supervised—that fear has an especially toxic effect. Despite the fact that adult Americans spend the overwhelming majority of their waking hours at work, and despite the fact that the business press openly confesses that "the workplace is never free of fear, and it shouldn't be" and that "fear can be a powerful management tool," the workplace remains a vast terra incognita protected from public scrutiny by high towers of legal argument and political indifference.[42] Wielding threats of firing, demotion, harassment, and other sanctions, employers and managers attempt to stifle speech and action, to ensure that workers don't talk back or act up. Employers do this not because they are cruel, but because they believe, as former Intel CEO Andrew Grove writes in his *Only the Paranoid Survive*, that fear spurs the fevered pace of contemporary industry, that it is an essential prop of our political economy.[43] Workplace fear creates an internal social order that can only be described, with little exaggeration, as feudal, a world less postmodern than premodern, whose master theorist is neither Karl Marx nor Adam Smith but Joseph de Maistre.

Consider the experience of a group of female employees at a Nabisco plant in Oxnard, California, maker of A-1 steak sauce and the world's supplier of Grey Poupon mustard. In a 1995 lawsuit, these workers complained that their supervisors consistently prevented them from going to the bathroom. Instructed to urinate into their clothes or face three day's suspension for unauthorized expeditions to the toilet, the workers opted to wear adult diapers. But incontinence pads were expensive, so the workers downgraded to Kotex and toilet paper, which pose severe health risks when soaked in urine. Indeed, several workers eventually contracted bladder and urinary tract infections. (Hearing of their plight, conservative commentator R. Emmett Tyrrell Jr. advised them to wear special diapers used by horses in New York's Central Park carriage trade.) Not until April 1998 did the federal government, under pressure from labor unions, even maintain that employers had to grant employees an ill-defined "timely access" to the bathroom. Since then, employers have managed to evade the law. As of 2002, for instance, managers at a Jim Beam bourbon distillery in Clermont, Kentucky, were still keeping spreadsheets monitoring employee use of the bathroom, and forty-five employees were disciplined for heeding nature's call outside company-approved break times. Female workers were even told to report the beginning of their menstrual cycles to the human resources department.[44] These are just some of the more notorious cases of workplace coercion that have been publicized; it is anyone's guess how many more workers suffer from similar constraints, but are too afraid to speak out against them. (In the most comprehensive survey of employees to date, two social scientists found that one in five workers considering filing a lawsuit against their employer did not do so for fear that their employer would retaliate against them; in many states and industries such reprisals are entirely legal.)[45]

It is not merely workers at the low end of the service economy who experience these forms of command and fear; so do white-collar employees.

Grove, for example, liked to run Intel the way Al Capone ran Chicago. On one occasion when an aide was late for a meeting, Grove waited, "holding a stave of wood the size of a baseball bat." After a time, Grove slammed "the wood onto the surface of the meeting-room table" and shouted, "I don't ever, ever, want to be in a meeting with this group that doesn't start and end when it's scheduled." Other employers are less bullying, but no less intimidating and controlling. Going high tech, they rely on computer technology to monitor their employees' every move. The Investigator software program—used by ExxonMobil and Delta—keeps track of not only workplace performance measures (like the number of employee key strokes and mouse clicks per second), but also troublemakers. Should an employee type "alert" words like "boss" or "union," Investigator automatically forwards her document— saved or unsaved, sent or not—to her supervisor. "Back in the fifteenth century," one PR executive explains, "they used to use a ball and chain, and now they use technology."[46]

In the corporate workplace, intimidation and spying coexist with phony affirmations of individualism, while employees terrified of losing their jobs are corralled into elaborate performances of faux bonhomie and loyalty to the firm. The results can often be humiliating and degrading. After NYNEX cut its workforce during the mid-1990s, for example, it required its MBAs and skilled technicians to attend a three-day-long retreat where they were encouraged to discover their own creativity by hopping around a room in different ways. Some hopped on one leg, others on two, still others with hands in the air, and one with a hand covering his eye. According to one participant, "The leaders would say things like, 'Look at how creative you are, how many different ways you can figure out to manage to jump around the room.' And we all did it. . . . We all did it." A marketing executive at a radio-station chain that had also undergone a round of firings recounts how a management consultant at a motivational seminar handed out water pistols to the employees and had them squirt each other—to help them get in touch with their more playful selves. "There were all these executives running around squirting each other," he says. He thought about not joining in, but reconsidered after asking himself, "If I don't squirt, will I be gone too?" Such games, he added, were "the most uncomfortable thing for professional men and women. A lot of us felt uncomfortable, embarrassed, reluctant to play the games. But they kept at it. It was almost like it was designed to break you down. I think it was a way of humiliating us." After a round of layoffs at the Bank of America, corporate higher-ups established a voluntary program for employees to "adopt" an ATM machine. More than 2,800 employees signed up, faithfully cleaning their own machine and its environs—on their own time, without extra pay—just to save their jobs.[47]

Understanding fear as we do—as a collective response to nonpolitical threats, as the polity's means of moral and spiritual regeneration—or responding solely to foreign objects of fear, we ignore or downplay these everyday forms of fear, which reinforce a repressive social order, constrain freedom, and create or perpetuate inequality. Focused on objects of fear perceived to be not political, looking to these fears as sources of civic instruction and collective renewal, our writers and leaders pay little attention to those forms of power that arouse repressive fears. All societies, including our own, are organized vertically, distributing more power, resources, and prestige to the few than to the many. Confronting external threats that presumably cannot be placated, writers and politicians enjoin a unity that is little more than a cover for these hierarchies and inequalities. Under cover of that unity, the powerful exact more and the powerless get less. That is what unity in the face of frightening, alien, apolitical dangers means. By looking upon fear as an opportunity for collective renewal in the face of nonpolitical threats, we help perpetuate the forms of fear that most constrain our aspirations and actions.

Much of this book was conceived prior to 9/11, and its various urgencies lie far afield from the threats of Islamic fundamentalism and terrorism. Nevertheless, our reactions to 9/11—the sense of renewal that many hoped it would bring, the insistence upon viewing terrorism as not political, the manipulation of the fear of terrorism by elites to create or consolidate repressive forms of power—presses us to confront the political dimensions of fear. This book gestures in that direction, urging us to give up our two basic assumptions about fear. The first is that political fear and its associated objects—danger, disaster, and evil—offer any hope of beginning, renewing, or restoring a robust republic of energetic virtue and galvanizing purpose. For too long, intellectuals and politicians have been trolling the swamps of fear in search of the headwaters of political and moral life. That such quests have now resulted in thoughtful, humane intellectuals celebrating a warrior culture born of mass carnage—indeed, in the case of George Packer, praying that we never go back to its predecessor culture of peace and prosperity—should give us pause. What exactly, we must ask ourselves, is missing from our world that we should require spilled blood and incinerated flesh, and the fear such havoc and loss create, to feel alive? How is it that Christopher Hitchens, one of the most literate and acclaimed voices of our time, could make a confession of the following sort, without raising an eyebrow of public concern, and indeed be feted for his acuity and humanity? "I should perhaps confess that on September 11 last, once I had experienced all the usual mammalian gamut of emotions, from rage to nausea, I also discovered that another sensation was contending for mastery. On examination, and to my own surprise and pleasure, it turned out to be exhilaration. Here was the most frightful enemy—theocratic barbarism—in plain view. . . . I realized that if the battle went on until the last day of my life, I would never get bored in prosecuting it to the utmost."[48] We have paid a terrible price for our flirtation with political fear, dishonoring its victims and disabling ourselves. Perhaps this is a good time to consider whether that price has been worth it.

Second, this book should disabuse us of the notion that the objects of our fear—and our fear of those objects—arise from dark, deeply apolitical or antipolitical forces, that fear is "a shimmering of nothingness," as Polish poet Zbigniew Herbert characterizes "The Monster of Mr. Cogito":

it is difficult to describe
escapes definition

it is like an immense depression
spread out over the country

it can't be pierced
with a pen

with an argument
or a spear.[49]

Though this idea of fear is fairly commonplace, it is just that—an idea, and a mistaken one at that. Political fear can be pierced with a pen, an argument, a spear. It is a meeting ground of the intellect and the passions, of our morals and our politics, not some inscrutable emanation from the psychological and cultural depths. It is a friend of the familiar—laws, elites, institutions, power, and authority—and a consort of the conventional—morality and ideology, no less amenable to political analysis than are any of these phenomena. To claim otherwise is to ascribe to fear a power it simply does not possess. Surrounding fear with an aura of the diabolical and the mysterious may satisfy that hunger for spectator disaster familiar to horror movie enthusiasts the world over, but it does not satisfy the demands of truth.

If we deprive fear of these surrounding myths, if we deprive the fear aroused by 9/11 of its political ballast, perhaps we will see more clearly what our assumptions have long obscured: the repressive fear of elites, experienced by American men and women as they go to work, learn in school, haggle with officials, and participate in the organizations that comprise our associated life. Perhaps we will see how our fear of terrorism, orchestrated and manipulated by the powerful, is being used to reorganize the structure of power in American society, giving more to those who already have much and taking away from those who have little. Perhaps we will even attend to—and make a political issue of—the inequalities of American life and the repressive fear those inequalities arouse and sustain. For one day, the war on terrorism will come to an end. All wars do. And when it does, we will find ourselves still living in fear: not of terrorism or radical Islam, but of the domestic rulers that fear has left behind.

# PART 1

# HISTORY OF AN IDEA

While I will have much to say in this book about how political fear works, part one is devoted to its first two themes—to how we think of political fear, and why we think of it as we do. It might seem strange that a book about political fear should assign so much space to our ideas about fear rather than to its practice. But recall what Burke said: It is not so much the actuality of a threat, but the imagined idea of that threat, that renews and restores. "If the pain and terror are so modified as not to be actually noxious; if the pain is not carried to violence, and the terror is not conversant about the present destruction of the person," then, and only then, do we experience a "delightful horror."[1] The condition of our being renewed by fear is not that we directly experience the object that threatens us, but that the object be kept at some remove from ourselves. By examining how we imagine the objects of our fear, I hope to bring those objects more closely into focus, to disentangle the skeins of misperception that have enabled us to believe, mistakenly, that we can be renewed by our fear of them.

Readers will note that I have subtitled this book "the history of a political idea." That is because I am concerned with fear as an idea that has changed over time. An intellectual history of fear may strike readers as a counterintuitive proposal. After all, few elements of the human experience seem less amenable to strictures of the intellect or of history. Fear is supposed to lurk beyond the reach of our rational faculties, a preternatural invader waiting to breach the borders of civilization. It has no history. It is, to quote Aron again, "a primal, and so to speak, subpolitical emotion."[2] Yet fear seldom intrudes upon the public square completely unadorned, as "fear itself," in Roosevelt's phrase. Fear arrives, as it did on 9/11, wrapped in layers of intellectual assumption, some woven centuries ago, that fashion our perceptions of and responses to it. As an item of public discussion, fear takes its shape from political and cultural elites, who take their cues from previous elites. Political fear, in other words, has a history, and to a surprising degree, it is a history of ideas. Knowing that history, we can see how our ideas have changed or not—enabling us to better assess our own ideas and change them if necessary.

The key protagonists in this history are four political philosophers: Thomas Hobbes, an Englishman from the seventeenth century; two Frenchmen, Montesquieu and Alexis de Tocqueville, the first from the eighteenth century, the second from the nineteenth; and Hannah Arendt, a German-Jewish émigré who fled Nazi Germany and ultimately settled in the United States. I could have chosen other philosophers—Machiavelli, de Maistre, Kierkegaard, Nietzsche, Freud, Schmitt, or Weil, to name a few. I could have looked at other genres—the plays of Brecht, for instance, or the novels of Kafka. While I have availed myself of the work of these writers, I have concentrated upon Hobbes, Montesquieu, Tocqueville, and Arendt because of the intellectual influence and political resonance of their accounts. These four figures wrote about fear and gave it a distinctive cast at moments when new political forms and ideas were emerging—for Hobbes, the modern state; for Montesquieu, the ideology of liberalism; for Tocqueville, egalitarian democracy; and for Arendt, totalitarianism. Because their thinking about fear was deeply marked by developments of modern political history, we can see in their accounts some of the changing dynamics of political fear. But as much as their thinking reflects history, so has it shaped our perception of that history. And it is this second feature of their thought that makes them especially instructive. Hobbes, Montesquieu, Tocqueville, and Arendt contributed to ways of thinking about fear we have inherited, languages we still speak today. Reading them, we gain some understanding of not only our past, but also our present.

I begin my account with Hobbes, a Janus-like theorist who looked backward to the ancients and forward to the moderns. Like Aristotle, Hobbes emphasized fear's political and moral components, demonstrating how fear required the help of elites, laws, institutions, and education. But Hobbes also was the first theorist to see political fear's galvanizing potential, how it could help establish the moral language and political codes of a society that had lost that language and those codes. I call the chapter on Hobbes "Fear," for it was Hobbes who formulated the most politically coherent account of fear we have, an account that informs my own approach to the problem, even though I disagree with some of its tenets. To some degree, Hobbes is the hero—or antihero—of this book, the great visionary who defined the problem of fear most acutely, and from whom we still have much to learn. His successors, by contrast, are fear's great mystifiers. Montesquieu, the first revisionist after Hobbes, offered an account of fear that I call "terror." Unlike Hobbesian fear, Montesquieu's terror was not the product of law, institutions, education, or even elites. It arose instead from a lone despot's use of lawless violence, which decimated institutions and elites and dispensed with education. Terror, for Montesquieu, was not the result of moral artifice or political calculation; it was an expression of the despot's distorted psyche, of his lust for destruction and penchant toward cruelty. But like Hobbesian fear, Montesquieu's terror was meant to serve as the catalyst of political and moral awakening. In the face of the despot, a liberal society would come to appreciate and pursue some of the principles we in the United States have come to cherish: the rule of law; a limited, constitutional state; social pluralism and diversity.

Despite their disagreements, Hobbes and Montesquieu believed that fear and terror were instruments of those wielding power from above. With the French Revolution and the age of democracy it spawned, political writers turned this assumption upside down. Political fear was now thought to emanate from below, from the psyche and culture of the mass. For Tocqueville, this new political fear was what I call "anxiety": a people's restless insecurity and nervousness, born of the overthrow of traditional authority and the isolation of modern society, with no clear object or focus. Anxiety was not the product of laws, elites, institutions, or education; it flourished in their absence. Nor was it a response to a despotic ruler, for the age of despotic rulers was supposed to have passed. Democracy—the impersonal, shapeless authority of the mass—was the order of the day, and anxiety was its natural psychic state. In response to this deep insecurity, Tocqueville argued, the mass longed for a firm disciplinarian who might bring some coherence and order to society. From that longing, a new kind of despotism would emerge—a state dictating each and every detail of daily life, a state more powerful, more invasive and intrusive than its predecessors. Where Hobbes and Montesquieu believed that the repressive actions of the powerful aroused fear or terror in the powerless, Tocqueville and his successors believed that the anxiety of those on the bottom authorized the repressive acts of those on the top. But like Hobbes and Montesquieu, Tocqueville believed that if we developed a proper and healthy fear of these prospects, we would cultivate the political instruments that might keep them at bay: local institutions, civic associations, and the dense civil society so many intellectuals praise today.

In Hannah Arendt's idea of "total terror," we reach the apotheosis of these intellectual developments. Like her predecessors, Arendt thought that the notion of total terror, embodied in Nazi Germany and Stalinist Russia, could serve as the ground of a new political morality. Like Montesquieu, she believed that terror was the product in part of violence. Like Tocqueville, she thought that the anxious mass created the political apparatus that acted so despotically. To this mix, she added the notion of ideology, the absolutist, fanatical faith in doctrines like communism and Nazism, which appealed to lonely men and women in desperate need of some reassuring truth. Though ultimately discredited by historians and social scientists, Arendt's vision of total terror found a wide audience during the Cold War and a new audience in the wake of the Cold War and 9/11. In "Remains of the Day," I look at this Arendt revival, as well as the enduring contemporary influence of Montesquieu's and Tocqueville's accounts of terror and anxiety. All of these recent diagnoses of fear, I argue, share the same deficits of their predecessors—a disregard for the political dimensions of fear, an obfuscation or elision of its repressive functions and inegalitarian consequences, and a hope that fear can serve as a ground for political renewal.

# 1     Fear

NO MATTER HOW IMPORTANT WEAPONS MAY
BE, IT IS NOT IN THEM, GENTLEMEN THE
JUDGES, THAT GREAT POWER RESIDES. NO!
NOT THE ABILITY OF THE MASSES TO KILL
OTHERS, BUT THEIR GREAT READINESS
THEMSELVES TO DIE, THIS SECURES IN THE
LAST INSTANCE THE VICTORY OF THE POPU-
LAR UPRISING.

—LEON TROTSKY

It was on April 5, 1588, the eve of the Spanish Armada's invasion of Britain, that Thomas Hobbes was born. Rumors of war had been circulating throughout the English countryside for months. Learned theologians pored over the book of Revelation, convinced that Spain was the Antichrist and the end of days near. So widespread was the fear of the coming onslaught it may well have sent Hobbes's mother into premature labor. "My mother was filled with such fear," Hobbes would write, "that she bore twins, me and together with me fear."[1] It was a joke Hobbes and his admirers were fond of repeating: Fear and the author of *Leviathan* and *Behemoth*—Job-like titles meant to invoke, if not arouse, the terrors of political life—were born twins together.

It wasn't exactly true. Though fear may have precipitated Hobbes's birth, the emotion had long been a subject of enquiry. Everyone from Thucydides to Machiavelli had written about it, and Hobbes's analysis was not quite as original as he claimed. But neither did he wholly exaggerate. Despite his debts to classical thinkers and to contemporaries like the Dutch philosopher Hugo Grotius, Hobbes did give fear special pride of place. While Thucydides and Machiavelli had identified fear as a political motivation,[2] only Hobbes was willing to claim that "the original of great and lasting societies consisted not in mutual good will men had toward each other, but in the mutual fear they had of each other."[3]

But more than Hobbes's insistence on fear's centrality makes his account so pertinent for us, for Hobbes was attuned to a problem we associate with our postmodern age, but which is as old as modernity itself: How can a polity or society survive when its members disagree, often quite radically, about basic moral principles? When they disagree not only about the meaning of good and evil, but also about the ground upon which to make such distinctions? Establishing communion among subscribers to the same political faith is difficult enough; a community of believers, after all, still argues about the meaning of its sacred texts. But what happens when that community no longer reads the same texts, when its members begin from such disparate starting points, pray to such different gods, that they cannot even carry on an argument, much less conclude it? Hobbes called this condition the "state of nature," a situation of radical conflict about the meaning of words and morals, producing corrosive distrust and open violence. "In the state of nature," Hobbes wrote, "every man is his own judge, and differeth from other concerning the names and appellations of things, and from those differences arise quarrels, and breach of peace."[4] This state of nature was not an extraordinary moment, no sudden storm over an otherwise placid sea. It was endemic to the human condition, constantly threatening a state of war. In fact, wrote Hobbes, it *was* a state of war.[5]

Hobbes warmed to the fear of death—not just the affective emotion, but the cognitive apprehension of bodily destruction—because he thought it offered a way out of this state of nature. Whatever people deem to be good, Hobbes argued, they should recognize that self-preservation is the precondition for their pursuit of it. They should realize that peace is the prerequisite of their preservation, and that peace is best guaranteed by their agreeing to submit absolutely—that is, by ceding a great deal of the rights that are by nature theirs—to the state, which he called Leviathan. That state would have complete authority to define the rules of political order, and total power to enforce those rules. Accepting this principle of self-preservation did not require men to give up their underlying faith, at least not in theory: it only asked them to acknowledge that their pursuit of that faith necessitated their being alive. When we act out of fear, Hobbes suggested, when we submit to government for fear of our own lives, we do not forsake our beliefs. We keep faith with them, ensuring that we remain alive so that we can pursue them. Fear does not betray the individual; it is his completion. It is not the antithesis of civilization but its fulfillment. This is Hobbes's counterintuitive claim about fear, cutting against the grain of later argument, but nevertheless finding an echo in the actual experience of men and women submitting to political power.

We shall consider here three other elements of Hobbes's treatment of fear, for they also speak to our political condition. First, Hobbes argued that fear had to be created. Fear was not a primitive passion, waiting to be tapped by a weapons-wielding sovereign. It was a rational, moral emotion, taught by influential men in churches and universities. Though the fear of death could be a powerful motivator, men often resisted it for the sake of honor and glory. To counter this tendency, the doctrine of self-preservation and the fear of death had to be propounded by preachers and teachers, and by laws instructing men in the ground of their civic duty. Fear had to be thought of as the touchstone of a people's commonality, the essence of their associated life. It had to address their needs and desires, and be perceived as defending the most precious achievements of civilization. Otherwise, it would never create the genuine *civitas* Hobbes believed it was meant to create.

Second, though Hobbes understood fear to be a reaction to real danger in the world, he also appreciated its theatrical qualities. Political fear depended upon illusion, where danger was magnified, even exaggerated, by the state. Because the dangers of life were many and various, because the subjects of the state did not naturally fear those dangers the state deemed worth fearing, the state had to choose people's objects of fear. It had to persuade people, through a necessary but subtle distortion, to fear certain objects over others. This gave the state considerable leeway to define, however it saw fit, the objects of fear that would dominate public concern.

Finally, Hobbes marshaled his arguments about fear not only to overcome the impasse of moral conflict, but also to defeat the revolutionary legions contending at the time against the British monarchy. The English Revolution broke out in 1643 between royalist forces allied with Charles I and Puritan armies marching on behalf of Parliament. It concluded in 1660 with the restoration of Charles's son to the throne. Between those years, Britain witnessed the war-related death of some 180,000 men and women, the beheading of Charles I, and the decade-long rule of Oliver Cromwell's Puritans.[6] Scholars have long debated whether this bloody struggle was a modern revolution or the last in a long line of religious conflicts unleashed by the Reformation. To be sure, Cromwell's forces did not seek a great leap forward: they hoped to return England to God's rule, conceiving themselves as restorative rather than progressive agents. Nevertheless, there was a revolutionary and democratic dimension to their actions, which Hobbes perceived and believed had to be countered. "By their harangues in the Parliament," he complained of the revolutionary leaders, "and by their discourses and communication with people in the country," the revolutionaries made ordinary people "in love with democracy."[7] Hobbes's arguments about fear were in no small measure directed at the revolutionary ethos of these Puritan warriors. And this lends his account a decidedly repressive, even counterrevolutionary character, the ramifications of which we shall see in the work of later theorists like Tocqueville and contemporary intellectuals writing today, as well as in the actual practice of political fear.

What Hobbes's arguments add up to is an acute analysis, never quite seen before or since, of fear's moral and political dimensions. Though Hobbes owed much to his predecessors, his appreciation of moral pluralism and conflict drove him to a new, and distinctly modern, conception of the relationship between fear and morality. Previous writers like Aristotle and Augustine believed that fear grew out of society's shared moral ethos, with the objects of a people's fear reflecting that ethos. Convinced that such an ethos no longer existed, Hobbes argued that it had to be created. Fear would serve as its constituent element, establishing a negative moral foundation upon which men could live together in peace. Thus, where previous writers treated fear as an emanation of a shared morality, Hobbes conceived of it as the catalyst of that morality. And though Hobbes was indebted to his contemporaries' analysis of self-preservation, he knew that the men of his age—tangled in revolution, indifferent to their own death—were not likely to accept it. This inspired some of his deepest reflections about how the fear of death could be generated and sustained by the sovereign and his allies throughout civil society. While Hobbes's analysis of fear owes more to classical and contemporary sources than we might think, his imagined orchestration of fear is more prophecy than reiteration, envisioning how modern elites will wield fear in order to rule, and how modern intellectuals will rely on fear, even as they distance themselves from Hobbes, to create a sense of common purpose.

## Skepticism and Civil War

Fear was central to Hobbes's political imagination for two reasons. First, it helped resolve a philosophical conflict about the foundation of morals.[8] Writing at a moment of intense skepticism about the objectivity of all perceptions and beliefs, Hobbes was aware of the irreconcilable differences among men about the meaning of good and evil.[9] Like Montaigne and Lipsius—indeed, like many writers today who reject the notion that there is any such thing that can be called truly good for all persons—Hobbes argued that good and evil were not moral properties inherent in the world. Good and evil were statements of personal preference and aversion, about which men could and did differ. "Every man, for his own part, calleth that which pleaseth, and is delightful to himself, GOOD; and that EVIL which displeaseth him: insomuch that while every man differeth from other in constitution, they differ also one from another concerning the common distinction of good and evil."[10] Where previous writers had taken moral disagreement to be a symptom of error, of man's inadequate understanding of the moral truth residing in the universe, Hobbes deemed it an inescapable human condition, "there being nothing simply and absolutely so; nor any common Rule of Good and Evill, to be taken from the nature of the objects themselves."[11]

Confronting disagreement about good and evil, Hobbes argued that the one principle upon which men could agree, indeed had to agree, was that each person was entitled, even bound, to seek his own preservation. However men defined the good—which could be as various, Hobbes acknowledged, as sensuous pleasure or pure knowledge[12]—it was in the nature of human action that they acted for the sake of that good.[13] But for men to seek and attain their good, they had to be alive. With the exception of eternal salvation, there was no good a man could pursue if he were dead.[14] Life, for Hobbes, was the highest good not because men always desired or pursued it nor because it brought them the greatest pleasure; indeed, he noted, life could be filled with pain, which might reasonably lead a man to kill himself.[15] Life was the highest good because it made possible the pursuit and fulfillment of all other goods. Recognizing its worth did not require men to give up their notions of good and evil so much as to acknowledge that however they defined those terms, they had to be alive in order to pursue the former and avoid the latter. Life, in other words, was not an intrinsic but an instrumental good.

But even if men agreed that self-preservation was a necessary condition of their pursuit of the good, even if they acknowledged that self-preservation required them to seek peace and submit to a sovereign state, Hobbes still confronted a problem. Men came to an appreciation of self-preservation only through reason.[16] But reason, Hobbes believed, often fell victim to passion, particularly the love of honor and glory.[17] At moments of calm or repose, a man might recognize that self-preservation was a good to be defended at all costs, even if that meant forgoing other goods that mattered to him. But at moments of intense humiliation, when his honor or reputation was at stake, he would forget or reject the value of self-preservation. He would risk his own death, challenge another man to a duel, and pursue his immediate rather than his long-term good.[18] Reason could thus never fully triumph over passion. What was required was to find and fund a passion that contained within itself elements of reason, or at least a passion that was hospitable to reason. "To reduce this doctrine to the rules and infallibility of reason, there is no way," Hobbes warned, "but first to put such principles down for a foundation, as passion not mistrusting, may not seek to displace."[19]

What passion carried the necessary energy to fuel human action and the requisite rationality to direct that action to its proper end, self-preservation? Fear. In his earliest treatises, Hobbes argued that two types of passion governed human deliberation and conduct: appetite, which drew a person toward an object or particular course of action, and aversion, which pushed him away.[20] From the point of view of self-preservation, the perils of appetite were plain. Though "the real good" of a person "must be sought in the long term, which is the job of reason," appetite focused the individual upon the short term, which often proved illusory or threatening to his long-term good. Appetite prevented him from "foreseeing the greater evils that necessarily attach" to the immediate goods he sought.[21] Aversion, by contrast, focused the individual on "displeasure present," and, when aversion took the form of fear, on "displeasure expected."[22] While fear could prove misleading—Hobbes was well aware that men often feared objects or outcomes as illusory as the goods they imagined[23]—it was best understood as a "certain foresight of future evil."[24] The purest form of fear was the fear of death, the ultimate future evil. Focused on the long-term, ultimate evil, the fear of death had an elective affinity with reason. It was the one passion that "not mistrusting" reason would not "seek to displace" it. The fear of death thus offered a perfect coincidence of thought and feeling, lending intellectual substance to Hobbes's observation that "one man calleth *Wisdome*, what another calleth *feare*."[25]

Hobbes's analysis of the fear of death as a rational emotion, enabling the individual to pursue his long-term good, looks backward, to Aristotle and Augustine, and forward, to Montesquieu and Tocqueville and beyond. Like his predecessors, Hobbes argued that fear took its bearings from our moral beliefs, attaining its value only by virtue of the goods that truly mattered to us. Unlike his predecessors, however, Hobbes argued that fear bore no intrinsic relationship to these beliefs. Fear was a neutral instrument of a person's good; it took no stand on the inherent worth of that good, except to point out to the individual the ways in which that good might undermine his preservation and thereby render his pursuit of that good impossible. And where previous writers argued that an individual's sense of the good arose from the objective moral beliefs of his society, Hobbes believed that a person's sense of the good was peculiarly his own. Because the good was not shared, self-preservation—and its companion, the fear of death—was no more than a regulative principle among different persons' irreconcilable conceptions of the good. It was a point of agreement among people who disagreed, requiring of them no substantive, shared, moral foundation, only an acknowledgment of their irresolvable differences. While Hobbes's successors would reject the backward-looking dimensions of his argument, they would never quite escape its forward-looking dimensions, the notion that fear could serve as a common ethic among people who otherwise lacked one.

Hobbes also hoped that the fear of death would serve as a weapon against that extraordinary group of men who plunged England into civil war, the political corollary of the state of nature. This was no simple task. Social movement in the seventeenth century was propelled by determined militants and disciplined activists, who believed that unprecedented levels of stamina and courage were required of them, that fear was to be shunned for the sake of glory and other heroic values. "Fortitude is resplendent," wrote John Milton, one of the parliamentary forces' most eloquent defenders, "not only in the field of battle and amid the clash of arms, but displays its energy under every difficulty and against every assailant." As John Arrowsmith warned his fellow revolutionaries in 1643, "I am confident you never dreamt of reforming a church and state with ease." War was the operative metaphor for their entire way of life. "The condition of the child of God," noted one radical, "is military in this life." Said another, "The world's peace is the keenest war against God." The Puritan revolutionaries found particular inspiration in the example of the Catholic St. Bernard, who had declared, "What can such soldiers fear who have consecrated their lives to Christ? . . . The Soldier of Christ kills with safety; he dies with more safety still."[26] Hobbes hoped to rely upon fear as an adjunct of reason, assuming fear to be the one passion that would not buck reason's injunction to seek preservation and peace. But here were men who "scarce thought of such death as comes invisibly in a bullet, and therefore were hardly driven out of the field."[27] It was not sufficient to create a sovereign state that could threaten men with death. That state would have to dissuade them of the value of courage, and persuade them that "the less they dare, the better it is both for the commonwealth and for themselves."[28] As much as the fear of death would have to be mobilized on behalf of reason, reason would have to be mobilized on behalf of the fear of death.

Hobbes thus thought about the fear of death and the demand of self-preservation not as a description of an already existing reality—of how human beings actually behaved in the world—but as a project of political and cultural reconstruction, requiring the creation of a new ethos and a new

man. Fear, he believed, would have to attain the imprimatur of moral legitimacy, to become as compelling as the call to Christian redemption, as ad-
mirable as classical feats of heroic glory. A generation raised on the writings
of ancient theorists of martial virtue would have to realize that there was
something irrational and foolish, perhaps insane, about a morality that
praised heroic death.[29] The courageous revolutionary would have to be seen
as reckless and incoherent, forever attuned to the appraising gaze of his
peers and distracted by their wayward sensibilities. The fearful man, by contrast, was to emerge as a truly rational agent, sensible and wise.

Hobbes's account of fear thus has an avowedly counterrevolutionary flavor. Given the scholarly debates about the revolutionary credentials of the
Puritans, I hesitate to assign Hobbes or his teaching such an anachronistic
appellation. Yet there is no escaping the fact that the Puritans saw politics as
a weapon of social transformation, that many of them were inspired by the
democratic currents of their day, and that courage was a cardinal revolutionary virtue. Raising the specter of liberty throughout what Milton called an
"anxious and listening Europe," the civil war offered these revolutionaries an
experience of political novelty not unlike that afforded to Wordsworth during
the first years of the French Revolution. Disciplined militants, organized in
parties and cells, introduced new concepts to western political thought, arguing for everything from universal male suffrage to unqualified religious freedom. While some spoke the language of local complaint, others invoked a
more universalist vocabulary, heralding the triumphant march of freedom
across land and water—from Britain to the continent, and from there to an
even wider expanse of nations. "From the columns of Hercules to the Indian
Ocean," wrote Milton, "the people of this island are transporting to other
countries a plant of more beneficial qualities and more noble growth than
that which Triptolemus is reported to have carried from region to region."
Inspired by visions of a redeemed nation, the Puritan New Model Army
hacked its way through the countryside, giving battle to royalist armies and
dispensations alike. In one of those strange moments of political intimacy
that revolutionary situations so often generate, soldiers and generals packed
the cramped pews of Putney Church to argue with each other about the
foundations of the new order, and to hear a lowly colonel tell his scandalized
superiors that "the poorest he that is in England hath a life to live, as the
greatest he."[30] This was the democratic, insurgent temper that Hobbes
hoped fear would counter.

The counterrevolutionary thrusts of Hobbes's argument contributed to
his thinking about fear in a second sense, forcing him to an unmatched soci-

ological awareness of how fear could be generated and sustained. If we compare Hobbes's account with that of Machiavelli, we can see this sociological
acuity most visibly at play. Machiavelli depicted political fear as a blunt tool,
aroused by the instruments of princely coercion. "Fear is held together,"
Machiavelli wrote to his imaginary prince, "by a fear of punishment which
will never abandon you."[31] Machiavellian fear was the prince's weapon, an
effect of his violence. It presumed a perpetual division between prince and
people, benefiting the former and threatening the latter. But Hobbes did not
believe any one ruler could ever possess enough coercive power to generate
sufficient fear among his subjects. "For if men know not their duty, what is
there that can force them to obey the laws? An army, you will say. But what
shall force the army?"[32] Nor did he think that fear could compel obedience if
people did not believe that submitting out of fear would somehow benefit
them. Absent some larger infrastructure of moral obligation, some willing
collaboration on the part of the ruled, princely fear would prove a hollow
hope for grounding submission.

Political fear would have to be understood, Hobbes concluded, not as the
surgical tool of an alien sovereign but as a form of collective life nourished
by the conscious participation of individual subjects, authoritative elites in
civil society, and institutions like the church and universities. The "better
sort" who originally stirred the countryside to civil war—those men who possessed the "most leisure to be idle" and "read the books written by famous
men of the ancient Grecian and Roman commonwealths"—would have to
become the intellectual vanguard of an aggressive counterinsurgency, steer-
ing subjects away from the mistakes of inherited assumption.[33] No state
could fully insinuate itself into the remote crevices of every community. A
more supple arrangement was called for, with leaders of civil society drafted
to preach the gospel of fear. Like their counterparts in the New Model Army
and the Puritan ministries, these teachers and preachers of fear would engi-
neer a profound transformation in popular sensibility.

To rouse fear in the countryside, these preachers would have to be
trained in the philosophical foundations of fearful obedience. This required
education, which required teachers, which required universities: "Men may
be brought to a love of obedience by preachers and gentlemen that imbibe
good principles in their youth at the Universities."[34] Leading up to the civil
war, Hobbes argued, the universities had taught subversion. They praised
classical theorists of democracy and peddled oxymorons like divided sovereignty to impressionable students. "The *Universities* have been to this nation
as the wooden horse was to the Trojans." Until the universities were "better

disciplined," until they began to teach the philosophy of fearful obedience, they would remain breeding grounds of treason, spreading the doctrines of ancient liberty and religious refusal. "I despair of any lasting peace among ourselves, till the Universities here shall bend and direct their studies to the . . . teaching of absolute obedience to the laws of the King."[35]

From properly trained teachers, ordinary people would learn that political fear was useful to them, that it helped secure some vital ingredient of their earthly happiness. Once ordinary people understood the moral importance of fear, they would collaborate in its cultivation. Each subject would deliver to his neighbors the message that anyone challenging the political order was under threat of almost certain punishment, if not annihilation. They thus would help to bring into being the very object of fear that kept them in thrall. As has often been noted, the frontispiece of the original edition of Hobbes's *Leviathan* depicts an apparitional king hovering over a walled city. This imposing sovereign keeps watch over the city's inhabitants and protects them from their enemies. The sovereign's body, however, is composed of thousands of individual figures, orderly men and women quietly staring upward toward its head. According to one interpreter, the image implies that the sovereign only exists through the subjects themselves.[36] But the image also suggests that the subjects are the authors of their own fear, their spectral gaze making Leviathan's otherwise benign visage not only imposing but threatening. It is an image, as we shall see, of astonishing prescience.

### Ecce Homo

To render democratic warriors receptive to the claims of fear, Hobbes believed that they would have to be transformed into reasonable creatures, conscious of their own good and capable of securing it. This required an inversion of values, with fear elevated to the status of a virtue, and the warrior principles of honor and glory denigrated as shameful vices. Fearful men were to be thought of not as cowards, but as purposive and reflective, focused upon their own ends. Such a claim may seem jarring, but, for Hobbes, fear was a friend, not an enemy, of the self. Passions like ambition, honor, and glory—inspiring the democratic ideology of revolution[37]—not only distracted from the needs of bodily preservation—not an incidental fact of selfhood, Hobbes reminds us[38]—but also stoked a giddy waywardness, depriving the self of steadfastness and coherence. Frightened of death, he could construct a purposeful life. He would be capable of rationality, even of that inner self-direction philosophers call positive liberty.[39] When men act out of fear, it is not because they have been crushed; it is because they have been saved.

In arguing on behalf of fear and against honor and glory, Hobbes seeks to show that the latter principles do not do for the individual what their advocates claim. According to Hobbes, men value honor and glory as symbols of power.[40] Power is valuable because it is an instrument of the self; it is a man's "present means, to obtain some future apparent Good."[41] But, Hobbes argues, there is a fundamental contradiction in seeking honor and glory for the sake of power. In order to be honored or deemed glorious, a person must demonstrate that he has power greater than that of his fellows—glory being "the imagination or conception of our own power, above the power of him that contendeth with us," honor being the "high rate" that men would pay "for the use of [our] Power."[42] Because glory and honor "consist in comparison and precellence," those who seek it must constantly measure themselves against their fellow men.[43] That comparative imperative focuses men on the status and achievements of their peers, away from themselves. It also makes men inordinately sensitive to insults and slights, the outward signs of lost honor or glory, and arouses a destabilizing rage.[44] Thus, an ethos meant to secure an individual the "present means, to obtain some future apparent Good"—*his* good, as opposed to what his neighbor deems to be good—generates in him an obsession with his peers and propels him to take dangerous, irrational acts, which undermine the very good he seeks.[45] Elevating recklessness to a virtue, honor and glory only betray the individual. He cannot keep faith with himself. He loses his inner compass and is forever distracted by those around him. There is nothing honorable or glorious about distraction: it bears all the attributes of madness.[46]

Fear is a disciplining agent, taming these destructive and distracting impulses. "As hope," which inspires honor and glory, "brings out anger, so fear controls it."[47] Fear lends the individual integrity and coherence, reminding him of that which matters to him most. Those who deem fear to be a second-rate virtue or a vice mistakenly believe that being afraid is "nothing else than to be affrighted." But those who are afraid, Hobbes insists, can also "distrust, suspect, take heed, provide so that they may not fear."[48] The fearful, in other words, do not simply freeze or flee. They move forward, maximizing whatever means they have at their disposal in order to obtain their future ends, which is the very definition of power.

It might sound strange to our ears to hear a counterrevolutionary advocate of a repressive state praise fear as the instrument of an autonomous self. As children of the Enlightenment, we believe, in the words of Franz Neumann, that "only a fearless man can decide freely."[49] But Hobbes's argument suggests a deeper traffic between the self and the fear-ridden subject of Leviathan. Radicals and revolutionaries tilt against the fear of death. Seeking to change a stubborn reality rather than accommodate it, they risk everything, including their lives, for the sake of an improbable transformation.[50] Though the revolutionary is not opposed to the self—indeed, she finds in revolution opportunities to express the best parts of herself—she is contemptuous of the cowardice and submission counterrevolutionaries like to pass off as self-interested realism and prudence. But the fearful counterrevolutionary has his own, competing claims to selfhood. Never quite the terrorized simpleton some imagine him to be, the counterrevolutionary has the argument of rationality on his side, as well as morality (by staying alive, he keeps faith with his conception of the good). Whether or not the counterrevolutionary is correct—as I will suggest in chapter six, there is more to the revolutionary's logic and less to the counterrevolutionary's than Hobbes would have us believe—it is the counterrevolutionary's claim to rationality, morality, and selfhood that makes fear such a compelling rationale for submitting to power. Though Hobbes's successors will attempt to sever fear from selfhood, they will do so at a price. They will overlook the real benefits—beyond mere life— to be gotten from fear, and obscure the reasons why men and women so often submit to its repressive dictates.

## Spectral States

Two questions about political fear haunt contemporary writers. First, why do people fear the things they fear? Why does the fear of crime, drugs, or terrorism dominate public concern, while other dangers get short shrift?[51] Second, why do the powerless submit to the powerful, particularly when the former outnumber the latter? True, the powerless may face retaliation or brutal retribution should they rebel. But were they to unite and pool their resources, they could turn their concerted power against their superiors. Why do they seldom do so?[52] Hobbes was particularly sensitive to these questions, and thought them intimately connected. Confronting a society where men often feared what he believed to be the wrong things, Hobbes was forced to think hard about how they could be persuaded to fear the right things. Men should fear death over dishonor. They also should realize that their death was most likely to come about in the state of nature, whose dangers they only dimly perceived, and at the hands of the sovereign—whose power they only minimally grasped—should they disobey him. Hobbes's task was to make the risks of the state of nature real to men, and to make the sovereign's power appear larger, more threatening, than it truly was. What these twin fears—of the state of nature and of the sovereign—required was what contemporary intellectuals would call the "construction" of fear. Hobbes, we might say, was the first writer to appreciate how fear could be swelled beyond the warrant of objective fact, where far-off dangers not immediately feared by people are transformed, in their minds, into imminent threats.

According to Hobbes, people can be persuaded to fear both the state of nature and the sovereign's punitive power—even when those dangers are neither clear nor present—because fear is a highly plastic emotion. Fear, Hobbes argues, is a species of aversion, a negative reaction to an object or proposed course of action we believe will harm us. "But Aversion," Hobbes reminds us, "wee have for things, not onely which we know have hurt us; but also that we do not know whether they will hurt us, or not."[53] This dimension of unknowable harm can make fear ripe for abuse, with demagogues encouraging us to fear mystical spirits in the afterlife. But it also provides an opening to make people afraid of that which they never have experienced as harmful. Such fears of unknowable harm must be plausible; they cannot, or should not, be invented out of thin air. The fear of the state of nature, for example, is an "*Inference*, made from the Passion." It is a speculation about the future, based on known facts of human nature.[54] But since the future is "but a fiction of the mind," whoever defines the objects of our fear necessarily traffics in the realm of imagination.[55] This makes the fear of unknowable harm a kind of rational fiction, a hypothetical speculation about the future, based upon experience and inference. Such speculations also involve a degree of moral evaluation, rooted in the ideologies of a particular place. Fear is a passion, and passion takes it shape not only from a person's nature, "but also from . . . differences of customes, and education."[56] If customs are made—often only recently—they can be unmade, and new customs introduced in their place. So it is with fear. Fear depends upon a society's broader ideological evaluations of virtue and vice, which are amenable to the sovereign's artifice and education.

Because fear is a pliable emotion, shaped and reshaped by moral instruction and ideology, the sovereign has great power to define its objects. No sovereign automatically possesses such power; indeed, he often competes with "private" men attempting to persuade people to fear objects he has not authorized them to fear. But if a sovereign fully assumes his legitimate powers, he will be able to define the objects of people's fear.[57] The sovereign must thus establish the fear of the state of nature and of his coercive power as his subjects' foremost fears. He must give the people "prospective glasses," forged of "Morall and Civill Science," of well considered moral and political doctrines, to help them "see a farre off the miseries that hang over" them but which they do not immediately perceive.[58]

How do the glasses of moral and civil science, provided by the sovereign, make people afraid of the state of nature? Not simply by showing them that the state of nature is miserable, but by demonstrating to them that they will experience a fear in the state of nature that is, strictly speaking, irrational and absurd. Where the fear of death is supposed to enable the individual to secure his own good, fear in the state of nature leads the individual to act in ways that subvert his good. In the state of nature, in other words, fear works contrary to its assigned purpose. Lacking a sovereign authority to define and enforce the rules of order, lacking any assurance of the good intentions of his fellows, the individual in the state of nature is forced to go on the offensive. Even if he knows that most people have friendly, or at least not hostile, intentions toward him, he can never know whether the individual he confronts is among those. To protect himself, he must treat everyone as if they were an enemy.[59] Because his fellows are in the same situation, they must treat him and their fellows as enemies as well.[60] The result is a war of all against all, which only perpetuates the very conditions that make people afraid. Fear in the state of nature does not protect men or enable them to secure their good; it forces them to act in ways that ensure their continuous fear, never allowing them to let down their guard and pursue their own good.[61] Such fear is all-consuming, leaving men no time or space to experience anything besides their fear. Fear in the state of nature severs the individual from his good, forcing him to think about nothing but his fear, nothing but life itself. He no longer fears death in order to enjoy the goods of life, for there are no such goods left for him to enjoy.[62] In the state of nature, then, fear betrays its stated purpose. It is this absurdity, this reversal of promise, that makes the state of nature something to be avoided at all costs. But it is an absurdity that can only be perceived by those donning the glasses of moral and civil science, which deem the fear of death a useful emotion, enabling men to secure their own good. It is the glasses, in other words, that turn a distant reality into a terrible threat.

And how do the glasses of moral and civil science turn the sovereign into a fearsome Leviathan, a creature no one would ever dream of challenging or crossing? By framing the subject's submission to the sovereign in such a way that the subject believes the sovereign is more powerful than he truly is. When the individual submits to the sovereign, he cedes his right to "use his own power, as he will himselfe, for the preservation of his own Nature."[63] He does not cede his narrow right to defend himself against immediate and certain physical attack, even if he is attacked by the sovereign; self-defense is a right no one can relinquish.[64] But he does give up his broader right to do whatever he believes is necessary to protect himself—to do whatever he understands protection to entail, against whatever dangers he believes he may at some point confront—and transfers that right to the sovereign. He agrees never to get in the way of the sovereign as the latter goes about doing whatever he believes is necessary for his own security, and by extension, for the security of the state. He agrees to stand aside and allow the sovereign to pass.[65] Under no circumstances is he to come to the aid of someone targeted by the sovereign for punishment, or to refuse to aid the sovereign, should he be asked, in subduing someone targeted for punishment—unless that someone is a family member or a person upon whom he is dependent. Though he retains the right to defend himself against the sovereign's physical assault, he must never use that right on behalf of another, except in the two cases just stipulated.[66]

Needless to say, if an individual retains the right to defend himself but no one outside his immediate circle is permitted to assist him, that individual will find himself confronting a form of power he cannot hope to resist with any efficacy. Each person's recognition of this fact—that when it comes to confrontations with the sovereign, he is essentially alone—helps generate an image of Leviathan's massive power. This magnified power augments the subject's fear of challenging the sovereign, making it less likely that he will ever do so. Guaranteed the right of passage, the sovereign is free to move about without resistance, a right enhanced by the fear each person feels. In an ideal world, the glasses of moral and civil science would be so powerful, the bonds of solidarity so frayed, the fear of failure so potent, no one would ever dream of challenging Leviathan.

Many of Hobbes's critics, in his time and our own, have dismissed his account of state power as shallow and hollow. James Harrington, an English political theorist of the seventeenth century, lampooned Leviathan as a "mere spitfrog," while later critics would complain that Hobbes's state could never energize a nation to do the things that nations do—fight wars, undertake large projects, launch noble expeditions.[67] But these criticisms, it seems to me, miss the point: Hobbesian state power was not intended for greatness, but to curtail challenges from below. It succeeded when its subjects merely stood still or got out of its way. Their immobility was the outward sign of their fear—a fear signaling their unwillingness to take up arms against the state, a fear all the more potent for the minimal power that aroused it. Yes, the Leviathan was like the Wizard of Oz, an illusion built from the calculations and imagination of those beholding it. But if there was not much behind the curtain, it did not really matter. For whatever was there, the beholder of the illusion could be certain that the sovereign possessed more power than he wielded himself.

## Fear and Civilization

Standing amid the killing fields of modern memory, we believe that politics of fear entails the overthrow of the rule of law, the elimination of the family, and the destruction of culture. Fear, we assume, is consistent with barbarism and antithetical to civilization. But Hobbes allows no such conceit. He insists that the proper cultivation of political fear depends upon clearly formulated laws and specified punishments. Laws, he writes, should be intelligible to ordinary subjects and published widely. State sanctions should be applied—equally and in accordance with prescribed rules—only to those violating those laws.[68] The rule of law is not an exception to rule by fear; it is the fulfillment of rule by fear: "The aym of Punishment is not a revenge, but terrour."[69] Hobbes believes it is perfectly possible for individuals to live under clear rules and still be afraid of challenging sovereign power. In fact, he hopes that precise rules will legitimate that fear, for arbitrary punishment will only subject the individual to a fear similar to that which he experiences in the state of nature. Arbitrary punishment is not punishment at all but a "hostile act" of the state.[70] If the sovereign hopes to use fear to pacify rather than arouse, to instill quiescence rather than awaken hatred, he must secure for the individual a better life than that which he finds in the state of nature. The rule of law is essential for that purpose.

Fear, for Hobbes, is also consistent with familial intimacy and the bonds of friendship. In the same way that the state cannot ask the individual to give up his right to defend himself against deadly assault, it cannot ask the individual to betray his family or those to whom he is obliged—financially or otherwise—for the maintenance of his life.[71] To compel an individual to betray his family or close friends is to turn the individual's fear of death into a weapon against himself, to ask him to choose between the fear of death and the goods of life. No state can ask the individual to strike such bargains and still maintain that fear is connected to the goods of life. Fear must support, not subvert, familial life and the claims of intimacy. This consonance between fear and family also betrays Hobbes's chilling realism, for the cultivation of familial life, he believes, can actually serve to enhance fear. As much as familial loyalty strengthens the bonds between family members so does it isolate the family from those outside its circle. The very exclusivity of familial bonds draws the family close and repels outsiders. It is thus not necessary to ask a son to kill his parents, for "there are others who being commanded will do that."[72]

Finally, Hobbes believes that a state built upon fear can support a world of humanistic endeavor; in fact, he argues, it is a necessary condition for such endeavors. One of Hobbes's central accusations of the state of nature, we should recall, is that it threatens high culture—"no Arts, no Letters; no Society," as he puts it.[73] Conversely, Hobbes sees the desire for culture as one of the collateral inspirations for the creation of Leviathan; culture requires leisure and comfort, which requires peace and security, which requires submission to the state. "Desire of Knowledge, and Arts of Peace, enclineth men to obey a common Power: For such Desire, containeth a desire of leasure; and consequently protection from some other Power than their own."[74] Although the subjects of Leviathan are suffused by intense fear, arts and letters can coexist with that fear. It was not, after all, until fear came to rule in ancient city-states like Athens that Plato and Aristotle could begin their work: "*Philosophy* was not risen to the *Graecians*, and other people of the West, whose *Common-wealths* (no greater perhaps than *Lucca*, or *Geneva*) had never *Peace*, but when their fears of one another were equall."[75]

## A Counterrevolution of Fear

One of the backdrops of modern political fear has been the ongoing struggle, armed and unarmed, between the forces of democratic transformation and the forces refusing to accommodate them. Violent or not, the parties of movement have often met resistance from the parties of order, who seek to subdue their opponents through fear.[76] While the last three centuries have seen insurgent movements wielding more than their fair share of fear—indeed, it was Robespierre who first declared that the Revolution should "subdue liberty's enemies by terror"[77]—this has caused them no end of trouble. Revolutionaries ask ordinary people to take extraordinary risks for the sake of remote, even implausible, goals. They not only demand courage, but identify courage as the very emblem of a good society.[78] When they employ the tactics of fear to repress dissent, as they often do, they are forced to defend an instrument antithetical to the spirit of defiance that originally inspired their movement. Counterrevolutionaries, by contrast, suffer from no such contradictions. They only require ordinary people to stand still, not to get in the way of their ferocious path. While they reserve the right to take militant action—indeed, their philosophy cries out for a guardian class willing to do whatever it takes to preserve social order and cohesion—counterrevolutionaries ask people merely to stay home, to abandon the public square for domestic comfort. When they use fear, they bear a lighter burden of justification than that born by their revolutionary counterparts, for fear is quite compatible with their domestic ethos of quiescence.

Counterrevolutionaries have often been myopically revanchist, but the more perceptive—like Hobbes—have recognized that the successful use of fear requires more than a simple restatement of traditional truths and a reiterated politics of deference. Counterrevolutionary theorists like Joseph de Maistre and Friedrich Nietzsche, and sophisticated practitioners like the Argentine generals who launched the Dirty War against the Left or J. Edgar Hoover, have been too attuned to the weaknesses of the old order not to see how its uninspired leadership and demobilized legions contributed to its demise. They have sought to rejuvenate submission with a more vital philosophy, to instill in ordinary men and women a reinvigorated fear of authority. They have followed the inspiration of Hobbes, administering precisely calibrated doses of exemplary punishment along with revamped notions of obligation. They have raised the specter of an all-encompassing disorder, claiming that should the democratic forces maintain, assume, or resume a governing position, the world will be not merely turned upside down but blown to bits. From the civil patrols of the Guatemalan highlands to old Russia's White Guards, counterrevolutionary fear has been an activist, collective affair, as extramural, complex, and moral as the old regime it defends and its opponents seek to displace.[79]

But Hobbes's doctrine evokes another side of modern politics—not the inaugural moment of counterinsurgent fear, when the forces of activist reform are defeated, but the succeeding era of quiet complacence and sober regard for family, business, locality, and self. After the demobilization of any popular movement, men and women tend to their own affairs, worrying about the everyday business of survival and success, forgoing larger visions of collective transformation. In her account of Pinochet's Chile, for example, journalist Tina Rosenberg writes of Jaime Pérez, a socialist student leader during Salvador Allende's last year in power. After the 1973 military coup, which ended 150 years of Chilean democracy, Pérez fled from public life. He did not protest, he "slept." He traded his old car for a new one—every year—and bought three color TVs. Explaining his silence, Pérez says, "All I knew was that life was good," and in certain respects, it was.[80]

The United States has also seen such moments—most famously in the wake of the McCarthy-era purges. Once the tumult of repressive politics died down, men and women retreated to the goods of family life and getting ahead. Critics lambasted the social types of the 1950s as conformists, coining phrases like "the man in the gray flannel suit," "the lonely crowd," and "status anxiety." But these were terms of moralistic accusation that evaded or sublimated the reality of McCarthyism. People were frightened during the 1950s, and they were frightened because of political repression. Their fear bore none of fear's obvious marks; they did not resemble the terrorized face in Edvard Münch's famous portrait *The Scream*. They looked instead like Hobbesian man—reasonable, purposive, and careful never to take a step in the wrong direction. Fear didn't destroy Cold War America: it tamed it. It secured for men and women some measure of what they deemed to be their own good. American citizens didn't betray their former principles: under the weight of intense coercion, their principles changed. Or they opted to forgo certain principles—political solidarity—for the sake of others—familial obligation, careerism, personal security. However they justified their decisions, their choices reveal the influence of Hobbesian fear. And if it sounds strange to contemporary ears to call it fear, that is only a testament to Hobbes's success.

In this regard, I can think of no more representative figure linking Hobbes's vision to the twentieth century than Galileo. According to his most celebrated biographer, Hobbes "extremely venerated and magnified" Galileo, whose influence is evident throughout Hobbes's work.[81] In the 1930s, Bertolt Brecht revived the story of Galileo as a twentieth-century parable of revolutionary courage and counterrevolutionary fear. Brecht turned Galileo into the improbable hero of a new proletarian science, a revolutionary slayer of medieval dragons. By threatening the church's authority, Brecht suggested, Galileo's teachings promised a world where "no altar boy will serve the mass/No servant girl will make the bed." But when "shown the instruments" of torture by the Inquisition, Galileo recanted his revolutionary scientific theories.[82]

At the end of Brecht's play, Galileo confesses to shame and remorse over his capitulation. "Even the Church will teach you that to be weak is not human," he spits out. "It is just evil." Though he managed after his recantation to pursue a clandestine science, the very solitariness of the pursuit—its separation from a larger project of collective, radical transformation—betrayed the scientific enterprise, which demands publicity, solidarity, and above all, courage. "Even a man who sells wool, however good he is at buying

wool cheap and selling it dear, must be concerned with the standing of the
wool trade. The practice of science would seem to call for valor." Most damn-
ing of all, Galileo realizes that he never was in as much danger from the Inquisition as he believed. Like the subjects of Leviathan, whose fear turns a
mere spitfrog into a terrifying giant, Galileo magnified his own weakness
and the strength of his opponents. "At that particular time, had one man put
up a fight, it could have had wide repercussions. I have come to believe that
I was never in real danger; for some years I was as strong as the authorities,"
he says. "I sold out," he wanly concludes.[83]

Whether Galileo is a coward or a realist (and in good Brechtian fashion,
the playwright suggests there might not be much difference between the
two), one thing is clear: Galileo's fear of death is connected to the goods he
valued in life. As much as he speaks on behalf of a larger political vision of
science, so does he subscribe to a more domestic conception of himself and
his ends. Brecht's Galileo is a bon vivant, a lover of the finer things—good
food, good wine, leisure. His science, he believes, depends upon his stomach. "I don't think well unless I eat well. Can I help it if I get my best ideas
over a good meal and a bottle of wine?" He adds, "I have no patience with a
man who doesn't use his brains to fill his belly." He hopes to use the proceeds from his science to secure a good dowry for his daughter, to buy books,
to acquire the necessary free time to pursue pure research. Thus, when he
chooses to abide by the dictates of the Inquisition and pursue his research on
the sly, he acts in accordance with a principle that has been his all along: science depends first and foremost on personal comfort.[84]

In choosing silence over solidarity, comfort over comradeship, Galileo
swaps one truth for another. It is not that fear silences his true self, that
self-interest gets the better of his moral code. It is that the only way he can
imagine fulfilling his ends is to capitulate to fear. That is how fear works in
a repressive state. The state changes the calculus of individual action, making fear seem the better instrument of selfhood. The emblematic gesture of
the fearful is thus not flight but exchange, its metaphorical backdrop not
the rack but the market. "Blessed be our bargaining, whitewashing, death-
fearing community," Galileo howls. And in the distance, one can see
Hobbes nodding in silent agreement, without the slightest hint of irony.[85]

# 2    Terror

Hobbes wrote about fear in the midst of political collapse, when the centripetal forces of civil war could no longer be contained by established norms of religion or history. So unnerving was this experience of political entropy that he sought to have it permanently imprinted on the European mind, there being "nothing more instructive towards loyalty and justice than . . . the memory, while it lasts, of that war."[1] Charles Louis de Secondat, baron de Montesquieu—a French aristocrat born in 1689, a full decade after Hobbes's death—took up the question of fear just as that memory began to fade. Montesquieu's was a world suffering not from the confusion of disorder but from the clarity of established rule. By the time of Montesquieu's birth, Louis XIV had turned a country that only narrowly escaped the revolution that wrecked Britain into the most orderly state in Europe. Convinced that "a little harshness was the greatest kindness I could do my subjects," Louis concentrated political power in his own hands, subduing nobles and commoners alike. He seized control of France's armies, turning semiprivate militias into soldiers of the crown. He banished the aristocracy from royal councils of power, relying instead on three trusted advisors and an efficient corps of officials in the countryside. He snatched veto power from local grandees accustomed to striking down royal edicts in regional *parlements*. He bankrupted the nobility through obscure methods of taxation; others he corrupted with frivolous titles, assigning them to positions of responsibility over his kitchen and stables. A class that had shared power with the royal family for generations was reduced to competing for such privileges as helping the king get dressed in the morning and perching on a footstool near the queen. Louis, the French historian Ernest Lavisse aptly noted, ruled with "the pride of a Pharaoh" and possessed, according to a character in Montesquieu's *The Persian Letters*, "a high degree of talent for making himself obeyed."[2]

Montesquieu had a visceral awareness of this aristocratic displacement. As a participant in the Bordeaux *parlement* and a substantial landowner involved in the wine trade, he chafed at royal interference in local matters, especially restrictions on the production and sale of wine. Everything about the reign of Louis XIV—the eclipse of the nobility, the drive toward centralized power, the loss of local institutions—he identified with despotism, and any limitation on royal power earned his support as the mark of reform. Combining a rearguard defense of noble privilege with a visionary critique of centralized power, he took positions sometimes traditional, sometimes reformist, but always opposed to the absolutism favored by Hobbes.[3]

This was the world and the politics that prompted Montesquieu to launch his reconsideration of Hobbesian fear, a revision so profound and complete it would shape intellectual perception for centuries to come. Political fear was no longer to be thought of as a passion bearing an elective affinity to reason; from now on, political fear was to be understood as despotic terror. Unlike Hobbesian fear, despotic terror was devoid of rationality and insusceptible to education. It was an involuntary, almost physiological response to unmitigated violence. The terrorized possessed none of the inner life that Hobbes attributed to the fearful. They were incapable of thought and moral reflection; they could not deliberate or even flee. They cowered and crouched, hoping only to fend off the blows of their tormentor. Montesquieu also reconceived the politics of fear. Where Hobbesian fear was a tool of political order, serving ruler and ruled alike, Montesquieu believed that terror satisfied only the depraved needs of a savage despot. Brutal and sadistic, the despot cared little for the polity. He had no political agenda; he sought only to quench his thirst for blood. The Hobbesian sovereign was aided by influential elites and learned men, scattered throughout civil society, who saw it in their interest to collaborate with him. The despot decimated elites and obliterated institutions, subduing any social organization not entirely his. While the Hobbesian sovereign generated fear through the rule of law and moral obligation, the despot dispensed with both.

Why this shift from fear to terror? Part of it was due to context. Creating political order in the wake of Louis XIV simply did not pose the same challenge to the Frenchman that it had to the Englishman. When Montesquieu tried to imagine a state of nature, as he did in the opening pages of *The Spirit of the Laws*, he could barely muster eight short paragraphs on the topic. The sheer brevity of his account—not to mention its benign descriptions—suggests how unfazed the political imagination of his day was by the specter of civil war.[4] But part of this shift was due to a change in political sensibility. Unlike Hobbes, who yearned for absolute government, Montesquieu sought to limit government power. Where Hobbes believed sovereigns should guard all political power as their own, Montesquieu argued for a government of "mediating" institutions. In his ideal polity, individuals and groups, housed in separate institutions, would share and compete for power. Forced to negotiate and compromise with each other, they would produce political moderation, the touchstone of personal freedom. Montesquieu argued for social pluralism and toleration—also checks, he believed, on the one-size-fits-all regime Louis XIV seemed bent on creating. With his vision of limited government, tolerance, political moderation, and personal freedom, Montesquieu was to become one of liberalism's chief spokespersons, about as similar to Hobbes as a butterfly is to a wasp.

And yet beneath their considerable differences lay a deep vein of agreement. Like Hobbes, Montesquieu turned to fear as a foundation for politics. Montesquieu was never explicit about this; Hobbesian candor was not his style. But in the same way that the fear of the state of nature was supposed to authorize Leviathan, the fear of despotism was meant to authorize Montesquieu's liberal state. Just as Hobbes depicted fear in the state of nature as a crippling emotion, Montesquieu depicted despotic terror as an all-consuming passion, reducing the individual to the raw apprehension of physical destruction. In both cases, the fear of a more radical, more debilitating form of fear was meant to inspire the individual to submit to a more civilized, protective state.

Why would a liberal opposed to the Hobbesian vision of absolute power resort to such a Hobbesian style of argument? Because Montesquieu, like Hobbes, lacked a positive conception of human ends, true for all people, in which to ground his political vision. Montesquieu's liberalism was not the egalitarian liberalism of the century to come, nor was it the conscience-stricken protoliberalism of the century it had left behind. Unlike Locke, whose argument for toleration was powered by a vision of religious truth, and unlike later figures such as Rousseau or Mill, whose arguments for freedom were driven by secular visions of human flourishing, Montesquieu pursued no beckoning light. He wrote in that limbo period separating two ages of revolution, when weariness with dogma and wariness of absolutism made positive commitments difficult to come by and even more difficult to sustain. His was a skeptical liberalism: ironic, worldly, elegant—and desperately in need of justification. Despotic terror supplied that justification, lending his vision of limited government moral immediacy, pumping blood into what might otherwise have seemed a bloodless politics. Montesquieu did not know—and did not care to enquire—whether we were free and equal, but he did know that terror was awful and had to be resisted. Thus was liberalism born in opposition to terror—and at the same time yoked to its menacing shadow.

But hitching liberalism to terror came at a price: It obscured the realities of political fear. Montesquieu painted an almost cartoonish picture of terror, complete with a brutish despot straight out of central casting, and brutalized subjects, so crazed by terror they couldn't think of or for themselves. So did he overlook the possibility that the very contrivances he recommended as antidotes to terror—toleration, mediating institutions, and social pluralism—could be mobilized on its behalf. An expression of the despot's deranged psyche, Montesquieu's terror was an entirely nonpolitical or antipolitical affair, circumventing political institutions and sidestepping the political concerns of men. The polemical impulse behind his account was clear: If Montesquieu could show that despotic terror destroyed everything men held dear, and if he could show that terror possessed none of the attributes of a liberal polity, terror could serve as the negative foundation of liberal government. The more malignant the regime, the more promising its liberal alternative. Built into Montesquieu's argument, then, was a necessary exaggeration of the evil against which it was arrayed.

Though repressive, the rule of Louis XIV did not entirely warrant Montesquieu's overheated depictions, prompting Voltaire to complain that Montesquieu "satirizes more than he judges" and that he "makes us wish that so noble a mind had tried to instruct rather than shock."[5] Montesquieu was not unaware of the flaws in his account. In a youthful work, *The Persian Letters*, he offered plentiful evidence to suggest that his mature conception of despotic terror, stated in *The Spirit of the Laws*, was as much political pornography as it was social vision. In *The Persian Letters*, Montesquieu described a form of fear quite similar to that depicted by Hobbes. Rational and moral, fear relied upon education; it aided rather than subdued the self; it depended upon a powerful ruler working in concert with elites; it required the collaboration of all sectors of society. But in his later years, Montesquieu could no longer abide this youthful gloss. So he rejected the earlier vision, as have subsequent writers, who would ignore or misinterpret *The Persian Letters*, resulting in the distorted vision of terror we possess to this day.[6] Montesquieu's, then, is a cautionary tale, revealing the pitfalls of a liberalism that

relies on terror and thereby misconstrues it, making the Frenchman a creature of not only his own time, but also our own.

## Terror Bound

*The Persian Letters* is a fictitious account of Usbek and Rica, two Persian gentlemen who travel to France. There they encounter novel ideas and exotic
practices, which they recount to each other and to their Persian friends in a
series of letters. Back in Persia, Usbek has a harem of wives, which his eunuchs maintain while he is away. A chief subtext of the letters is the parallel
between Usbek's domestic tyranny and that which he finds in France: the
Persian harem is European despotism writ small. Through the characters of
Usbek, his eunuchs, and his wives—and his depiction of the harem's laws,
moral ethos, and pluralist structures—Montesquieu provides a political account of despotic terror, dramatically different from the one he will offer in
*The Spirit of the Laws.*

Usbek is a gentleman and a scholar. He is a charming husband, faithful
friend, and beloved teacher. He is committed to the strenuous search for wisdom, not the easy contemplation of familiar ideals. So devoted is he to truth
that he disrupts his life in Persia and travels to Europe to find it. He is a partisan of modern science and high culture. He condemns slavery because it
induces "eternal lethargy" and praises commercial societies because they
promote "abundance and industry." A thorough-going moralist, he would
rather relinquish political power at the Persian court than compromise his
principles. He is, in short, the prototypical modern intellectual—not a stereo-
typical Enlightenment rationalist like Helvetius or Condorcet, but a genuine
pluralist, a Diderot or Montesquieu himself. He delights in the world's multiplicity and diversities, and revels in the strange and the new.[7]

But Usbek is also a purveyor of terror. He castrates men to make them
serve him more faithfully. He has his eunuchs violently punish his wives.
He does not tolerate disagreement or challenge, and makes sure that his law
reigns supreme in the harem. How could this learned, sensitive individual
preside over such a regime of terror? How could a humanist be a rapist, an
intellectual a despot?

Many scholars have interpreted Usbek's contradictions as symptomatic
of the hypocrisy and self-delusion of despotic rule: drunk with power, the
despot is necessarily opaque to himself.[8] But that interpretation evades a
darker truth: Usbek's partition of his life into separate spheres—the life of
the mind, the polity, the harem—is the key to his despotism. Usbek does

not demand the reconciliation of opposing principles. He tolerates contradiction and accepts the plurality of disparate worlds. It is this genial tolerance that facilitates his exercise of violence at home and speculation about peace abroad. The reason he can brutalize his wives and eunuchs while advocating toleration is that the harem demands a different cultural logic from that of the Persian court or Regency France. Contrary to the claims of many of Montesquieu's interpreters and exponents[9]—not to mention *The Spirit of the Laws*—pluralism and tolerance support rather than undermine the practice of despotism.

Montesquieu's account in *The Persian Letters* of the relationship between terror, the rule of law, and morality also runs counter to his later arguments. The harem is nothing but rules and endless homilies about upholding the rules. Punishments are severe, but not arbitrary. Designed to uphold the harem's code, they are meted out in response to specific transgressions. "You command," Usbek tells the eunuch, "whenever you fear a weakening of the laws of decency and modesty." When Usbek learns that one of his wives, Zachi, has allowed a white eunuch into her room—one of the harem's cardinal crimes—he does not react precipitously. He exercises restraint, hoping to prevent future transgression without having the eunuchs punish her. He sends Zachi a long letter, identifying her crime, interrogating and rebutting her possible excuses. He extends mercy to her—but with the warning that she should not expect such benevolence in the future. He reminds her that she benefits from his despotic rule, that the harem is "a happy shelter against the attacks of vice, a sacred temple where your sex loses its weakness and becomes invincible despite all the disadvantages of its nature."[10]

Montesquieu's portrayal of the eunuchs in *The Persian Letters* also bears little resemblance to the despot's enforcers in *The Spirit of the Laws*. In his later work, Montesquieu will suggest that the personal incapacities of the enforcers—their lack of self-esteem, honor and ambition—keep them in thrall to the despot. But in *The Persian Letters*, Usbek stokes the eunuchs' ambition in order to gain their cooperation, and he uses the authority of the older, more senior eunuchs to discipline the younger ones. In a letter to one of his fellow eunuchs, a senior eunuch explains that he became a eunuch as a young slave after Usbek asked him to assume responsibility over the harem wives. In deciding to be castrated, the eunuch made several calculations. Usbek had threatened him, claiming that he would face severe punishments if he did not agree to be castrated. But he was also tired of being a slave. The work was difficult and wearying, and he wanted a change. He was ambitious, hoping to work his way up to a higher position. "I had planned," he writes,

"to sacrifice my passions to tranquility and fortune." Hoping for a promotion, he accepted the surgery. Ambition actually increased his fear, suggesting to him that if he didn't cooperate with Usbek, he not only would face un-
bearable pain but also would miss out on an excellent opportunity. The
promise of advance thus made castration seem a desirable option, enabling
him to "see the recompense but not the loss."[11]

Ambition is not a naturally occurring idea among the eunuchs; it must be
taught by the older eunuchs and learned by the younger ones. For example,
when a younger slave, Pharan, resists the offer of promotion to eunuch, his
mentor tries to persuade him to "allow himself to be consecrated to that office" because it would "be to [Pharan's] advantage." To teach ambition, the
senior eunuchs must soften the younger eunuchs' violent reactions to the
idea of castration, which impede their rational calculations. According to one
of the older eunuchs, when the time came for "the blade" to separate Jaron,
a younger colleague, from his "nature," the younger man cried and resisted.
But the older one soothed him: "I quieted your tears and your outcries," he
writes. By calming emotion and enabling the younger eunuch to remember
what he would gain by castration, the older eunuch used compassion to sustain the despotism's fear. "I thought of you," writes the older eunuch to
Jaron, "as having a second birth and taking leave of a servitude in which you
always had to obey, to enter another kind of servitude, where you were to
command."[12]

If anyone in the harem should exhibit the personal qualities that Montesquieu will ascribe to terror in *The Spirit of the Laws*—paralyzed will and
crippled rationality—it should be the harem women, for they are its true victims. Yet Usbek's wives are independent, willful, assertive, and knowing.
They launch tiny rebellions and commit small acts of disobedience. They
have affairs and take every opportunity to fulfill their own desires. They are
resourceful and strategic, manipulating Usbek and the eunuchs to advance
their own purposes. In return for not harassing the eunuchs with special requests all through the night, they receive special privileges. If the eunuchs
are too zealous in their punishment of the wives, the women tempt Usbek to
bed and, at the moment of his greatest pleasure, extract promises that he will
put the eunuchs in check, by violence if need be. As one eunuch observes, "I
have everything to fear from their tears, from their sighs, from their embraces, from their very pleasure. . . . Their charms can become terrible for
me." The wives' "present services" to Usbek, he adds, "wipe out in one moment all my services of the past." He is frightened by their "amorous negotiations," by their ability to craft a "treaty made with sighs."[13]

Even when the wives seem most degraded and stripped of selfhood, they evince a desire for self-promotion. One wife, Zachi, reminds Usbek of a beauty contest he once conducted among the wives. Each woman was forced to strip in front of him, decorating her body with makeup, jewelry, and exotic accessories. Usbek examined each of them meticulously. His "curious regard" was "extended" to their "most secret spots." He had them "assume a thousand different positions—ever a new command and ever a new submission." In the annals of political literature, it would be hard to find a more unvarnished portrait of human degradation. The beauty contest appears to be the perfect metaphor for the stripping down of self, which has come to be emblematic of the totalitarian state.[14] Yet Zachi confesses that even at this moment of submission, her only thought was to win the contest, for victory would bring her greater status in the harem. Like the eunuchs, she accepts her own degradation as a means of rising above others. She is not weighed down by her humiliation; instead she sees in it a blazing path of personal advance.[15] But Zachi's ambition—like that of the other wives and of the eunuchs—has a price: it keeps Usbek in power. The desire of the wives and eunuchs for promotion can only be satisfied by Usbek's remaining in charge. Being afraid and submissive thus fits well with being ambitious and upwardly mobile. Fear is structured not by the absence of rationality and aspiration but by a short-term, limited rationality, which tracks a narrow path of self-advance rather than the spacious avenue of collective emancipation.

Like the eunuchs, the wives do not automatically subscribe to or follow the dictates of this short-term rationality. They, too, must be taught the harem rules by the older wives. One wife, Zelis, explains that she intends to enroll her young daughter in the harem's sexual politics before the usual age girls are inducted. She fears that if her daughter gets too much of a taste for freedom, she will experience her submission to the harem rules as a form of violence. But if the girl learns early the practice of docility, her submission will acquire the "gentle effect of habit." She will internalize its rules and strictures, and be happily acculturated to wifedom: "We practice our role of subordinate so that it may hold us firm through the critical period when passions begin to appear and encourage us toward independence."[16]

From *The Spirit of the Laws*, we have come to think that familial love does not survive despotic terror, for if it did, it would pose an obstacle to terror. But *The Persian Letters* shows that familial love not only persists under terror but actually sustains it. Zelis is inspired by a deep love for her daughter. It is precisely her desire to protect the child from the violence of a late induction that inspires the mother to train her at an earlier age. Kindness, not cruelty, leads her to assist Usbek in the propagation of fear. Far from relying upon an entirely different, and lower, order of human motivation, despotism can be bolstered by the most ordinary—and elevated—emotions.

*The Persian Letters*, then, leaves us with the following account of fear, which helps us see not only the limits of *The Spirit of the Laws* and later accounts of fear, but also, I would suggest, the true faces of fear. First, fear is not antithetical to reason. It thrives on an instrumental, cost-benefit analysis. Fear does not just coexist with this rationality; it is, as the eunuchs demonstrate, structured and enhanced by it. This rationality is certainly limited: it reproduces the conditions that prevent the wives and eunuchs from achieving a fuller happiness. But given the costs of challenging its dictates, it makes some sense for them to act in accordance with it. Second, fear arises from and is connected to the broad range of sympathies, desires, and aspirations that ordinarily motivate men and women. The fearful do not lack virtue, honor, ambition, love, or loyalty. They are fearful precisely because they possess these characteristics. Third, fear is not solely aroused by cruelty or sadistic violence. Kindness and well-meaning compassion help create and sustain it. Fear does not solely arise from actions intended to inspire fear. It just as easily follows from the all-too-human desire to lessen the suffering of one's own. Fourth, despotic power need not be arbitrary, concentrated, or centralized, and it need not be free of legal or moral restrictions. The harem depends upon multiple wielders of power, including the eunuchs and the wives, each of whom submits to a code, both legal and moral. Finally, the social universe underlying despotic power has all the characteristics of pluralist spheres, multiple associations, and hierarchical elites that Montesquieu and his followers later will claim are checks against despotic fear. In the world of fear, the avenues of social influence are as crooked and entangled as the streets of prerevolutionary Paris.

## Terror Unbound

When Louis XIV died in 1715, his death raised expectations among the nobility that they might regain some of the privileges lost during his reign. They had good reason for hope. Louis's successor, Philip of Orleans, was sympathetic to their complaints. He abandoned Versailles for Paris, moving the seat of royal power closer to the nobility, and established councils designed to give the aristocracy some share of political power. In addition, he loosened the dour morals and religious orthodoxy that had sustained Louis through his more than half-century of absolute rule.[17] Published in 1721, *The Persian*

*Letters* registered the promise of this moment. Though filled with dire warn-ings of a despotic future, *The Persian Letters* evinced a sense that reforming the French monarchy was possible. Nimbly touring despotism's political structure, Montesquieu exposed its building blocks and, by implication, the ease with which they could be dismantled.

*The Spirit of the Laws* was published in 1748, twenty-seven years after *The Persian Letters*. During that interim, Orleans had died, and with him all hopes for constitutional reform. His successors, first Cardinal Fleury and then Louis XV, set about undoing what Orleans had done, and it soon became apparent that reforming the monarchy would require a more strenuous assertion of po-litical will than Montesquieu's circle evidently was capable of mustering. Even under Orleans, there had been signs of trouble. The administrative councils proved to be an abject failure. Newly resurgent *parlements* tried to challenge royal authority, but ultimately did little more than play the part of a Greek cho-rus.[18] This failure of reform—coupled with Montesquieu's two-year stay in England, which "radicalized" him[19]—produced in him a growing impatience with the stalled pace of change, a combination of frustrated hope and acceler-ated expectation, which influenced the writing of *The Spirit of the Laws*. Despotism, Montesquieu came to believe, did not depend upon the familiar forms of rule and authority described in *The Persian Letters*; it was hardly amenable to political analysis at all. Instead, it was powered by the deepest currents—psychological, cultural, even biological—of human experience. It was not an elastic structure but an intractable regime. It could not be taken apart by the delicate arts of reform: it had to be gutted and destroyed. Mon-tesquieu was no friend of revolution, but the unintended consequence of his account was to lend credence to the claims of his younger, more radical, brethren, calling for a wholesale transformation of France's Old Regime rather than its piecemeal reform.[20] Terror was not just another mode of poli-tics: it was a nightmare from which Europe had better soon awake lest it be consigned to darkness. When it came to despotism, time was not on the side of its opponents—a lesson not lost on Robespierre, Saint-Just, and the Jaco-bins, who would sponsor that revolutionary bloodbath meant to cleanse France of its despotic inheritance.

*The Spirit of the Laws* thus belongs to the great moral artistry of the En-lightenment, to that moment when the liberal imagination was first seized by its critical and enduring passions—a hatred of cruelty and fanaticism, a dis-trust of all things clerical, a deep and humane sympathy for the claims of dis-senters, and a cosmopolitan solidarity with victims across the globe. To this list of liberal aversions Montesquieu added a distinctive blend of programmatic solutions: the rule of law, tolerance, a government of mediating institutions and separated powers, a system of countervailing elites to check central authority, and social pluralism. Montesquieu advocated these reforms on behalf of a new kind of freedom—freedom as personal security, the calm and untroubled assurance that one is protected from the predations of state power. This was not the freedom of Hobbes or Locke—neither the unimpeded motion of the human body nor the right to use one's reason in accordance with God's law—but a freedom that could be enjoyed only when political power was fragmented and checked by multiple institutions, the rule of law, and a diverse society. It was a freedom defined wholly by the absence of fear: "Political liberty is that tranquillity of spirit which comes from the opinion each one has of his security, and in order for him to have this liberty the government must be such that one citizen cannot fear another citizen."[21]

But what exactly was this fear, this despotic terror? Curiously, *The Spirit of the Laws* never defines it.[22] Part of Montesquieu's unwillingness to define it was due no doubt to his intellectual temperament. He was repelled by the austere architecture of Hobbesian thought, in which unadorned definitions gave rise to severe edifices of theoretical conclusion, a style of deductive reasoning he believed mirrored the harsh simplicity of despotic rule.[23] But Montesquieu's refusal to define terror registered an even deeper conviction. Terror, he had come to believe, was a great nullifying force, so oriented toward destruction and negation it could not sustain anything suggesting presence or concreteness. "Everything around" despotism, he observed, was "empty." Terror's most telling sign was silence, the desolation of verbal space signaling both the dissolution of men capable of speech and the disappearance of a world capable of description. No words, no definitions, could withstand terror's decimating energies.[24]

Hobbesian fear—and the fear Montesquieu described in the harem—traveled in a world of things, among men with ends to pursue and goods to be sought. Absence and loss were certainly fear's companions: there was, after all, no more categorical loss than death. But the fear of death was a powerful emotion for Hobbes precisely because it conveyed to its sufferer the prospect of losing the goods he valued in life. The fact that the generation of Hobbesian fear required the cooperation of elites and institutions only added to this sense that fear flourished in a world of things. The denser the world, the more opportunities for depriving men of the objects that mattered to them, the greater the possibilities for arousing fear. In an empty space where human affections were thin and the objects of human attachment few, fear would find an inhospitable terrain.

In *The Spirit of the Laws*, Montesquieu conceived an altogether different relationship between terror, self, and world. Terror preyed upon a person stripped of selfhood—of reason, moral aspiration, the capacity for agency, and a fondness for things in the world. The more self a person possessed, the more capable he was of resisting terror. The more connected he was to the world and its objects, the more resources he would have to challenge the despot. Deprived of self and world, he was the perfect victim of despotic terror. The ideal environment for terror was a society in which social classes and complicating hierarchies had been eviscerated and the individual was forced to stand alone—not unlike the world, Montesquieu believed, of Louis XIV. Liberated from the thick constitution of medieval ranks and orders, the despot would be free to wield his sword with unequivocal force. The most fertile climate for despotic terror, then, was not a dense atmosphere of desiring selves, collaborating elites, and robust institutions, but a vast expanse of nothingness, from which liberalism derived its somethingness.

## An Unmade Self

At the center of Montesquieu's despotism crouched its victim: the unmade self. The despot's victims were like physical objects, obeying him "as infallibly as . . . one ball thrown against another." When they submitted, there was no resistance, no opposition, just physical motion in response to physical motion. Ideally, the mere threat of violence, rather than violence itself, was enough to compel their obedience. "One has received the order and that is enough."[25] To produce this perfect physics of power, "one must take everything away" from the victim: his will, his selfhood, his very humanity. The despot thus threatened more than the body. He robbed the victim of "a will of his own," rendering him incapable of formulating preferences, making decisions, or acting upon those decisions. The victim was divested of those internal drives—tastes, beliefs, desires—that inspire people to oppose themselves against the world. Stripped of these thorny idiosyncrasies, which make a person the peculiar being he is, the victim could not "prefer [himself] to others" but could only prefer himself "to nothing." He was incapable of imagining his future, of thinking about his long-term aims and ends. He was so absorbed in responding to violence or its threat that he could not see how his actions undercut his long-term ends. "When the savages of Louisiana want fruit, they cut down the tree and gather the fruit. There you have despotic government." The victim could not think in causal or linear terms. "As for the sequence of events, [he] cannot follow it, foresee it, or even think about it." Reason itself was crowded out by terror, for a reasoning person might be able to challenge and overcome the despot. "In a despotic government, it is equally pernicious whether one reasons well or badly; it suffices that one reason to run counter to the principle of the government." The victim lacked emotions like love and ambition, and virtues like honor and loyalty, which linked him to other men and women in the world, and could potentially inspire him to oppose the despot. "Honor would be dangerous" in a despotism, threatening despot and victim alike. Ambition also was stamped out; it only encouraged subjects to act courageously. The victim had no feeling for family; neither loyalty nor love could move him. "It is useless to counter" the victims' slavishness, Montesquieu concludes, "with natural feelings, respect for a father, tenderness for one's children and women, laws of honor, or the state of one's health."[26]

Hobbes thought that a person's fear of death was an expression of that person's most intimate desires and wishes. All fearless people were alike— brash, foolish, enthralled by death—but a fearful person was fearful in his own distinctive way. For Montesquieu, it was the reverse. Because the terrified were incapable of reason, agency, and formulating their own ends, they possessed none of the irregularities distinguishing one person from the next. Terror fed on the dull sameness of animals motivated by nothing but the biological imperative of staying alive. The victim's "portion, like beasts,'" was "instinct, obedience, and chastisement." The fear of death could not be linked to the goods of a particular life, for it flourished only in the absence of those goods: "In despotic countries one is so unhappy that one fears death more than one cherishes life." In free societies, obedience was "naturally subject to eccentricities." Free subjects thought too highly of themselves to slavishly obey; they forced their rulers to accommodate their demands. Not so in despotism. A de-individualizing experience, despotic terror made no room for pluralism, difference, and individuality.[27]

In recent years, intellectuals of varying stripes have taken the liberal tradition to task for its celebration of the independent, autonomous self. A figure of titanic but chilly remoteness, the liberal self is supposed to be Kant's bleak gift to modern morals. According to Michael Sandel, the liberal self is "an active, willing agent," who chooses her beliefs rather than embrace or discover those she has inherited from parents, teachers, and friends. She is not bound by her "interests and ends." She "possesses" such ends but is not "possessed" by them. She lurks, like a spider, behind all the strands connecting her to the objects of the world—content in her remove, autonomous at the center of her austere web.[28] The original vision of a self detached from its ends and the world, however, was born not in triumph but in grief. Long before Kant, long before the liberal subject of communitarian complaint, there was Montesquieu's victim, a fragile being severed from its basic goods and the world's objects. Dispossessed of contingent aims, ends, and desires, the victim was divested of every unique relationship and circumstance that made him who he was. For only after shaving off these distinctive layers of self could the despot act upon a creature of pure physicality.

Despite these differences between the proverbial liberal self and Montesquieu's brittle victim of terror, the two figures did share an elusive affinity. Kant's self may not have been the victim Montesquieu envisioned, but Kant could only think of the self as he did because Montesquieu had redefined terror to be an entirely physical phenomenon. By stripping terror of the emblems of selfhood and by conceiving those emblems as checks against terror,[29] Montesquieu made it possible for subsequent theorists to think of fear, redefined as terror, as an experience unhinged from the life of the mind. If a person were rational or moral, Montesquieu suggested, he was not likely to be found among the terrorized. Kant picked up on this contrast between terror, on the one hand, and selfhood, on the other, only he turned it in an entirely different direction. Like the despot, Kant sought to strip the self of its contingent features—its particular ends, its attachment to immediate circumstances, its objects of desire. But where the despot uncovered a creature ripe for terror, Kant discovered an agent of moral freedom, a pure good will, attuned solely to the dictates of reason, who could act upon the requirements of duty without the "admixture of sensuous things." Such a person, Kant believed, would be incapable of fear, precisely because he had been liberated from the things of this world, including his physical self.[30] But where Montesquieu's stripped-down self was prepared for a descent into hell, Kant's rose gloriously to the kingdom of ends. Thus was the liberal self conceived in the shadow of terror.

### An Unmade World

Contrary to Hobbes, Montesquieu sought to show in *The Spirit of the Laws* that terror served no useful or intelligible political purpose. It did not meet the needs of individual members of the polity: physical safety, economic well-being, moral self-definition, personal advance. Nor did it establish public order, fortify boundaries, or promote a common existence. Its sole function was to enable the despot, a creature of intense want, to fulfill his every desire. Isolated from the polity and ignorant of its needs, the despot responded only to the stirrings of his physical self—to the pleasures of lust and sadism, to the sensations of taste, touch, and smell. In describing the despot in this way, Montesquieu sought less to demonstrate his dark criminality than to stress his political remove, which symbolized the apolitical, private function of terror. Despotic terror could not benefit an entire people—as fear did, according to Hobbes and to Montesquieu in *The Persian Letters*—because it spoke to the most remote, least civic passions of a depraved being. By ascribing despotism's origins to the despot's physical passions, one could pinpoint terror's source and easily remove it, without threatening the interests of anyone beyond the despot himself. It was this possibility of easy remove that made despotic terror such a desirable foundation for liberal politics. Despotism was easy to mobilize against, in Montesquieu's account, precisely because it lacked any supportive trapping in the population and could be so painlessly extracted.

The despot who aroused terror bore no resemblance to the Hobbesian sovereign or to Usbek. He was not schooled in the arts of rule. He never read philosophy. He did not build roads, was cavalier about taxes, and showed no concern for the needs of his subjects. Where kings sought to build monuments for the ages—cathedrals and empires, vast commercial enterprises— the despot had no interest in glory, neither his own nor his realm's.[31] His sole concern was to satisfy his infinite needs, arising from the vast geography of his misshapen psyche. This was a man who was "naturally lazy, ignorant, and voluptuous," an animal "drunk with pleasures." He was not governed by the imperatives of reason or prudence. "A creature that wants," he could not bear reason's inevitable delay to his own gratification. A "man whose five senses constantly tell him that he is everything and that others are nothing" could not think about his subjects. Like an infant, he simply could not perceive or accommodate the demands of anyone besides himself.[32]

Prior to Montesquieu, political theorists had written about lawless tyrants ravishing entire peoples for their own pleasure. But what gave the actions of these tyrants their criminal flavor was the persistent backdrop of laws. The tyrants of yore were transgressors, and transgression required laws or limits.[33] Montesquieu's despot, by contrast, was neither transgressive nor criminal. He acted without limits because there were none. His power was not subject to laws. His reign was "disorderly," "extreme," and "agitated." It had "no rule, and his caprices destroy all the others," enabling him to "take life away" at a moment's notice. The despot's power was also not subject to any kind of moral restriction. Ethical principles could not survive the intense violence of the regime. Lawlessness and absence of morality made for a peculiar kind of education. Unlike the sophisticated instruction provided by Hobbes's teachers of fear or the harem to its members, the despot purged his subjects of their moral reflexes. Religion was eliminated, as was any form of knowledge, ethical or otherwise. "Knowledge will be dangerous . . . and, as for the virtues, Aristotle cannot believe that any are proper to slaves." The despot only taught the few simple precepts of unquestioning obedience, seeking not to "elevate the heart" but to "bring it down." The simpler the ideas, the more powerful the terror, making education in despotism "in a way, null."[34]

In addition to being arbitrary and amoral, the despot's power was concentrated. A moderate monarch exercised power through "mediate channels." He issued edicts, but they had to be carried out by political institutions like local courts, which modified and tempered his wishes. "Just as the sea, which seems to want to cover the whole earth, is checked by the grasses and the smallest bits of gravel on the shore, so monarchs, whose power seems boundless, are checked by the slightest obstacles." The despot, by contrast, did not work through independent forms of power. His rule was not "counterbalanced" by local or intermediate political institutions.[35] Nor did it rely upon that complex order of social institutions and classes upon which the Hobbesian sovereign depended. Such institutions and classes would only get in the despot's way.[36] By dispensing with them, the despot isolated his victims, depriving them of the collective resources and power that might help them resist his rule. The despot eliminated all forms of human concert, political or otherwise, for concert, by its very nature, threatened his power. It was this vision of social devestation that lends Montesquieu's account its novelty, for no one before him had ever quite imagined such a wasteland.

In place of this complex social order, the despot relied upon a retinue of subordinates or "vizirs," who executed the despot's orders with startling precision. In order to do so, they had to wield virtually all of the violent instruments that the despot had accumulated in his own hands. The despot's "immense power passes intact to those to whom he entrusts it." Montesquieu never explained why men possessing more power than the despot did nothing to challenge him. The vizirs certainly were not bound to the despot by ties of moral or political obligation. They did not see themselves as participants in a project of state construction. And since they possessed the instruments of violence, why were they subject to the peculiarly physical fear of violence that Montesquieu believed was the essence of terror? Montesquieu never resolved this paradox. He only suggested that unlike the harem's eunuchs, the vizirs lacked reason, ambition, and a sense of self, and so could not turn the instruments of violence on the despot or band together to overthrow him. Without these attributes of character—which the monarch's aristocracy possessed in abundance—they could not rebel.[37]

### Life Against Death

Hobbes began from the premise that no individual possessed sufficient natural strength—of body or mind—to force everyone else to submit to his power. Rule by fear was not natural: it had to be created by giving one man an artificial monopoly of power. Making a state capable of generating fear required an act of genuine creativity, and like all creative acts, this one necessitated vision and skill, imagination and art.[38] But political order did not pose the same theoretical challenge to Montesquieu that it had to Hobbes. He confronted no civil war, and though Louis XIV had done much to curtail France's medieval aristocracy, Montesquieu could still presume the ageless reign of a feudal monarch acting in concert with a robust nobility—a monarchy, to be sure, reformed by the rule of law and separated institutions, but nevertheless present and viable. (Montesquieu, Bentham would later remark, mistakenly identified feudalism as a "fine oak" rather than a "fatal tree.")[39] For Montesquieu, the good society inhered in a political structure of deep historical resonance. It did not have to be created out of nothing: it required only the steady cultivation of the rich historical soil Europe had been gifted. Because order did not have to be created, it did not require the aid of terror. Terror was superfluous to order—and antithetical to it, despoiling Europe's historical inheritance and leaving nothing in its place, save terror and its earthly embodiments: the despot, his viziers, and their victims.

But Montesquieu's analysis contained an unacknowledged irony: if terror was what remained after the traditional order of things had been taken apart, then terror was a more elemental presence in human affairs, a primitive form lying beneath the historical development of a polity. For Montesquieu, terror acted like death. But while death destroys that which is, it is also the condition toward which all living things are drifting. Terror was likewise the end, in both senses of the word, of political things. It eliminated politics: "Politics with its springs and laws should here be very limited," for "not many laws are needed for timid, ignorant, beaten-down people." And it was that which remained after politics had been eliminated: "Rivers run together into the seas; monarchies are lost in despotism."[40] Thus, even though Montesquieu began with the assumption that political order is natural and that terror destroys that order, deep within his account was an assumption that terror was somehow more natural. Resorting to the most relentless metaphors of nature, he described terror as the political condition toward which Europe's most prominent regimes were tending.

While politics—laws, deliberation, even violence—required action, the aim of terror was a deathlike stillness. "While the principle of despotic government is fear," Montesquieu wrote, "its end is tranquillity." Not a peaceful tranquility, but a tranquility connoting the end of human action. If despotism achieved this primordial stasis, something besides politics—something requiring no human action, not even the despot's—would have to govern it. That something was culture. In a perfect despotism, Montesquieu wrote, "there are no laws, so to speak; there are only mores and manners." This was not the culture that Hobbes had in mind—where principles of moral obligation were taught by state-sanctioned instructors, instilling fear through norms and rules. This was culture understood as the mute, undetectable layers of assumption arising from the endowments of biology, climate, and primeval history. Laws and institutions—even violence—were the creations of discrete individuals or groups. They were promulgated at specific moments in time, and had a definite shape and clear effect. They were "the particular and precise institutions of the legislator." Manners and mores, by contrast, emerged from the distant past. No one instituted them. They surfaced from the deepest recesses of a people, reflecting elemental structures of apprehension. "Laws are established, mores are inspired; the latter depend more on the general spirit, the former depend more on the particular institution."[41] Mores had no specific coherence. They could not be articulated as sentences or propositions. They were the vaguest of sensibilities. In a culture of fear, all concrete, specific actions—even of the despot—disappeared, as did all concrete ideas. This was a perfect system, operating without the intervention of any agent, the emanation of primitive being. This was a vision of fear-ridden societies—stripped of politics, swimming in nature, drowning in culture—to which later writers, from Tocqueville to Arendt to intellectuals today, would return again and again.

While Sigmund Freud is associated with the twentieth century's assault on the sunny rationalism that Montesquieu and the Enlightenment supposedly inaugurated, we see here how closely Freud's worldview paralleled Montesquieu's, how much Montesquieu anticipated the sensibilities of our own time. ("There is hardly an event of any importance in our recent history," Hannah Arendt would later write, "that would not fit into the scheme of Montesquieu's apprehensions.")[42] Writing after World War I, Freud claimed that the fundamental conflict within men and women was between the instincts of life and death. The life instinct propelled the self out into the world for the sake of sexual and emotional congress, political and social union. The death instinct sought to return the self to a condition of utter stillness and separation, before birth, where the tensions and conflicts associated with life had ceased. What made the death instinct so powerful was the dim memory of the inorganic state that preceded all life. "It must be an *old* state of things," Freud wrote, "an initial state from which the living entity has at one time or other departed and to which it is striving to return," that explained why "the goal of all life is death." That memory of a prior inorganic state lay behind the human drive toward self-destruction, as evidenced by World War I: it was why men and women not only traveled toward death, but also sought to advance the pace of the journey.[43]

Montesquieu's despotic terror was like the death instinct, an adjutant of decomposition, restoring self and society to a primal stillness. Liberal politics, by contrast, was like the life instinct: It sought to put things together, to build up rather than break down. It worked against the coercive impulse to ease oneself back into a lifeless past, and for that reason, was difficult and counterintuitive. Taking something apart is always easier than putting it together, for disassembly returns things to their simplest forms. A liberal polity demanded that its leaders "combine powers, regulate them, temper them, make them act." It required "a masterpiece of legislation that chance rarely produces." Despotism, by contrast, "leaps to view." Where moderate polities required "enlightened" leaders and officials "infinitely more skillful and experienced in public affairs than they are in the despotic state," despotism settled for the "most brutal passions."[44]

Hobbes is often considered a more pessimistic theorist of politics than Montesquieu, but it was the Frenchman who truly possessed the more terrifying vision. No matter how absolutist or repressive his Leviathan, Hobbes believed in the indissoluble presence of men and women, of discrete agents whose participation was necessary for the creation of any political world, no matter how frightening. They were confused, vain, and obnoxious, but their recklessness spoke to a more capacious truth—that dissolution was not the way of the world. Montesquieu spoke on behalf of a darker dispensation. For all the evil the despot was supposed to unleash, he was in the end a mere catalyst, setting in motion forces of nature that were far beyond his control and that would ultimately engulf him as well. If there was any genuine actor in Montesquieu's story of this descent into hell, it was not human beings but the impersonal drive toward nothingness, which forced its way through the most civilized facades and corresponded to the elemental processes of life itself.

Montesquieu's liberalism thus bore a peculiar relationship to terror. On the one hand, terror had to be fought, consuming, if necessary, Europe's entire fund of political energy. On the other hand, terror seemed more real, more in sync with the deep movements of nature, than liberal ideals of moderation and freedom. But if ought entails can, how could liberalism take up a struggle against such an indefatigable foe? The solution was, first, to localize terror, and, second, to externalize it. Even though terror threatened all polities, particularly monarchies, Montesquieu thought it could be enclosed within one type of regime, despotism, and that a liberal or moderate regime could keep it at bay.[45] For someone who believed that terror was the universal tendency of all political movement, this was an ironic conclusion, overturning centuries of teaching about how fear ought to be managed. Fear had previously been conceived as a problem for all moral beings. Its challenges were universal, its boundaries ethical. Even Montaigne, usually invoked as Montesquieu's predecessor, believed that though fear was a great "fit," it could be overcome by recalling one's "sense of duty and honor." Montesquieu envisioned the domain of fear along radically different lines. He suggested that terror was a passion with a specific locale, that it could be contained by the concrete borders of a moderate regime. Thus, when Hegel later ended his discussion of African despotism by writing, "We shall therefore leave Africa at this point, and it need not be mentioned again," he was invoking more than a literary turn of phrase. He was voicing Europe's new conviction that fear tracked the lines of territorial rather than moral geography.[46]

Hegel's comment pointed to a second element of Montesquieu's strategy: his externalization of terror. Though Montesquieu believed much of Europe was heading toward despotism, he depicted terror as lying primarily outside of Europe, particularly in Asia. Montesquieu may not have invented the concept of Oriental despotism, but he gave it a new lease on life, portraying an entire region and people languishing in primitivism and barbarism. Abraham-Hyacinthe Anquetil-Duperron, one of Montesquieu's early critics, decried his use of dehumanizing stereotypes, claiming that Montesquieu had so distorted the East, he inadvertently offered a justification for colonialism from the West. A theory designed to denounce despotic terror at home unintentionally provided an excuse for practicing it abroad.[47] But there was more than crypto-colonialism going on here, for Montesquieu seemed to believe that by situating terror abroad, Europe could escape its effects at home. This may not have been the first time that a writer turned upon the rest of the world for relief from his own, projecting crude stereotypes he secretly feared were true of his native land; it certainly would not be the last.

## The Fate of an Idea

Since the eighteenth century, western intellectuals have been drawn again and again to *The Spirit of the Laws*, depicting terror as a savage enterprise destroying the canons of liberal civilization. Diderot criticized much of Montesquieu's analysis but nonetheless suggested that the temptation to wield terror was a psychological disease, a form of "madness" to "which sovereigns were especially prone." In his famous address to the French Convention, Robespierre attempted to blur Montesquieu's contrast between terror and virtue, arguing that the Jacobins should "subdue liberty's enemies by terror." But Saint-Just insisted on maintaining the distinction. "A republican government," he declared, could have "virtue for its principle, or else terror," but not both: they were too opposed. After the fall of Napoleon, Madame de Staël subjected the French Revolution's Reign of Terror to withering criticism. But though its sponsors were children of the Enlightenment, she deemed despotic terror "incompatible with human reason," stagnation its only gift to society. Hegel, in his grand narrative of human history, claimed that despotic terror was primarily found in Africa, "an unhistorical continent," mired in primitive superstition and barbarian instincts, "with no movement or development of its own."[48]

Today, the ideas of *The Spirit of the Laws* still captivate intellectuals, for no amount of postmodernist self-awareness can dampen the conviction that terror haunts civilization, rather than resides within it. Elaine Scarry's *The Body in Pain*, arguably the past quarter-century's most literate treatment of torture, is an extended meditation on the notion that torture—terror's most awful instrument—destroys self and world. Anthropologist Michael Taussig's description of voluptuous barbarism in Latin America suggests that terror traffics in sultry mystery and shadowy uncertainty; so foreign and exotic are its dark arts, he claims, one must drop the "cause-and-effect thinking in historical and social analysis" in order to understand it. Even sophisticated journalists like Tina Rosenberg and Amy Wilentz, who write about state terror with great acuity, cannot abstain from titles—*Children of Cain, The Rainy Season*—evoking the primeval, the natural, and the exotic.[49] Montesquieu's positive prescriptions against despotic terror—the rule of law, pluralism, separated powers, and toleration—also remain salient, deriving much of their force from the concept of despotism he pioneered. Much of the recent revival of civil society is littered with his conception of mediating institutions and pluralism as checks against tyranny.[50] These ideas also lie at the heart of the U.S. Constitution. Madison called Montesquieu "the oracle who is always consulted and cited" on questions of the separation of powers. Indeed, with the exception of the Bible, Montesquieu was the most invoked authority of the entire founding generation, and probably remains so today.[51]

Whether they have read *The Spirit of the Laws* or not, these writers are its children. With its trawling allusions to the febrile and the fervid, *The Spirit of the Laws* successfully aroused the conviction that terror was synonymous with barbarism, and that its cures were to be found entirely within liberalism. Thus was a new political and literary aesthetic born, a rhetoric of hyperbole suggesting that terror's escorts were inevitably remoteness, irrationality, and darkness, and its enemies, familiarity, reason, and light. Perhaps it was this aesthetic that a young Edmund Burke had in mind when he wrote, two years after Montesquieu's death, "To make any thing very terrible, obscurity seems in general to be necessary. When we know the full extent of any danger, when we can accustom our eyes to it, a great deal of the apprehension vanishes."[52]

# 3   Anxiety

Just fifty years separate Montesquieu's death in 1755 from Tocqueville's birth in 1805, but in that intervening half-century, armed revolutionaries marched the transatlantic world into modernity. New World colonials fired the first shot of national liberation at the British Empire, depriving it of its main beachhead in North America. Militants in France lit the torch of equality, and Napoleon carried it throughout the rest of Europe. Black Jacobins in the Caribbean led the first successful slave revolution in the Americas and declared Haiti an independent state. The Age of Democratic Revolution, as it would come to be known, saw borders transformed, colonies liberated, nations created. Warfare took on an ideological fervor not seen in over a century, with men and women staking their lives on the radical promise of the Enlightenment. But more than any particular advance, it was a new sense of time and space that distinguished this revolutionary world from its predecessor.[1]

Montesquieu came of age in the twilight of Louis XIV's sixty-three-year reign. The uninterrupted length of Louis's rule left a deep impression on *The Spirit of the Laws*—of time standing still, of politics moving at a glacial pace. The Age of Democratic Revolution set a new tempo for political life. Jacobins in France announced a new calendar, proclaiming 1792 the Year One. They tossed out laws bearing the traces of time immemorial. They took new names, affected new manners, and voiced new ideas. History books still register this extraordinary compression of time, with dynasties rising and falling within months and years rather than decades or centuries. Even Kant, with his obsessive punctuality, reportedly could not keep up with the pace of events: on the morning in 1789 when he heard of the fall of the Bastille, he stepped out the door for his daily walk later than usual.[2]

Politics not only accelerated; it thickened, as amateurs rushed on stage, demanding recognition as political actors in their own right. Prior to the Age of Democratic Revolution, political life was a graceful but delicate dance between king and court. But suddenly the lower classes were given the opportunity to make, rather than watch, history. According to Thomas Paine, politics would no longer be "the property of any particular man or family, but of the whole community." With plebeian recruits jostling for space, "the soil of common life," Wordsworth noted, grew "too hot to tread upon."[3] As late as France's Revolution of 1848, even the most liberal of aristocrats would feel squeezed by this inrush of new bodies. On the morning of February 24, just after the Parisian insurrections had begun, street demonstrators confronted Alexis de Tocqueville, soon to be minister of foreign affairs, on his stroll to the Chamber of Deputies.

> They surrounded me and greedily pressed me for news; I told them that we had obtained all we wanted, that the ministry was changed, that all the abuses complained of were to be reformed, and that the only danger we now ran was lest people should go too far, and that it was for them to prevent it. I soon saw that this view did not appeal to them.
>
> "That's all very well, sir," said they, "the Government has got itself into this scrape through its own fault, let it get out of it as best it can."
>
> "... If Paris is delivered into anarchy," I said, "and all the Kingdom is in confusion, do you think that none but the King will suffer?"[4]

Whether Tocqueville's "we" was a reference to his interlocutors in the street or colleagues in the Chamber of Deputies, it suggested the populist familiarity that high politics had now acquired, a political immediacy simply unthinkable under the Old Regime.[5]

These changed dimensions of time and space would utterly transform how Tocqueville—indeed, how his entire generation, and generations after them—thought about political fear. It would do so in two ways: first, in his sense that it was the mass, and not the individual, that drove events; second, in his recasting of Hobbes's fear and Montesquieu's terror as mass anxiety. Tocqueville believed that the crashing entrance of so many untrained political actors made it impossible for anyone to undertake, on his own, significant political action. "We live in a time," he noted, "and in a democratic society where individuals, even the greatest, are very little of anything." Or, as Michelet, describing the plight of the individual amid the mass, put it: "Poor and alone, surrounded by immense objects, enormous collective forces which drag him along."[6] For all their differences, Hobbes's sovereign and Montesquieu's despot were singular figures of epic proportion, projecting their shadow across an entire landscape. The mass eclipsed such figures, allowing no one, not even a despot, to put his stamp on the world. There simply wasn't enough room. For Tocqueville, the mass meant more than political congestion: it threatened to dissolve the very boundaries of the self. Not by crushing the self, as Montesquieu had envisioned, but by merging self and society. Unlike the frontispiece of *Leviathan*, where the individuals composing the sovereign's silhouette insisted upon their own form, the canvas of revolutionary democracy depicted a gathered hulk, with no recognizable human feature or discrete part. So complete was each person's assimilation to the mass, it simply did not make sense to speak anymore of individuals. "By dint of not following their own nature," John Stuart Mill gloomily concluded, men and women no longer had a "nature to follow."[7]

The new political tempo of the Age of Democratic Revolution, Tocqueville claimed, also produced a new kind of fear. With everything in the world changing so fast, no one could get his bearings. This confusion and loss of control made for free-floating anxiety, with no specific object. Montesquieu's victims were terrified of tangible threats: punishment, torture, prison, death; Hobbes's subjects feared specific dangers: the state of nature and the coercive state. The anxiety of Tocqueville's citizens, by contrast, was not focused upon any concrete harm. Theirs was a vague foreboding about the pace of change and the liquefying of common referents. Uncertain about the contours of their world, they sought to fuse themselves with the mass, for only in unity could they find some sense of connection. Or they submitted to an all-powerful, repressive state, which restored to them a sense of authority and permanence. Anxiety, then, was aroused not by intimidating power—as fear had been for Hobbes and terror had been for Montesquieu—but by the existential condition of modern men and women. Anxiety was not a response to state repression; it induced it.

With mass anxiety giving rise to political repression, with the experience of those below forcing the actions of those above, Tocqueville completely transformed fear's political meaning and function, signaling a permanent departure from the worlds of Hobbes and Montesquieu. Redefined as anxiety, fear was no longer thought of as a tool of power; instead, it was a permanent psychic state of the mass. And when the government acted repressively in response to this anxiety, the purpose was not to inhibit potential acts of opposition by keeping people down (Hobbes) or apart (Montesquieu), but to press people together, giving them a feeling of constancy and structure, relieving them, at least temporarily, of their raging anxiety. Thus did Tocqueville take yet one more step away from the political analysis of fear offered by Hobbes, and set the stage for Hannah Arendt, who would complete the journey.

Like Montesquieu, however, and to a certain degree like Hobbes, Tocqueville took these steps away from politics in order to serve the ends of politics. Like Montesquieu, Tocqueville believed that he could use this image of anxiety to mobilize men and women on behalf of a more benign polity. Tocqueville favored a government of limited and separated powers, and the vibrant associations and participatory politics of democracy. In the local whir of ordinary men and women, in their concerted efforts to build bridges, erect schools, and pass laws, Tocqueville saw a substitute for the lost cohesion of the Old Regime. Thus, like Montesquieu and Hobbes, Tocqueville turned to a form of fear as the negative foundation for his imagined polity. "Fear," he wrote in a note to himself, "must be put to work on behalf of liberty."[8]

## From the Tyranny of the Majority to the Lonely Crowd

Like Montesquieu, Tocqueville offered two distinct accounts of political fear at two distinct moments in time—only in Tocqueville's case, both accounts found their way into the same book, *Democracy in America*, which was published as two volumes, the first in 1835, the second in 1840. In the first volume, Tocqueville identified anxiety as a political problem that could be resolved by political means: anxiety was the political weapon of a tyrannical majority, which drew its power from law, ideology, and institutions, and subjected minority dissenters to the threat of ostracism. How to fend off this tyrannical majority? By dividing and decentralizing political power, and by encouraging participatory and local organizations, which would put less power at the majority's disposal, and more at the dissenters'. This wasn't an altogether happy picture, but it did hold out the possibility that if political power were fragmented, freedom might thrive and anxiety diminish.

But even in the first volume, Tocqueville's analysis contained a corrosive subtext: the individual conformed not because of any distribution of power, not because of laws, ideology, and institutions, but because he was too weak, psychologically, to insist upon his freedom. In the second volume, published in 1840, this weak psyche metastasized into an entire culture, beyond politics and power, almost beyond hope. With his desperate emotional need to belong, the modern, democratic self did not have to be actively frightened into submission: he was already anxious by virtue of his inability to stand on his own, already prepared, with no encouragement, to hand over his freedom. While in the first volume laws, ideology, and institutions helped create a culture of quiescence, the second was dominated by a darker vision, where political solutions were almost helpless against a preexisting culture of loneliness. The second volume represented more than a simple change of focus. It was a wholesale rejection of the first, which Tocqueville had come to believe was "distorted, common, and false," offering in its place "the true and original picture" of modern life.[9]

Why such a dramatic shift, and in such a short period of time? Tocqueville wrote the first volume in a flush of optimism, at a moment when the forces of liberal reform seemed poised to assume control of France. During the late 1820s and early 1830s, Tocqueville and his circle argued that France needed to make peace with its revolution in order to build a genuine liberal democracy. They pushed for freedom of the press, the right of assembly, extending the franchise, and other measures associated with the humane liberalism of Benjamin Constant, Madame de Staël, and François Guizot. This was a program, Tocqueville hoped, that would preserve the reforming spirit of the revolution without its violent side-effects.[10] But it was not to be. By the late 1830s, it became clear that many conservatives would never reconcile themselves to the revolution. Even Tocqueville's liberal allies, who would assume power in 1840, seemed more frightened of a possible revolution among France's laboring classes than called by the promise of reform. Guizot, once an eloquent spokesperson for the liberalism Tocqueville envisioned, took up the banner of reaction, declaring that "what was formerly democracy would now be anarchy" and that the "democratic spirit" was "nothing but the revolutionary spirit." Tocqueville felt betrayed and deflated by such men, many of them his former mentors. "They irritate my nerves with their moral peevishness and their actions," he wrote in 1838, and later he described them as "poltroons who tremble at the least agitation of the human heart," who cared only that "the phantom of socialism that disturbed their enjoyment by threatening their future would disappear."[11]

Tocqueville wrote the second volume, then, in the shadow of political defeat, which spread across his analysis a spirit of fatalism.[12] Rather than confront the immediate political reasons for his program's collapse—the combination of conservative reaction and liberal timidity—Tocqueville opted for a more cosmic indictment of democratic decline. It was not politics and institutions that mattered, he came to believe, not elites and their ideologies, but the culture of democracy itself, the deep assumptions of its people, which were impervious to political action. As he would write in 1853:

> You say that institutions are only half of my subject. I go farther than you, and I say that they are not even half. You know my ideas well enough to know that I accord institutions only a secondary influence on the destiny of men. Would to God I believed more in the omnipotence of institutions! I would have more hope for our future, because by chance we might, someday, stumble onto the precious piece of paper that would contain the recipe for all wrongs, or on the man who knew the recipe. But, alas, there is no such thing, and I am quite convinced that political societies are not what their laws make them, but what sentiments, beliefs, ideas, habits of the heart, and the spirit of the men who form them, prepare them in advance to be, as well as what nature and education have made them.[13]

Whatever effort he had made in the first volume to find the political underpinnings of the mass's power, Tocqueville had come to the conclusion that modern anxiety transcended any political arrangement. Equality, democracy, the self—these were artifacts of culture and psychology, not politics. They were the underground of modern life, which no political intervention could disinter.

## TYRANNY OF THE MAJORITY

As Tocqueville rode throughout the United States during 1831 and 1832, taking notes and preparing for the first volume of *Democracy in America*, he had the French Revolution very much in mind.[14] The revolution had not been kind to Tocqueville's family, an old line of Norman aristocrats stretching back to the time of William the Conqueror. Tocqueville's maternal grandfather defended Louis XVI before the French Convention, and like his illustrious client, was sent to the guillotine. Though initially sympathetic to the revolution, Tocqueville's father quickly soured on it. He joined an émigré regiment in Brussels, and later served in the military guard of Louis XVI. During the Reign of Terror, he and his wife were imprisoned, leaving his hair white and her nerves shattered. By the time he left for the United States, the twenty-six-year-old Alexis had lost much of his family's hostility to the revolution,[15] but he was nevertheless still fearful of popular majorities. The commercial and political elites with whom he spoke during his trip only confirmed his premonitions. These were soured old Federalists, who greeted Andrew Jackson's rule with about as much enthusiasm as Tocqueville's family did Robespierre's. Even though their evidence was thin, Tocqueville adopted their exaggerated view of popular forces in control of the country's destiny, which he called the tyranny of the majority[16]

The tyrannical mass, Tocqueville believed, represented a new kind of political animal, brandishing new instruments. It did not wield the "clumsy weapons of chains and hangmen."[17] Instead, it roamed about the land, arranging a dull sameness through sentiments. The new agent of fear was a majority wielding power not through traditional offices or weapons of state, but through the social mechanisms of popular opinion and common belief.

Within the majority, it was not possible to identify any individual leader. "No one can be found," Tocqueville wrote, "exercising very great or, more particularly, very lasting influence over the masses." The members of the majority did not deliberate among themselves, arguing about the finer or broader points of their ideology. Instead, they possessed an "involuntary accord which springs from like feelings and familiar passions." Without making any reasoned, even conscious, decisions, without heeding the counsel or call of leaders, each person morphed into the whole, losing whatever particularity he might have previously possessed. It was this absolute unity that made the majority such a potent political form, for while "everything is in motion around you," Tocqueville noted, "the motive force is nowhere apparent." The majority possessed authority, but no one knew "where to find its representative."[18]

To grasp the novelty of this view, we need only compare it to Hobbes's. Hobbes believed that without a leader to speak on behalf of a people, the people would dissolve into a chaos of particulars. For a people to assume an intelligible form, someone would have to be authorized, by them, to represent them. "A multitude of men, are made One Person, when they are by one man, or one Person, Represented; so that it be done with the consent of every one of that Multitude in particular. For it is the Unity of the Representer, not the Unity of the Represented, that maketh the Person One. And it is the Representer that beareth the Person, and but one Person: And Unity, cannot otherwise be understood in Multitude."[19] By contrast, Tocqueville believed that not only was a leader not necessary to forge a majority, but the majority precluded the very idea of leadership. They achieved their unanimity without leaders or any conscious agreement to submit to the majority. This absence of leaders, deliberation, reasoned and conscious agreement—indeed, of particular individuals—made the majority a more insidious and threatening power than tyrants of old.

Though Tocqueville did not believe that the majority came into being through political mechanisms, he did believe that the foundation of its power was political. As Tocqueville saw it, the majority was able to assume its preeminence because democratic constitutions granted it a higher claim to sovereignty and because it possessed the moral imprimatur of egalitarian principles.[20] The U.S. Constitution, for example, famously opens with "We the People," and, as Alexander Hamilton argued in *Federalist* 22, "The fabric of American empire ought to rest on the solid basis of the consent of the people. The streams of authority ought to flow immediately from the pure, original fountain of all legitimate authority."[21] This combination of constitutional design and political ideology turned the state into the automatic instrument of the majority, making it difficult for elite elements in government—in the executive and judicial branches, in the upper house of the legislature—to resist its will. The majority independently orchestrated its agenda, which it transmitted to the legislature, which then imposed it upon the entire government. As Tocqueville wrote in a draft of *Democracy in America*, "All the force of government is confided to the society itself. . . . In America all danger comes from the people; it is never born outside of them."[22] Where power in the Old Regime flowed from state to society, power in democracy flowed from society to the state.

Just as the foundation of the majority's power was political, so were the weapons it wielded against dissenters. The majority threatened dissenters not with physical violence or prison but with isolation, telling those who challenged it, "You are a stranger among us." It did not deprive dissenters of their rights; through ostracism, it made those rights ineffective. In democracies like the United States, Tocqueville believed, exercising power depended upon the cooperation of like-minded men and women. Without the ability to talk to fellow citizens, the dissenter was politically crippled, incapable of advancing his goals. "You can keep your privileges in the township," the majority would declare to the dissenter, "but they will be useless to you, for if you solicit your fellow citizens' votes, they will not give them to you, and if you only ask for their esteem, they will make excuses for refusing that." The dissenter's potential allies were well aware that if they joined him, they too would face isolation and be equally crippled, and so they kept their distance from him.[23]

Tocqueville's portrait of the tyrannical majority, then, captured his complex, and confused, sensibility about this new democratic age. On the one hand, Tocqueville held an exaggerated view of the omnipotence of the majority, mistakenly assuming that the political struggle between the forces of equality and elitism was over, and that equality had won. The victims of fear were not those on the bottom but those on the top. Where dissenters under the Old Regime could find a foothold—"No monarch is so absolute that he can hold all the forces of society in his hands, and overcome all resistance"—dissenting elites in a democracy could find none.[24] The struggle against fear would have to be waged on behalf of this silent minority, which despite its great wealth and social standing was nevertheless conceived by Tocqueville to be the casualty of an impersonal democratic juggernaut. Had Tocqueville's imagination of the democratic majority been less inflamed, he might have seen that the forces of equality were not nearly as powerful or unanimous as he believed, and that elites in the United States, and certainly in France, still possessed considerable clout.[25] But his imagination was not less inflamed, and so he could not see the all-too-real obstacles to majority rule.

On the other hand, by emphasizing the political sources of the majority's power—constitutional design and ideology—and the political reasons dissenters would fear ostracism—the threat of powerlessness—Tocqueville offered a fairly optimistic appraisal of the possibilities for countering the majority. If fear was a function of politics and power, it could be mitigated by more felicitous political arrangements. If state centralization could be staved off, and civic associations encouraged, the majority's hold on state power would prove more difficult to achieve. If elites and civic institutions, particularly lawyers and juries, were strengthened, they would provide alternative sources of power, thereby lessening the threat that ostracism posed to the dissenter. Thus, even if the majority did monopolize state power, decentralization and political pluralism would make that monopoly less lethal.[26]

## STRANGE INTERLUDE

But Tocqueville's portrait of majority tyranny in the first volume did not end there. The first volume also contained a blistering portrait of the democratic self, a conformist who capitulated to the majority not because he lacked power, but because he lacked character. Aristocrats under the Old Regime were buoyed by a sense of personal honor, a muscular self-confidence that gave "extraordinary strength to individual resistance." The old Federalists who led the American Revolution, aristocrats in all but name, had a "greatness all their own," a "virile candor and manly independence of thought." This sense of honor and independence was partially a function of the greater resources and power these men possessed, but it was also in their bones. Even in a democratic age, the remnant aristocracy, dispossessed of power, believed in itself in a way that democrats simply did not and could not. "In spite of their impotence," these aristocrats held "a high idea of their individual worth." Isolated and ostracized, they were still able to "resist the pressure of public authority."[27]

The modern democrat, by contrast, was consumed by feelings of weakness that did not correspond to any objective lack of power. So great was this lack of self-confidence, who could say where the "yielding of weakness" would "stop?"[28] Naturally inclined not to resist the demands of others, the democrat did not have to be threatened with ostracism in order to conform to the wishes of the mass. By virtue of his character, or lack thereof, he naturally feared doing anything that might challenge the majority. The majority's authority, then, hung like a moist air around the democratic self. Without any encouragement or threat, he internalized its beliefs. So complete was his willingness to submit that he gradually lost any of the specific tastes and opinions that might have put him in opposition to the majority. The majority "acts as much upon the will as upon behavior and at the same moment prevents both the act and the desire to do it." The majority did not require formal censorship of "licentious books" because no one was "tempted to write them." Or, as Tocqueville would later write, "this all-powerful opinion finally infuses itself into the thoughts even of those whose interest it is to fight against it; it both modifies their judgment and subdues their will."[29]

Tocqueville offered this vision of the total conscription of self as a direct contrast to the methods and morals of the Old Regime. In fact, when set against the mind control exercised by the majority, the Old Regime appeared restrained, almost benevolent; for the kings and lords of old sought to control only the body, allowing a tremendous freedom of mind. The majority was less violent, but practiced a more intimate supervision. It "left the body alone" and went "straight for the soul."[30] Long before the experiences of twentieth-century totalitarianism, then, Tocqueville suggested that the particular vices of the democratic self would make for a world infinitely more terrifying—not because of any increase in cruelty or violence, but because the self's contours and boundaries had been blurred.

### THE LONELY CROWD

Three larger shifts in Tocqueville's thinking inform the second volume of *Democracy in America*, with its aggressively nonpolitical conception of anxiety. First, in the earlier volume, Tocqueville viewed equality as a political phenomenon, as both an ideological doctrine and a political practice. Insofar as equality referred to the material conditions of life, they were understood to be products of political events and changes. The egalitarian "social state" of America, Tocqueville explained, arose from the abolition of primogeniture, the rise of ideological doctrines of popular sovereignty, and the burst of egalitarian movements that accompanied the American Revolution.[31] But in the second volume, Tocqueville depicted equality as merely the material conditions of a people, which created among them similar tastes and opinions. He did not explain how these conditions came into being; he merely asserted that a mysterious "middling" process, outside of politics, had gradually eliminated economic extremes. As the economic conditions of men and women grew "more or less similar," their identities fused, their sensibilities converged, and they grew to be "like each other."[32]

Second, Tocqueville adopted a new analysis of the mass's authority. Where the authority of the mass in the first volume was rooted in constitutional design and political ideology, the mass's authority in the second volume arose from socioeconomic equality and the psychology of the mass. Material sameness encouraged men and women to distrust each other as individuals but to trust the mass. This faith in the mass had nothing to do with its ideology or power. It arose from an inner impulse, connected to the material conditions of equality. "The nearer men are to a common level of uniformity," the "readier" they are "to trust the mass." "In times of equality men, being so like each other, have no confidence in others, but this same likeness leads them to place almost unlimited confidence in the judgment of the public."[33] Regardless of the distribution of power in democracy, its forms of governance or political doctrines, this combination of material equality and psychological impulse led individual men and women to grant authority to the mass. "*However powers within a democracy are organized and weighted,*" he wrote, "it will always be very difficult for a man to believe what the mass rejects and to profess what it condemns."[34]

Finally, as the structural organization of the two volumes demonstrates, Tocqueville's view of the relationship between politics and culture changed. In the first volume, Tocqueville claimed that politics shaped culture; in the second, he argued the opposite. In volume two, after discussing the cultural sentiments of democratic societies, Tocqueville introduced their political consequences by claiming, "I could not properly fulfill the purpose of this book if, having pointed out the ideas and feelings prompted by equality, I did not in conclusion indicate the influence which these ideas and feelings may exercise upon the government of human societies."[35] In volume one, Tocqueville's guiding intuition was that democracy was a political development, which created a larger culture of egalitarian manners and morals. He thus devoted the bulk of that volume to a discussion of laws, institutions, and ideologies as the catalysts of human energies and passions.[36] In the second volume, political developments were depicted as the inevitable products of a preexisting cultural milieu.

In the second volume, then, it was the facts of material sameness, the psychology of the democratic self, and the larger culture that psychology created that explained the individual's submission to the mass. But what about his psychology made the modern democrat so prone to submission? According to Tocqueville, it was his constant and inescapable feeling of loneliness. This was not the ostracism that Tocqueville invoked in the first volume of *Democracy in America*. This new isolation was not a punishment imposed on dissenters: it was the proverbial anxiety of modernity, what Kierkegaard, Nietzsche, Simmel, Tönnies, Durkheim, Heidegger, Arendt, and a host of other social theorists would curse as the burden of living in a postfeudal age.

Tocqueville saw the lonely crowd as a direct counterpoint to the emotive community of the Old Regime. Before the modern age—before the revolution, equality, and secularism—men and women were members of a hierarchical society. They were bound to each other by three distinct links, each giving them a deep and abiding sense of connection. They were connected horizontally to the members of their class, which created a "little fatherland" among them. They were connected vertically to those above or below them, creating duties of paternalism and obligation. And they were connected in time to their ancestors and descendants. Individuals may have felt constricted by these ties, but never alone. And relief from loneliness—from being consigned to oneself—was the best measure of the Old Regime's benignity: "People living in an aristocratic age are almost always closely involved in something outside themselves."[37]

Equality and secularism severed these links. By eliminating the generational transmission of hierarchy, equality broke "the woof of time," the temporal connections between past, present, and future. It also cut the vertical links of duty and obligation, which bound "everybody, from peasant to king." By destroying these temporal and vertical links, equality eliminated the most important link of all—the horizontal one connecting each individual to the other. Among equal men and women, Tocqueville concluded, there are no "natural links" whatsoever, for equality put "men side by side without a common link to hold them firm." The loss of religious authority, so closely connected to the decline of the Old Regime, added to this sense of isolation. Religion bound men and women to one another through a chain of obligations. It drew a person "away, from time to time, from thinking about himself." In a secular society, by contrast, each person was "forever thrown back on himself alone," with "shut up in solitude of his own heart."[38]

Without social hierarchy, without genuine links of affect and content, men and women became unsure of themselves and their surroundings. "Doubt invades the highest faculties of the mind and half paralyzes all the rest." They saw nothing to check their impulses and desires; nothing to ground their choices; nothing to give content, meaning, and direction to their actions. Instead, they saw a vast, open plain, where anything and everything was possible, where the landscape changed daily, turning quickly into a white blur. This absence of structure translated into an absence of authority, the most anxiety-inducing experience of all. "When there is no authority in religion or in politics, men are soon frightened by the limitless independence with which they are faced." Tocqueville here alluded to what would come to be known as the fear of freedom, the vertigo that is supposed to afflict anyone forced to make a choice without the comfort of established foundations and authority: everyone was now "frightened of their own free will," "afraid of themselves."[39]

In the face of anxiety about the absence of structure, authority, tradition, cohesion, and meaning, the state was forced to step in to reestablish a firm structure of authority, to remind men and women that they were not alone. "With everything on the move in the realm of the mind," men and women felt "inevitably enervate[d]." Constant trembling produced paralysis, a "relaxing" of the "springs of the will." It was not long before men and women realized that the reestablishment of authority—the firmer, the better—would, if nothing else, mitigate their considerable anxiety. They turned to a dictator, or, more likely, to a paternalistic welfare state, which in the name of helping people, extracted their power. Those who wanted "the material order at least to be firm and stable" soon became a "people for bondage." Not only did they "let their freedom be taken from them, but often they actually hand[ed] it over themselves," Toqueville wrote. "Despairing of remaining free, from the bottom of their hearts they already worship the master who is bound soon to appear."[40] A century later, when Hannah Arendt began surveying the sources of Hitler's and Stalin's appeal, she would pick up right here, arguing that it was mass anxiety that had propelled these men into power.

## From Fear and Terror to Anxiety

In several respects, Tocqueville's second volume of *Democracy in America* followed the path taken by Montesquieu in *The Spirit of the Laws*. Like Montesquieu against Hobbes, Tocqueville saw fear as a free-floating insecurity rather than a focused apprehension of harm. So did Tocqueville divest fear of any moral component. In fact, it was the absence of any coherent conception of, or firm conviction about, the good that made anxiety possible. Like Montesquieu against Hobbes, Tocqueville believed anxiety bore an inverse relationship to selfhood. The more sense of self a person possessed, the less likely he was to experience anxiety; the less sense of self he had, the more likely he was to experience anxiety. Like Montesquieu against Hobbes, Tocqueville believed anxiety arose in the absence of integrative institutions, cohesive elites, and structures of authority. Like Montesquieu against Hobbes, Tocqueville linked anxiety to the facts of culture rather than to those of power and politics, albeit to a much greater degree than did Montesquieu.

But Tocqueville also departed from assumptions about fear that both Hobbes and Montesquieu, despite their considerable differences, had shared. Unlike Hobbes or Montesquieu, Tocqueville saw the lines of anxiety's genesis, cultivation, and transmission extending upward, from the deepest recesses of the mass psyche to the state. Hobbes and Montesquieu believed that the state needed to take certain actions to arouse fear or terror, that the initiative came from above. Tocqueville turned that assumption upside down, claiming that anxiety was the automatic condition of lonely men and women, who either forced or facilitated the state's repressive actions. To the degree that the state acted repressively, it was merely responding to the demands of the mass. Because the mass was leaderless, divested of guiding elites and discrete authorities, state repression was a genuinely popular, democratic affair.

Unlike Montesquieu or Hobbes, Tocqueville suggested that the individual members of the mass who sought to lose themselves in the state's repressive authority were culturally and psychologically prone to submission. Hobbes and Montesquieu believed that the individual who was to be afraid or terrified had to be created through the instruments of politics—elites, ideology, and institutions in Hobbes's case, violence in Montesquieu's. But in Tocqueville's eyes, politics did not have to do anything at all. The anxious self was already on hand. No matter how politics and power were configured, the self would be anxious by virtue of his psychology and culture.

Ultimately, it was this vision of the democratic individual amid the lonely crowd that made Tocqueville's vision of mass anxiety so terrifying. In claiming that anxiety did not have to be crafted, that it was a constitutive feature of the democratic self and its culture, Tocqueville suggested that danger came from within, that the enemy was a psychological fifth column lurking in the heart of every man and woman. As he wrote in a notebook, "This time the barbarians will not come from the frozen North; they will rise in the bosom of our countryside and in the midst of our cities."[41] Hobbes had tried to focus people's fear on a state of nature that lay in the future and in the past and on a real sovereign in the present, Montesquieu on a despotic terror that lay in the future or in the far-off lands of Asia. Both sought to focus people's fear on objects outside themselves or their countries. Tocqueville turned people's attention inward, toward the quotidian betrayals of liberty inside their anxious psyches. If there was an object to be feared, it was the self's penchant for submission. From now on, individuals would have to be on guard against themselves, vigilantly policing the boundaries separating them from the mass. At the height of the Cold War, American intellectuals would revive this line of thought, arguing that the greatest danger to Americans was their own anxious self, ever ready to hand over its freedom to a tyrant. Warning against the "anxieties which drive people in free society to become traitors to freedom," Arthur Schlesinger concluded that there was, in the United States, a "Stalin in every breast."[42]

The other object to be feared was the egalitarian culture from which the democratic self arose.[43] Tocqueville did not call for a reversal of democratic gains or a retreat from equality. He was too much the realist and believer in the revolution's gains to join the chorus of royalist reaction. Instead, he argued that to preserve the gains of the revolution, to help the democratic individual fulfill his promise as a genuine agent, the self would have to be shored up by creating firm structures of authority, restoring to it a sense of local affiliation, fostering religion and other sources of meaning, situating the self in civic associations whose function was less political than psychological and integrative.[44] To counter mass anxiety, egalitarians and liberals, democrats and republicans, should cease their assault on society's few remaining hierarchies. They should not participate in the socialist movement to centralize and enhance the power of a redistributive state. Instead, they should actively cultivate localism, institutions, and elite authority; these remnants of the Old Regime were the only bulwark against an anxiety threatening to introduce the worst forms of tyranny seen yet. The task, in other words, was not to continue the assault on the Old Regime but to stop it, to focus attention not on overturning the remains of privilege—local institutions and elites, religion, social hierarchies—but on enhancing them: these were the only social facts standing between democracy and despotism, freedom and anxiety.[45] One hundred and fifty years later, communitarian intellectuals in North American and Western Europe would offer a similar argument.

## Portrait of the Romantic Liberal as a Counterrevolutionary Man

As we have seen, Tocqueville's retreat from the first to the second volume of *Democracy in America* was a symptom of his dwindling political fortune during the second half of the 1830s. Reeling from defeat but unable to confront its political causes—conservative intransigence and liberal diffidence—he resorted to cultural and psychological explanations of the political quiet surrounding him. In this regard, he was not that dissimilar from Montesquieu, who also found in culture an explanation for the political setbacks of his day, or from Arendt in the 1940s and North American and Western European intellectuals in the 1990s. At moments of political deceleration, when the forces of reform are stalled, liberal and radical intellectuals often abandon political analysis for the all-encompassing interpretations of psychology and culture. Stunned by defeat, which they do not believe can be reversed, they come to believe that nothing as contingent or plastic as politics can explain their loss. With their brooding appeals to the profound and intractable, the categories of psychology and culture seem more attuned to deeper currents of the human condition and to the despondent mood of defeated intellectuals.

But Tocqueville's despair in the 1830s also represents a novel sensibility, forged in the wake of the French Revolution, that can only be described as a species of liberal romanticism.[46] A mix of radicalism and disappointment, Tocqueville's romanticism betrayed a simultaneous longing for and loathing of revolution, a love/hatred of freedom and equality. Enchanted by the theory of liberal democracy, Tocqueville was bored by its practice. He thus looked elsewhere—to imperial expeditions abroad and counterrevolutionary exploits at home—to relieve himself of his raging ennui. Because this sensibility prefigures that of so many intellectuals writing after Tocqueville, because it runs throughout his and so many later conceptions of anxiety, it is worth further consideration.

Tocqueville was a junior attaché of that strange generation of European intellectuals awakened by the French Revolution who suffered the disappointment of its final rout when Napoleon was defeated at Waterloo in 1815.[47] Revolutionary politics unleashed in them a desire for political freedom, for public action on a grand scale, that simply could not be fulfilled in the thirty years' quiet of post-Napoleonic Europe. With its weird mix of longing, melancholy, and rage, romanticism spoke to this mood of stalled advance. It offered a language of radical judgment and accusation, condemning the compromise and timidity of the first half of the nineteenth century. But unlike the revolutionary spirit that inspired them, the romantics wrote in anticipation of political failure; no matter how momentous their vision, it never lost the aura of awaited defeat.

Despite the fact that he was only ten when Napoleon was defeated, Tocqueville navigated these mingled currents of revolution and romanticism, evincing in his own life the same balance of ardor and despair that characterized his older brethren. Publicly presenting himself as the consummate realist, with little patience for enthusiasm of any sort, he was in fact a closet Werther. He confessed to his brother that he often shared their father's "devouring impatience," his "need for lively and recurring sensations." "Gnashing [his] teeth behind the bars of reason" (which, he admitted, had "always been for me like a cage"), he longed for "the sight of combat" ; it "always excites me," he wrote.[48]

Given his family's experiences during the revolution, it seems only natural that Tocqueville would have loathed it and its associated pathologies. Often, he did. But Tocqueville's response to the revolution was noteworthy less for its antipathy than for its praise. Part of his enthusiasm was due no doubt to his conviction that the Old Regime was dead, that any viable politics would have to acknowledge that there was no going back to the period before 1789.[49] But though Tocqueville publicly spoke the cautionary words of prudence in order to defend the revolution, the secret language of his commitment belonged to an altogether more passionate idiom. Well into his midfifties, Tocqueville was channeling the spirit of the early Wordsworth, claiming about the revolution that "youth was at the helm in that age of fervid enthusiasm, of proud and generous aspirations, whose memory, despite its extravagances, men will forever cherish." The year 1789 was one of great intemperateness and "incomparable grandeur." Tocqueville lamented the end of the Reign of Terror, claiming that "men thus crushed can not only no longer attain great virtues, but they seem to have become almost incapable of great crimes." Even Napoleon, the "most extraordinary being who has appeared in the world for many centuries," earned his admiration. By contrast, who could find inspiration in the parliamentary plotting of his age, where politics had been reduced to trivial machination and unprincipled compromise? That "little democratic and bourgeois pot of soup" was how he described the political scene. "Do you believe," he asked in 1840, "that the political world will long remain as destitute of true passions as it is at this moment?" Parliaments asked of men nothing, and they got it. Revolutions asked all, and got more. Thus he wrote, "I would like a state of revolution one hundred thousand times better than the wretchedness that surrounds us."[50]

Why did revolutions summon such extraordinary reserves of human energy? Because they were novel events, moments of stark originality when people acted with unprecedented ingenuity and courage. Revolutions forced upon their participants the obligation of, and opportunity for, genuine political creativity. Relying on their own judgments and instincts, leaders and citizens discovered "a spirit of healthy independence, high ambitions, faith in oneself and in a cause." Nonrevolutionary times asked men to follow convention and custom. In the give-and-take of moderation, there was "no action," nothing that could "bring about anything noteworthy." And "what is politics without action?" Where originality was the emblem of freedom, imitation was the harbinger of submission. This was a deeply personal issue for Tocqueville, for he often feared that he was a mere actor in politics, not an author, repeating the lines that another had written for him. Indeed, when he turned on the revolutionaries of 1848, it was because he did not consider them genuine revolutionaries at all, but rather, in words that found a famous echo in the opening lines of Marx's *Eighteenth Brumaire*, "provincial actors" in a "bad tragedy," ersatz revolutionaries "engaged in acting the French Revolution, rather than continuing it."[51]

Throughout his career, Tocqueville sought a political outlet for these romantic longings, where deliberation and concerted action could be carried out on a grand scale. Tocqueville was not interested, as some have argued, in reviving the civic republican traditions of Aristotle and Machiavelli.[52] He hoped to find in politics dimensions of sensibility and experience these earlier theorists would simply not have recognized. Politics was to be a place for passion and panache, an activity to stave off the torpor and stagnation threatening to engulf France and indeed all of Europe. It was to be a sphere for individual expression and artistry, where the individual, rather than the community, could recover his eviscerated capacities. As Tocqueville wrote in a draft of *Democracy in America*, "To conserve something for [the individual's] independence, his force, his originality; such must be the constant effort of all the friends of humanity in democratic times." Tocqueville did not fear, as did republicans of yore, civic corruption—the ravages of time and fate—nearly as much as he did ennui, despair, the lassitude of safety and compromise. If politics could inject a note of danger, of risk and adventure, it might force Europe out of its frivolous stupor and help it recover the verve of its revolutionary years. The goal, in short, was a politics in which he would have the "opportunity to use . . . this internal flame I feel within me that does not know where to find what feeds it."[53] This was the voice not of Aristotle or Machiavelli, but of Hugo, Stendhal, and Lamartine.[54]

As Tocqueville was the first to admit, his project of joining romantic passion to political moderation was a failure, the victim of reactionary refusal and liberal trepidation. But there was another dimension to Tocqueville's failure to find true love in parliament: despite his formal commitment to moderation, Tocqueville felt suffocated by it. He may have mouthed the words of parliamentary procedure, but they did not inspire them. Without revolution, politics was simply not the grand drama he imagined it had been between 1789 and 1815. "Our fathers observed such extraordinary things that compared with them all of our works seem commonplace." The politics of moderation produced moderation aplenty; it did not produce much in the way of politics, at least as Tocqueville defined that term. During the 1830s and 1840s, he wrote, "what was most wanting . . . was political life itself." There was "no battlefield for contending parties to meet upon." As a result, politics was forever "deprived" of "all originality, of all reality, and therefore of all genuine passions." There was something almost comical about Tocqueville's effort to infuse moderate reform with revolutionary passion, and he knew it. For where "revolutionary times . . . do not permit indifference and egoism in politics," nonrevolutionary times most assuredly did.[55]

Never quite able to forge a liberalism of passion, Tocqueville did find satisfaction in two kinds of politics—imperialism and counterrevolution—which, not coincidentally, had little to do with the spirit of moderation he so often championed. Imperialism—France had just begun its 130-year-long affair with Algeria—spoke to many of Tocqueville's concerns: the desire for national glory, the demands of realpolitik, the scramble for Africa.[56] But he saw in imperial expansion much more than the promise of French destiny or national greatness. In the domination of foreign lands, Tocqueville envisioned the regeneration of the European race, a continental awakening from the flaccid sleep that followed the defeat of Napoleon. Witnessing Europe's armies march across the globe, Tocqueville thought less as a Frenchman or a republican than as a European. He cared less about which nation was doing the conquering than that conquering was being done. As the British prepared to fight the Opium War, he wrote, "I can only rejoice in the thought of the invasion of the Celestial Empire by a European army. So at last the mobility of Europe has come to grips with Chinese immobility!" It was a "great event," "pushing the European race out of its home" and "submitting all the other races to its empire or its influence." Against those—like himself—who normally would "slander our century" because of its piddling politics, Tocqueville insisted that "something more vast, more extraordinary than the establishment of the Roman Empire is growing out of our times, without anyone noticing it; it is the enslavement of four parts of the world by the fifth." Upon the conclusion of the Treaty of London, which threatened to diminish France's role in the Middle East and aroused cries for war throughout France, Tocqueville wrote to Mill that though he was wary of his countrymen's rush to war, he thought it "even more dangerous" to "chime in with those who were loudly asking for peace, at any price." Not because peace undermined national security, but because "the greatest malady that threatens a people organized as we are is the gradual softening of mores, the abasement of mind, the mediocrity of tastes."[57]

But in a long career of public life, nothing quite awakened Tocqueville's enthusiasm like the Revolution of 1848, when liberals and radicals throughout the continent, including France, tried once again to topple Europe's persistent old regimes. Tocqueville did not support the uprising: in fact, he was among its most vociferous opponents. He voted for the full suspension of civil liberties, including the suppression of freedom of assembly and of the press—which, he happily announced, was done "with even more energy than had been done under the Monarchy"—and welcomed talk of a "dictatorship" to preserve "the alienable right of Society to protect itself."[58] Why did he assume this stance? To protect the very liberalism and parliamentary politics that he had spent the better part of two decades lamenting. Defending liberalism against radicalism, Tocqueville was given a chance to use illiberal means for liberal ends, and it's not entirely clear whether it was the means or the ends that most stirred him. Tocqueville fully understood the power of this fusion between liberal ideal—or, as he called it, "republican faith"—and counterrevolutionary purpose. For when the two came together, he wrote, liberalism was able to channel its most potent political energies: "This bold profession of anti-revolutionary had been preceded by one of republican faith; the sincerity of the one seemed to bear witness to that of the other."[59]

Counterrevolution gave Tocqueville the opportunity to exhibit all of those qualities he so admired in revolutionaries of times past, but that he had never found in times present. In 1848, he felt exhilarated, heroic, not bored.

> Let me say, then, that when I came to search carefully into the depths of my own heart, I discovered, with some surprise, a certain sense of relief, a sort of gladness mingled with all the griefs and fears to which the Revolution had given rise. I suffered from this terrible event for my country, but clearly not for myself; on the contrary, I seemed to breathe more freely than before the catastrophe. I had always felt myself stifled in the atmosphere of the parliamentary world which had just been destroyed: I had found it full of disappointments, both where others and where I myself was concerned.[60]

He found himself "caught in the currents of a majority," and despite his oft-voiced misgivings about majorities, he loved the company. A self-styled poet of the tentative, the subtle, and the complex, he burned with illumination upon discovering the simplicity of a society firmly divided into two camps, the thrill of choosing between good and evil. Where timid parliaments sowed a gray confusion, counterrevolution forced upon society the bracing clarity of black and white. "There was no field left for uncertainty of mind: on this side lay the salvation of the country; on that, its destruction. There was no longer any mistake possible as to the road to follow; we were to walk in broad daylight, supported and encouraged by the crowd. The road seemed dangerous, it is true, but my mind is so constructed that it is less afraid of danger than of doubt."[61]

But revolutions, to paraphrase Jefferson, come at best once every twenty years, and so the work of a liberal counterrevolutionary would always remain intermittent and unsteady. Without the threat of popular rebellion—or the possibility of imperialist adventure—to lend frisson to liberal ideals, Tocqueville's romantic longings could never be satisfied through liberal politics. So he turned inward, attacking the democratic self with the same fervor he would attack the revolutionaries of 1848, and with the same passion with which he would recommend France's expeditions in Algeria. This inward turn, this final implosion of radical messianism, found its way into Tocqueville's account of anxiety, making the two volumes of *Democracy in America* a shared projection of revolutionary hope and counterrevolutionary disdain.

The conformist cowed by the tyrannical majority in volume one and the isolated self standing amid the lonely crowd in volume two were the simultaneous creations of a revolutionary modernist and disappointed romantic. Criticisms of the modern self, these images of conformity and isolation nevertheless bore the marks of the very modern self the revolution had unleashed. Prior to the revolution, philosophers had often praised the conformist for showing a healthy respect for the opinions of his peers. Writing in 1757, Edmund Burke called this respect for the opinion of others "imitation," which he celebrated as "one of the strongest links of society." Though Burke warned that too much imitation could prove detrimental to progress, he nevertheless affirmed it as "a species of mutual compliance which all men yield to each other, without constraint to themselves, which is extremely flattering to all."[62] Before the revolution, the isolated self depicted in volume two—consumed by doubt, uncertain about truth, unable to decide—would have been the stuff of Shakespearean tragedy, the emblem of a human, all too human, condition. But in the wake of the revolution, imitation came to be seen as conformity, Hamletic doubt crippling anxiety. "What is a crime among the multitude," as Disraeli put it, "is only a vice among the few."[63] Only someone first awakened and then betrayed by the revolution could have engineered such transformations making the conformist and the isolate the targets of romantic disappointment.

With revolutions, Tocqueville once wrote, men are ruined less by "the faults and the crimes that they commit in the heat of passion or of their political convictions" than by "the contempt . . . they acquire for the very convictions and passions which moved them" in the first place. Having tried and failed to bring freedom into the world, "they turn against themselves and consider their hopes as having been childish—their enthusiasm and above all, their devotion, absurd."[64] This was a fitting epitaph for himself—and for all the disillusioned liberals and radicals who would become fixtures of the nineteenth and twentieth centuries. Tocqueville ached for the flair and conviction that romantics have always attributed to revolutionaries. But he also knew the fate of the revolution—not only that it ended in a bloodbath, but that it ended. This knowledge left him in an impossible situation. Even though he could scarcely breathe in the humid summer enveloping France after 1815, he could not fully break with the era's antirevolutionary underpinnings. Instead of wrestling with this ambivalence, he turned on the self. For in targeting the self as the prime conduit of modern anxiety, he was able to settle scores with the revolution he believed had unleashed that self—and that, by leaving liberal democracy in its place, had done so much to enervate it.

At the heart of Tocqueville's writing, this unresolved ambivalence—about revolution, democracy, liberalism, and the self—has long given his account of anxiety a tremendous ecumenical appeal. From Mill to Nietzsche to Arendt, from Ortega y Gassett and T. S. Eliot to the Frankfurt School and Foucault, from liberal intellectuals writing during the Cold War to communitarian intellectuals writing in its wake, Tocqueville's image of society's colonization of the anxious self has dominated the cultural landscape, particularly at moments of political retreat. It has appealed to conservatives, liberals, and radicals, who find in its criticisms of modern society a recipe for localism or federalism, community or hierarchy, liberal institutions or resistance to the welfare state. Whenever these writers have tired of Tocqueville's solutions, whenever they have decided that his solutions cannot actually deliver them from tedium and despair, they have resorted to his critique of the modern self, its anxious psychology and culture. And, whenever they have tired of his critiques, they have found succor in his two other favored outlets: counterrevolution and imperialism.

# 4 Total Terror

It was a sign of his good fortune—and terrible destiny—that Nikolai Bukharin was pursued throughout his short career by characters from the Old Testament. Among the youngest of the "Old Bolsheviks," Bukharin was, in Lenin's words, "the favorite of the whole party." A dissident economist and accomplished critic, this impish revolutionary, standing just over five feet, charmed everyone. Even Stalin. The two men had pet names for each other, their families socialized together, and Stalin had Bukharin stay at his country house during long stretches of the Russian summer. So beloved throughout the party was Bukharin that he was called the "Benjamin" of the Bolsheviks. If Trotsky was Joseph, the literary seer and visionary organizer whose arrogance aroused his brothers' envy, Bukharin was undoubtedly the cherished baby of the family.[1]

Not for long. Beginning in the late 1920s, as he sought to slow Stalin's forced march through the Russian countryside, Bukharin tumbled from power. Banished from the party in 1937 and left to the tender mercies of the Soviet secret police, he confessed in a 1938 show trial to a career of extraordinary counterrevolutionary crime. He was promptly shot, just one of the 328,618 official executions of that year. Not long before his murder, Bukharin invoked a rather different biblical parallel to describe his fate. In a letter to Stalin, Bukharin recalled the binding of Isaac, the unwitting son whose father, Abraham, prepares him, on God's instruction, for sacrifice. At the last minute, an angel stops Abraham, declaring, "Lay not thine hand upon the lad, neither do thou any thing unto him: for now I know that thou fearest

God, seeing thou hast not withheld thy son, thine only son from me." Reflecting upon his own impending doom, however, Bukharin envisioned no such heavenly intervention: "No angel will appear now to snatch Abraham's sword from his hand."[2]

The biblical reference, with its suggested equivalence of Stalin and Abraham, was certainly unorthodox. But in the aftermath of Bukharin's execution it proved apt, for no other crime of the Stalin years so captivated western intellectuals as the blood sacrifice of Bukharin. It was not just that this darling of the communist movement, "the party's most valuable and biggest theoretician," as Lenin put it, had been brought down.[3] Stalin, after all, had already felled the far more formidable Trotsky. It was that Bukharin confessed to fantastic crimes he did not commit. For generations of intellectuals, Bukharin's confession would symbolize the depredations of communism, how it not only murdered its favored sons, but also conscripted them in their own demise. Here was an action, it seemed to many, undertaken not for the self, but against it, on behalf not of personal gain, but of self-destruction. Turning Bukharin's confession into a parable of the entire communist experience, Arthur Koestler, in his 1941 novel *Darkness at Noon*, popularized the notion—later taken up by Maurice Merleau-Ponty in *Humanism and Terror* and Jean-Luc Godard in his 1967 film *La Chinoise*—that Bukharin offered his guilt as a final service to the party. In this formulation it was not Stalin, but Bukharin, who was the true Abraham, the devout believer who gave up to his jealous god that which was most precious to him.

But where Abraham's readiness to make the ultimate sacrifice has aroused persistent admiration—Kierkegaard deemed him a "knight of faith," prepared to violate the most sacred of norms for the sake of his fantastic devotion—Bukharin's has provoked almost universal horror.[4] Not just of Stalin and the Bolshevik leadership, but of Bukharin himself—and of all the true believers who turned the twentieth century into a wasteland of ideology. Moralists may praise familiar episodes of suicidal sacrifice such as the Greatest Generation storming Omaha Beach, but the willingness of the Bukharins of this world to give up their lives for the sake of their ideology remains, for many, the final statement of modern self-abasement. Not because the sacrifice was cruel or senseless—not even because it was undertaken for an unjust cause or was premised on a lie—but because of the selfless fanaticism and political idolatry, the thoughtless immolation and personal diminution, that are said to inspire it. Communists, the argument goes, collaborated in their own destruction because they believed; they believed because they had to; they had to because they were small. According to Arthur Schlesinger, communism "fills empty lives"—even in the United States, with "its quota of lonely and frustrated people, craving social, intellectual and even sexual fulfillment they cannot obtain in existing society. For these people, party discipline is no obstacle: it is an attraction. The great majority of members in America, as in Europe, *want* to be disciplined." Or, as cultural critic Leslie Fiedler wrote of the Rosenbergs after their execution, "their relationship to everything, including themselves, was false." Once they turned into party liners, "blasphemously den[ying] their own humanity," "what was there left to die?"[5] Abraham believed in his faith and was deemed a righteous man; the communist believed in his and was discharged from the precincts of humanity.

As we now know, Bukharin's confession, like so many others of the Stalin era, was not quite the abnegation intellectuals have imagined. From 1930 to 1937, Bukharin resisted, to the best of his abilities, the more outlandish charges of the Soviet leadership. As late as his February 1937 secret appearance before the Plenum of the Central Committee, Bukharin insisted, "I protest with all the strength of my soul against being charged with such things as treason to my homeland, sabotage, terrorism, and so on." When he finally did admit to these crimes—in a public confession, replete with qualifications casting doubt upon Stalin's legitimacy—it was after a yearlong imprisonment, in which he was subject to brutal interrogations and threats against his family. Bukharin had reason to believe that his confession might protect him and his loved ones. Soviet leaders who confessed were sometimes spared, and Stalin had intervened on previous occasions to shield Bukharin from more vicious treatment. Threats against family members, moreover, were one of the most effective means for securing cooperation with the Soviet regime; in fact, many of those who refused to confess had no children. Instead of manic self-liquidation, then, Bukharin's confession was a strategic attempt to preserve himself and his family, an act not of selfless fanaticism but of self-interested hope.[6]

But for many intellectuals at the time, these calculations simply did not register. For them, the archetypical evil of the twentieth century was not murder on an unprecedented scale, but the cession of mind and heart to the movement. Reading the great midcentury indictments of the Soviet catastrophe—*Darkness at Noon, The God That Failed, 1984, The Captive Mind*—one is struck less by their appreciation of Stalinist mass murder—it would be years before Solzhenitsyn turned the abstraction of the gulag into dossiers of particular suffering—than by their horror of the liquidated personality that was supposed to be the new Soviet man. André Gide noted that in every Soviet collective he visited "there are the same ugly pieces of furniture, the same picture of Stalin and absolutely nothing else—not the smallest vestige of ornament or personal belonging."[7] (Writers consistently viewed public housing, whether in the Soviet Union or in the United States, as a proxy for leftist dissolution. Fiedler, for instance, made much of the fact that the Rosenbergs lived in a "melancholy block of identical dwelling units that seem the visible manifestation of the Stalinized petty-bourgeois mind: rigid, conventional, hopelessly self-righteous.")[8] Perversely taking Stalin at his word—that a million deaths was just a statistic—intellectuals concluded that the gulag, or Auschwitz, was merely the outward symbol of a more profound, more ghastly subtraction of self. Even in the camps, Hannah Arendt wrote, "suffering, of which there has been always too much on earth, is not the issue, nor is the number of victims." It was instead that the camps were "laboratories where changes in human nature" were "tested" and "the transformation of human nature" engineered for the sake of an ideology.[9]

If we owe any one thinker our thanks, or skepticism, for the notion that totalitarianism was first and foremost an assault, inspired by ideology, against the integrity of the self, it is most assuredly Hannah Arendt. A Jewish German émigré to the United States, Arendt was not the first to make such claims about totalitarianism.[10] But by tracing the ideologue's self-destruction against a backdrop of imperial misadventure and massacre in Africa, waning aristocracies and dissolute bourgeoisies in Europe, and atomized mass societies throughout the world, Arendt gave this vision history and heft. With a cast of characters—from Lawrence of Arabia and Cecil Rhodes to Benjamin Disraeli and Marcel Proust—drawn from the European landscape, Arendt's *The Origins of Totalitarianism* made it impossible for anyone to assume that Nazism and Stalinism were dark emanations of the German soil or Russian soul, geographic accidents that could be ascribed to one country's unfortunate traditions. Totalitarianism was, as the title of the book's British edition put it, "the burden of our times." Not exactly a product of modernity—Arendt repeatedly tried to dampen the causal vibrato of her original title, and she was as much a lover of modernity as she was its critic[11]—but its permanent guest.

Yet it would be a mistake to read *The Origins of Totalitarianism* as a transparent report of the totalitarian experience. As Arendt was the first to acknowledge, she came to the bar of political judgment schooled in "the tradition of German philosophy," taught to her by Heidegger and Jaspers amid the crashing edifice of the Weimar republic.[12] Making her way through a rubble of German existentialism and Weimar modernism, Arendt gave totalitarianism its distinctive cast, a curious blend of the novel and familiar, the startling and self-evident. Arendt's would become the definitive statement—so fitting, so exact—not because it was so fitting or exact, but because it mixed real elements of Stalinism and Nazism with leading ideas of modern thought: not so much twentieth-century German philosophy, as we shall see, but the notions of terror and anxiety Montesquieu and Tocqueville developed in the wake of Hobbes. As Arendt confessed in private letters, she discovered "the instruments of distinguishing totalitarianism from all—even the most tyrannical—governments of the past" in Montesquieu's writings, and Tocqueville, whose work she read while drafting *The Origins of Totalitarianism*, was a "great influence" on her.[13]

But within a decade of publishing *The Origins of Totalitarianism*, Arendt changed course. After traveling to Israel in 1961 to report on the trial of Adolph Eichmann for *The New Yorker*, she wrote *Eichmann in Jerusalem*, which turned out to be not a trial report at all, but a wholesale reconsideration of the dynamics of political fear.[14] Not unlike Montesquieu's *Persian Letters* or the first half of Tocqueville's *Democracy in America*, *Eichmann in Jerusalem* posed a direct challenge to the account of fear that had earned its author her greatest acclaim. It produced a storm of outrage, much of it focused on Arendt's depiction of Eichmann, her savage sense of irony, and her criticism of the Jewish leadership during the Holocaust. But an allied, if unspoken, source of fury was the widespread hostility to Arendt's effort to upend the familiar canons of political fear: for in *Eichmann*, Arendt showed that much that Montesquieu and Tocqueville—and she herself—had written about political fear was simply false, serving the political needs of western intellectuals rather than the truth. Arendt paid dearly for her efforts. She lost friends, was deemed a traitor to the Jewish people, and was hounded at public lectures.[15] But it was worth the cost, for in *Eichmann* Arendt managed "a paean of transcendence," as Mary McCarthy put it, offering men and women a way of thinking about fear in a manner worthy of grown-ups rather than children.[16] That so many would reject it is hardly surprising: little since Hobbes had prepared readers for the genuine novelty that was *Eichmann in Jerusalem*. Forty years later, we're still not prepared.

## Of Ideologues and Idiocy

If Hobbes hoped to create a world where men feared death above all else, he would have been sorely disappointed, and utterly mystified, by *The Origins of Totalitarianism*.[17] What could he possibly have made of men and women so fastened to a political movement like Nazism or Bolshevism that they lacked, in Arendt's words, "the very capacity for experience, even if it be as extreme as torture or the fear of death?"[18] Hobbes was no stranger to adventures of ideology, but his ideologues were avatars of the self, attracted to ideas that enlarged them. Though ready to die for their faith, they hoped to be remembered as martyrs to a glorious cause. For Arendt, however, ideology was not a statement of aspiration; it was a confession of irreversible smallness. Men and women were attracted to Bolshevism and Nazism, she maintained, because these ideologies confirmed their feelings of personal worthlessness. Inspired by ideology, they went happily to their own deaths—not as martyrs to a glorious cause, but as the inglorious confirmation of a bloody axiom. Hobbes, who worked so hard to reduce the outsized heroism of his contemporaries, would hardly have recognized these ideologues, who saw in their own death a trivial chronicle of a larger truth foretold.

What propelled Arendt in this direction, away from Hobbes? Not the criminal largesse of the twentieth century—she repeatedly insisted that it was not the body counts of Hitler and Stalin that distinguished their regimes from earlier tyrannies[19]—but rather a vision, inherited from her predecessors, of the weak and permeable self. Between the time of Hobbes and that of Arendt, the self had suffered two blows, the first from Montesquieu, the second from Tocqueville. Montesquieu never contemplated the soul-crushing effects of ideology, but he certainly imagined souls crushed. It was he who first argued, against Hobbes, that fear, redefined as terror, did not enlarge but reduce the self, and that the fear of death was not an expression of human possibility but of desperate finality. Tocqueville retained Montesquieu's image of the fragile self, only he viewed its weakness as a democratic innovation. Where Montesquieu had thought the abridged self was a creation of despotic terror, Tocqueville believed it was a product of modern democracy. The democratic individual, according to Tocqueville, lacked the capacious inner life and fortified perimeter of his aristocratic predecessor. Weak and small, he was ready for submission from the get-go. So strong was this conviction about the weakness of the modern self that Arendt was able to apply it, as we shall see, not only to terror's victims but, even more wildly, to its wielders as well.

Melding Montesquieu's theory of despotic terror and Tocqueville's account of mass anxiety, Arendt turned Nazism and Stalinism into spectacular triumphs of antipolitical fear, what she called "total terror," which could not "be comprehended by political categories."[20] Total terror, in her eyes, was not an instrument of political rule or even a weapon of genocide. One will look in vain throughout the last third of *The Origins of Totalitarianism*, where Arendt addresses the problem of total terror, for any reckoning with the elimination of an entire people. Total terror, for Arendt, was designed to escape the psychological burdens of the self, to destroy individual freedom and responsibility. It was a form of "radical evil," which sought to eradicate not the Jews or the kulaks but the human condition. If Arendt's totalitarianism constituted an apotheosis, it was not of human beastliness. It was of a tradition of thought—established by Montesquieu, elaborated by Tocqueville—that had been preparing for the disappearance of the self from virtually the moment the self had first been imagined.

## SELF AMID MASS

Arendt opened her discussion of totalitarianism with a lengthy consideration of the mass, the primary source of all totalitarian movements and regimes. For Arendt, the mass denoted less a political grouping or sociological category than a pathological orientation of self. Arendt's mass man experienced a feeling of "selflessness in the sense that oneself does not matter." This selflessness extended from the highest to the lowest concerns of the individual, from the masses' "lost interest in their own well-being" to their "lack of self-interest" and "decisive weakening of the instinct for self-preservation." So weak was the mass man's desire to preserve, let alone advance, himself that any "organization" to which he belonged "could succeed in extinguishing individual identity permanently."[21] Like its individual members, the mass as a whole lacked concrete interests and discrete goals. "Masses are not held together by a consciousness of common interest and they lack that specific class articulateness which is expressed in determined, limited, and obtainable goals." Unlike other groups, the mass was decidedly apolitical, inspired by no shared concerns, interested in no specific goals.[22]

Given this lack of concentrated political purpose, what made the mass such a potent political fuel? According to Arendt, it was the anxiety of its individual members, that "terrifying negative solidarity" of a people without roots and affiliations. "The chief characteristic of the mass man," she wrote, is "his isolation and lack of normal social relationships."[23] Though the mass did not share a politics, it did possess a distinctive psychology, born of the anomie and rootlessness of fin de siècle Europe.[24] Totalitarian movements attracted "completely unorganized" men and women by providing a psychological solution to the anxiety of isolation. With their demands for total loyalty and absolute submission, totalitarian movements joined men and women with a "band of iron," giving them that sense of structure and common identity they lacked but craved. Allowing no room for separation or individuation, these movements—and the totalitarian state they helped create—allayed, or attempted to allay, anomic anxiety.[25]

Thus did Arendt announce, early on, her Tocquevillian orientation: It was Tocqueville who first seized upon the mass as the generative source of modern tyranny, and who argued that the primary experience of the mass was neither Hobbesian fear nor Montesquieu's terror—both responses to power from above—but rather the anxiety of rootlessness. Like Tocqueville, Arendt believed that the mass was the primary engine of modern tyranny, and that anomic anxiety was its fuel. Though she appreciated the fact that totalitarian rulers like Stalin had created the social conditions of this anxiety—and that other totalitarian regimes could do the same[26]—the primary thrust of her argument was that mass anxiety was the result of a preexisting anomie, and that this anxiety produced movements on behalf of totalitarian terror.

Yet Arendt offered three critical emendations to Tocqueville's script. First, where Tocqueville had deemed the anxiety of rootlessness a product of equality, Arendt insisted that anxiety was not connected to equality. Though she agreed that mass anxiety arose from the breakdown of class structures, it was the absence of integrative institutions—not equality per se—that made the mass so prone to feelings of rootlessness and isolation.[27] Equality could produce quite different forms of political and social organization, and it was only class snobbery—not to mention a factual mistake—to assume that the modern democrat alone suffered from the vertigo of anomie.[28]

Second, Arendt's conception of rootlessness and isolation—what she called "superfluousness" and "loneliness"—was far more radical than Tocqueville's. Tocqueville's mass may have been socially unmoored and psychologically unhinged, but its members had jobs to do, livings to earn, mouths to feed. Though the props of the old order had been pulled, his mass was still a vital participant in an industrializing economy. Not so Arendt's. Her mass suffered the indignity of being expendable, of not being necessary even for the reproduction of everyday life. In an age of mass industry, individual workers were reduced, at best, to the anonymous labor of the assembly line, and, at worst, to permanent unemployment. Where Tocqueville's rootlessness left the individual alone with his work, providing him with that "most elementary form of human creativity, which is the capacity to add something of one's own to the common world," Arendt's superfluousness took even this away, removing from men and women all "contact with the world as the human artifice."[29] That superfluousness induced feelings of loneliness, "the experience of not belonging to the world at all, which is among the most radical and desperate experiences of man."[30] Loneliness was distinct from isolation, for isolated men and women still worked and thus knew their own power and appreciated the solidity and reality of the external world. Deprived of work and fellowship, Arendt's lonely person could not confirm the truth that he or the world truly existed, that he was a self at all.[31] He suffered a desperate and strange form of selflessness—not the altruism of old, but the existential incoherence of old age.[32]

Finally, Arendt reversed Tocqueville's claim about the mass's transition from activity to passivity. For all of its weak-willed shapelessness, Tocqueville's mass was an active agent, the only such agent in a revolutionary world that had seen agency disappear. What in part provoked Tocqueville's horror was how this active agent managed to pacify itself and those around it. Arendt's mass, by contrast, was inert, a vast lake of underground anxiety waiting to be tapped. When it was tapped, it did not produce the weird stasis that Tocqueville described in *Democracy in America*. Instead, it became that distinctive creature of twentieth-century politics, the mass movement, an entity, Arendt insisted, with no structure—structure was a feature of permanence—only direction.[33]

## IDEOLOGY

Among ideology's great appeals was that it spoke to the mass's sense of superfluousness and loneliness. Men and women, Arendt argued, were not drawn to ideologies like anti-Semitism or communism because they offered attractive ideals of a new world—a classless society—or promised concrete benefits—that German Aryans would one day rule the earth. Rather, it was the act of believing in ideology, she argued, not the content of the ideology itself, that mattered. It wasn't what the ideology said, but what it did: relieve the mass of its anxiety. Like so many who would write about mass ideologies after her—whether fascism or communism, antiglobalization or militant Islam—Arendt approached ideology less as a set of specific ideas than as a state of mind to be analyzed, a mode of thought impervious to all experience save the intense anxiety of its proponent.[34]

According to Arendt, ideologies like Nazism and communism envisioned a world of lawful, relentless, forward movement. Previous schemes of the cosmos—religion, Platonic philosophy, ancient Greek mythology—conceived of laws, human and divine, as pillars of stability and permanence amid interminable flux, as impositions of order upon an otherwise chaotic world. Arendt's ideologues, by contrast, imagined laws as natural and historical processes of ceaseless development. Every particular creation was in an advanced state of decay, preparing for the birth of some new, more advanced, life form. The world, in this view, was caught in an upward spiral of evolution, where everything was not what it was, but what it was becoming.[35] Because becoming signaled nothing so much as the death of older forms, everything was always dying. Thus, where Hobbes's ideologues were attracted to ideas that increased them, that celebrated the integrity of the human personality and the solidity of its artifice, Arendt's were charmed by visions of human eclipse, by ideas that cast death, including their own, not as an irreversible or regrettable fact of life, but as a way, the way, of life.

Totalitarian ideologies thus made no appeal to their followers' interests, to their concrete goals or particular needs. To the contrary, ideologies preyed upon and advanced the "complete loss of individual claims and ambition," "extinguishing individual identity permanently."[36] Fearing neither their own death nor the demise of their race or class, Arendt's ideologues feared the disconfirmation or absence of ideology—not because they were drawn to its particular content, but because they were so agreeably flattened by its horizons. Indeed, when an ideological movement was defeated, the affections of its adherents immediately evaporated; released from one grand idea, they were ready for the next. So long as ideology kept the world moving, they followed.

Ironically, the very same ideologies that dissolved the world into ceaseless motion also provided the individual with a sense of solidity and connection. Ideological propaganda "gave the masses of atomized, undefinable, unstable and futile individuals a means of self-definition and identification which not only restored some sense of the self-respect they had formerly derived from their function in society, but also created a kind of spurious stability which made them better candidates for an organization."[37] Ideology created a coherent world, albeit an entirely fictitious one. It ferreted out a putative order amid meaningless chaos—not the imposed order of human or divine rule, but the impersonal and indisputable order of mathematics, in which two plus two equals four. Impervious to the surprise and incoherence of everyday life, ideology provided a "strait jacket of logic" in which men and women found meaning in a meaningless world. In more traditional societies, men and women enjoyed the assurance of common sense and conventional opinion, which helped assimilate the world's happenstance. Deprived of that common sense, the mass felt compelled to "exchang[e] the freedom inherent in man's capacity to think" for a relentless conveyor belt of logic.[38]

It was no wonder, according to Arendt, that so many of Stalin's victims willingly confessed to crimes they did not commit. True mass men, they concluded that it was better to die with ideology's premises and logic intact than to resist the coercion of its fictitious truth. Drawing a page from *Darkness at Noon*, Arendt wrote of the mode of thought that had allegedly induced the likes of Bukharin to confess: "You can't say A without saying B and C and so on, down to the end of the murderous alphabet. . . . The coercive force of the argument is: if you refuse, you contradict yourself and, through this contradiction, render your whole life meaningless; the A which you said dominates your whole life through the consequences of B and C which it logically engenders."[39] The only resources that might enable an individual to refuse these compulsions of logic were Tocqueville's old standby's: "great strength of character to resist constant threats" and "great confidence in the existence of fellow human beings—relatives or friends or neighbors."[40] In other words, a heroic cast of mind and a close-knit association of fellows.

## TOTAL TERROR

Though totalitarianism had mass roots, its final flower was "total terror," which was most visibly achieved in the camps, for only within Auschwitz and the gulag did the Nazis and the Bolsheviks possess sufficient power to turn their crackpot theories into accomplished fact. Analyzing this transformation of mass anxiety into total terror, Arendt left the world of Tocqueville and entered that of Montesquieu. Like Montesquieu, Arendt believed that total terror divested its victims of those accumulations of civilization— intimacy, reason, interest, identity—that go by the name of humanity. And like Montesquieu, she argued that by eliminating these human attributes, total terror reduced men and women to the barest strips of nature. Or, put more chillingly, by eliminating these attributes, total terror unleashed those elements of nature present in all men and women that civilization usually contains. In the camps, she claimed, the psyche was destroyed "without the destruction of the physical man." Denizens of the camps could "no longer be psychologically understood" because they were "inanimate men"—"bundles of reactions"—who responded only to physical threats. They became entirely alike, as predictable as nature itself, lacking that human capacity "to begin something new out of" one's "own resources, something that cannot be explained on the basis of reactions to environment and events." After being subjected to unrelenting violence, "nothing . . . remains but ghastly marionettes with human faces, which all behave like the dog in Pavlov's experiments, which all react with perfect reliability even when going to their own death, and which do nothing but react."[41] Where the mass was all psychology, the camps were all biology.

What was so remarkable about Arendt's account of the victims inside the camps, however, was how closely it paralleled her discussion of the mass outside the camps. In the camps, men and women lacked individuality, will, identity. Men and women in all their plurality were transformed into Man, the species. Not only did individuals disappear, but so did the memory of them; their death was as anonymous as their life.[42] Each of these elements was characteristic of mass society. It was as if the victims of the camps experienced a death in life only slightly more toxic than the one they already suffered outside the camps. "Extermination," she wrote elsewhere, "happens to human beings who for all practical purposes are already 'dead,'" which was how she understood the broken lives of mass society. For that reason, she concluded, "terror fits the situation of these ever-growing masses to perfection."[43]

Like Montesquieu, then, Arendt was forced to the inadvertent suggestion that total terror possessed a subterranean pull, that the men and women of mass society had been lying in wait throughout the nineteenth century, desperate to destroy themselves in the twentieth. Civilization and humanity, she noted again and again, were wrenching elevations, while total terror trafficked in the lower depths. Humanness required men and women to look beyond the biological drives for food, shelter, and the reproduction of the species, and revealed itself in the stylized creations—as opposed to the physiological reactions—of free men and women. "Man's 'nature,'" she wrote, "is only 'human' insofar as it opens up to man the possibility of becoming something highly unnatural, that is, a man." But Auschwitz and the gulag "show that human beings can be transformed into specimens of the human animal."[44] Total terror reveled in the disassembly of civilization's great, and difficult, work, in the destruction of centuries of effort on behalf of the created and the designed. Though total terror was not, strictly speaking, natural—it was an ally of an ideological conception of the natural[45]—it fraternized with the natural, preying upon the desire of men and women to immerse themselves in nature's anonymous rhythms and currents. As we shall see, Arendt hoped that fighting total terror would become the great, unnatural project of a renewed humanity. But given her conception of total terror's natural affinities, was she recommending anything more than a shaking of fists at the weather?

Though Montesquieu laid the groundwork for Arendt's account of total terror, her analysis of the politics of total terror would have been, at first glance, as bewildering to the Frenchman as her account of ideology would have been to Hobbes. Montesquieu's despot was a tyrant of the old school, a Caligula of lust and sadism whose imprint was felt throughout society. Despite the despot's cruelty, his was a fairly conventional set of crimes, intelligible enough to anyone familiar with the seven deadly sins. Terror was a tool of his pleasure, satisfying his enormous appetite for violence, ensuring that he could have whatever he wanted. For all his depravity, the long shadow it cast was oddly reassuring, for it suggested that at least one person had had a hand in creating a world where so many suffered. The particular identity of his victims may have disappeared, but his remained.

Arendt's totalitarian leaders, by contrast, were almost entirely inconsequential. "Nothing is more characteristic of the totalitarian movements in general and of the quality of fame of their leaders in particular than the startling swiftness with which they are forgotten and the startling ease with which they can be replaced." Regimes of total terror were not organized like traditional hierarchies, with lines of authority pointing gloriously north. Nor were they centralized, ready to carry out the orders of an ever watchful, visible leader. Instead, they were like an "onion," with each peel revealing ever more remote points of power. No one official obeyed the orders of his immediate superior. Instead, each official was forced to divine the wishes, never expressed, of the leader. The leader, in turn, was equally mysterious. He was sure that he existed through the mass, and they through him, which meant only that it was impossible to tell the two apart. The totalitarian state was not a discrete entity: proliferating offices, it merged with the shadowy mass movement that propelled it.[46] Amid this vast democracy of crime, Arendt's leaders were practically invisible.

Totalitarian leaders also lacked the despot's appetite for violence. Himmler was famously unnerved by the sight of blood; Hitler was unfailingly vegetarian in his personal dealings. Like their victims, totalitarian leaders had no "evil motives of self-interest, greed, covetousness, resentment, lust for power." Stalin and the Bolsheviks did not launch the purges in order to protect their power, trounce their enemies, or fulfill their desires. Hitler and his followers did not build concentration camps in order to make themselves a master race, for they did not "care if they themselves" were "alive or dead, if they ever lived or never were born."[47] Total terror had no utilitarian purpose whatsoever. It wreaked havoc upon the economy, undermined national security, and usually worked to the detriment of its wielders.[48]

According to Arendt, the sole purpose of total terror was to serve the totalitarian ideologies of motion that inspired it, "to make it possible for the force of nature or of history to race freely through mankind, unhindered by any spontaneous human action." Indeed, total terror was designed not only to "liberate the historical and natural forces" described by ideology, but also "to accelerate them to a speed they never would reach if left to themselves." Total terror was not supposed to maintain order. It was not designed to help Hitler carry out the destruction of the Jews or help Stalin undertake forced collectivization. Its purpose was to eliminate the spontaneity of human freedom itself, to turn men and women into transmission belts of nature and history. To accomplish this end, men and women would have to be purged of all but the most limited and basic reactions. This requirement applied to the victims—and to the victimizers. The concentration camps could not tolerate guards and commandants who enjoyed the sight or act of killing. If the camps were turned into "amusement parks for beasts in human form," if lustful sadists were allowed to run amok, the movement of death in life would be slowed. Auschwitz was a factory of racism, built not for the benefit of its foremen, bosses, and owners, but for the sake of the product itself: "The Nazis did not think that the Germans were a master race, to whom the world belonged, but that they should be led by a master race, as should all other nations, and that this race was only on the point of being born."[49] Ultimately, Arendt concluded, if the real beneficiary of terror was motion itself, then terror's wielders would have to be prepared to have the knives turned on themselves—if for no other reason than to keep things moving. And so they were: "The process may decide that those who today eliminate races and individuals or the members of dying classes and decadent peoples are tomorrow those who must be sacrificed. What totalitarian rule needs to guide the behavior of its subjects is a preparation to fit each of them equally well for the role of executioner and the role of victim. This two-sided preparation . . . is the ideology."[50]

In arguing that total terror's wielders shared the fate and characteristics of its victims, Arendt both repudiated and extended Montequieu's analysis of despotic terror. On the one hand, she collapsed Montesquieu's distinction between terrorizer and terrorized, undercutting his argument that terror was designed for the benefit and pleasure of its wielder. On the other hand, she applied to its wielders the same analysis that Montesquieu had applied to its victims, claiming that total terror turned both parties into mindless bearers of a preordained destiny. Thus did she amplify a premonition in Montesquieu's own writing—that terror was "not so much something which people may fear, but a way of life."[51] Total terror was not political; it was neither a tool of governance nor a means to an end. It was instead the expression of the deepest drives of a humanity that had been reduced to the status of animals. If total terror was more horrifying than despotic terror, it was only because

Arendt pursued Montesquieu's theory of terror to its logical conclusion, claiming that total terror was its own impersonal lord and master, turning individuals as powerful as Hitler and Stalin into the merest of implements.[52]

## TERROR AS FOUNDATION

As we have seen, Hobbes, Montesquieu, and Tocqueville were convinced that established political moralities were no longer capable of grounding political arguments and political forms, and that fear could provide the basis for of a new morality and politics. Each theorist mobilized an image of terrible consequence—the state of nature, despotism, mass democracy—on behalf of a new political form—the sovereign state, a liberal regime, pluralist democracy. Arendt was no different. As she argued in *The Origins of Totalitarianism*—and would elaborate with ever-growing force in her subsequent work—Auschwitz and the gulag revealed that the foundations of western civilization were shattered, that Europe had finally reached an "end in history."[53] In the face of crimes so unprecedented, it was no longer possible to argue or to act according to the familiar categories of liberalism, conservatism, or socialism, or tired moral antidotes like "love thy neighbor as thyself." It was necessary to establish a new foundation, and in total terror, Arendt found it. "Every end in history," whether Auschwitz or the gulag, "necessarily contains a new beginning."[54] Though in her wiser moments she realized that "no conceivable chronicle of any kind could succeed in turning six million dead people into a political argument," that "horror, or the dwelling on it . . . cannot become the basis of a political community or party in a narrower sense," she nevertheless affirmed that the fear of that horror could help establish a new political morality.[55] "The fear of concentration camps and the resulting insight into the nature of total domination might serve to invalidate all obsolete political differentiations from right to left and to introduce beside and above them the politically most important yardstick for judging events in our time, namely: whether they serve totalitarian domination or not."[56]

To seize opportunity from catastrophe, Arendt argued, it was necessary to recognize that the threat of total terror no longer lay, as fear did for Hobbes, in a hypothetical future, or, as terror did for Montesquieu, in a distant geography. The germs of total terror, like Tocqueville's mass anxiety, were already here, in the "everyday experience of the evergrowing masses of our century." The possibility of total terror would not come to an end with the death of Stalin or Hitler, and indeed might "assume" a more "authentic form" with their passing. For when "the authentic mass man takes over," she wrote, "he will have more in common with the meticulous, calculating correctness of Himmler than with the hysterical fanaticism of Hitler, will more resemble the stubborn dullness of Molotov than the sensual vindictive cruelty of Stalin." This was a danger that was "only too likely to stay with us from now on."[57]

As she set about establishing a new political morality in the shadow of total terror, however, Arendt became aware of a problem that had plagued Hobbes, Montesquieu, and Tocqueville, and that Burke—not to mention makers of horror films—understood all too well: once terrors become familiar, they cease to arouse dread. The theorist who tries to establish fear as a foundation for a new politics must always find a demon darker than that of her predecessors, discover ever more novel, and more frightening, forms of fear. Thus Montesquieu, seeking to outdo Hobbes, imagined a form of terror that threatened the very basis of that which made us human. In Arendt's case, it was her closing image of interchangeable victims and victimizers—of terror serving no interest and no party, not even its wielders; of a world ruled by no one and nothing, save the impersonal laws of motion—that yielded the necessary "radical evil" from which a new politics could emerge.[58]

But as her friend and mentor Karl Jaspers was quick to recognize, Arendt had come upon this notion of radical evil at a terrible cost: it made moral judgment of the perpetrators of total terror nearly impossible.[59] According to *Origins*, total terror rendered everyone—from Hitler down through the Jews, from Stalin to the kulaks—incapable of acting. Indeed, as Arendt admitted in 1963, "There exists a widespread theory, to which I also contributed [in *Origins*], that these crimes defy the possibility of human judgment and explode the frame of our legal institutions."[60] Total terror may have done what fear, terror, and anxiety did for her predecessors—found a new politics—but, as Arendt would come to realize in *Eichmann in Jerusalem*, it was a false foundation, inspiring an operatic sense of catastrophe, that ultimately let the perpetrators off the hook by obscuring the hard political realities of rule by fear.

## Of Careerists and Collaboration

In *Eichmann in Jerusalem*, Arendt radically revised these arguments—about the self amid the mass, about ideology, about the purpose and politics of terror, and about terror as a foundation. Instead of the selfless individual, Arendt gave us Eichmann the social-climbing careerist. Instead of the anomic mass, she depicted a snobbish party hierarchy, with deep roots in what she called "respectable society." Instead of ideologies of incidental content confirming the worthlessness of the individual, she now claimed that ideology appealed to its adherents' sense of their own grandeur. Total terror was not an expression of abstract motion: it was the instrument of a concrete political end, genocide. That end was imagined by Hitler and his cronies, and implemented by middle managers like Eichmann, collaborators throughout Europe, and leaders within the Jewish community itself. Instead of turning everyone into passive implements of an impersonal destiny, total terror turned everyone into active agents. Most important, total terror could not serve as the foundation of a new morality or politics. It was not "radical evil," but a symptom of the "banality of evil," of the trivia that ultimately underlies and accompanies the terrible. By insisting on total terror's banality, she sought not to minimize it, but rather to deny it moral depth, to see in it not an argument for the new, but the unhappy persistence of the old.[61]

What accounts for this shift in Arendt's perspective, from the antipolitics of total terror to the politics of careerism and collaboration? *Eichmann in Jerusalem* was written at a moment of political hope, in the early 1960s, as movements for radical reform in the United States and elsewhere began to awake from the decade-long sleep of the Cold War. Interestingly enough, *The Origins of Totalitarianism* was also conceived and partially written at a moment of hope, in the first half of the 1940s, when the European resistance against the Nazis, from which Arendt drew much sustenance, first appeared. But the section of *Origins* in which Arendt set out the views on totalitarianism and total terror we have been discussing here was completed in the second half of the 1940s, at a moment of despair, after the Cold War had begun. A brief rehearsal of the composition of *Origins* and *Eichmann* reveals the impact of immediate political events on Arendt's thinking, suggesting a trajectory not unlike Montesquieu's and Tocqueville's—though in Arendt's case, the direction went not from politics to psychology and culture, but from politics to psychology and culture and then back to politics again.

In the early 1940s, when Arendt began thinking about *Origins*, she was consumed with the problem of European fascism, not totalitarianism. As her original prospectus makes clear, she saw fascism as a symptom of two nineteenth-century European developments: the racism of anti-Semitism and imperialism. So central were racism and imperialism to her analysis that she even considered calling *Origins* "Imperialism" and a planned chapter on the Nazis' "Race-Imperialism." Nowhere in this original conception and composition of the book was there any discussion of Stalinism or of totalitarianism and total terror. Arendt was interested solely in understanding how European elites—rather than the mass—came to be attracted to racist ideologies—understood as specific and coherent ideas, rather than logics of impersonal motion—and how they sought to escape the constraints of liberal civilization through imperial expeditions in Africa and the Middle East. Though she never quite got, at this initial stage, to her chapter on "Race-Imperialism," the Nazi genocide was clearly her intended destination.[62]

While an air of pending catastrophe hangs over these first two sections of *Origins*, Arendt wrote them, odd as it may sound, at a moment of hope for a new Europe, which she thought might flourish after the war. As she explained in a 1945 *Partisan Review* article, World War II saw not only the Nazi apocalypse but also the birth of antifascist struggles throughout Europe. Centered in France, the resistance was opposed not to Germany, but to fascism, which it saw as a European problem. It envisioned a postwar political order not of conservative nation-states but of an egalitarian, federated continent which would pursue a radical program of economic redistribution, including "control of wealth" and "public ownership of basic resources and major industries," "liquidating the Junkers and industrialists as social classes, complete disarmament, and control of industrial output." Members of the resistance drew their inspiration from their struggle against the Nazis. "Under Nazi oppression," Arendt explained, they "not only relearned the meaning of freedom but also won back their self-respect as well as a new appetite for responsibility."[63] Later, she would call this experience and the vision that resulted from it the "treasure" of the resistance: the feeling of freedom and self-discovery that comes not only from opposing tyranny, but also from acting without the guidance of things past, with the conviction that it is one's actions, and one's actions only, that stand between darkness and light.[64]

At the close of her *Partisan Review* article, however, Arendt warned that the resistance vision of postwar Europe might not come to pass. She feared that the Allies would put into power the "governments-in-exile," which had tried to oversee continental opposition to the Nazis from afar. These governments, she warned, could "quickly put a stop to this new feeling of European solidarity," for their goal was simply "the restoration of the status quo." Arendt was particularly concerned that a new emphasis on "collective security," which, she reminded her readers, was a holdover from the Holy Alliance, would find postwar traction in the fear of the Soviet Union. Already, she noted, the Kremlin had begun to demarcate its sphere of interest in Eastern Europe, and in the background she heard the western powers following suit. The upshot of this restoration, she believed, would be a revival of the very forces—elites, ethnic and national chauvinism, economic conservatism—that propelled European fascism in the first place. "The only alternative to these anti-quated methods," she concluded, "which could not even preserve peace, let alone guarantee freedom, is the course taken by the European resistance."[65]

Though fascism did not enjoy the postwar revival Arendt predicted, and though parts of Western Europe would ultimately implement some measure of social democracy, much of what she warned of came to pass. Thanks in part to Stalin's moves in Eastern Europe, fear of the Soviet Union liquidated the European renaissance she had envisioned, and the Allies quickly consolidated the traditional power politics of prewar Europe. In the United States, the shift to anticommunism was particularly dramatic, evidenced most powerfully in the revival of a conservative Republican Party and the collapse of the progressive wing of the Democratic Party. Where the years of 1944–46 had seen the stirrings of the labor movement on behalf of industrial democracy, culminating in the biggest strike wave in American history, the congressional elections of 1946, which returned the Republican Party to power, and the Truman Doctrine of 1947 shut that radicalism down. Economic revanchism and political reaction were the result. As Arendt would write to Jaspers in 1953, "The [Eisenhower] administration itself, with the golf playing president at its head, is . . . a government of big business whose sole concern is to make big business bigger." Because of this postwar retraction, no one was able to resist McCarthyism. "Can you see . . . how far the disintegration has gone and with what breathtaking speed it has occurred? And up to now hardly any resistance. Everything melts away like butter in the sun."[66]

Though Arendt opposed much of this postwar order, she herself was not immune to its effects, and this, I would argue, influenced the writing of the last third of *The Origins of Totalitarianism*, in which for the first time she began to consider Stalinism—as well as Nazism—as a variant of the much larger phenomenon of totalitarianism. Arendt composed the last section of *Origins* between 1948 and 1949, published the book in 1951, and added a new last chapter, "Ideology and Terror," in 1953. By this time, her perspective had shifted from Hitler to Stalin—indeed, it was her reading of reports from the gulag that first stirred her interest in the camps as sites of terror— and her hope for postwar Europe had all but disappeared.[67] Her sense of ideology as a vision of impersonal motion, her emphasis on the masses as opposed to elites, her notion of terror as an end unto itself, her silence about genocide—all these were symptoms of the Cold War and her shift from the West to the East. For Arendt, the confrontation with Stalinism was deeply personal. Though she was never a Communist, her husband was, and from her involvement in the antifascist movements of the 1930s and 1940s, she had acquired the antibourgeois spirit of Marxist politics. Stalinist tyranny thus posed a profound personal challenge to her wartime optimism about the possibilities of a united, antifascist front, rooted in the Left.[68] Her sense of disappointment, moreover, about the failure of the resistance to bring about a new political order—"The Resistance," she bitterly noted in 1946, "has not achieved the European Revolution"[69]—led to her conviction that only total terror, rather than the positive vision of a federated Europe, could supply the grounds for a new politics and morality.[70] Like Montesquieu after *The Persian Letters*, like Tocqueville after the first volume of *Democracy in America*, she lost the hope she derived from her initial political triumphs. The treasure of the resistance had become a "lost treasure."[71] This wan sensibility, wrought by political failure and the onset of the Cold War, lay at the heart of the last third of *Origins*, as she herself confessed in the opening paragraph of the preface to the book's first edition: "Two world wars in one generation, separated by an uninterrupted chain of local wars and revolutions, followed by no peace treaty for the vanquished and no respite for the victor, have ended in the anticipation of a third World War between the two remaining world powers. This moment of anticipation is like the calm that settles after all hopes have died."[72]

Looking back, it is easy to overlook this brief interregnum between World War II and the Cold War, to see *Origins* as an uninterrupted meditation on the seamless horror of Auschwitz and the gulag. But for men and women at the time, including Arendt, that destruction and that horror seemed neither uninterrupted nor seamless. The view of hindsight blinds us to the genuine optimism that briefly seized the Left during the mid-1940s, which the Cold War shut down, and to the disappointment that followed. As Arendt would write of the postwar fate of the resistance ideal, "It did not last long. After a few short years they were liberated from what they originally had thought to be a 'burden' and thrown back into what they now knew to be the weightless irrelevance of their personal affairs, once more separated from 'the world of reality' by an *épaisseur triste*, the 'sad opaqueness' of a private life centered about nothing but itself."[73] Such a description of life after the war found its way into the last third of *Origins*, with its account of the mass's superfluousness and separation from reality—a description, I would argue, that would have been inconceivable during and immediately after the war, when Arendt and other intellectuals were engaged in struggle and felt anything but superfluous and unreal. Far from describing the reality of the mass, Arendt's psychological analysis in *Origins* may simply have been the sad testament of one who had fought and lost. To paraphrase Paul Lazarsfeld, where a fighting revolution requires politics, a defeated revolution calls for psychology.[74]

It is also important to remember this moment of hope because it would be revived for Arendt in the early 1960s, when she wrote *Eichmann in Jerusalem*. Scholars often overlook the significance of the years 1961 to 1963, during which *Eichmann* was conceived, composed, and published. These were the *anni mirabiles* of American politics and letters, witnessing the publication of Rachel Carson's *Silent Spring*, Michael Harrington's *The Other America*, Betty Friedan's *The Feminine Mystique*, and *The Port Huron Statement*, and the appearance of the civil rights movement and the student movement on an international stage. In Germany, a younger generation began to question the actions of its parents during World War II. Issues of collaboration—which the last third of *Origins* had all but rendered moot; how, after all, could the automatons of mass society do anything as willful as work with elites in the Nazi party?—were suddenly on the table.[75] These included not just the ethics of collaboration, but the mindset—racist and careerist—that had given rise to it, and the hierarchical institutions—the party, the firm, the academy—that housed it. These were, not coincidentally, the kinds of issues that the student and other movements were raising in the United States: how a concern for private careers and class comfort had encouraged many to support, and blinded others to, the racism of American society; how a veneer of affluence hid pervasive inequality and hierarchy; how the anticommunism of the Cold War was plunging the United States into another war that, to its victims, looked like nothing so much as the racist imperialism of old Europe. Indeed, many members of the student left often cited *Eichmann* in their criticisms of American society.[76] Though Arendt would never fully embrace the oppositional movements of the 1960s, her analysis in *Eichmann* lies squarely, I would argue, within their firmament.

## THE CAREERIST AND THE SOCIAL CLIMBER

Today, the watchwords of political fear—totalitarianism, genocide, terror—possess a strange and awful grandeur, evoking an alien but potent world of crazed fanatics, suicidal ideologues, and frenzied murder. It was the singular achievement of *Eichmann in Jerusalem*, however, to remind readers that the atrocities of the twentieth century grew out of the most mundane considerations and familiar institutions: careerism and the workplace. "What for Eichmann was a job, with its daily routine, its ups and downs," wrote Arendt, "was for the Jews quite literally the end of the world."[77] For there to be tyranny, terror, and genocide, Arendt realized, someone had to tyrannize, terrorize, and kill. Individuals were paid to do this work, promoted if they did it well. Thus did fear become a job, even a career. Much of *Eichmann in Jerusalem* centers upon this claim, for it speaks to the aspirational dimensions of political fear—that its perpetrators and collaborators seek not only to live, but also to live well—and to the institutional hierarchies in which such aspirations find their home. The careerist, according to Arendt, was no passive spectator. He actively sought more for himself. And it was this quest for more that led him to participate in terror. Terror, in other words, did not constrain its wielders' desires or limit the self: it preyed upon their desires and stoked their sense of self. Like all hierarchies, regimes of terror relied upon the enterprising spirit of the hustler, who found in their promise of power and status a ticket out of the humdrum world into which he had been born, even if the price of that ticket was to manage a genocide or two.

Prior to Arendt, few theorists had explored how careerism might inspire men to participate in regimes of fear. George Winstanley, leader of one of those visionary sects that so vexed Hobbes, had alluded to the perils of ambition, how a pinched desire for advance could induce oppression of those below and submission to those above. "Covetousness," he declared, "begets fear lest others should cross them in their design, or else begets a fear of want, and this makes a man to draw the creatures to him by hook or crook, and to please the strongest side, looking what others do, not minding what himself does." A century later, Rousseau stated the case more plainly: "Citizens only allow themselves to be oppressed to the degree that they are carried away by blind ambition."[78] But these were stray comments, outposts of malcontent wisdom rather than full-blown political philosophy. Indeed, most theorists—from Montesquieu and the Framers to twentieth-century pluralists and free-marketeers—have deemed ambition an antidote to tyranny and fear. Self-interested desires, according to this school of thought, give men and women a personal stake in their freedom. Contending interests and competing ambitions produce cooperation or stalemate, both of which are supposed to be opposed to the intimidation that inspires fear.[79] Even Marxists, whose commitments render them hostile to careerism and social climbing, have usually worried more about the threats these impulses pose to class solidarity than about their contributions to rule by fear. Thus, with the exception of *The Persian Letters* and Brecht's *Galileo*—works of literature, it should be recalled, not political theory—*Eichmann in Jerusalem* is our sole sustained enquiry into the relationship between careerism and rule by fear.

Arendt's analysis of careerism in *Eichmann* was also at odds with her analysis in *The Origins of Totalitarianism*, where jobholding hardly made an appearance.[80] If what Arendt had claimed in *Origins* about the loss of self were true, Eichmann, as she portrayed him in 1963, would have been an impossibility. Eichmann was self-interested and self-serving, virtually every move he made calibrated to bring some good to himself.[81] The measures of Eichmann's self-advance, moreover, were the vertical rungs of the Nazi party and good society. "What he fervently believed in up to the end was success, the chief standard of 'good society' as he knew it."[82] Eichmann sought, in other words, to ascend those very hierarchies that Arendt had claimed in *Origins* did not exist.

A classic social climber, Eichmann was a careerist of the first order. Possessing a knack for negotiating with local functionaries and organizing large-scale operations, he was chiefly responsible for the deportation and transit of millions of Jews to Auschwitz and other concentration camps. But unlike Mussolini, that other fascist who made the trains run on time, this one "had no motives at all," wrote Arendt, "except for an extraordinary diligence in looking out for his personal advancement."[83] Eichmann joined the Nazis because he "was fed up with his job as traveling salesman" and saw in Nazism an opportunity to "start from scratch and still make a career." Hitler had also worked his way up, and it was his upward mobility that made him and his movement, in Eichmann's eyes, worthy of esteem: "His success alone," Eichmann said, "proved to me that I should subordinate myself to this man." Eichmann's encounter with Nazism, as he understood it, was a story of luck and pluck. He had little memory for the political details of Nazi history, whether the Wansee Conference or the deportation of a few thousand Jews from France. What he remembered were drinks with the wellborn and bowling with a high government official in Slovakia. Nearing the end of the war, as various Nazi functionaries brooded in Berlin over their impending fate and that of Germany, Eichmann fretted over superiors refusing to invite him to lunch.[84]

Eichmann's careerism found a welcome reception in the Third Reich, according to Arendt, because Nazi Germany was riddled with snobbish hierarchies. Despite the fact, for example, that Eichmann's father had been close to the father of Ernst Kaltenbrunner, a party luminary eventually tried and hanged at Nuremberg, "the relationship of the sons was rather cool: Eichmann was unmistakably treated by Kaltenbrunner as his social inferior."[85] Even after the destruction of the Nazi regime, one could still find traces of these hierarchies within Germany. Recounting a story from the end of the war, Arendt wrote about a Königsberg woman, suffering from varicose veins, who accosted a physician for help. Telling her to forget her veins, the physician warned her about the oncoming Red Army and urged her to run for her life. "*The Russians will never get us*,'" the woman replied. "*The Führer will never permit it. Much sooner he will gas us.*'" While the physician was struck by the woman's suicidal priorities, Arendt was more impressed by her highbrow disdain. "The story, one feels, like most true stories, is incomplete. There should have been one more voice, preferably a female one, which, sighing heavily, replied: And now all that good, expensive gas has been wasted on the Jews!" In the 1950s and 1960s, according to Arendt, elite Germans thought that the real crime of the Nazis was not the extermination of six million Jews but sending "'prominent' Jews" into exile. "There are more than a few people," she wrote, "who still publicly regret the fact that Germany sent Einstein packing, without realizing that it was a much greater crime to kill little Hans Cohn from around the corner, even though he was no genius."[86] (Writing from Paris in 1970, Mary McCarthy told Arendt a similar tale of snobbery and genocide, this time from postwar Britain. According to McCarthy, George Orwell's widow had heard, by way of Stephen Spender, someone in Britain say, "Auschwitz, oh, dear *no*! That person was never in Auschwitz. Only in some very *minor* death camp.")[87] All of these reports of social arrogance reinforced Arendt's argument that Nazism was an affair of the classes, not the masses.

But perhaps, it might be argued, Eichmann's careerism was a symptom of his psychological weakness. Eichmann, according to this interpretation, would have been little different from the classic conformists of American social commentary, those bankrupt figures from *Democracy in America*, *Babbitt*, and *The Lonely Crowd* who craved the approval of others. (This reading might explain the American penchant, which Arendt disliked, for ferreting out that elusive "Eichmann in every one of us.")[88] Eichmann, however, did not need the approval of all others, just of those who might have done him some good. With a nose for power, he aimed for ascendance, not acceptance, seeking nothing so much as a governor generalship much like that possessed by Hans Frank over Poland or Reinhardt Heydrich over Czechoslovakia.[89] To transform his careerism into an inner weakness misses its aspirational qualities, how he sought to accumulate power and prestige. To reduce that aspiration to a psychological flaw is to substitute a therapeutic diagnosis for a moral judgment. Eichmann's careerism was certainly worthy of contempt—not, however, because it signaled internal pathology, but because it registered a base set of values hitched to a genocidal project. To the extent that Eichmann's careerism reflected a retrograde social consensus, it was a vice of morals and politics, not a failure of psychology or personality.

With her discussion of careerism and social climbing, Arendt reversed the tendency—seen in Montesquieu's *The Spirit of the Laws*, the second volume of *Democracy in America*, and *The Origins of Totalitarianism*—to equate the politics of fear with a loss of self and institutional hierarchies. By demonstrating that regimes of fear appealed to the ambition of men like Eichmann, she returned to the insights of Hobbes and *The Persian Letters*. Regimes of fear, she came to realize, thrive not on a destroyed humanity, but on the desire of individuals to advance themselves. Not only do these regimes require real work, in the sense of compensated, volitional action, but they also depend upon the workplace as the primary institution of most adult lives. Only by overlooking work and the workplace could earlier theorists, including Arendt, claim that fear entailed a loss of self and absence of traditional hierarchies. By restoring work to its proper place, Arendt made it possible for us to see the willed effort and institutional politics that inevitably propel regimes of fear.

## IDEOLOGY RECONSIDERED

In her analysis of ideology in *Eichmann*, Arendt also emphasized these categories of ambitious selfhood and institutional hierarchy. To the extent that Eichmann believed in the ideology of Nazism, she argued, it was not because it denied him any concrete benefits or preyed upon his weak sense of self. To the contrary, Nazi propaganda cast the Germans as heroic creators of a grand future. In Nazism, men like Eichmann could imagine themselves as bigger than they were. Ideology, she also claimed, was a moral narcotic, altering its adherents' sense of ethical reality so that they could do terrible things with minimal disruptions of conscience. It anaesthetized or palliated their moral sense, shielding them from the reality of what they were doing. In *Origins*, Arendt argued that ideology created a fictitious reality for those who no longer believed in the credibility of the world and their own existence. In *Eichmann*, ideology was also a fiction but of a politically instrumental sort: it enabled the individual to overcome his "innate repugnance" to committing horrendous crimes.[90] While Arendt's new conception of ideology had its flaws—particularly its failure, shared with *Origins*, to take seriously the integrity of anti-Semitism as an idea—it brought to her analysis an element of old-fashioned realism. Ideology was no longer the Wagnerian apocalypse depicted in *Origins of Totalitarianism*: it was now just another form of political mystification.

At first glance, *Eichmann in Jerusalem* seemed to confirm what Arendt had written about ideology in *Origins*. Eichmann, she wrote, was an "idealist," someone who, in his own words, "*lived* for his idea . . . who was prepared to sacrifice for his idea everything and, especially, everybody," including his family and himself. But Arendt made this point in order to draw a contrast between the idealist and "the businessman," who aspired to nothing grand, not even the high-flown career that Eichmann imagined for himself. Ideology, in other words, was significant less for its sacrifice of self—the ideologue still held onto "his personal feelings and emotions"—than for the grandeur of its adherents' ambitions.[91] The ideologue sought to do something significant, and looked about for ideas—like eliminating the Jews—that allowed him to fulfill that desire. Unlike the ideologue in *Origins*, who saw greatness in the impersonal forces that crushed him, the ideologue in *Eichmann* saw greatness in the world he created, which would remember his deeds with gratitude and reverence. No one, Arendt claimed, understood this urge as well as Himmler. In speech after speech, Himmler impressed upon his followers the grand task they were about to perform. If the job of slaughtering the Jews was "difficult to bear," he claimed, the SS could warm to the thought that it was "historic, grandiose, unique" and that it was they who were doing it.[92] It was not just the task, in other words, that appealed to the SS; it was also the fact that it was they who would perform it.

Such words were particularly resonant to a braggart like Eichmann. (So strong was Eichmann's braying impulse that Arendt wondered how he had managed to remain in hiding for so long after the war).[93] Eichmann bragged because he sought to elevate himself above those who played by the rules of the game.[94] He thus suffered from the familiar vices of self, which Arendt claimed in *Origins* had been eliminated by mass society and total terror. Behind the grand declamations of ideology stood a man with an unfortunate, though hardly peculiar, penchant for self-aggrandizement. As in *Origins*, Arendt made a direct connection between ideology and motion, but here it was not just the impersonal motion of nature or history, but also the upward mobility of the careerist. "From a humdrum life without significance and consequence the wind had blown him into History, as he understood it, namely, into a Movement that always kept moving and in which somebody like him—already a failure in the eyes of his social class, of his family, and hence in his own eyes as well—could start from scratch and still make a career."[95] In *Eichmann*, then, Arendt brought ideology down to earth, back to the familiar self with his familiar longings, vices, and interests. Perhaps that is why Arendt made a point of noting that Himmler's grand ideological statements were always delivered toward the end of the year, "presumably along with a Christmas bonus."[96]

In *Origins*, Arendt argued that ideology was a substitute for a world that was not there, a salve to a lonely being who no longer believed in anything, including the evidence of his own senses. In *Eichmann*, however, Arendt depicted Nazism as an ideology of diversion and exculpation, which presumed that the world in all its ugliness—and the individual in all his inwardness—was still there. Its purpose was to accommodate the individual to that ugly reality. Most Nazis, Arendt argued, had an "innate repugnance toward crime."[97] The aim of ideology, then, was to overcome that repugnance by turning mass murder into a positive moral duty. Killing Jews required the same refusal to yield to inner temptation—in this case, the desire not to kill—that not stealing required in another era. Killing all Jews, without exception, even had the imprimatur of Kant's categorical imperative, of which Eichmann possessed a fairly coherent, if simple, understanding. Thus, to kill a few Jews out of sadism or rage was less morally worthy than killing all the Jews, without emotion and for only the purest—that is, the most lawlike and universalizable—of reasons.[98] While fanatical Jew-killing was reminiscent of the internal renunciation described by Arendt in *Origins*, it was of an altogether more traditional sort, resembling nothing so much as the Christian ideal of doing the good, however malignantly defined, for its own sake. So persuasive, if upside down, was this moral world that someone like Eichmann, according to Arendt, could committ "his crimes under circumstances that [made] it well-nigh impossible for him to know or to feel that he [was] doing wrong."[99]

But for the most part, Arendt realized, the Nazis' moral inversions were not successful: party functionaries still sensed, however dimly, that they were committing evil. Had the Nazis, after all, not possessed some notion that they were doing wrong, would they have resorted to euphemistic "language rules," where nothing—not murder, concentration camps, nor gas chambers—could be called by its proper name? One of the purposes of this linguistic obfuscation, no doubt, was to confuse foreign visitors and to conceal the Nazis' crimes: the Nazis were worried about bad publicity and feared that should they lose the war, they would be judged in a less than positive light. But the Nazis used these words even among themselves. The Final Solution required an extensive bureaucracy, with far-flung offices throughout occupied Europe, and not every employee was a reliable foot soldier. The Nazis resorted to code words because they could not guarantee that their own ranks would accept the horror of what they were doing: euphemism was an "enormous help in the maintenance of order and sanity."[100] Arendt's discussion thus suggested that the purpose of ideology was to deflect attention from—or to justify—moral horror so that its executioners could carry on their murderous business.

What made Nazi ideology persuasive to men like Eichmann, Arendt concluded, was the simple fact that so many of the men he respected seemed to believe in it. "His conscience was indeed set at rest when he saw the zeal and eagerness with which 'good society' everywhere reacted as he did. He did not need to 'close his ears to the voice of conscience,' . . . not because he had none, but because his conscience spoke with a 'respectable voice,' with the voice of respectable society around him."[101] Eichmann genuinely believed in the authority of his social betters, that their opinions were worthy of respect and emulation. They also had power, so it behooved him to subscribe to the beliefs that accompanied that power. These twin elements in Eichmann's ideological makeup—the sincere and the instrumental, the moral and the careerist—were inseparable, for in Eichmann's eyes, success was a moral good, the standard by which men were judged worthy or not. As he claimed of Hitler: "[He] may have been wrong all down the line, but one thing is beyond dispute: the man was able to work his way up from lance corporal in the German Army to Führer of a people of almost eighty million. . . . His success alone proved to me that I should subordinate myself to this man."[102]

## TERROR RECONSIDERED

Having discovered the role of careerism and reinterpreted ideology, Arendt was finally prepared to rethink the purpose and politics of total terror. In *Origins*, as we have seen, the aim of total terror was to eliminate human freedom and individuality, to liberate the motion of nature or history from the drag of the self. Total terror was an end unto itself. In *Eichmann*, however, Arendt argued that total terror was not an end unto itself, but an instrument of genocide. Nazism, she wrote, was "an enterprise whose open purpose was to eliminate forever certain 'races' from the surface of the earth." Eichmann "supported and carried out a policy of not wanting to share the earth with the Jewish people and the people of a number of other nations." While these statements are so obvious today as to approach banality, they signaled Arendt's newfound appreciation that Nazism was "an attack upon human diversity as such," an attack on the irreducible plurality of peoples rather than on persons, on men and women conceived as members of a race rather than as agents and selves.[103]

With her clarity about the Nazis' genocidal aims restored—genocide being the intended terminus of her original plan for *Origins*—Arendt was able to appreciate terror's instrumental qualities, that it was a rational means to a mind-boggling end. The Nazis faced a significant obstacle in their quest to eliminate the Jews: in Europe, there were more non-Nazis or anti-Nazis than Nazis, and in the concentration camps, more victims than perpetrators. Like all wielders of fear, the Nazis worried that disgruntlement with their rule might coalesce into organized opposition. As the Nazis accumulated more power and territory, they had good reason to be nervous, for they were attempting morally perilous and unprecedented tasks in strange lands. Terror was a means of overcoming these obstacles. It enabled the Nazis to maximize the impact of the resource they did have—violence—and minimize the impact of the resource they did not have—people. It was thus a utilitarian adaptation of means and ends, turning potential opponents, Jew and non-Jew alike, into either collaborators or cooperators.

For many readers, Arendt's discussion in *Eichmann* of collaborators and cooperators, particularly among the Jews, deflected attention from the Nazis themselves, and unfairly cast the Jews as the corrupt agents of their own demise. As one of her most vehement critics noted, "Our enemies have for years been engaged in a campaign of whitewashing the culprits and blaming the victims. The latter, brutally murdered not so long ago, are now being killed for a second time by the defilers. Among these enemies Hannah Arendt now places herself."[104] But by focusing on collaborators, Arendt was not seeking to minimize the role of the Nazis. She was instead trying to show that terror did not entail the simple monopoly of power by the fear wielders and the total lack of power among the fear sufferers. Terror was an affair of collusion, with no "clear-cut division between persecutors and victims." Like Hobbes, Arendt believed that nonresistance was useful to the powerful, that it inflated their power, inspiring an image of their grim irresistibility, which intimidated potential opponents. Obedience was the result of nonresistance, and "in politics," Arendt wrote, "obedience and support are the same." With terror, obedience and support were not quite the same, but neither were they antithetical: in the few cases where potential collaborators and cooperators resisted their assigned roles—in Denmark, for instance, where the entire country, from king to commoner, mobilized to protect the Jews—the Nazis' power eroded, their terror proved ineffective, and the genocidal project collapsed. "The Nazis, it turned out, possessed neither the manpower nor the will power to remain 'tough' when they met determined opposition." It was for that reason that the Nazis, according to Eichmann, "regarded this cooperation [between the Jewish councils and the Nazis] as the very cornerstone of their Jewish policy."[105]

Arendt was certainly aware of the constraints the Jews faced, that when

they tried to resist, they were not only killed, but also tortured. She thought
the question "Why did the Jews not resist?" obscene. It ignored the obvious
fact that no one else acted otherwise, and that "there exist many things considerably worse than death"—like torture—which the SS made sure were
never "very far from their victims' minds and imagination." In not resisting, the Jews had chosen, with good reason, "the comparatively easy death
the Nazis offered them—before the firing squad or in the gas chamber."[106]
It was important to raise the issue of the nonresistance of the Jews, however, in order to show that it contributed to the efficacy of terror and that the
Jews exercised agency in opting for it. The Jews faced a choice between not
resisting and heading to the gas chamber or resisting and being tortured. It
was not a good choice, and the choice they made was more than under-
standable. But it was a choice, and treating it as if it were not only ascribed
to the victims a passivity they did not possess and to the Nazis an omnipotence they never had. Such a view almost turned the Jews into the animals
the Nazis imagined them to be. It also minimized the true evil of regimes of
fear, which was that they asked their victims to cooperate, willfully, in their
own death. The Nazis did not grant the Jews the grace of passivity or disappeared agency. They demanded far more, that the Jews "organize their own
destruction."[107]

But Arendt had a second problem with the question "Why did the Jews
not resist?" She thought it presumed that the Jews acted as a cohesive whole.
In fact, she argued, the Jews, like all peoples, were divided between elites and
followers, and it was the leaders of the Jewish councils and Jewish organizations who counseled their followers to take the path of cooperation and nonresistance. Terror worked best, she argued, when it conscripted indigenous
leaders whom the victims trusted. Contrary to what centuries of political theorists had taught—that terror requires the obliteration of civil society—and
what she had claimed in *Origins*, she argued that social organizations and
their leaders were the transmission lines of terror. The Jewish councils were
not the simple puppets of the Nazis; had they been, the Jews would not have
trusted them as they did. It was precisely that the councils were somewhat
independent, that they were run by men of high standing, that made them
such potent authorities among the Jews. Far from the Nazi regime requiring
the total abolition of autonomous social organizations, it actively fostered
them, so that when the time came for more severe measures, they would
have garnered enough social capital among the Jews to help implement
those measures. "The whole truth," Arendt gloomily concluded, "was that if
the Jewish people had really been unorganized and leaderless, there would

have been chaos and plenty of misery but the total number of victims would hardly have been between four and a half and six million people."[108]

The Jewish leadership, according to Arendt, chose to collaborate with the Nazis for several reasons. First, they lacked allies in the wider population. In the few cases, in fact, where the surrounding cities and countryside came to their aid, Jewish leaders were able to mount a challenge. Second, they subscribed to a belief in eternal Jewish victimhood, and viewed anti-Semitism as an intractable gentile animus. This belief induced a kind of fatalism, in which working with the Nazis seemed like the only course of action. Finally, the Jewish leadership suffered from the illusions of realism. In the name of being realistic, they sometimes forsook genuine opportunities for rebellion or opposition. If nothing else, they failed to see that had they done nothing, the fate of the Jewish people could have been no worse, and might have been a good deal better. Their realism, in other words, was more than realism: it provided active support to the Nazis.[109] Though subsequent scholars—and critics at the time—have demonstrated the faulty assumptions and factual errors underlying this last argument,[110] it usefully suggests the distance Arendt had traveled from *Origins* to *Eichmann*. No longer were the victims of terror simple, unthinking automatons. Instead, they were rational agents, making calculations similar to those described by Hobbes. They assumed that if they cooperated in the here and now, they might buy enough time to survive until the Allies arrived. It was not a crazy calculus, but its claims to rationality supported a logic of fear and induced obedience.

## FEAR AND FOUNDATION

When the history of twentieth-century fear is written, Arendt suggested in *Eichmann*, it would be better to dispense with grandiose notions like total terror and radical evil, and confront instead the dull realities of careerists and collaborators. By insisting on this nexus between terror and triviality, Arendt did not seek to discount the gravity of the Holocaust or, by implication, of Stalinism. She sought instead to deprive fear of any legs, to show that it could not underwrite politics. Arising from and depending upon the normal exchanges of ordinary human beings, fear lacked the mythic power she had ascribed to it in *Origins*. Eichmann, the Nazis, even genocide, did not deserve the imprimatur of radical evil, which inspired a terror verging on awe. Evil, as she wrote to Gershom Scholem, did not belong to a netherworld: it was very much a part of our world, the outgrowth of mundane compromises and human, all too human, vices. "I changed my mind and do no longer speak of 'radical evil.' . . . It is indeed my opinion now that evil is never 'radical,' that it is only extreme, and that it possesses neither depth nor any demonic dimension. . . . It is 'thought-defying,' as I said, because thought tries to reach some depth, to go to the roots, and the moment it concerns itself with evil, it is frustrated because there is nothing. That is its 'banality.' Only the good has depth and can be radical."[111]

Arendt thus dispelled the sacred aura that so many before her—and since—have found in the politics of fear, refusing to grant to it the primordial, religious overtones that linger around words like Holocaust. Her much-maligned tone of irony, her bitter laughter at the sheer comedy of Eichmann the man, reflected her effort to deny evil—and the fear of evil—the last word, something *Origins* had come close to granting. Laughter, as Arendt wrote in an essay on Kafka, "permits man to prove his essential freedom through a kind of serene superiority to his own failures." Looking hard at Eichmann, Arendt finally heeded the wise counsel of Jaspers, who had warned her in 1946 not to allow the Nazis to take "on a streak of 'greatness'—of satanic greatness—which is, for me, as inappropriate for the Nazis as all the talk about the 'demonic' elements in Hitler and so forth. It seems to me that we have to see things in their total banality, in their prosaic triviality, because that's what truly characterizes them. Bacteria can cause epidemics that wipe out nations, but they remain merely bacteria. I regard any hint of myth and legend with horror, and everything unspecific is just such a hint."[112] Though Arendt had never allowed the Nazis to take on a streak of "satanic greatness," she had granted that mantle to total terror. In following Jasper's advice, then, Arendt abandoned total terror—and fear, more generally—as a foundation for politics, but it also abandoned her as a source of nightmare. Perhaps it was this liberation from the total terror of her own imagination that explains the "curious state of euphoria" she experienced upon writing *Eichmann in Jerusalem.*[113]

## Two Ideas and Their Strange Careers

In the three decades since her death, Arendt's two attempts to make sense of twentieth-century political fear have enjoyed a curious fate. On the one hand, scholars of Nazism and Stalinism have rejected most of the central arguments of *The Origins of Totalitarianism.* Despite their differences, for instance, Christopher Browning and Daniel Goldhagen agree that men and women in Nazi Germany did not suffer from anomic loneliness: Nazism grew out of and depended upon a socially integrated civil society.[114] Against Arendt's view of Nazism as a mass-driven phenomenon, many historians now emphasize its elite dimensions, how intellectuals, government and military officials, professionals, clergymen, and business magnates organized the "consensus" for the Holocaust.[115] Contrary to her claims that the content of Nazi ideology was less important than its psychological function, scholars agree that anti-Semitism was a coherent ideology with great substantive appeal, particularly among traditional conservatives of the German Right. Drawing from a deep vein of counter-Enlightenment thinking, speaking to decades of discontent over the liberating promise of the French Revolution, "redemptive anti-Semitism" was critical to the Nazi worldview.[116] Finally, as Tzvetan Todorov has argued, in the camps, agency, even moral agency, survived.[117]

Using archives opened after the collapse of communism, Soviet historians lend even less support to Arendt's theses in *Origins*. Against her notion that the individual leader of terror regimes is of little consequence, one historian has written, "Stalin hovers like a specter over these events. As the most powerful political leader of the state and the center of a growing quasi-religious cult, he was personally responsible for much of the bloodshed." Though Stalinism was primarily a top-down affair, it also had its bottom-up aspects, though not in the atomistic, mass sense that Arendt described. Terror was a two-way street, where low-level, grassroots activists waged war against midlevel regional bureaucrats, whom they hoped to displace.[118] Selfhood did not die in the 1930s: it survived, sometimes by going into hiding, other times out in the open. Indeed, according to one historian, the president of the Central Executive Committee of the Soviets annually received, up until 1935, approximately 77,000 letters filled with "complaints, petitions, denunciations, confessions, and advice." One worker, for example, instructed Molotov, the foreign minister, in the fine arts of diplomacy, while another warned party leaders that they were growing out of touch with the rank and file, and compared them to the figure of Antaeus from Greek mythology, "who perished after he lost contact with the earth."[119] Within two years of Arendt's claiming that Stalin's death might signal the beginning of an even more concerted campaign against the self, Soviet newspapers began publishing letters to the editor in which ordinary citizens complained of Bolshevik perfidy and malfeasance.[120] Terror did not rend the fabric of everyday life, shredding the ties that bind for the sake of new ideological cloth: it threaded its way into that fabric, with citizens denouncing each other to the authorities over perceived slights, marital squabbles, and the like. Everyday complaints supplied the content of ideology, transforming trivial conflicts into grand war. As one survivor put it, "You should never step on anybody's toes. Even a minor incident may be fatal. Your wife has an argument with her neighbor and that neighbor will write an anonymous letter to the NKVD and you will have no end of trouble."[121]

Despite this evidence, many intellectuals, particularly those of a more literary or philosophical bent, continue to insist on the relevance of *Origins* for understanding not only Hitler and Stalin but twentieth-century terror as a whole. The atomized society; the breakdown of traditional hierarchies; the lonely self, evacuated for the sake of an incoming ideology; a terror so impersonal that nothing but an inscrutable evil can be said to rule—these are the favored tropes of intellectuals claiming *Origins* "*not* as a *past* document but as an aid in our own *present* thinking."[122] Whether they are talking about the reaction against globalization, the revival of nationalism and ethnic identity, civil society, or the threat of radical Islam, intellectuals worry about a dangerous anomie and its potential contributions to political extremism.[123] Across the political spectrum, from Jeanne Kirkpatrick's stated preference for authoritarian over totalitarian dictatorships—the former, customary, patriarchal, and familiar; the latter, utopian, antitraditional, and ideological—to Foucault's administrative power—serving no one and nothing, save the release of bodily motion and biopower—Arendt's marriage of ideology and terror sits at the center of contemporary consciousness, often in defiance of the facts. Indeed, for some intellectuals, the empirical flaws of Arendt's argument in *Origins* only testify to her deeper, more visionary grasp of totalitarian evil. Arendt's was a special gift, they claim, for "metaphysical insight," a capacity, similar to that of a fiction writer, to see the truth or meaning underneath or beyond the verifiable fact. "To penetrate to the devil's soul," wrote Irving Howe in 1991, "you need a touch of the devil yourself; to grasp the inner meaning of totalitarianism . . . you must yield yourself a little imaginatively."[124]

And what of *Eichmann in Jerusalem*? What of the terror of careerism, collaboration, and cooperation? Of the self-interest that lurks behind or about ideological pronouncement, of the ambition that propels or accompanies belief? Of the persistent hierarchies and class structures? Of the victims who make choices, sometimes securing their survival, sometimes not, often at the cost of collaboration? Of the indigenous elites who steer their followers away from opposition and toward cooperation? Of the violence that does not destroy reason, selfhood, and agency but elicits and depends upon it? Despite a range of studies confirming the presence of these elements—not just in Stalinist Russia and Nazi Germany, but in Pinochet's Chile, in the dirty wars of Argentina and Uruguay, in the Eastern Europe of the Brezhnev years and beyond[125]—contemporary intellectuals remain uninterested in these categories. Though certain arguments of *Eichmann* continue to draw attention—the banality of evil, for example, usually referenced as a slogan rather than an idea—none has achieved sufficient velocity to dislodge the vast, submerged consensus about total terror that *Origins* helped to create.

Why is that? Because, for many contemporary intellectuals, the selfless ideologue is more instructive than the ambitious careerist. The ideologue warns us of the perils of wanting too much, politically, reminding us of the terrible things that happen when we stop thinking shortsightedly. Like Hobbes's state of nature, the ideologue is a condensed statement of admonition and alarm, alerting us to the dangers of impending trespass, that we are approaching, once again, the killing fields. Whether it is the 1988 French film *Le process de Mai*, a cinematic judgment on the excesses of May 1968, with voiceovers from France's Jacobin past ("Terror finds its beginnings in virtue"), or criticism of Ralph Nader's 2000 presidential campaign, inveighing against the "fanaticism" and "left-wing utopianism" of third parties, the sense of mortal danger aroused by ideology is palpable and useful.[126] The careerist may not be the most attractive figure—indeed, as we shall see in the next chapter, he can be a source of considerable disappointment for closet romantics, who revile political enthusiasm but pine for it once it disappears—but his preferred walking path is the marketplace rather than the corridors of state power. He cares for himself, not grand ideas. He is realistic and pragmatic, not utopian or fanatic. That careerism itself may be an ideology, that realism may be just as lethal as abstraction, that ambition may induce collusion with evil, that some of the worst cases of fear are the product of ordinary vices rather than extraordinary ideas—these were the suggestive implications of *Eichmann in Jerusalem*. But running afoul of the self-image of the age, they are ignored.

# 5    Remains of the Day

WHILE I WAS FEARING IT, IT CAME,
BUT CAME WITH LESS OF FEAR,
BECAUSE THAT FEARING IT SO LONG
HAD ALMOST MADE IT DEAR.

—EMILY DICKINSON

After every great battle comes a great despair. Particularly if the war is civil and insurgent, whether it is waged with words or arms, both sides feel desolate. Among the vanquished, comrade accuses comrade of treachery or cowardice, soldiers denounce generals for marching them toward folly, and everyone is soon seized by what Tocqueville described as the "contempt" that broken revolutionaries "acquire for the very convictions and passions which moved them" in the first place. Forced to abandon the cause for which they gave up so much, failed rebels "turn against themselves and consider their hopes as having been childish—their enthusiasm and above all, their devotion, absurd." Unlike the losers, whose defeat is a permanent reminder of their struggle's unrequited sacrifice, the victors suffer from short memories. Forgetting the hardships of battle, they mourn its lost noise. We felt more alive in the jaws of death, they cry, than we do now, in the lap of comfort. "Let me have a war" one of Aufidius's servants notes in *Coriolanus*. "It exceeds peace as far as day does night; it's spritely, waking, audible, and full of vent. Peace is a very apoplexy, lethargy; mulled, deaf, sleepy, insensible; a getter of more bastard children than war's a destroyer of men."[1] Though the winners complain of victory's deceleration, the real source of their unhappiness is its disenchantment. Victory forces victors to see that the good for which they fought is tarnished and soiled, that every promised land looks better from afar than up close. Perhaps that is why God never allows Moses off Mount Nebo: had he entered Canaan, he might have seen the waiting disappointment. Thus do victor and vanquished converge upon the same realization:

the battle we fought was for naught; nothing in the real world compares to the dream awakened by our effort to change it.

In the last third of the twentieth century, both Left and Right have suffered victory and defeat. The Left helped stop the Vietnam War—the only popular movement, with the exception of the Russian Revolution, ever to prompt a government to quit the battlefield. It ended one hundred years of Jim Crow, shattered glass ceilings for women, and introduced gays and lesbians to the world. But it was also defeated at the polls and routed in the streets. Today, equality no longer propels political argument; freedom, that other sometime watchword of the Left, is the private property of the Right. Triumphant or trounced, the Left has responded with a mix of sadness and agitation. As early as 1968, a sober Julian Bond caught a whiff of victory's despair in the split within the civil rights movement over that year's presidential campaign. While Bond and his Georgia comrades campaigned for Hubert Humphrey and a compromised Democratic Party, militants in the North couldn't reconcile the meagerness of this stance with the movement's great sacrifices. "We are called 'shills' and 'prostitutes' by our Northern brothers and sisters," wrote Bond, "which is an indication, I believe, that now that the sit-in demonstrations and Freedom Rides have paled, and voter registration efforts lost their excitement . . . there isn't much interest up yonder in us folks down here." In the antiwar movement, the despair was more palpable, if flakier. In 1971, with the engines of radical advance at full throttle, Jerry Rubin announced his readiness to jump off the train: it was getting too close to the station. "Peace has become respectable," he complained after the May Day mobilization against the Vietnam War—an early warning of the nervousness so often occasioned by political success.[2]

Thirty years later, it is the sour smell of defeat that makes leftists snort. With much of the world renouncing everything they once fought for, ex-leftists, repentant leftists, and liberals subject themselves and former comrades to an anxious scrutiny. The Left, they complain, allowed its extremists, or divisive splits over gender and identity, to alienate the rest of America. Forgetting that loss is usually the fate of all rebels from below, these critics imagine a Left less histrionic, more moderate and inclusive, able to do what had never been done before: change the world without provoking a howling backlash. A Left more appetizing and decent, they argue, might have eliminated white supremacy, stopped the war, transformed the welfare state into a participatory social democracy—and somehow avoided the political exile ultimately visited upon it. Unable to reconcile themselves to their loss, critics are now seized by the contempt and embarrassment

Tocqueville detected in an earlier generation of defeat. One writer cringes over the "androidal" complexion of sixties sectarians, with their "short hair-cuts" and "flabby muscles," their "flat tones" of Marxism so "oddly remote from American English." Another renounces his one-time fascination with "the Dostoevskian moral absolutism of the Weather Underground." Others wince at the Left's lack of patriotic fervor and national identification, the hostility to all things American.[3]

Lest this agony over victory and defeat be dismissed as a peculiar indul-gence of the Left, consider some of the recent melancholy on the Right. Hav-ing fought for more than a half-century to eliminate communism, social democracy, and the welfare state, today's conservatives can claim a large and credible success. The free market is the lingua franca of our time. The Berlin Wall is no more. Religion is once again fashionable. But for the fathers of modern conservatism—and their sons—the end of the Cold War has been an unhappy time. Irving Kristol complains that the collapse of communism "deprived us"—conservatives—"of an enemy." And "in politics," he says, "being deprived of an enemy is a very serious matter. You tend to get relaxed and dispirited. Turn inward." Having won universal recognition of the free market, conservatives now realize that capitalist societies are not all they are cracked up to be. Markets don't launch fleets of daring entrepreneurs; in-stead, they foster a desire for comfort and ease, discouraging the élan and panache that were supposed to flourish after the end of communism and the welfare state. "The trouble with the emphasis in conservatism on the mar-ket," observes a jaded William F. Buckley, "is that it becomes rather boring. You hear it once, you master the idea. The notion of devoting your life to it is horrifying if only because it's so repetitious. It's like sex."[4]

Some conservatives even find themselves pining for the old days of ideo-logical war. They miss the Left, for the Left, writes Francis Fukuyama, aroused supermen like "Lenin or Trotsky, striving for something . . . purer and higher," and provoked soldiers of vision and courage to battle against them. Its defeat has left the world with no "large causes for which to fight" and men content to "satisfy their needs through economic activity." Perhaps another progressive revolt would resurrect these titans of the past, for the Left's "struggle against injustice is what calls forth what is highest in man." Such a revolt might also summon another Sakharov or Solzhenitsyn, whose refusal to compromise made him "the most free and therefore the most human of beings." But when men like Solzhenitsyn succeed, "as they even-tually must," and when the leftist regimes against which they contend fall, as they eventually do, "struggle and work in the old sense" will fade, as will "the possibility of their again being as free and as human as in their revolutionary struggle." And then there will only be "dishwashers and VCRs and private automobiles," the very promised land conservatives have spent the better part of a half-century trying to enter.[5]

Times like these—with the party of movement ascendant, then subdued; the party of order defensive, then triumphant; and both parties mourning the end of their warring affair—are ripe for talk of fear, though talk of a peculiar, and evasive, sort. Whether it is the French Revolution and its counterrevolutionary aftermath, an insurgent New Deal beaten back by McCarthyism, or the sixties undone by a resurgent Right, the long cycle of radical awakening and conservative sleep produces a discussion that follows a remarkably tight script. Erstwhile members of the party of movement witness political quiescence, social immobility, and private retreat, and conclude that their party mistakenly stripped men and women of the comforts of the old regime, leaving them with a crippling sense of isolation and despair. Hoping to protect citizens from Tocquevillian anxiety, these critics argue for a revival of integrative institutions. No simple reactionaries, they defend a chastened liberalism—one that seeks less to overturn injustice in the name of rights or equality than to reinforce society in the name of the fragile self. To the degree that this liberalism of anxiety is successful, however, it saddles intellectuals and elites with a great fund of unused political energy. Writers and activists who once sought a radical reform of society now find themselves with little to do except promote local communities and civic institutions. They require a more martial counterpart to the liberalism of anxiety—the liberalism of terror—through which they can expend their excess political reserves. So they aim their insurgent artilleries, once directed at domestic inequity, at tyrannies in far-off lands. Recalling the relief Tocqueville derived from Europe's imperial adventures, they look abroad to fight for an Enlightenment that cannot be defended at home.

This describes, I think, the state of contemporary political argument in the United States and parts of Western Europe. Ever since the sixties went on seventy, scholars and intellectuals have inched toward the liberalism of anxiety, shying away from the liberal activism of rights and equality, embracing the softer virtues of community and civil society. At the same time, they have embraced the liberalism of terror, diverting their activist energies to Bosnia and the Balkans, and now to the Middle East and the Muslim world. With the free market the reigning language at home—an antipolitical language that makes little room for the crusades that once animated the West—intellectuals on the Left and Right look to the rest of the world as a theater of social experiment and political reform. They leave domestic arrangements intact, all the while justifying foreign expeditions in the name of an enlightenment erstwhile antagonists can support.

There are many other reasons why contemporary intellectuals have opted for the liberalisms of anxiety and terror, not least of which are the genuine weaknesses and liabilities of our movements for domestic reform and the wretched state of much of the world. I do not discuss these reasons here; they have been addressed elsewhere and presumably are familiar to most readers. More important, I do not want to obstruct our view of how the liberalisms of anxiety and terror mirror those moments in the past when intellectuals turned to fear as a source of reflection and action, and thereby obscured its political origins and functions. Looking at the liberalism of anxiety and the liberalism of terror in light of this past, we will see that whatever else they are, these are languages of detoured radicalism, which, like all detours, pave a convenient path to an obstructed destination.

## The Liberalism of Anxiety

Though the liberalism of anxiety borrows from the reaction against the French Revolution, though it takes aim at philosophers like Kant and Descartes, the immediate occasion of its misgiving is the 1960s. Anxious liberals make frequent, unhappy references to gains won and goods lost throughout that decade and its aftermath—entitlements to welfare without corresponding duties, expansive rights "to 'do our own thing,'" and other smaller liberations. According to Amitai Etzioni, individual freedom and communal life are "out of balance after decades in which self-interest and expressive individualism have prevailed." That imbalance, adds Jean Bethke Elshtain, is a product of the "new attitude toward rights that has taken hold in the United States during the past several decades." The sixties, in this view, is not simply a historical moment, but an ongoing project of individual emancipation, which has not been beaten back in any significant way. At a time when Democrats and Republicans have stripped suspected criminals of procedural protections, when a presidential candidate's membership in the ACLU suggests membership in the Communist Party, and when there are fewer counties in the United States with abortion providers than there were in 1973, the liberalism of anxiety worries about a "rights-absolutist climate of opinion" that has not dissipated.[6]

While its discontent is plainly addressed to the 1960s, the liberalism of anxiety is no simple antagonist of that decade. In the same way that Tocqueville was ambivalent about the French Revolution so are the liberals of anxiety conflicted about the rights revolutions of forty years ago. Contrary to the claims of their critics, these writers are not entirely hostile to liberalism or its recent achievements.[7] They express no desire to return to a segregated or sexist America. Some, like Michael Walzer, were among the most eloquent voices of the 1960s, and still argue for the elaboration and extension of its achievements. Others, like Etzioni, claim that communities should be fostered and nurtured, but not at the expense of individual rights. Majorities can be tyrannical, Etzioni warns, which is why the Constitution has wisely deemed "some choices" to be "out of bounds for the majority." Nor should we return public argument, write Etzioni and Michael Sandel, to premodern canons of natural law or religious authority; instead, we should embrace the irreducible pluralism—and contentious debates—that liberalism at its best insistently honors. Walzer argues that communitarianism, the most prominent version of the liberalism of anxiety, is an "intermittent feature of liberal politics," which, "like the pleating of trousers," seeks not to overthrow liberalism but to texture it with sociological and moral depth. And in their effort to incorporate communitarian criticisms into liberal arguments, philosophers like William Galston and Will Kymlicka have proven Walzer correct.[8]

The ambivalence of the liberals of anxiety toward the sixties runs even deeper. Though they often argue for a revival of community and civic virtue by reference to Aristotle or Machiavelli, their vocabulary is often drawn from the very individualist ethos they question.[9] The anxious liberals care much for the fate of the self, which they believe rights-based liberalism has deprived of full agency and force. They do not praise community and civic culture as goods unto themselves: community is worthy in their eyes because it lends a necessary theater to the self's appearance. According to Etzioni, "Individuals who are bonded into comprehensive and stable relationships and into cohesive groups and communities are much more able to make reasoned choices, to render moral judgments, and to be free." Kymlicka claims, "Cultures are valuable, not in and of themselves, but because it is only through having access to a societal culture that people have access to a range of meaningful options." Membership in a common culture, particularly a culture of diverse subcultures, helps us make "intelligent judgments about how to lead our lives." Without close-knit communities, writes Walzer, the individual suffers a radical "decline in 'the sense of efficacy.'"[10]

Anxious liberals thus do not spurn the individualism of the 1960s: they question its political sociology. For them, social order—which can range from the nation, a common culture, or subculture, to an institution, a voluntary association, or a local community—is the seedbed of the self. It provides the deep grammar of individualism, the nurturing ground upon which the self learns who she is and what she believes. From preestablished moral prescriptions and social ties—that which is given, as opposed to that which she chooses—the individual learns to express herself and her needs in a publicly intelligible language. Once she has internalized these prescriptions and ties, she can think and act for herself. She no longer requires an authoritative structure to direct her every step; she can take her own steps, even steps that contradict or challenge those assigned to her, for a properly pluralist social order offers the individual a variety of scripts—doctor, lawyer, Christian, Muslim, Democrat, Republican, and so on—to perform. It even tolerates her efforts to revise or write new scripts.[11] Like parents and teachers, the agents of social order use their power to guide rather than repress, with the goal of turning the student or child into a rational, autonomous adult.[12]

But the liberalism of anxiety also stows a darker, more subversive account of social order. Recalling an argument made by everyone from Tocqueville to the Frankfurt School to Christopher Lasch, anxious liberals quietly cherish social order as a necessary antagonist of the self. Social order makes demands upon the self, they claim, exacting obedience, asking the individual to abide by its rules. Such constraints often provoke the appearance of a more fractious, defiant self, who knows what she believes and is willing to risk all to pursue it. A Martin Luther or Anna Karenina—those great refusals of history and literature who declare, "Here I stand. I can do no other." In the revolt against constraint, the self defines her own beliefs, articulates her own principles—far more vigorously than she would under the soporific gaze of an excessively tolerant parent. The prerequisite of such a deeply felt intransigence is a social structure that weighs heavily upon her. Without that structure, rebellions will be shallow and trivial, freedom an empty gesture. "Radical freedom," Walzer insists, "is thin stuff unless it exists within a world that offers it significant resistance." He adds, "the easier the easiness" of breaking loose, the less strong the individual will be. Or, as Galston writes, "Rational deliberation among ways of life is far more meaningful (I am tempted to say that it can *only* be meaningful) if the stakes are meaningful—that is, if the deliberator has strong convictions against which competing claims can be weighed."[13]

The radical pursuit of freedom, these critics argue, and corresponding decline of social order, breed anxiety, crippling the self. The "vaunting of 'free individuality,'" writes Kymlicka, "will result not in the confident affirmation and pursuit of worthy courses of action but rather in existential uncertainty and anomie, in doubt about the very value of one's life and its purposes." "Self-determination," he adds, "has generated more doubt about the value of

our projects than before." It destroys the personal intimacy and social prox-
imity we need to become full individuals.[14] The result, writes Walzer, are
identities "mostly unearned, without depth." This observation does not
prompt conservative nostalgia. Instead, it asks us to make good on the promise of comprehensive individuality and robust agency that the sixties were
supposed to deliver. If we were once again "participants in a common life,"
we would witness a true flourishing of human capacities, for men and
women "are stronger, more confident, more savvy" when they "are responsible to and for other people."[15]

In the 1950s, at a comparable moment of political retreat, American intellectuals responded in like fashion to the end of the New Deal and a rampant
McCarthyism. Like our contemporary liberalism of anxiety, the Cold War
version took its cues from Tocqueville.[16] Intellectuals argued that the average American felt isolated and alienated, that the greatest threat to individual
agency was the anxiety of anomie. "A fluid social structure," wrote David
Riesman, "creates anxiety and bewilderment." The solution was not to return to the past, but to create what Talcott Parsons called an "institutional-
ized individualism," to situate the individual within institutions. A "strong
emphasis on freedom and responsibility," Parsons insisted, required "a
framework of both normative order and collective organizations."[17] The Cold
War intellectuals did not see the quiescence of the 1950s or McCarthyism as
the product of a resurgent Republican Party in Congress, the overthrow of a
dynamic labor movement, or the capitulations of liberal Democrats to red
baiting. Instead, they assumed that it was the continuing momentum of liberalism that generated anxiety and crippled individual agency. For liberalism, in the words of Lionel Trilling, was "at this time . . . not only dominant
but even the sole intellectual tradition" in the United States.[18]

Like other reactions to failed emancipations past—one also thinks of
Tocqueville's diagnosis of democracy after the French Revolution, Arendt's
meditations on spent modernity after World War II—the liberalism of anxiety is the voice of a ruined insurgency. It conveys the promise of liberated
human capacity, and the disappointment of seeing that promise betrayed.
But what makes the liberalism of anxiety a reaction against the insurgencies
of the 1960s—as opposed to a symptom of their decline—is its peculiar understanding of the threats to the self's agency, an understanding drawn from
Tocqueville's analysis of anxiety. Where Hobbes understood the fearful self
as a being of fixed contour, frightened and threatened by forms of external
power that thwarted it, the liberalism of anxiety imagines a weak self of almost vaporous indeterminateness. This weak self, rather than external coer-

cion or repression, is the Trojan Horse of unfreedom. What makes the self so weak and anxious, in this view, is the absence of external structure and order, the absence of coercion and repression. What would make the self strong? A revival and strengthening of integrative institutions like churches and families, which could once again press upon the individual and propel her to be a full self.

The insurgents of the 1960s presumed that the self was an agent who knew, and was passionately committed to, her interests and beliefs. Indeed, it was this knowledge and commitment that hurled her against the barriers of constraint—Jim Crow, the family, the Pentagon—for she believed those barriers prevented her from achieving her aims. If the self did not act, it was because these barriers—or her fear of them—stopped her from doing so. Challenging barriers meant taking risks and making sacrifices, resulting perhaps in the loss of career and opportunity, or, in some cases, life itself. Knowing that danger made men and women afraid, sometimes to the point of not acting.[19] Fear thus required two actors of real presence—a determinate self and the agents of social order. But the liberalism of anxiety has turned the self's knowledge of her beliefs and interests into a problem, the agents of social order into an indeterminate ether, and, with that, fear into anxiety. Because anxious liberals believe contemporary America lacks integrative institutions, they imagine the self to be a thin figure of disintegration. Conversely, because the self has grown thin, she cannot participate in integrative institutions.[20] Where there was presence, now there is absence; where there was fear, now there is anxiety.

One of the most telling symptoms of this shift from fear to anxiety is the discussions over the last two decades about the problem of identity. The occasions of these discussions have been various: pitched battles over political correctness, scholarly debates about nationalism and ethnicity, meditations on the politics of recognition versus the politics of distribution. But the underlying vocabulary and assumptions of these arguments have been consistent. The most pressing questions of politics, according to many participants in these debates, concern not the distribution of power and resources or the aggressive contest for equality and expropriation. Politics instead involves those agitated questions of membership and exclusion—of who belongs and who does not, who I am and who you are, and the unrelenting anxiety over borders (of self and society, group and nation) that such questions entail. In the words of David Miller: "It matters less, it seems, whether the state embraces the free market, or the planned economy, or something in between. It matters more where the boundaries of the state are drawn, who gets included and who gets excluded, what language is used, what religion endorsed, what culture promoted."[21] "The negotiation of identity/difference," writes Seyla Benhabib, "is the political problem facing democracies on a global scale." Unlike "the struggles over wealth, political position, and access that characterized bourgeois and working-class politics throughout the nineteenth and the first half of the twentieth century," she claims, today's struggles are about what Jürgen Habermas calls "the grammar of forms of life." Or, as Samuel Huntington puts it, "In the post–Cold War world, the most important distinctions among peoples are not ideological, political, or economic. They are cultural."[22]

Though oppositional intellectuals during the 1960s were not uninterested in identity, they spoke of it as an instrument of rule. Dominant groups, these earlier thinkers believed, organized differences—of race, class, and gender—vertically, placing one group on top of another, distributing more resources, status, and power to those at the top. As late as 1982, feminist theorist Catharine MacKinnon gave voice to this dispensation in a debate with Phyllis Schlafly. Feminists, according to MacKinnon, had little interest in socially generated differences as desirable or undesirable in themselves. They worried about differences that "enforced subordination, limited options," and generated "social powerlessness."[23] This political understanding of difference prompted an interest in fear, rather than anxiety, for fear arose from and reinforced society's vertical cleavages. Fear was a tool of the powerful against the powerless, and a reaction of the powerful to the possibility that the powerless would one day dispossess them of their privileges.[24] But contemporary theorists of identity conceive of society horizontally, which is why anxiety is their preferred emotion. We are divided into groups not at the bottom and the top, they argue, but at the centers and the margins. Whether the group is a race, ethnicity, religion, nation, or culture, it is never sure of the coherence or durability of its borders. It worries that its perimeter is too permeable, that foreigners will slip through its porous frontiers and jeopardize its existential character and basic unity. Because men and women are not sure where they begin and end, there is a pressing need to "differentiat[e] oneself from what one is not."[25] The struggle for identity, in other words, results from the anxiety over borders, which produces a redoubled effort to guard those borders. Reviving unwittingly an argument from an earlier moment of political retreat,[26] theorists of identity ascribe a nagging political salience, trumping all other conflicts, to anxieties about self and other, in group and out group, nation and enemy.

To be sure, intellectuals did not initiate these arguments over identity in a vacuum: with post–Cold War debates over inclusion and exclusion threaten-ing to dissolve entire societies into chaos, theorists felt legitimately called upon to offer some guiding intelligence.[27] But these theorists have gone fur-ther, interpreting identity claims as the political return of the deepest, most elemental disquiet of the human condition. Huntington writes that "peoples and nations are attempting to answer the most basic questions *humans can face*: Who are we?" Identity, argues Charles Taylor, "designates something like an understanding of who we are." Those who struggle on its behalf are roused by the sense that "there is a certain way of being human that is *my* way." When we refuse to recognize that way of being, we harm the person, imprisoning her "in a false, distorted, and reduced mode of being." Politics should accommodate men and women who seek to identify themselves with a nation or some other culturing grouping, explains Miller, because "identi-fying with a nation, feeling yourself inextricably part of it, is a legitimate way of understanding your place in the world."[28] Or, put more strongly, politics *is* the effort to define oneself with the nation or some other cultural grouping.

Because the liberalism of anxiety values the expressive self of the 1960s—but worries about its disruptiveness—it seeks a politics that allows for individual expressiveness without its disintegrative consequences. For that reason, anx-ious liberals prize institutions of civil society that are nonpolitical or antipolit-ical, and cares and concerns that are social and cultural, but not ideological or partisan. It is these institutions and concerns that combine the virtues of ex-pression and connection, allowing the individual to disclose who she is with-out provoking disorder and disintegration. Civil society is valuable, according to Etzioni, because it encourages us to "attend to nonpolitical institutions." Local communities should be supported, Elshtain suggests, because they are not ideologically maximalist: their "ethos is preserving, not acquiring," their goal is "to defend and sustain what remains of a way of life." Civic associa-tions, writes Taylor, are important because they are "often dedicated to ends which we generally consider nonpolitical."[29] The ideal form of civil society is a conversation between two people: "A conversation is not the coordination of actions of different individuals, but a common action in this strong, irre-ducible sense; it is *our* action. It is of a kind with—to take a more obvious ex-ample—the dance of a group or a couple, or the action of two men sawing a log."[30] Conversations can range from Mozart to the weather, for "in human terms, we stand on a different footing when we start talking about the weather." In conversation, we don't just impart information to a separate self. Instead, we create a shared universe of intimate meaning between ourselves.

Conversations model the ideal form of politics, which should be expressive and embedded, collective but not divisive. "What has all this [talk of conversation] to do with republics?" Taylor asks. "It is essential to them," for "they are animated by a sense of a shared immediate common good."[31]

This bias against political action and debate is by no means uniform among proponents of the liberalism of anxiety. Some, like Walzer, praise the rough and tumble of democratic politics. But even when Walzer embraces disruptive and redistributive organizations—labor unions, for instance—it is partially their integrative function, their support for "cooperative coping," that he praises. And when the state supports unions, he adds, it helps men and women overcome their isolation. For Walzer, the 1935 Wagner Act, which gave workers the right to organize and join unions without fear of employer retribution, does more than protect workers from intimidation by their employers: it also "counter[s] the dissociative tendencies of liberal society," protecting "communities of feeling and belief" from the centripetal force of individual mobility.[32]

It is these quietist tendencies within the liberalism of anxiety—the love of intimate conversation, the praise of non-ideological associations, the embrace of integration over conflict—that ultimately render it a stillborn philosophy of politics. The liberalism of anxiety was aroused by remorse over the disappearance of the passionate conviction and crusading movements of the 1960s, and still longs for the individual and political vitality of an earlier age. It seeks a stronger self, a more defiant individual. But little of that is to be found in the PTAs and Rotary Clubs it so fulsomely praises. Whatever their value as modes of social integration, these organizations are not weapons of social conflict or training grounds of strenuous selfhood. They may be partial to conversation and cocktails, perhaps some cooperative coping, but they eschew antagonism, conflict, and political confrontation. Civil society must thus remain an object of permanent disappointment for its defenders. Because it disappoints, its advocates are driven to embrace an alternative ethos, the liberalism of terror. Formulated by a different group of writers in response to a different set of concerns, the liberalism of terror provides the bracing resolve and militant politics liberals of anxiety seek but cannot find in private associations, civil society, and conversations about the weather.

## The Liberalism of Terror

Where the liberalism of anxiety responds to the failures of the 1960s, the liberalism of terror feeds off the successes of the 1980s and 1990s. In the last two decades, the United States and its allies defeated the Soviet Union and its allies, and the patrons of the free market defeated the sponsors of social democracy. By 2002, the twin victories of liberal democracy and free-market capitalism were so complete that George W. Bush could invoke them, to no discernible opposition, as "a single sustainable model for national success."[33] Considering how much energy the United States devoted to fighting the Cold War, its unexpected, victorious end should have been the occasion of much celebration. And for a brief time it was. But no sooner had the United States declared victory than American leaders began to publicly worry that they no longer possessed a clear international charge or definition of national security. Testifying before Congress in 1992, then defense secretary Richard Cheney confessed, "We've gained so much strategic depth that the threats to our security, now relatively distant, are harder to define." Eight years later, Condoleezza Rice would write, "The United States has found it exceedingly difficult to define its 'national interest' in the absence of Soviet power." So unsure of America's international role did political elites become that by century's end, Joseph Nye, a former Clinton defense aide and subsequent dean of Harvard's Kennedy School, would declare the national interest to be whatever "citizens, after proper deliberation, say it is," an abdication simply unthinkable during the Cold War reign of the proverbial Wise Men.[34] Where these worries were concrete, the anguish of cultural elites was more amorphous. The Cold War, many intellectuals now claimed, was a reassuring time, organizing a complex world into a clear conflict between the United States and the Soviet Union. Without communism, we no longer knew who we were, what we were about. Insecurity and self-doubt were the inevitable result. As a character in Don DeLillo's *Underworld* declares of the Cold War, "It's the one constant thing. It's honest, it's dependable. Because when the tension and rivalry come to an end, that's when your worst nightmares begin."[35]

While these reactions to the conclusion of a prolonged international engagement were perhaps to be expected, the rancor of intellectuals, particularly conservative intellectuals, over the triumph of capitalism was truly surprising. Writers who had fought for years against socialism and on behalf of the free market suddenly began blasting the blind materialism and insipid consumerism of American capitalism. They found it trite and shallow, insufficiently dark and brooding. It made American politics pedestrian, rendering citizens and leaders unwilling or unable to think about large and great causes like defeating communism, to engage militarily the world beyond their shores. In an influential manifesto decrying the alleged decline of American military might after the Cold War, Donald and Frederick Kagan could barely contain their hostility for "the happy international situation that emerged in 1991," "characterized by the spread of democracy, free trade, and peace." How "congenial to America," they added, with its love of "domestic comfort." Robert Kaplan emitted barb after barb about the "children of suburbia," the "healthy, well fed" denizens of "bourgeois society," too consumed with their own comfort and pleasure to lend a hand—or shoulder a gun—to make the world a safer place.[36]

It was into this gap—the absent foundation, the vanished cause—that a small group of intellectuals, brandishing the scourge of terror as the *causus causans* of liberal politics, stepped. Disavowing all utopias, but sensitive to the charge that liberalism was an insufficiently fighting, and grounded, faith, these theorists hoped to restore liberalism to Montesquieu's original animating purposes: the defense of freedom, the rule of law, toleration, and limited state power. Justifying these values as the hard-earned wisdom of experience, they insisted that liberalism arose from no positive vision of social transformation, no philosophically derived notion of the individual or freedom or justice. It was instead the sad, dystopian knowledge of the twentieth century—the unhappy recognition that state tyranny and the cruelty of fanatics were all one needed to know in order to defend liberal arrangements, at home and abroad. Liberal politics was best understood as "a recipe for survival" rather than "a project for the perfectibility of mankind," a liberalism of terror rather than a liberalism of rights or equality.[37]

The original, and most forceful, exponent of the liberalism of terror was Harvard political theorist Judith Shklar. A Jewish refugee from Nazi Europe, Shklar had little patience for talk of spent causes, lost militarism, and the like. The plaints and pleas of the last quarter of the twentieth century reminded her of nothing so much as the soured romanticism that consumed Europe during the first half.[38] But for all her impatience with the dreamy qualities of contemporary discussion, Shklar was hardly immune to the challenges posed by the end of the Cold War and the sixties, and the triumph of the free market. For she also believed that contemporary liberalism lacked moral confidence and political momentum, that it required a new foundation. In terror— though she called it fear, she self-consciously styled her analysis of fear on Montesquieu's account of despotic terror—she found the foundation she needed. "What liberalism requires," she wrote, "is the possibility of making the evil of cruelty and fear the basic norm of its political practices and prescriptions."[39] As a category of political discussion, terror possessed a distinct utility: it answered those who criticized liberalism for lacking sufficient moral justification, a rationally grounded vision of the good life. It did so not by providing a vision of the good life, but by enlightening liberalism's critics about the perils of looking for that life in politics. Resting politics on the negative foundation of terror deflated our aspirations—not to goodness per se, but to achieving goodness through, and looking for it in, politics. Witnessing the terrors unleashed throughout the twentieth century in the name of the working class or a higher race, the sober observer would realize that whenever utopian aspirations entered the public sphere, terror inevitably followed. This was, Shklar insisted, no philosophical claim: it was the incontrovertible conclusion to the evidence of history.

Shklar was hardly the first to point out the relationship between terror and idealism—it was Robespierre, after all, who pronounced terror and virtue the revolution's twin children—but she derived from this knowledge a larger conclusion about the kind of foundation liberalism required. Too many philosophers, Shklar suggested, had searched for political foundations by looking beyond the factual and the actual to the moral and the principled. Instead of immersing themselves in history or politics, they asked what reason required or goodness entailed, and then sought to instantiate their conclusions in the political realm. From that manner of proceeding, she argued, all sorts of political mischief followed. Would it not make more sense, she asked, to begin with the cruelty and violence by which ideals had so often been pursued? Rather than peering up to the city of God, why not walk among Europe's killing fields, inspecting the tortured victims of utopias past and present? By doing so, she argued, "one closes off any appeal to any order other than that of actuality." The liberalism of terror, she concluded, entailed "a ramble through a moral minefield, not a march toward a destination."[40]

As much as Shklar might not have cared to admit it, the advantage of putting terror first was distinctly epistemological. Shklar believed that terror possessed an easy intelligibility which made for quick and universal agreement about principles. Terror required no philosophy, no leap of reason, to establish its evil: everyone knew what it was and that it was bad. "The fear of fear does not require any further justification, because it is irreducible." Cruelty, terror's most common weapon, "repels instantly and easily because it is 'ugly,'" prompting an indisputable argument on behalf of any politics that might prevent it. "Because the fear of systematic cruelty is so universal, moral claims based on its prohibition have an immediate appeal and can gain recognition without much argument." Unlike goodness or rights, which provoked endless disagreement, terror settled arguments, making it the ideal foundation. The liberalism of terror, she wrote, "does not, to be sure, offer a *summum bonum* toward which all political agents should strive, but it certainly does begin with a *summum malum,* which all of us know and would avoid if only we could." All of us knew it—that was the key. And from that knowledge, morality and politics followed: "The liberalism of fear, which makes cruelty the first vice, quite rightly recognizes that fear reduces us to mere reactive units of sensation and that this does impose a public ethos on us."[41]

While Shklar wrote out of a genuine concern for the victims of terror, her theory served a more domestic purpose: it responded to the widespread sense that liberalism was a tottering faith, that in the wake of the sixties and the twilight of the Cold War, its ideals no longer compelled. For many intellectuals, the crisis of contemporary liberalism was a crisis of knowledge, of uncertainty about positive programs and principles. Terror and the practices associated with it—cruelty, suffering, pain—provided certainty, resolved doubt. Intellectuals writing in Shklar's wake often invoked the simple clarity of these negative experiences—as opposed to the elusive obscurity of positive principles—as the reason for adopting them as a foundational premise. Among the arguments cited by Israeli political theorist Avishai Margalit for resting politics upon the negative foundation of humiliation was that " . . . it is easier to identify humiliating than respectful behavior, just as it is easier to identify illness than health. Health and honor are both concepts involving defense. We defend our honor and protect our health. Disease and humiliation are concepts involving attack. It is easier to identify attack situations than defense situations, since the former are based on a clear contrast between the attacker and the attacked, while the latter can exist even without an identifiable attacker."[42] Richard Rorty likewise argued that negative experiences like cruelty made it possible to affirm liberal principles without resorting to an architectonic philosophy. Solidarity with the victims of cruelty, he wrote, was "to be achieved not by inquiry"—the traditional route of liberals like Rawls or Dworkin—"but by imagination, the imaginative ability to see strange people as fellow sufferers." The liberal need no longer worry about the grounds of her ideals once she realized that she was "more afraid of being cruel than of anything else." All she needed to recognize was that "traditional differences (of tribe, religion, race, customs, and the like)" were "unimportant when compared with similarities with respect to pain and humiliation." She could forego the unanswerable philosophical question "Do you believe and desire what we believe and desire?" and ask instead, "Are you suffering?"[43] Or, as Michael Ignatieff put it: "In the twentieth century, the idea of human universality rests less on hope than on fear, less on optimism about the human capacity for good than on dread of human capacity for evil, less on a vision of man as maker of his history than of man the wolf toward his own kind. The way stations on the road to this internationalism were Armenia, Verdun, the Russian front, Auschwitz, Hiroshima, Vietnam, Cambodia, Lebanon, Rwanda, and Bosnia."[44]

Despite Shklar's impatience with the self-indulgence of contemporary argument, then, many seized upon her liberalism of terror precisely because it responded to their own quest for political assurance. Accounts of terror—in the Balkans or Rwanda—offered by writers in Shklar's wake were not simply tales of far-off lands. They became tales about the West, the witnesses to the terror. *Slaughterhouse*, David Rieff's acclaimed account of Bosnian ethnic cleansing, was subtitled "the Failure of the West." Reviewing *Slaughterhouse* in *The New Republic*, veteran journalist Anthony Lewis called it "an epitaph for Bosnia, or for us."[45] Samantha Power, author of an award-winning book on the lackluster American response to genocides throughout the twentieth century, confessed to the *New York Times* that she was "a child of Bosnia" who "came of age" in the Balkans.[46] As if to underscore the point, two of the most prominent books about ethnic cleansing in the nineties—Philip Gourevitch's *We Wish to Inform You That Tomorrow We Will Be Killed With Our Families* and Michael Ignatieff's *The Warrior's Honor*—made their authors the central characters of their tales. Where Cold War accounts of Nazi or Stalinist atrocities often kept their author off stage and featured austere, impersonal narratives—one thinks of Solzhenitsyn's *Gulag Archipelago* or Arendt's *Origins of Totalitarianism*, the first by a victim of Stalin, the second by a refugee from Hitler—literary treatments of terror after the Cold War pushed their authors to center stage, reminding readers that the chief protagonist in these tales was not the victim, but the teller, standing in for the rest of us.

Few writers made these connections between terror and personal renewal more palpable than Gourevitch, in his harrowing report on the 1994 Rwandan genocide. For Gourevitch, Rwanda was a classroom of the western self, where someone like him—or us—could acquire greater clarity about his beliefs and the veracity of his own experience. At the outset of *We Wish to Inform You*, Gourevitch confessed that his real topic was not the Rwandan genocide but moral epistemology. "This is a book about how people imagine themselves and one another," he explained, "a book about how we imagine our world." Though genocide might seem an inauspicious occasion to raise such rarified questions of the imagination, Gourevitch believed it was appropriate, for genocide forced one to confront "the peculiar necessity of imagining what is, in fact, real." Staring at a pile of bones, Gourevitch "wondered whether I could really see what I was seeing while I saw it." Unlike the average person who saw a tree, and took it for granted that she was seeing a tree, the witness to genocide had to do more than look in order to see: looking was insufficient, for what one saw was too horrible to be believed. To truly see genocide, one had to acknowledge that, yes, human beings had done—and could do—these things to each other. Sight, in other words, required ethical comprehension, a leap of the moral imagination. That melding of morality and vision, Gourevitch explained, "is what fascinates me most in existence" and what drew him to Rwanda.[47]

As difficult as it was to see genocide, once one saw it, one enjoyed a far greater confidence about the truth of one's perceptions, and came away with a more bracing sense of reality. The sight of mass death solidified Gourevitch's sense of his own experience, applying a clarifying shock of reality that he would never, could never, lose. Nor did he wish to: "These dead Rwandans will be with me forever, I expect. That was why I had felt compelled to come to Nyarubuye: to be stuck with them—*not with their experience, but with the experience of looking at them.*" The benefit of sight, in other words, redounded to the seer, not to the seen. He was the audience; they, the objects of display. "The dead at Nyarubuye were, I'm afraid, beautiful. There was no getting around it. The skeleton is a beautiful thing." Traveling on a dangerous road in the Rwandan countryside, surrounded by death and destruction, Gourevitch simply felt alive, more alive than at any point in his life: "I was glad to be out there, on an impassable road in an often impossible-seeming country, hearing and smelling—and feeling my skin tighten against—the sort of dank, drifting midnight that every Rwandan must know and I had never experienced so unprotectedly."[48]

Perhaps it was inevitable that Gourevitch would look among African skeletons for a clarifying mirror of himself, for as Shklar discovered when she embarked upon her ramble in a moral minefield, there was a deep vein of narcissism running throughout the liberalism of terror. For all their talk of victims, Shklar pointed out, philosophers often "protect [themselves] against utter despondency" by seizing upon victims as answers to their own concerns. For the liberal of terror, the victim was an argument, "a way of . . . finding an ethos that . . . leads neither to zeal nor to cruelty." The liberal of terror thus impressed the victim into a service the latter did not choose. "Forced to serve the onlookers," the victim was "used untruthfully, as a means to nourish our self-esteem and to control our own fears."[49]

To make terror a negative foundation of liberal politics, it was essential that it participate in none of the morals or politics men and women valued. Mix terror with any virtue, connect it to any cherished institution, and it lost that conspicuous intelligibility and apartness that made it a desirable foundation in the first place. Again, Shklar's account proved useful. Shklar focused upon exclusively physical forms of terror, the violence committed by tyrants against defenseless victims. Though at times she talked about "moral cruelty"—the "deliberate and persistent humiliation" of other persons[50]—Shklar wrote mostly about the physical terror profiled by Montesquieu in *The Spirit of the Laws*. Montesquieu understood terror, according to Shklar, as a "physiological reaction" to violence or the threat of violence. "This is where our physical and moral impulses meet and struggle, and where the former triumph." This kind of terror did not partake of the morals or politics that ordinarily inspire human beings, for there was "something uniquely physical about a fear-ridden despotism that separates it from every other form of government in Montesquieu's gallery of regimes."[51]

In explaining the causes of terror, Shklar further separated it from morals and politics. Shklar claimed that terror was aroused by cruelty, which she defined as "the willful inflicting of physical pain on a weaker being in order to cause anguish and fear."[52] Philosophers might dismiss this argument as circular—terror was aroused by cruelty, and cruelty was the use of physical pain to arouse terror—but circularity was critical to Shklar's account. It suggested, like nothing else, the close-knit world to which terror and cruelty exclusively belonged. Terror was enclosed in a self-sustaining sphere, borrowing from nothing—certainly nothing of human value—outside its own circle. It had nothing to do with the requirements of political rule. Tyrants often relied upon terror, Shklar claimed, because of their "princely fear, not only of foreign enemies, but, as in Agamemnon's case, for the ruler's own prestige." Princely fear was irrational, a dishonorable cowardice, rather than a reasonable reflection upon necessities of state. None of the actions Agamemnon took in response to his fear, Shklar noted, qualified as "rational responses to any necessities," and he used violence against victims, like defenseless women and children, from whom he had nothing to fear.[53]

Occasionally, Shklar did attempt to provide a thicker political description of terror, pointing to the connections between terror, inequality, and the state's monopoly of power. Terror, she noted, was inspired by its wielder's belief in the inferiority of his victims. The "difference" between "the weak and the powerful" often "invites" the "abuse of power and intimidation," and those differences are "built into the system of coercion upon which all governments have to rely to fulfill their essential functions."[54] But even as she opened the door to politics, Shklar closed it: Shklar held inequality to be significant because it increased the "social distance" between victim and victimizer. Inequality separated the victim, emotionally and cognitively, from her tormentor, making it possible for the latter to act upon an internal impulse toward cruelty, which predated inequality. Inequality made the victim alien to the victimizer, enabling him to implement his pre-political, personal desires. Inequality did not inspire the despot to use terror in order to protect his superior position. Instead, it facilitated his use of terror, creating around him a "vacuum that separates him from his subjects, and this is the prerequisite for the maximum both of inequality and of potential and actual cruelty."[55] Terror came first, before inequality; it was made possible, but not activated, by inequality.

Though Shklar insisted that terror was not to be understood as the product of a sadistic mind or a personal derangement, she could not escape the psychological reductiveness of Montesquieu's account. Terror for Shklar, like despotism for Montesquieu, was a universal solvent, a psychic impulse that found an outlet in the concentration of state power and accumulated inequality. It was, she claimed in a revealing phrase, the "underlying psychological and moral medium that makes vice all but unavoidable."[56] Terror was its own instigator of political evil, serving no purpose except the creation of a cowed and victimized population. Because it was a universal medium, the only remedy was to construct dams and dikes throughout the body politic to check its coursing movement. Thus did Shklar, like Montesquieu and Tocqueville before her, use the language of terror to justify the rule of law, fragmented state power, tolerance, and social pluralism.[57]

Shklar wrote her most bracing pieces on terror during the mid to late 1980s, just as the Cold War was coming to an end. Fresh in her mind were Hitler and Stalin, those "agents of the modern state" who, with "unique resources of physical might and persuasion at their disposal," acted so often with such "deadly effect."[58] But for those who sought to make terror a negative foundation in the wake of the Cold War—when the breakdown of modern states in the Balkans, Rwanda, and elsewhere unleashed waves of ethnic cleansing—the problem was not the unbounded states Shklar had warned of but "failed states." Failed states liberated men and women from all restraint, giving rise, it was argued, to a more arbitrary and vicious violence and, hence, more virulent terror.[59] What seemed to prompt this genocidal savagery, moreover, was an obsession with the purity of collective identities, the unity—ethnic, religious, or national—of a particular group. Unlike the idealogical utopianism of the twentieth century, this new breed of conflict was fueled by considerations more ethereal and symbolic, which seemed less amenable to traditional political calculations.

To explain this new development, writers did not abandon Shklar's depoliticized account of terror. They merely supplemented it with a psychocultural analysis of anxiety derived from Tocqueville. The terror wrought from ethnic warfare and conflicts over identity, Samuel Huntington argued, was a response to the disruptions of modernity. As westernizing elites attempted to export the rule of law, toleration, free markets, and secularism to underdeveloped parts of the world, men and women there were uprooted from traditional ways of life. Stripped of nurturing institutions like the patriarchal family or village, shorn of the beliefs that organized their universe, the victims of this imposed modernity reacted with the same anxiety described by Tocqueville in *Democracy in America*. They grew nervous about their place in the universe, felt confused and uncertain about who they were. As globalization assaulted traditional identities, making men and women more alike, they grew even more anxious. Homogeneity meant their own destruction, the loss of their specific identity; assimilation spelled existential death. In response to the anxieties of anomie and assimilation, men and women cleaved to their traditions and beliefs, particularly religion, and feared whatever they perceived to be the "other"—the West, an opposing ethnicity, a different religion. Opting for repressive modes of identity like Serbian nationalism and Islamic fundamentalism, the uprooted of modernity inflicted savage cruelty and terror upon these others, hoping to ward off whatever threatened their identity.[60]

Though many liberals of terror rejected Huntington's claim of a "clash of civilizations," they were more indebted to his account than they realized. Ignatieff, for example, opened his account of the ethnic conflicts of the 1990s, particularly the Balkan wars, on a note of ostensible opposition to Huntington. "Theorists like Samuel Huntington," Ignatieff wrote, "would lead me to believe that there is a fault line running through the back gardens of Mirkovci [a village in eastern Crotia], with the Croats in the bunker representing the civilization of the Catholic Roman West and the Serbs nearby representing Byzantium, Orthodoxy, and the Cyrillic East." But, Ignatieff went on, "here in Mirkovci, I don't see civilizational fault lines, geological templates that have split apart. These metaphors take for granted what needs to be explained: how neighbors once ignorant of the very idea that they belong to opposed civilizations begin to think—and hate—in these terms, how they vilify and demonize people they once called friends; how, in short, the seeds of mutual paranoia are sown, grain by grain, on the soil of common life."[61] Claiming that identities did not grow out of ancient hatreds but were recent creations, Ignatieff argued that the collapse of the Yugoslavian state made individuals uncertain about their prospects of survival. They turned for protection to political entrepreneurs like Slobodan Milosevic, who saw ethnic identity and hatred as a lever for exercising power and diverting attention from the growing economic crisis in the Balkans. Ignatieff also acknowledged that power and privilege in the Balkans had long been distributed along ethnic lines, which helped explain the mutual distrust and dislike among the peoples of the former Yugoslavia. "Communities of fear," wrote Ignatieff, "are created out of communities of interest," and ethnic fear was the result.[62]

But beneath or beside Ignatieff's political account of ethnic revanchism stood a far less political account, closely paralleling Huntington's—and Shklar's—approach. An early clue to Ignatieff's assumptions came in his invocation of the biblical story of Cain and Abel. Though Cain was a farmer and Abel a sheepherder, these brothers were essentially the same—that is, until God, for no apparent reason, chose Abel as the object of his blessing. Enraged at this arbitrary elevation, Cain killed Abel. For Ignatieff—and Gourevitch—the story of Cain and Abel suggested the sheer meaninglessness of conflict between peoples whose differences were so small.[63] Ignatieff's and Gourevitch's invocation of Cain and Abel was emblematic of their depoliticized, antihistorical approach to ethnic terror. After all, they could have chosen other stories of fratricidal conflict from Genesis, in which the source of hatred between brothers is neither arbitrary nor otherworldly. In the case of Jacob and Esau, for instance, or of Joseph and his eleven brothers, it is a father's—rather than God's—decision to favor one son over another that impels the hatred of the second for the first, and the decision of the second to eliminate the first. In these stories, hatred and conflict arise from what the Declaration of Independence called "a long train of abuses," and seem neither so mysterious nor theologically hallowed as they do in the Cain and Abel parable. In the case of Jacob and Esau or Joseph and his brothers, it was neither the sameness nor difference of the brothers that awakened hatred, but the inequality between them. Inspired by these stories, Ignatieff and Gourevitch might have adopted a more historically sensitive analysis of the Rwandan or Balkan conflicts, identifying the sources of violence and terror in the accumulation of inequities over time, and in the desire for vengeance such accumulations generate. But Ignatieff and Gourevitch were not interested in history and politics. Gourevitch conducted a brisk fifteen-page tour—in a 350-page book—through a hundred years of European colonialism, leading him to conclude that the Rwandan genocide was fueled by an "idea" that "may be criminal and objectively very stupid." Ignatieff was even less impressed by history and politics, dispensing with them in less than ten pages.[64]

Having established the mythic resonance and political emptiness of genocidal warfare, Ignatieff resorted, like Huntington, to an equal mix of psychology and speculation about the perils of modernity to explain the Balkan wars. Invoking Freud's theory of the "narcissism of minor differences," Ignatieff asked why small differences between peoples are so often "accompanied by such large amounts of anxiety?" "Why is it that minor difference should be strange *and therefore* threatening?" Ignatieff never answered his own question, perhaps because he assumed the question answered itself. Instead, he merely asserted, as if it were a truism, that the convergence of identities aroused anxiety, forcing the threatened individual to distinguish himself, with great ferocity, from whatever or whomever he imagined as the other. As if "narcissistic anxiety" were a natural response to this cultural convergence, as if ethnic cleansing were a natural response to narcissistic anxiety. Despite his qualification that he was invoking narcissistic anxiety not as an "explanatory theory" but "only as a phrase, with a certain heuristic usefulness," Ignatieff did use the theory of narcissistic anxiety as an explanatory account. Like Huntington, he argued that as "globalism . . . brings us closer together, makes us all neighbors, destroys the old boundaries of identity marked out by national or regional consumption styles, we react by clinging to the margins of difference that remain." It was the "uprootings of modernity," he claimed, that aroused anxiety. Modernity unleashed an underlying psychic mechanism, which prompted the turn to ethnic violence. It was the psychological threat modernity posed to the self—the psychic insecurity, the dissolving of boundaries, the loss of self—that truly made it such a source of mischief.[65]

By painting terror as an eruption from the psyche and culture, Huntington and Ignatieff, and writers like Robert Kaplan, fulfilled the imperative that made terror such an ideal political foundation in the first place. Terror, in their hands, remained an intrusion into politics. It did not emerge from the requirements of politics or from the conflicts politics so often generate: it stood outside of politics. In the words of Kaplan, in premodern Europe "there was no 'politics' as we have come to understand the term, just as there is less and less 'politics' today in Liberia, Sierra Leone, Somalia, Sri Lanka, the Balkans, and the Caucasus, among other places."[66] These writers were also quick to point out that the western military interventions designed to end ethnic cleansing might also have a domestic benefit: restoring the flagging spirits of the West. According to Ignatieff: "When policy [in the Balkans or other troubled spots of the world] was driven by moral motives, it was often driven by narcissism. We intervened not only to save others, but to save ourselves, or rather an image of ourselves as defenders of universal decencies. We wanted to show that the West 'meant' something. This imaginary West, this narcissistic image of ourselves, we believed was incarnated in the myth of a multiethnic, multiconfessional Bosnia."[67] For Ignatieff, this moral exhilaration and domestic renewal were closely linked to the revival of a liberal activism discredited since the 1960s. The military incursions in Bosnia, he noted, were "a theater of displacement, in which political energies that might otherwise have been expended in defending multiethnic society at home were directed instead at defending mythic multiculturalism far away. Bosnia became the latest *bel espoir* of a generation that had tried ecology, socialism, and civil rights only to watch all these lose their romantic momentum."[68] Resigned to a complete rollback of domestic liberalism, liberal activists hoped to do elsewhere what they could not do at home.

This would not be the first time that liberals looked to benighted regimes abroad to compensate for the stalled pace of domestic advance. Back in 1792, the French Girondins, the liberals of their day, sensed that their revolution was in peril. Looking to long-suffering peoples to the east, they decided to export progress—and promptly declared war on Austria. And it was Robespierre, so often denounced as a utopian scourge, who issued this prescient warning to his distracted comrades: "No one loves armed missionaries."[69] Likewise, in 1941, with a resurgent Republican Party and impending war turning American liberalism into an imperiled project, New Dealer Rexford Tugwell concluded that it was no longer possible to conduct his experiments in social democracy on the mainland. So he packed his bags and set off for Puerto Rico, hoping to perform on that island colony that which he could not achieve at home.[70]

Where Ignatieff and his liberal colleagues imagined the battle against ethnic cleansing as an occasion of progressive renewal, Kaplan and his counterparts saw it as an opportunity for conservative renewal. A new generation of imperial warriors, they believed, might deliver the West from its cultural mediocrity and easy living. More pagan than bourgeois, more intuitive than rational, these warriors would be no Colin Powells—no strict professionals, equally comfortable in the bureaucracy of the Pentagon and the corridors of the United Nations. They would recall instead "something old and traditional." American Special Forces in the Third World, Kaplan argued, were "recreating colonial expeditionary forces with men who are chameleons, modeled after the spy, linguist, and master of disguise Sir Richard Francis Burton. 'Ambiguity,' 'subjective' and 'intuitive' thinking, and decisions made when only 20 percent of the evidence is in are encouraged: by the time more information is available, it will be too late to act."[71] These romantic impresarios of war would find their diplomatic counterparts in men like Henry Kissinger and Richard Nixon, who practiced statecraft the old-fashioned way. Kissinger, Kaplan wrote, treated foreign policy as if it were "lovemaking"—inventive and creative, "intensely human," sensitive to the peculiar genius of each individual and the particularity of each situation, rather than drably rule-bound.[72] Illegally bombing Cambodia, continuing the Vietnam War long after it was necessary, Kissinger and Nixon displayed an aristocratic contempt for the mass, demonstrating that it was still possible in a disenchanted universe to show true character. "Now, isn't that exactly how we want—or at least how we say we want—our leaders to act? Isn't what angers so many people about President Bill Clinton and other current politicians the fact that they make policy according to the result of public-opinion polls rather than to their own conviction?"[73] In a decade that had seen "an increasingly sallow form of mediocrity," Kaplan concluded, we should savor the "unflinching firmness" of a Kissinger or Nixon, their willingness to "go to cruel extremes."[74]

What the new wars of ethnic purity—and the corresponding duty of imperial involvement—promised for the Left as well as the Right was nothing less than a regeneration of the West. For liberals, terror offered a posture of militant, crusading purpose, an opportunity to impose the Enlightenment abroad precisely because it could not be defended at home. For conservatives, it was a chance to restore martial valor and aristocratic heroism jeopardized by the free market and the end of the Cold War. Whatever the source of their new fervor, Left and Right were now united in a worldwide revolutionary project to bring America to the rest of the world. This was not the first time that western intellectuals had looked to terror abroad for answers to their own domestic despair. It would not be the last.

## A War on Terror?

Immediately following the terrorist attacks of 9/11, commentators insisted that everyone abandon inherited categories of political interpretation. Whatever one's views of domestic and international politics, the argument went, 9/11 represented something new in the world. It was a historical marker, not simply of life as it had been lived before and would be lived after, but of how we used to think and now would have to think. As Christopher Hitchens put it, "The American polity is now divided between those who can recognize a new situation when they see it, and those who cannot or will not."[75] But what was so remarkable about the response to 9/11, especially among American intellectuals and journalists, was how just little it departed from the political script we have been tracing throughout this chapter, indeed throughout this book. Long before 9/11, exponents of the liberalism of anxiety and liberalism of terror had set out the interpretive framework that would dominate the post-9/11 era. In fact, prior to 9/11, some of most far-reaching theorists of these persuasions had imagined a foreign policy disaster that would deliver the United States from the moral lethargy and creeping despair that al-legedly set in after the 1960s, the Cold War, and the triumph of the free market. In 2000, for instance, Robert Putnam wrote, "Creating (or recreating) social capital"—restoring to the American community its frayed bonds of membership—"is no simple task. It would be eased by a palpable national crisis, like war or depression or natural disaster." "But for better *and* for worse," he concluded, "America at the dawn of the new century faces no such galvanizing crisis."[76]

Within a year, America did face such a crisis, and for many pundits, it seemed to come as a welcome relief. Though many commentators accused the radical Left of hailing the attacks of 9/11 as a case of the "chickens come home to roost,"[77] the main quarter from which such elation could be heard was the mainstream media. Almost as soon as the hijackers brought down the World Trade Center and gouged a hole in the Pentagon, journalists and writers seized upon the day's events as a comment on the cultural miasma and decadent materialism of the United States. David Brooks noted that even the most casual observers of the pre-9/11 domestic scene, including Al Qaeda, "could have concluded that America was not an entirely serious country." The United States had just emerged from a decade in which we "renovated our kitchens, refurbished our home entertainment systems, in-vested in patio furniture, Jacuzzis and gas grills." Maureen Dowd wrote that 9/11 exposed the "narcissistic us-me culture" of the nineties, when baby boomers hoped "to overcome flab with diet and exercise, wrinkles with collagen and Botox, sagging skin with surgery, impotence with Via-gra, mood swings with anti-depressants, myopia with laser surgery, decay with human growth hormone, disease with stem cell research and bioengi-neering." Francis Fukuyama complained that the decade's "peace and prosperity encourage[d] preoccupation with one's own petty affairs" and "self-indulgent behaviour." Making the connection between America's limp character and the terrorist attack explicit, Brooks concluded, "You can imagine how it [the United States] must have looked to the Islamic extremists leading the hard life in Afghan terrorist camps." Such speculations were not peculiar to media commentators. Even Bush administration officials like Lewis Libby—and later Bush himself, as well as Republican leader Tom DeLay—claimed that an ethos of lethargy, embodied in Bill Clinton's foreign policy, had made "it easier for someone like Osama bin Laden to rise up and say credibly, 'The Americans don't have the stomach to defend themselves. They won't take casualties to defend their interests. They are morally weak.'"[78]

By inflicting deadly violence and rousing intense fear, the 9/11 terrorists, according to these commentators, promised to deliver the United States from its tedium and selfishness, its individualism and despair. For Brooks, "the fear that is so prevalent in the country" was "a cleanser, washing away a lot of the self-indulgence of the past decade." Revivifying fear, Brooks argued, would now supersede crippling anxiety, replacing a disabling emotion with a bracing passion. "We have traded the anxieties of affluence for the real fears of war," he wrote.[79] "Now upscalers who once spent hours agonizing over which Moen faucet head would go with their copper farmhouse-kitchen sink are suddenly worried about whether the water coming out of pipes has been poisoned. People who longed for Prada bags at Bloomingdale's are suddenly spooked by unattended bags at the airport. America, the sweet land of liberty, is getting a crash course in fear."[80]

Writers repeatedly welcomed the galvanizing moral electricity now coursing through the body politic: an electricity of public resolve and civic commitment, fueling a more considered gravitas; a restoration of trust in government (perhaps, according to some progressives, a revamped welfare state); a culture of patriotism and connection; a new bipartisan consensus; the end of irony and the culture wars; and a more elevated presidency.[81] According to a reporter at USA Today, President Bush was especially keen on the promise of 9/11, offering himself and his generation as exhibit A in the project of domestic cultural renewal. "Bush has told advisors that he believes confronting the enemy is a chance for him and his fellow baby boomers to refocus their lives and prove they have the same kind of valor and commitment their fathers showed in WWII."[82] With its shocking spectacle of death and consequent fear, 9/11 offered a dead or dying culture the chance to live again. After that day in September, Andrew Sullivan noted in the New York Times Magazine, America was "more mobilized, more conscious and therefore more alive." In the same pages, George

Packer remarked upon "the alertness, grief, resolve, even love" awakened by 9/11. He quoted a survivor of the attack on the World Trade Center, who said, "I like this state. I've never been more cognizant in my life," to which Packer added, "I've lived through this state" too, "and I like it." In fact, Packer noted, "what I dread now is a return to the normality we're all supposed to seek."[83] On the first anniversary of the attacks, as the families and friends of victims mourned their loss, Hitchens reaffirmed the thrill he experienced on 9/11 and in the year of liberating war that followed:

> On that day I shared the general register of feeling, from disgust to rage, but was also aware of something that would not quite disclose itself. It only became fully evident quite late that evening. And to my surprise (and pleasure), it was exhilaration. I am not particularly a war lover, and on the occasions when I have seen warfare as a traveling writer, I have tended to shudder. But here was a direct, unmistakable confrontation between everything I loved and everything I hated. On one side, the ethics of the multicultural, the secular, the skeptical, and the cosmopolitan. (Those are the ones I love, by the way.) On the other, the arid monochrome of dull and vicious theocratic fascism. I am prepared for this war to go on for a very long time. I will never become tired of waging it, because it is a fight over essentials. And because it is so very *interesting*.[84]

In analyzing what drove the nineteen hijackers, writers portrayed the angry young men of radical Islam as the anxious residue of an advancing modernity. Cobbling together an account similar to that of Huntington and Ignatieff—and of Tocqueville and Arendt—intellectuals insisted that politics had nothing to do with the events of 9/11. The men who seized the planes, their leaders and wealthy patrons, and the recruits who threatened to join them were not interested in politics in any sense of the word. They were motivated by the torment of their inner psyches, brought about by the cultural shock of modernity. "Their grievance," explained Thomas Friedman, "is rooted in psychology, not politics," and they "blame America for the failure of their societies to master modernity."[85] The Islamicists did not hate the United States because of its policies: a history of interventions in Muslim countries like Iran, Saudi Arabia, and Indonesia; unstinting support for Israel; or sponsorship of repressive regimes throughout the Middle East. They hated the United States for what it was. And what the United States was, according to these writers, was the emblem of modernity: liberal, tolerant, democratic, secular. In the words of one reporter, the terrorists acted "solely out of . . . hatred for the values cherished in the West as freedom, tolerance, prosperity, religious pluralism and universal suffrage, but abhorred by religious fundamentalists (and not only Muslim fundamentalists) as licentiousness, corruption, greed and apostasy." Given this existential hatred, it made no sense to talk of changing American policies in the Middle East or the Muslim world. As Friedman noted, "Their terrorism is not aimed at reversing any specific U.S. policy," and, added another reporter, "changes in Western policy, though not to be ruled out completely, would not necessarily resolve the disputes" between the Islamicists and the West.[86]

Why were the terrorists and Islamicists so hateful toward modernity? Because it made them anxious. What made them anxious? The loss of premodernity, the ruined solidarity of dead or dying traditions, the unscripted free-for-all of individualism. The Islamicists were not threatened directly by the United States, but the United States was a convenient scapegoat for their own anxieties. "Trapped between the traditional world in which they born," wrote one editorialist, "and the confusing world of modernity in which they inescapably live, they seek a single cause for their confusion, their resentments, their frustrated ambitions and their problems of cultural identity." One reporter noted, "Freedom itself can be considered deeply disturbing, even threatening, in many of the world's poorer societies that are anchored to the old pillars of faith, tradition and submission." And "this anxiety," he concluded, "has found a ready focus in American rock music." This anxiety was most evident, argued Fouad Ajami, in Mohamed Atta, the Egyptian-born ringleader of the 9/11 attacks. "The modern world unsettled Atta," Ajami claimed. Growing up in "a drab, austere society that had suddenly been plunged into a more competitive, glamorized world in the 1970s and 1980s," Atta had been "placed perilously close to modernity." From this collision between the modern and the traditional "there emerged an anxious, belligerent piety." The absolute truths of Islamic fundamentalism were a source of comfort, a way of creating meaning in a meaningless world. Like Arendt's totalitarian, Atta "needed the faith" of radical Islam "as consolation."[87]

These twin doctrines—that fear could be a source of domestic renewal and that terrorism was inspired by an anxiety over modernity—complemented each other well. America needed an antidote to its own cultural despair, which the fear of terrorism supplied. But for that fear not to cripple, it required an answering war. By insisting that Islamic fundamentalism was the existential anxiety of modernity, writers ensured that, intellectually speaking, no political or diplomatic response would be envisioned to it. According to them, modernity was an irreversible process, and anxiety its inevitable result. The best way to subdue modernity's discontent, especially its murderous veins, was to kill it. A permanent war against terror would thus convert domestic anxiety into bracing fear; remake liberalism, which had seen such hard times since the 1960s, as a fighting faith; restore to a fraying society its sense of collective and individual purpose; unite conservatives and liberals behind a worldwide crusade for the Enlightenment. From one end of the political spectrum, the former Trotskyist but still radical Hitchens called out in defense of the war on terrorism: "Americanization is the most revolutionary force in the world. There's almost no country where adopting the Americans wouldn't be the most radical thing they could do."[88] And from the other end of the spectrum came the answering reply:

> The political agenda of American conservatives is no less revolutionary. From the beginning, Americans regarded their values and institutions as embodying universal aspirations that would one day have a significance far beyond the shores of the United States. The Great Seal on the back of the dollar bill bears the inscription *novus ordo seclorum*—"new order of the ages"—that expresses a very unconservative sentiment with potentially revolutionary consequences. In this view, democracy, constitutional government and the individual rights on which they rest are good not just for North Americans by virtue of their peculiar habits and traditions, but for all people around the world. Hence the United States in its foreign policy has been anything but a status quo power.[89]

"The radicalism of the American revolution," Francis Fukuyama would conclude, "is still present, expressed today in U.S. promotion of a global economy and in a muscular foreign policy that seeks to shape the world in an American image."[90] With the Soviet Union no longer around, with anxiety and terror revived as the foundation of politics, intellectuals who once shuddered at the violent utopianism of the Bolshevik Revolution were now prepared to take up, and prosecute with arms more lethal, what Thomas Paine once called the "cause of all mankind."[91]

# PART 2

# FEAR, AMERICAN STYLE

We've seen how modern theorists and writers separate fear from elites, ideology, laws, and institutions, and thereby obscure its political origins and uses. We've seen how they overlook the ways in which fear enables one group to rule another, how it stops the ruled from pursuing, through political action, the happiness so often denied them. One of the reasons for this evasion, I've argued, is that fear often serves as a ground for intellectuals in need of grounding arguments. At moments of doubt about the ability of positive principles to animate moral perception or inspire public action, fear has seemed an ideal source of political insight and energy. But there may be a second reason, peculiar to the United States. Advocates and defenders of free societies often define themselves in opposition to the repressive rule that fear entails. Whatever else a liberal society is, it is not one where citizens consistently fear their superiors, where they must calibrate their speech and action to avoid the displeasure of their betters. Nor is it one where power is so distributed—or the means of coercion so available—as to systematically arouse this kind of fear. Thanks to its Constitution and social pluralism, many intellectuals argue, the United States is free of such fear. There may be elite influence and manipulation here, what some scholars call "hegemony" and others "the third face of power." There may be passivity among the many, activity for the few. But there is little of the overt intimidation that characterized Europe's old regimes and still keeps so many in thrall throughout the world. Even our most searing critics have ascribed to contemporary America what C. Wright Mills mistakenly claimed for its nineteenth-century predecessor: "The relation of one man to another was a relation not of command and obedience but of man-to-man bargaining. Any one man's decisions, with reference to every other man, were decisions of freedom and of equality." According to Christopher Lasch, the United States long ago traded "the old paternalism of kings, priests, authoritarian fathers, slavemasters, and landed overlords" for "a new ruling class of administrators, bureaucrats, technicians, and experts" possessing "few of the attributes formerly associated with a ruling class—pride of place, the 'habit of command,' disdain for the lower orders." This new class still rules, but not through "ties of personal dependence." Instead, it relies upon "new modes of social control, which deal with the deviant as a patient and substitute medical rehabilitation for punishment."[1]

In what follows, I argue that politically repressive fear is far more present in the United States than we like to believe. This may be a fear of threats to the physical security or moral well-being of the population, against which elites position themselves as protectors, or it may be the fear among the powerful of the less powerful, and vice versa. These two kinds of fear—the first uniting the nation, the second dividing it—reinforce each other, with elites reaping the benefit of their combined force. The collective fear of danger distracts from the fear between elites and the lower orders, or it gives the latter added reason to fear the former. "The end of Obedience is Protection," Hobbes wrote, referring to the protection states provide against external attack and domestic anarchy.[2] But since the power by which elites protect us is linked to the power they brandish over us, our need for the first often bolsters our fear of the second. Whether political fear is of the first or second sort, or some combination thereof, it supports and perpetuates elite rule, inducing inferiors to submit to superiors, not to protest or challenge their power but to accommodate it. Fear ensures that those with power maintain it, and prevents those without power from doing much, if anything, to get it.

To get a handle on political fear in the United States, we must recognize that it is not a thoughtless passion but a rational, moral emotion. As I argue in chapter six, political fear reflects the interests and reasoned judgments of the fearful about what is good for them, and responds to real dangers in the world: to genuine threats to the nation's security and well-being, to the coercive power wielded by elites and the lurking challenge the lower orders pose to those elites. So does political fear reflect people's ethics and principles, which focus them on certain dangers over others and influence their response to those dangers. Political fear entails more than a simple, top-down politics, in which a cohesive cabal threatens punitive sanctions or conjures fantastic enemies in order to preserve their rule. It is an affair of collusion, involving the grunt work of collaborators, the cooperation of victims, and aid from those bystanders who do nothing to protest fear's repressive hold. In chapter seven, I show how these coalitions of fear work through the very contrivances that are supposed to check fear: the fragmented state—limited by the separation of powers, federalism, and the rule of law—and a pluralistic civil society, which provides the wielders of fear coercive instruments often not available to government officials. Many of my examples in chapters six and seven are drawn from the McCarthy period, not because I believe McCarthyism is still rampant but because its mechanisms are still in place. By focusing on its minutiae, I hope to show that political fear is neither strange nor aberrant but familiar and embedded, that it is a problem not solely of the past but also of the present. Chapter eight turns us to the contemporary American workplace, for it is there, in the coercive relationship between employer and employee, that we see today the most visible and pervasive evidence of fear in the United States—and the persistence of those mechanisms that have caused us such trouble in the past.

I call these elements—the rational and moral nature of fear; the collusion between elites, collaborators, bystanders, and victims; the fragmented state and a pluralist civil society; and fear in the workplace—"Fear, American Style." Each element is a symptom of the American experience: of our decentralized political culture; of the constitutional limitations placed upon the American state; of the diversity and revanchism of our elites; and of a fluid social structure, offering plentiful opportunities for people to cooperate in the complex pluralism that is Fear, American Style. While I label this combination "American," its individual elements are present elsewhere, in even the nastiest regimes. It may seem counterintuitive to suggest that fragmented states, pluralist societies, rationality, or morality compose any part of the Nazi or Stalinist experience, or of the myriad tyrannies that still dot the globe. Yet they do. The particular amalgam that is Fear, American Style may be our unique contribution to the earth's share of unhappiness, but its components are by no means peculiar to the United States.

A note of caution: readers looking in these chapters for atrocities in the United States on the order of Nazi Germany or Stalinist Russia will not find them. Though I discuss violence against African Americans, who have borne the most systematic fear of any group in the United States, and though I cite examples of political violence from societies more repressive than our own, I focus more on small coercion and petty tyranny, for my interest is in fear that stifles political options, fear that has what constitutional lawyers and scholars call a "chilling effect." And what we find in the United States is that it only takes a little bit of coercion to produce a great deal of fear. This is one of the paradoxes of American life, puzzling everyone from Tocqueville to Richard Hofstadter and Louis Hartz: how a country with so many freedoms can generate such widespread political inhibitions. But where these other analysts have looked to the cultural anxiety of an insecure democracy—on the assumption that the absence of operatic violence equals a dearth of political repression—I mole about in the quotidian coercions of everyday life. Such acts do not qualify as gross violations of human rights, but grand savagery is not, I would argue, the only reason to worry about political fear. It is fear's repressive consequences, not just the personal suffering it inflicts, that make it a toxic fact of life that must be opposed.

If we are to oppose Fear, American Style, we must reconsider two basic suppositions. First, we must confront the collusion between American liberalism and fear. American liberalism is a double-edged sword—on the one hand, promising and sometimes delivering a society of free and equal men and women, on the other hand, defending a set of arrangements, like the fragmented state and social pluralism, that routinely betray that promise. At its best, liberalism has liberated slaves from bondage and second-class citizens from Jim Crow, given women the vote and workers the right to unionize, and generally made the United States a more humane society. But with its suspicion of strong, centralized states, wariness of social movements, and commitment to moderation, it has also lent support to the forces of fear. As Martin Luther King noted in 1963: "I have almost reached the regrettable conclusion that the Negro's great stumbling block in the stride toward freedom is not the White Citizen's Counciler or the Ku Klux Klanner, but the white moderate who is more devoted to 'order' than to justice; who prefers a negative peace which is the absence of tension to a positive peace which is the presence of justice; who constantly says, 'I agree with you in the goal you seek, but I can't agree with your methods of direct action.'"[3] Reckoning with Fear, American Style demands a more honest accounting of liberalism's contradictory inheritance and a greater skepticism toward some of its dearest faiths. I say this neither to discredit liberalism nor to recommend that we discard it. The protections it affords are real and not to be dismissed. If I have less to say here about those protections, it is only because that ground has already been well covered, and I see no good reason to write "a book from which one learns what other books contain."[4] A meditation on this doubleness of American life, in which liberalism and fear are so closely tethered, need not be taken as a sign of illiberalism or anti-Americanism. It is instead, it seems to me, the merest prerequisite of maturity, of the wisdom that should come to a nation after several centuries of constitutional rule. Particularly now, as the United States prepares yet another campaign to deliver the world from fear, it is worth seeing how the institutions we hail abroad have fared at home.

Second, we must abandon the notion that fear can be a foundation of political life. Not only does such a notion propel us to overlook the nitty-gritty politics of fear, but it also fails to deliver on the promise of liberating us from fear. Men and women are seldom inspired to confront fear merely because they believe it to be evil; without some answering vision of positive justice, some ideologically grounded hope for radical change, they have a difficult time identifying fear as an evil to be opposed, and so put up with it. When Abraham Lincoln committed the nation to eliminating slavery, he did not speak of negative foundations or a *summum malum*. Instead, he promised that "all the wealth piled by the bond-man's two hundred and fifty years of unrequited toil shall be sunk," that "every drop of blood drawn with the lash, shall be paid by another drawn with the sword, as was said three thousand years ago, so still it must be said 'the judgments of the Lord, are true and righteous altogether.'"[5] Though Lincoln hallowed the shedding of blood with a religious language many no longer share, we possess today more secular, and less violent, vocabularies of freedom and equality—like those offered by John Rawls, Ronald Dworkin, and Jürgen Habermas—that serve the same function as Lincoln's. These visions of positive justice not only enjoin us to envision and strive for a life with less fear, but also help to identify that which we fear in the first place. As Michael Walzer has rightly noted, "The liberalism of fear depends upon what we might call the liberalism of hope," for "what we are afraid of is that the things we have come to value, our accomplishments until now, and our plans for the future will be destroyed."[6] Justice, in other words, and not fear, must come first.

# 6    Sentimental Educations

(*HOW COULD MERE TOIL ALIGN THY CHOIRING STRINGS!*)

—HART CRANE

## A Rational, Moral Emotion

Roy Huggins—screenwriter, producer, director—may not have been the most talented man in Hollywood, but over the course of a midcentury career he managed to compile a resume of some achievement. In 1958, he won an Emmy Award for *Maverick*; later he produced *The Fugitive* and *The Rockford Files*. But it was not for these accomplishments that Huggins would be remembered. He would go down in history—if he made it that far—for his 1952 appearance before the House Committee on Un-American Activities (HUAC). As a young screenwriter in the 1930s, Huggins joined the Communist Party, at the time one of the few forces in American life organizing against European fascism. In 1939, after Stalin signed his nonaggression pact with Hitler and the party reversed its stance, Huggins quit the party. Eight years later, when HUAC launched its investigation of communism in Hollywood, the studios announced that they would no longer employ party members—and, as it came to pass, anyone refusing to cooperate with HUAC. With this and other sanctions in mind, Huggins named names. Nineteen to be exact, though some he refused to spell for the committee. He deemed it more principled, one observer notes, "to give the names but not the letters."[1]

Why did Huggins cooperate with HUAC? Because he detested the Soviet Union, he says, and the United States was at war in Korea. The Communist Party was allied with America's enemies, in some cases committing espionage on their behalf, and it was run by hypocrites, praising Stalin and the

Bill of Rights. But Huggins had other concerns as well. He had a family, and though he may have daydreamed about the political theater of going to jail rather than betraying former comrades—witnesses refusing to name names could be cited for contempt of Congress and imprisoned—he wondered, "Who the hell is going to take care of two small children, a mother, and a wife, all of whom are totally dependent upon me?" Congress had also passed legislation, dubbed the "concentration camp bill" by an aide to President Truman, that gave the attorney general emergency powers to round up and detain suspected subversives.[2] "Do I really want to go to a concentration camp for who knows how many years?" he asked himself. "The terror was undoubtedly upon me," he says, his decision to cooperate "a failure of nerve." As soon as he testified, he regretted it, and he continued to do so throughout his life. He may not have liked Stalinism, but he was hardly sanguine about McCarthyism.[3] Nor did he like being an informer. "Jesus Christ," he said to himself, "you had your moment of truth—it came, and you should have said, Stick it up your ass, and you didn't."[4]

As Huggins tells it, he cooperated with HUAC because he was afraid, and he was afraid because he faced real threats. His fear was thus rational in the sense of being reasonable. What it was not, he insists, was moral. In itself, his fear was amoral, an involuntary reaction—"the terror was undoubtedly upon me"—to overweening power. Its consequences, however, were decidedly immoral, for fear, according to Huggins, inspired him to betray his beliefs. He may have been a victim or a coward, a casualty of repression or a man without qualities, but it was fear that led, or forced, him to forsake his principles.

Much in Huggins's experience—and the historical record—bears out his claim about the rationality of his fear. But can his fear be so neatly separated from his moral beliefs? After all, testifying before HUAC did not betray Huggins's opposition to communism. Nor did it undermine his commitment to the United States and its defense. If anything, these beliefs may have contributed to his fear of HUAC. Huggins had a fear of violating his duty to the state: either a heartfelt fear of doing wrong, born of the desire to do right,[5] or a fear of the inner torment or external disgrace he would experience were he to do wrong. Huggins also believed that challenging HUAC would call into question the legitimacy of American institutions, a luxury he thought the United States could ill afford during the Cold War.[6] Huggins feared the power of the state but also feared the loss of that power, a fear aroused by his commitment to American democracy and opposition to communism. Because Huggins's fear of weakening the state contributed to his fear of challenging it, we can say that far from being opposed to his beliefs, his fear of the state arose in part from them.[7]

Since September 11, we have seen a similar fusion of fears, in which the rational and the moral reinforce each other. Between September and December 2001, according to a study sponsored by the Pew Charitable Trust, 74 percent of television coverage about 9/11 and America's response was "all pro-U.S." or "mostly pro-U.S.," while 7 percent was "mostly dissenting" or "all dissenting."[8] Network executives have admitted to tailoring their coverage in order to avoid the appearance of criticizing U.S. foreign policy—not because they face state-sponsored coercion but because they fear a conservative-led backlash, which might result in lower ratings. According to Erick Sorenson, president of MSNBC, "Any misstep and you get into trouble with these guys and have the Patriotism Police hunt you down."[9] But more than cold calculus inspires these fears of conservative criticism: such fears are accompanied, reinforced, or aroused by a heartfelt belief in the legitimacy of those criticisms and in the need to support U.S. foreign policy. After issuing instructions to pair any scene of civilian destruction in Afghanistan for which the U.S. military was responsible with reminders of the devastation of 9/11 and of the relationship between the Taliban and Al Qaeda, CNN chair Walter Isaacson testified to the mix of rational and moral considerations underlying his network's coverage. "If you get on the wrong side of public opinion," he admitted, "you are going to get into trouble." At the same time, he said, it "seems perverse to focus on the casualties or hardship in Afghanistan." It was the Taliban, after all, that was "responsible for the situation Afghanistan is now in."[10] After ABC News president David Westin declared that he had no opinion about whether the Pentagon should be considered a legitimate target for enemy attack, he was roundly condemned by Rush Limbaugh and others, and quickly apologized. According to the *New York Times*, "Executives at ABC News said Mr. Westin decided to apologize because he realized that the comment—made in answer to a question—seemed unduly cold and even wrong. But they also acknowledged that they were eager to stop an onslaught of negative public attention."[11]

It is impossible to know in these cases which concern, the rational or the moral, is determinative; in all likelihood, they are equally influential, making fear and capitulation seem the rational and moral response to pressure.[12] As leading journalist Michael Kinsley has admitted, "As a writer and editor, I have been censoring myself and others quite a bit since Sept. 11. By 'censoring' I mean deciding not to write or publish things for reasons other than my own judgments of their merits. What reasons? Sometimes it has been a sincere feeling that an ordinarily appropriate remark is inappropriate at this extraordinary moment. Sometimes it is genuine respect for readers who might feel that way even if I don't. But sometimes it is simple cowardice."[13] In the words of CBS News anchor Dan Rather:

> It is an obscene comparison—you know I am not sure I like it—but you know there was a time in South Africa that people would put flaming tyres around people's necks if they dissented. And in some ways the fear is that you will be necklaced here, you will have a flaming tyre of lack of patriotism put around your neck. . . . Now it is that fear that keeps journalists from asking the toughest of the tough questions.
>
> It starts with a feeling of patriotism within oneself. It carries through with a certain knowledge that the country as a whole—and for all the right reasons—felt and continues to feel this surge of patriotism within themselves. And one finds oneself saying, "I know the right question, but you know what? This is not exactly the right time to ask it."[14]

This melding of fears is not peculiar to liberal democracies: even the most repressive regimes can inspire it. Take Vladimir Stern, one of the founders of Czechoslovakia's secret police. The son of a Communist who died at the hands of the Gestapo, Stern was a life-long idealist, a believer in communism, and after the abortive Prague Spring of 1968, a devotee of its more dissident strains. Until 1954, Stern ran one of the secret police's prestigious academies, educating officers in Marxism-Leninism and the arts of deception, torture, and murder. He knew that what he was teaching his students was a betrayal of the humane socialism that inspired him to join the party and staff its upper echelons. Like Huggins, he kept quiet because he was afraid of what the state might do to him. But his fear of the state was inseparable from his commitment to it. "Maybe I was a coward," he acknowledges. But, he adds, "Maybe I thought that to step out and say what you think would harm the Party. I made excuses for the Party. I stayed in even though there were things I disagreed with. I don't want to defend the murdering and torturing, but basically the system was correct."[15] Like Huggins and the U.S. news media, Stern feared to oppose the very system that made him afraid because he believed in the legitimacy of that system.

Huggins's moral beliefs may be connected to his fear in yet another way. One of his main fears of going to jail, he says, was that his family would suffer. This fear entailed a complex moral judgment—that Huggins had a duty, trumping all others, to his family, that that duty was primarily financial, and that it was he who was responsible for their economic well-being. Huggins did not consider that his wife could have worked. Nor did he believe that he might have a duty to teach his children the virtue of making personal sacrifices for freedom or of not informing on former friends and comrades. By contrast, when director Elia Kazan told his colleague Kermit Bloomgarden that he was thinking of naming names because "I've got to think of my kids," Bloomgarden responded, "This too shall pass, and then you'll be an informer in the eyes of your kids, think of that."[16] Bloomgarden did not discount the obligations to one's family: he merely understood those obligations in more than economic terms. Because Huggins did not, opting for jail seemed to him slovenly, immature, and irresponsible: "When you're thinking of becoming a hero, you feel like a slob. You feel, do you really have a right to do that?"[17] The fear of jail, by contrast, seemed wise, moral, even elevated.

It could be argued, of course, that Huggins's concern for his family was merely a pretext for his own fear of going to jail. Yet men and women with family ties often submit to repressive regimes when those without such ties do not. Stalin, for example, corralled many individuals to cooperate with his tyranny by threatening their families, and had less success among those with no families. In a 1947 letter, the head of Soviet counterintelligence recommended invoking suspects' "family and personal ties" during interrogation sessions. Soviet interrogators would put on their desks, in full view, the personal effects of suspects' relatives as well as a copy of a decree legalizing the execution of children.[18] The fact that other men and women, facing worse penalties, only choose Huggins's path when their loved ones are threatened suggests that a concern for family is not a pretext but a genuine contributing factor to fear.[19]

Perhaps the Soviet experience, though, teaches the opposite lesson: that a fear for one's family is inspired less by morality than by a natural or biological inclination to protect one's own. That would be an overreading of the evidence, however. For starters, it ignores the fact that while men and women submit to repression out of a fear for their families, they also betray their families out of a fear for themselves. David Greenglass famously betrayed his sister, Ethel Rosenberg; Stalin arrested or killed the spouses and siblings of four of his closest associates, only one of whom protested with any zeal.[20] It also overlooks the fact that what we often fear is not just harm to our families, but the shame or guilt our violation of familial duty will bring to them and us. It is precisely this fear of shame that Crito marshals against Socrates, only in his case, it is for the sake of disobedience to the state. After Socrates is convicted by the Athenian jury and prepares to accept his punishment of drinking the hemlock, Crito recommends that he forgo his commitment to abide by the verdict and honor instead his commitment to his family's well-being by taking them into exile. "I think you are betraying your sons by going away and leaving them," says Crito, referring to Socrates' decision to accept death, "when you could bring them up and educate them. You thus show no concern for what their fate may be." Crito concludes—in language Huggins would appreciate, though with a recommendation he would not—that Socrates is not acting morally at all. Socrates, says Crito, merely wishes to play the part of a martyr, reneging on his real obligations, to his family: "You seem to me to choose the easier path, whereas one should choose the path a good and courageous man would choose, particularly when one claims throughout one's life to care for virtue."[21] Of course, the virtuous example of Socrates and vicious example of David Greenglass no more disprove the thesis of there being a natural impulse to preserve one's family than does anorexia disprove the notion of our having a natural impulse to eat. What these cases do suggest is that the fear for one's family is more responsive to politics and ideology than we might think.

Huggins's fear was certainly self-interested, though even here a moral conception, of self and interest, may have been at work. The most immediate threat Huggins faced in refusing to cooperate with HUAC was not jail but the blacklist. What made the blacklist such a potent threat was not merely that it might send a person and her family into poverty, but also that it preyed on her particular sense of what mattered to her in life. Blacklisted men and women could survive by selling vacuum cleaners or waiting tables but often felt that they were not living the life they were meant to live. Rutgers professor Richard Schlatter, for instance, had been a Communist while a graduate student at Harvard during the 1930s. In 1953, he was called before HUAC and cooperated. "It was not just the question of losing my job," he says, "one can always find a way to live. But the only way in which I could do anything I felt worth doing was by being a teacher, a scholar, an academic. The thought that all that might come to a sudden end had a dampening effect." While some on the blacklist could surreptitiously pursue their vocations, writing under pseudonyms, for example, others could not. "I am a man of a thousand faces," actor Zero Mostel declared, "all of them blacklisted." Or as actor Lee J. Cobb put it, "It's the only face I have."[22]

When we think about fear and the action it inspires, we often think of it as Huggins did, as an involuntary acquiescence, amoral or immoral, to overwhelming power.[23] Though we may later regret the fear that forced us to betray our beliefs, we do not doubt that it is a pure reflection of reality, dictating submission. But this view obscures our moral collusion with fear: how we construe our interests, how we legitimize the power that threatens those interests, how we choose to respond to that power. Why, then, do we insist upon viewing fear and its attending actions as an expression of passivity? Perhaps because that view enables us to think of ourselves as blameless, as physical objects obeying the laws of nature. If fear is an unwilled reaction to pure power, if submitting out of fear is the only possible response to that power, we cannot be held morally responsible for our capitulation. "Being told that you are a slave," Joseph Brodsky notes, "is less disheartening news than being told that morally you are a zero."[24] But Huggins's—and our—regret suggests the flaw in this conception. If fear and the actions it conditions were truly a forced surrender to external circumstance, few of us would hold ourselves responsible for those actions. If the reality Huggins confronted were as non-negotiable as he suggests, it would make no sense to accuse himself of moral failure. Fear certainly cannot be separated from this reality; it is instead a fusion of our rational and moral apprehensions about this reality.

By Huggins's own account, his was a lonely choice. He felt obligated to his family but did not turn to them for advice. Most of us, however, make decisions about what to fear and how we respond to fear with the help of trusted intimates and advisers, Hobbes's teachers and preachers. Sometimes we consult immediate figures in our lives, like parents, therapists, lawyers, and priests. Other times, we look to more distant mentors, influential men and women in our imagined communities who advise us, indirectly, by their words and deeds. What they do, how they respond to their fear, sets the tone for the rest of us. If they believe a danger we are confronting is worthy of fear and not to be challenged, we may follow their lead. Miriam Lewin, a leftist imprisoned and tortured during Argentina's Dirty War, remembers well how one influential person's capitulation to fear deflated her and the lower ranks of the Left.

> In 1974 those who were captured didn't break. We thought we were growing; we thought the people were with us. The situation was different; morale was high. Later we began to feel that each person who fell was just one more of thousands who fell. If your chief fell before you and turned you in, and you've lost thirty-five friends, your husband, and your brother, by the time you fall you already have a sense of death and defeat. After a while you start to think, How is it that my chief collaborated and me, I'm just a poor foot soldier, why shouldn't I save my life?[25]

If these figures do not capitulate—one thinks of the eight lonely individuals who stood in Red Square in 1968 to protest the Soviet invasion of Czechoslovakia and as a result, reports one survivor of the gulag, "made millions stop being afraid"[26]—we may be emboldened to resist or overcome that danger, which can have the tonic effect of lessening our fear. Whether near or far-off, advisers do just that: advise. They do not dictate or force, they merely help us think about which dangers we should fear and how to respond to our fear. Fear poses complex moral dilemmas of the sort that Huggins confronted, in which self-interest and moral principle cannot be so easily separated. It is in this space that our teachers and preachers of fear work, throwing their weight behind one interest over another, making one principle seem higher than the other.

Huggins may not have sought or taken such counsel, but screen actor Sterling Hayden, whose credits range from *The Asphalt Jungle* to *Dr. Strangelove* and *The Godfather*, certainly did. A self-styled man of action, Hayden ran off to sea as a young man and was discovered by talent scouts while working on the Brooklyn docks. In 1941, he broke his contract with Paramount to join the Marines and later fought with Tito's partisans against the Nazis. Back in Hollywood in 1946, Hayden joined the Communist Party and then quickly dropped out. In 1951, he was called before HUAC. He named seven names, including Bea Winters, his former lover and party recruiter, a decision he regretted to the end of his life.[27] Sorting out the motives behind Hayden's capitulation presents something of a puzzle. True, he and his wife had entered into divorce proceedings, and Hayden feared that unfavorable publicity might cost him custody of his children. He worried about losing his job, particularly since he had just begun an expensive psychoanalysis, and he feared going to jail.[28] Yet this was the man who a decade earlier had abandoned a promising Hollywood career to help lead a guerilla campaign in Yugoslavia. When a Paramount executive at the time tried to persuade Hayden to reconsider his decision to leave, Hayden responded, "Goddamn it, sir, but I can't act and keep my self-respect. It's the only thing I have and I guess I'd better hang on to it." "What good is the rest, the money and the schooner and the living, if I don't like to look in the mirror when I'm shaving?" he said.[29]

Much had happened in the intervening years to persuade Hayden of the virtues of being afraid and acting in accordance with that fear. Hayden had joined Tito and the Communist Party at the high tide of American liberalism, when radicals teamed up with Democrats to make the astonishing transformation in politics and culture that was the New Deal. During the 1930s and '40s, most of Hollywood leaned left, and Hayden leaned with it. By the late

1940s, Hollywood had righted itself, with industry employers refusing to hire Communists and anyone not cooperating with the government.[30] The effect of the industry's surrender was palpable. It deprived uncooperative witnesses of the one protection—job security—that might have persuaded them to carry through their opposition. It demonstrated the coercive power of the government, and magnified it. If Hollywood's power brokers, with all their resources, could not stand up to Congress and the FBI, how could individual leftists? Though Humphrey Bogart had initially rallied against HUAC, the studios' acquiescence convinced him that he was a "dope." Someone like FDR, said the man who immortalized on screen the refusal to bow down before any authority, could "handle those babies in Washington, but they're too smart for guys like me." The surrender of the studio heads morally deflated the government's opponents, persuading them that there was no honor, only theater, in pressing their resistance. This was the context, these the distant voices Hayden heard, when he decided to testify.[31]

The more immediate influences on Hayden's decision, however, were Martin Gang, his lawyer, and Phil Cohen, his therapist. When Hayden first began to suspect that he was being blacklisted, he turned to Gang for advice. Gang suggested that he draft a letter to J. Edgar Hoover, explaining his past involvement in the party and expressing sincere repentance. Cooperating with the FBI, said Gang, would keep Hayden under HUAC's radar and out of the television lights. Unconvinced, Hayden turned to Cohen, who assured him that Gang's recommendation was reasonable. So advised, Hayden submitted the letter. But on the day he was scheduled to speak with the FBI, he had second thoughts. "Martin," he told his lawyer,

"I still don't feel right about –"
"Sterling, now listen to me. We've been over this thing time and time again. You make entirely too much of it. The time to have felt this way was before we wrote the letter."
"Yes, I guess you're right."
"You know I'm right. You made the mistake. Nobody told you to join the Party. You're not telling the F.B.I. anything they don't already know."

Hayden spoke with the FBI, which only made him feel worse and turned him against his therapist. "I'll say this, too," he told Cohen, "that if it hadn't been for you I wouldn't have turned into a stoolie for J. Edgar Hoover. I don't think you have the foggiest notion of the contempt I have had for myself since the day I did that thing." Not long after, HUAC issued him a subpoena.

Cohen again tried to pacify him. "Now then," said Cohen, "may I remind you there's really not much difference, so far as you yourself are concerned, between talking to the F.B.I. in private and taking the stand in Washington. You have already informed, after all. You have excellent counsel, you know."[32] Again, Hayden capitulated.

In recent years, scholar and writers have extolled the virtues of an independent civil society, in which private circles of intimate association are supposed to shield men and women from a repressive state. To the extent that these links are explicitly political and oppositional, this account of civil society holds true. Few of us have the inner strength or sustaining vision to opt for the lonely path of a Socrates or a Solzhenitsyn. Deprived of the solidarity of comrades, our visions seem idiosyncratic and quixotic; fortified by our political affiliations, they seem moral and viable. But what analysts of civil society often ignore is the experience of Hayden and others like him, how our everyday connections can echo or amplify our inner counsels of fear. "Friends and family worry about me," writes Mino Akhtar, a Pakistani American management consultant in New Jersey who has campaigned against the war in Iraq and the secret detention of Arabs and Muslims after 9/11. "They tell me to be careful, that I'm taking risks. They say that if my face and name keep coming up in public I won't get any more consulting jobs. I think about that sometimes. You work hard to establish yourself, you have the good job, big home, these mortgage payments; it's scary to think you can lose it all."[33] It is precisely the nonpolitical, personal nature of these connections that makes them so powerful a voice for cooperation. Afraid, we think about our lives and livelihoods, loved ones and friends, and we doubt the meaning or efficacy of our politics. When comrades advise us to resist, we discard their counsel as so much political rhetoric; when trusted intimates advise us to submit, we hear the innocent, apolitical voice of natural reason. Because these counsels of submission are not seen as political recommendations, they are ideal packages of covert political transmission.[34]

Though it may be possible to identify the rational and moral elements of Huggins's fear, are not some fears, like those we experience when our lives are threatened, purely rational, and the capitulations they authorize blameless concessions to threatening force? I take it as a given that the desire to preserve one's life and to avoid physical pain is an imperative few of us ignore or override with any ease. Faced with the proverbial demand for our money or our lives, most of us would choose the latter, for in that context, it hardly seems a choice. But our analysis of the fear of death cannot end there.

For in politics, the fear of death and bodily harm is seldom as straightforward, the choices seldom as simple, as that which we experience when a lone gunman threatens our lives. In politics, our fear of death is surrounded by moral obligations, authorizing us to act on that fear in certain situations and not in others. Our legal system, for example, makes distinctions between fears of death that entitle us to kill in self-defense and those that do not, on the assumption, as Hobbes noted, that "not every fear justifies the Action it produceth."[35] Even the concentration camps and the gulag authorized actions born of the fear of death in certain instances and not others.[36] These obligations and restrictions do more than grant or refuse us license to act upon that fear: they also enhance or minimize it.

On the battlefield, for example, soldiers are enjoined by the imperative of courage not to run in the face of enemy fire or to leave their comrades behind. But does courage entail the suppression, management, or elimination of the fear of death? Is courage a severe duty requiring us to continue fighting in the face of our fear, or a cultivated ethos, subduing our fear of death? Aristotle, still our premier theorist of courage, never quite made up his mind on this question. He thought true courage required that we stand fast in the face of known and feared danger. The courageous man "endures and fears," and no man "endures what is terrifying more steadfastly" than he. Courage asked us not to have no fear, but to persist in the face of fear. But Aristotle also defined the courageous man as one who "fearlessly faces" death on the battlefield and in "any situations that bring a sudden death." Because of his ethical training, the courageous man felt no fear in the face of his own death or on the battlefield.[37]

In politics, we know that both versions of courage obtain: where individuals fear death but resist its counsels for the sake of their obligations, and where their obligations and worldviews extinguish their fear of death. Usually, men and women experience some mix of these kinds of courage all at once, suggesting that Aristotle was not so much confused as he was clear. Take Thomas Chatmon, a black activist from Albany, Georgia, who traveled the state to organize opposition against Jim Crow. Driving along a back road one day, Chatmon was stopped by two white men. One of the men, according to Chatmon, "slapped me so hard, boy, I seen stars" and said to him, "You the damn nigger from Albany, came down here and made that speech last week." Deciding not to kill Chatmon after a white woman unexpectedly appeared on the scene, the men let him go with a warning: "Now you be careful, boy, you be careful." By his own admission, Chatmon was scared, but his belief in God enabled him to persist in the face of his fear. "I know

God protected me all those times. I have been protected many times in dangerous spots like that. And the only somebody that could have brought me through was God himself." Likewise, whenever his wife expressed fear that something bad might happen to him, he would tell her, "Don't think like that, think positive because you can't allow this fear to get to you." But Chapmon also went beyond mere endurance, finding the serenity that comes from not being afraid. "That's what Franklin Roosevelt told us years ago," he explains. "'The only thing you had to fear was fear itself.' You got to get rid of that. You can't be afraid."[38]

Whether they achieve a courage of steadfastness or serenity, soldiers of the literal and metaphorical variety contend against the fear of death because they do not wish to live a life in which they have betrayed their comrades or beliefs. Montesquieu, as we have seen, thought that when we accede to our fear of death, we do so as purely physical beings. Hobbes knew better: The reason we fear death and submit to its dictates is that we value the projects and purposes, the friends and families, that make our lives worthwhile. Were we to lose those sustaining connections, we might very well lose our fear of death. This is what happened to Nadezhda Mandelstam in 1934, when she and her husband, the poet Osip Mandelstam, were sent into internal exile by the Soviet authorities.

> Until a short time before, I had been full of concern for all my friends and relatives, for my work, for everything I set store by. Now this concern was gone—and fear, too. . . . Having entered a realm of non-being, I had lost the sense of death. In the face of doom, even fear disappears. Fear is a gleam of hope, the will to live, self-assertion. It is a deeply European feeling, nurtured on a self-respect, the sense of one's own worth, rights, needs and desires. A man clings to what is his, and fears to lose it. Fear and hope are bound up with each other. Losing hope, we lose fear as well—there is nothing to be afraid for.[39]

So important to us are these connections that Hobbes thought they contained an unassailable argument for why we should do everything possible to stay alive. It simply made no sense, he claimed, to risk or embrace death for the sake of an abstract principle, for how could we pursue or enjoy that principle if we were dead? But Hobbes overlooked another possible conclusion to his own insight. Might not some purposes be so important to us that we can't imagine giving them up and still leading a worthy life? Do not some concessions to fear require betrayals of principle so great that, once made, we can no longer claim those principles as our own? Having lost them, do our lives not seem worthless and no longer truly ours? "Is life," Socrates asks Crito, "worth living for us with that part of us corrupted that [our] unjust action harms and just action benefits?" No, replies Crito, as have other men and women the world over.[40]

## Elites and Collaborators, Bystanders and Victims

Thus far, we have taken a worm's eye view of fear. But political fear is more than an individual experience, and it affects more than personal lives. The morals contributing to it descend from tradition and popular belief, and the rational calculus underlying it reflects the realities of social and political power. Whether by design or consequence—for sometimes the outcome is intended, other times not—political fear reinforces a society's distribution of power and resources, influences public debate, and compels public policy. Political fear usually takes one of two forms. First, it governs relationships between the higher and lower orders of society, whose mutual fear of each other helps maintain the inequalities from which it arises. Second, political fear can arise from forces external or internal to a society, where an entire people are threatened by a foreign enemy or dangerous presence like crime, drugs, or moral decay. In actual practice, as we shall see, these two kinds of fear are often fused and reinforce each other.

Creating and sustaining political fear may require immediate applications of direct coercion like those levied against Chatmon, but more often, fear bleeds into the fabric of everyday life, without need of personal interdictions. That is the function of political fear: not to quell one individual, but to make an example of her, to send a message to everyone else that they should be careful, or they might be next.[41] During the 1970s and early 1980s, the Uruguayan military detained one in every fifty citizens, and sent one in every five hundred to jail. Their target was not just the victims themselves, but individuals like this Montevideo psychoanalyst and his wife, who, though never detained or imprisoned, kept politically silent for years: "Our own lives became increasingly constricted. The process of self-censorship was incredibly insidious: it wasn't just that you stopped talking about certain things with other people—you stopped *thinking* them yourself. Your internal dialogue just dried up."[42] Mandelstam likewise reports that most men and women under Stalin were kept in line not by the regime threatening them personally but by exemplary acts of coercion, which made it so that "none of us ever submitted petitions and pleas, expressed our opinion about something or took any other action before finding out what people thought 'at the top.'"[43] This condition of generalized fear may even be inspired by some act of ancient violence, passed on through underground lore to contemporary consciousness. In the western part of El Salvador, peasants remembered, long after the fact, the army's 1931 massacre of their families, which took over ten thousand lives. So powerful was that memory fifty years later that when the rest of the country rose up against the military, scarcely anyone in the region took up arms.[44]

Such ripple effects, even if unintended, are especially potent when their target belongs to an already vulnerable group. Since 9/11, for example, journalists and activists have reported extensive fear throughout Arab and Muslim communities in the United States, inspired by the detention of 1,200 to 5,000 Muslim and Arab men.[45] This is a fear not just of detention, deportation, or vigilante violence, but of speaking out on politically controversial issues of American foreign policy, which might—and often does[46]—attract scrutiny, surveillance, or harassment from the federal government and police. "There's fear in the Arab community," reports Mino Akhtar, the aforementioned Pakistani American. "What I hear Arabs and Muslims saying is, 'Let's keep a low profile. Don't step out there. We need to stay quiet and let this blow over," a claim confirmed by numerous press reports.[47] Against such a backdrop of fear, even the most innocuous actions can generate additional fear, with equally repressive results. In December 2001, for example, Mohadar Mohamed Abdoulah, a Yemeni immigrant living in San Diego, was granted $500,000 bail after being detained for two months as a 9/11 material witness and for having lied on his asylum application. Initially, the local Muslim community rallied to Abdoulah's cause, pledging $400,000 for his bail fund with promises to raise more. But once it was announced that each contributor would have to provide his or her name to the government and perhaps appear before the judge, many in the community balked. "When people were told they'd have to go to court and answer questions from the judge," said Abdoulah's lawyer, "they chilled out." "One day," added the lawyer, "it's all about the solidarity and standing tall. Then they run. This community isn't split. This is about abject fear."[48] Because of the state's detentions and deportations, and because of vigilante attacks, this simple request to identify themselves to the court was enough to arouse fear throughout the Muslim community in San Diego.

Generating fear across time and space in this way requires the involvement, even cooperation, of the entire society: elites and collaborators, bystanders and victims. To command more than a small, immediate audience, political fear must mobilize generals and foot soldiers, and a supporting army of secretaries, cooks, and maids to tend to them. Political fear also relies upon bystanders, whose passivity paves a path for elites and their collaborators, and the targeted community of victims, who transmit didactic tales of fear among themselves, thereby increasing its reverberating effects. Inspired by the victims' desire to shield themselves from sanctions, these small acts of education among the victims are central to the economy of fear. They minimize the amount of actual coercion perpetrators must apply, and they maximize the effect. One black North Carolina woman recounts that under Jim Crow her parents and grandparents warned her, at an early age, that if she disobeyed the rules of segregation, she would get arrested. "So," she concluded, "any time you saw 'white' and 'colored,' unless you wanted to be arrested and be in jail, you didn't dare."[49]

## ELITES

By elites, I mean those figures of influence who own or control the lion's share of power and resources, who are well positioned to act politically on their own—and society's—behalf. More than any other group, they take the initiative and reap the benefits of political fear. If fear is of the top-down variety, elites create it through direct and immediate coercion, and they sustain it over time through laws and ideologies. If fear is of the community-alien variety, elites still take the initiative and derive the greater benefit. Designated protectors of a community's safety, they determine which threats are most salient, emphasizing, for example, the threat of Iraq over that of North Korea, of Islamic terrorism over domestic terrorism.[50] They characterize the nature of the threat, whence it comes, how it is to be fought. They also mobilize the population against that threat. Because their success as protectors adds to their legitimacy and enhances their power, this kind of fear benefits them, politically, more than it does others.

Elites who create and sustain fear comprise neither a conspiracy nor a cabal. In fact, they often have surprisingly little in common, in terms of their interests, affiliations, and worldviews. The elites who spearheaded political fear during the McCarthy years, for instance, included antimodern, pro–big business, and often racist officials like J. Edgar Hoover and Mississippi congressman John Rankin; liberals like Harry Truman, Hubert Humphrey, and Herbert Lehman; industrial magnates; Hollywood moguls; university presidents; and newspaper columnists. Each of them had their own, often conflicting agendas. But creating or sustaining fear requires elites to share neither unity of purpose nor identity of interest. It merely requires that they cooperate—despite their differences, or because of them. After all, elites possess particular kinds of power, housed in particular institutions, and they lead different constituencies. These particularities and differences make their power local and limited. To be truly effective, they must combine their power, doing together what each cannot do alone.

This cooperation in fear takes the form of most cooperation in the United States: it arises from bargaining and exchange, where one set of elites gives to the other what the other lacks, and vice versa. Hoover, for instance, was an empire builder of the first order, but his empire required the cooperation of Congress, which pays the bills. So Hoover put pluralism in the service of repression. He strategically leaked information to key congressmen, and he had FBI agents chauffer individual representatives around Washington and do odd jobs for them. Hoover, claimed Truman's attorney general Tom Clark, was "rather meticulous about his relationships with Congress." And it paid off. After the war, when Truman submitted to Congress his budgets for the FBI and the OSS, the precursor to the CIA, Congress cut the latter budget by $4 million and increased the former by seven million. Of the last twenty-two budgets that Hoover proposed, only two were ever revised by Congress—both upward.[51]

When bargaining and exchange do not work, elites can always turn the weapons of coercion they use on their victims upon their fellow elites. One of Truman's most fateful decisions, for example, was his March 1947 issuance of Executive Order 9835, which launched investigations of every federal employee for signs of political subversion and authorized the firing of and refusal to hire anyone suspected of communist sympathies. More than any single government policy, EO 9835 chilled the political air, making it difficult to sustain leftist views without fear of sanction. But Truman was reluctant to issue EO 9835. Convinced that the threat of communist infiltration had been overstated and could easily be contained by less repressive measures, he worried that EO 9835 would only empower the FBI, which he likened to the Gestapo and the Soviet secret police. Though historians still disagree about why he issued it, one of his motivations was his fear of retribution—to himself, his party, and the executive branch—from Hoover and congressional Republicans.[52]

Elites who organize these coalitions of fear—like Hoover and congressional conservatives, as opposed to the liberal Democrats who reluctantly joined them—anticipate not just an immediate loss of privileges, but a threat to their power and standing, which allow them to enjoy those privileges in the future. Such situations elicit a combination of rational concern and moral revulsion, which is the hallmark of political fear. Elites cherish the material components of privilege but also believe that they are entitled to privilege. That belief is sustained by their larger image of the political cosmos, in which their high standing is equated with the well-being and survival of society. Inequality, in their eyes, is not simply a ladder of inequities but a form of rule, in which those above expect and receive deference from those below. It is that rule, in the minds of these elites, that makes for social cohesion and civic vitality. Without it, all would be lost. When Abigail Adams, for example, suggested to her husband John that he and his colleagues "Remember the Ladies" as they drafted laws for the new nation, he instantly spied the specter of social breakdown in her request. "Our Struggle," he complained, referring to the American Revolution, "has loosened the bands of Government every where." "Children and Apprentices" are now "disobedient," "schools and Colledges" have "grown turbulent," black slaves "insolent to their Masters." "There will be no end of it," he gloomily concluded.[53] More recently, when the Supreme Court overturned the Texas law banning same-sex sodomy, Justice Antonin Scalia foresaw "a massive disruption of the current social order" and an end to laws prohibiting "bigamy, same-sex marriage, adult incest, prostitution, masturbation, adultery, fornication, bestiality, and obscenity."[54] Even in our postmodern age, it seems, the most limited effort to minimize inequality can arouse the same specter of cosmic disorder as that which exercised this anonymous high priest of premodernity: "Thus became rebellion, as you see, both the first and greatest, and the very root of all other sins, and the first and principal cause both of all worldly and bodily miseries (sorrows, disease, sicknesses and deaths), and, which is infinitely worse than all these, as is said, the very cause of death and damnation eternal also."[55]

Among elites, few circumstances elicit this sense of cosmic threat—and the corresponding imperative for elite cooperation—more forcefully than war and its rumors, for war bears a contradictory relationship to social order. On the one hand, meeting the threat or reality of foreign attack requires the unity of society, a unity that can dampen dissent. On the other hand, wars shake up established arrangements, threatening to bring new groups to power and topple old elites. From the white planters after the Civil War to the tsar during World War I to Lyndon Johnson after the Vietnam War, history is littered with examples of elites taking a fall upon losing a war or failing to win it with sufficient speed. In addition, modern war has a way of imposing itself upon the everyday experience of men and women, throwing upon the stage new actors and classes.[56] Roused by the grand drama of history, ordinary people send their sons and daughters into combat or factory production—and begin to air their long suppressed claims for advance. Compressing decades of inequality and conflict, wars simultaneously push the lower classes to stand up and bow down, giving elites more reason to fear for their own power—and more instruments to advance it. To stem these challenges from below, elites must perform a delicate alchemy, fusing the nation's fear of its enemies with their own fear of movements for domestic reform. This alchemy is not cynical: many elites sincerely believe that reform movements pose a threat to their power, national unity, and civic order; and in wartime, these three items comprise a seamless triptych.

We can see particular evidence of this elite fusion of foreign and domestic fears during the Cold War. J. Edgar Hoover, still an unappreciated influence on the course of American anticommunism, was born and raised in turn-of-the-century Washington, D.C., at the time the northernmost outpost of "Southern, white, Christian, small-town" civilization. Racism and segregation were his articles of faith; religious pluralism meant that Lutherans, Presbyterians, and Methodists worshiped within walking distance of each other. When Hoover deemed communism a menace to civilization, it was this civilization he thought menaced. So he turned the FBI on everyone from the NAACP and Martin Luther King to Sammy Davis, Jr. and Cesar Chavez, all of whom he deemed, as he would later declare of the women's movement, "part of the enemy, a challenge to American values" and thus a threat to the "internal security of the nation."[57] Hoover found many allies for his campaigns among congressional conservatives, who saw red in virtually every brush stroke of the New Deal. As one influential anticommunist North Carolina senator put it, "Once we abandon the voluntary principles [of laissez-faire capitalism], we run squarely into Communism. . . . There can be no half-way control." The reformist policies of the New Deal National Labor Relations Board, claimed one congressional report, were "tinged with a philosophical view of the employer-employee relationship as a class struggle," which was "foreign to the proper American concept of industrial enterprise" and out of step with "the preservation of the capitalist system of private enterprise."[58]

Such views actively influenced the course of repressive anticommunism in the United States, leading to the suppression of not only the Communist Party but the labor and civil rights movements as well. Government loyalty boards asked employees whether they believed the blood supply of the Red Cross ought to be desegregated, the poll tax abolished, and federal antilynching legislation passed—all policies advocated by the Communist Party. Affirmative answers to such questions prompted further investigation and firing.

As the chair of one board explained, "Of course, the fact that a person believes in racial equality doesn't *prove* that he's a Communist, but it certainly makes you look twice, doesn't it? You can't get away from the fact that racial equality is part of the Communist line." Or, in the words of the chair of a state legislative committee, "If someone insists that there is discrimination against the Negroes in this country, or that there is inequality of wealth, there is every reason to believe that person is a Communist."[59] The effect of such ideologically fused fears, where civil rights and labor unions were associated with foreign threats, could be devastating. Throughout the 1930s and 1940s, to cite just one example, Local 22 of the communist-led Food, Tobacco, and Agricultural Workers Union organized thousands of mostly women and black workers at the RJ Reynolds tobacco plant in Winston-Salem, North Carolina. The union also encouraged its members to join the local chapter of the NAACP, turning a moribund seminar of eleven into a movement of almost two thousand. In 1947, after the union led a strike against RJ Reynolds, HUAC paid a visit. Holding widely publicized hearings on the links between the Communist Party and the union's officers, HUAC made the workers think twice about supporting leaders whose affiliations had provoked a government investigation. Not long after, more quiescent leaders assumed control of the local, and by 1950, virtually nothing remained of its original dynamism. And what happened to the NAACP chapter? Its ranks fell to below five hundred.[60]

In other parts of the world, elite fusions of foreign and domestic fears were even more pronounced. In 1957, one of the leading doctrinaires of the Argentine counterinsurgency argued, "We must emphasize that the character of this conflict [between capitalism and communism] corresponds to the religious wars of the past. . . . Its probable consequences: the survival or disappearance of Western civilization."[61] Emphasizing the inequalities that civilization entailed, a successor of his wrote in 1964:

*Communism wants to destroy the human being, family, fatherland, property, the state and God. . . . Nothing exists in Communism to link women with home and family because, proclaiming her emancipation, Communism separates her from domestic life and child raising to throw her into public life and collective production, just like men. . . . The father is the natural head of the family. The mother finds herself an associate of this authority. . . . According to the will of God, the rich should use their excess to alleviate misery. The poor should know that poverty does not dishonor, nor making a living with work, as the example of the son of God proved. The poor are more loved by God.[62]*

The Uruguayan military claimed its main mission was to combat "subversion," which it defined as "actions, violent or not, with ultimate purposes of a political nature, in all fields of human activity within the internal sphere of a state and whose aims are perceived as not convenient for the overall political system." The Brazilian military provided officers with 222 hours of instruction in internal security, 21 in defense against external aggression. Equating the free market with the national interest, the high command thought it more important to learn how to suppress a mobilized domestic opposition against capitalism than to defend against foreign attack. For them, the suppression of a mobilized opposition was the essence of defense against foreign attack.[63]

Elites cannot simply rely upon a popular belief in the connections between reformist movements and foreign threats. They must create such associations in people's minds, through public relations and coercion. In 1946, Hoover launched a major campaign to make the threat of communism real to Americans, who he believed did not sufficiently appreciate its perils. Hoover instructed his subordinates to "prepare education materials which can be released through available channels so that in the event of an emergency we will have an informed public opinion" about communist subversion. Hoover deemed it especially important to convince the "people who think," for scholars and intellectuals would help transmit the fear of communism throughout the wider society. He personally authored some sixty articles in law reviews and professional journals, while the FBI helped Hollywood make four films.[64] Such campaigns are seldom pure propaganda: they usually cite real facts about groups like the Communist Party, which not only had financial and political connections to the Soviet Union, but also spied on its behalf. But elites also exaggerate—not necessarily deliberately—these facts, as did the FBI bureau chief who declared Martin Luther King "the most dangerous Negro in the future of this Nation from the standpoint of communism, the Negro, and national security."[65]

Also helpful in generating popular fear of these movements is the use of government and private coercion. The sheer fact that the government and private elites are willing to punish their opponents often convinces ordinary citizens that the threat these groups pose is real. As much as repression is inspired by fear, so does it inspire fear, inculcating a sense in the wider population that those being targeted must have done something to deserve such attention. "Say what you like," a woman comments to Mandelstam about Soviet prisoners, "there's no smoke without fire."[66] In 1949, for example, the Justice Department invoked a little-known piece of legislation called the

Smith Act to prosecute the Communist Party leadership in court—not for espionage or attempting a violent overthrow the government, but for conspiring to organize a party to advocate the violent overthrow of the government. The sheer number of nouns and verbs the law and indictment cited to link the defendants to an actual crime—"conspiracy," "organize," "party," "advocate"—suggests just how far removed the defendants were in this case from anything resembling criminal activity. It didn't matter because the purpose of the trials, explained one of Hoover's deputies, was not prosecution but pedagogy, or pedagogy through prosecution. They were meant to teach Americans "that Communism is dangerous," that the "patriotism of Communists is not directed towards the United States but towards the Soviet Union."[67]

Today, the United States is again at war, and once again we see this elite fusion of domestic and foreign fears. Though the connection between external threats and reformist dissent is today more tenuous than it was during the Cold War, and though such dissent poses much less of a challenge to the powerful than it did in the past, many elites have connected domestic dissent to terrorism and have implemented policies with a potential chilling effect upon that dissent. As in the Cold War, it is difficult to know whether this effect is intentional or unintentional; sometimes it is, other times not. When the FBI, for example, pays a visit to a bookstore worker in Atlanta after he is seen toting an article titled "Weapons of Mass Stupidity" decrying the war on Iraq, the combination of motives inspiring the bureau's investigation seems fairly benign: one nervous or zealous citizen sees the pairing of "weapon" and "mass" and alerts the FBI to suspicious activity; low-level officials, reeling from accusations that FBI negligence contributed to 9/11, follow up the tip; and suddenly Marc Schultz finds himself explaining to two FBI men why he reads what he reads, opening his car to an FBI search, and wondering how he can keep off their radar screen in the future.[68] In other cases, as we shall see, the repression of dissent is clearly intended. But in a certain sense, the intent behind these acts is irrelevant, for it is their repressive consequences, the fear that they arouse, that make them so lethal to political reform. And even when those consequences are intended, the elites who produce them often believe, sincerely, that they are acting on behalf of the national interest, which they equate with their own power and standing.

Since 9/11, conservative elites and even some liberal voices in the media have followed the twin tracks of public relations and coercion—as did their predecessors during the Cold War—to awaken the American public to the connections between foreign terrorism and reformist ideas and movements at home. One group, Americans for Victory Over Terrorism (AVOT)—led by William J. Bennett, Frank Gaffney, and R. James Woolsey, all former officials from the Reagan, Bush, and Clinton administrations—took a full-page ad out in the *New York Times* declaring that "the threats we face today are both external and internal." The latter threat includes "those who blame America first and who do not understand—or who are unwilling to defend—our fundamental principles." Such domestic dissenters, the ad claimed, are inspired by "either a hatred for the American ideals of freedom and equality, or a misunderstanding of those ideals and their practice." Promising to "take" such individuals "to task," AVOT also called for holding "scholarly research" about Islam "to a serious and rigorous standard." Another group, chaired by Lynne Cheney, wife of Vice President Richard Cheney, and Democratic senator Joseph Lieberman, has decried liberal and leftist academics as the "weak link" in the war on terror. These public relations campaigns are designed not simply to arouse public awareness, but also to influence government action. And they have. After taking hours of testimony from conservative intellectuals decrying the pernicious influence of the late Columbia University scholar Edward Said on Middle Eastern studies, the House of Representatives unanimously adopted in the fall of 2003 a bill requiring academic departments receiving federal funding to tailor their scholarship and curriculum to "better reflect the national needs related to homeland security." Under that rubric, according to a report in *Salon*, the government could use the carrot and stick of federal money to make sure that "international studies departments . . . show more support for American foreign policy."[69]

*The New Republic* has opened a different domestic front in the war on terrorism, targeting the antiglobalization movement. Condemning a planned protest in Washington, D.C., in late September 2001 against the IMF and the World Bank, the magazine's editor declared that if the protest came off, the antiglobalization movement would "in the eyes of the nation, have joined the terrorists in a united front." He continued: "This nation is now at war. And in such an environment, domestic political dissent is immoral without a prior statement of national solidarity, a choosing of sides. By canceling the upcoming protests—and acknowledging that it is less important to ruin the meetings of the IMF and the World Bank than to let Washington recover—that is exactly the statement the antiglobalization movement would be making."[70] Antiglobalization activists and intellectuals quickly felt the power of such rhetoric: many, including the AFL-CIO, stayed away from the protest, and the movement has since fallen into abeyance.[71] Though editorials in little magazines rarely have much effect on national politics, U.S. trade representative

Robert Zoellick credits this one with convincing him of the links between terrorism and the movement against globalization. In a speech before a Washington think tank, Zoellick hinted at the "intellectual connections" between Al Qaeda and "others who have turned to violence to attack international finance, globalization, and the United States." In the *Washington Post*, he urged Congress to grant President Bush "fast track authority" to negotiate trade agreements, arguing that this would "send an unmistakable signal to the world that America will lead." During the congressional debate in late fall 2001 on fast-track renewal, Republican Speaker of the House Dennis Hastert took up Zoellick's theme, declaring, "This Congress will either support our president who is fighting a courageous war on terrorism and redefining American world leadership, or will undercut this president at the worst possible time." New York Democratic congressman Charlie Rangel—and even free-traders like *New York Times* columnist Paul Krugman—denounced such tactics for casting globalization's critics as unpatriotic and dangerous to national security, but to no avail. Where the antiglobalization movement and congressional Democrats had managed to deny fast-track authority to President Clinton in his second term, the combination of a silenced opposition and an emboldened Republican Party ensured the granting of such authority to President Bush by the summer of 2002.[72]

Beyond these exercises in the war of ideas, various security agencies operating in the interest of national security have leveraged their coercive power in ways that target dissenters posing no conceivable threat of terrorism. FBI officials and local police departments have repeatedly taken individual statements of opposition to U.S. foreign policy or the Bush administration as a sign of possible terrorist inclinations, leaving the individuals targeted for investigation with a fear of being watched and pursued for their beliefs.[73] Various government agencies have established "no fly" lists, so that members of the ACLU, Amnesty International, the Green Party, and the Catholic Church are stopped at airports and held for lengthy questioning, sometimes overnight.[74] The FBI has targeted the antiwar movement in the United States for especially close scrutiny. Even though an internal FBI memorandum acknowledges that the bureau "possesses no information indicating that violent or terrorist activities are being planned as part of these [antiwar] protests" and that "most protests are peaceful events," the FBI has carefully tracked the movement's activities, alerting local police to the use of video cameras by protestors to monitor possible police brutality and to the movement's use of the Internet "to recruit, raise funds and coordinate their activities prior to demonstrations."[75] Few of these cases approach the level of concerted coercion used against dissenters during the McCarthy or Vietnam years, and often they seem inspired by the bureau's fear of being caught sleeping on the job. Nevertheless, they do indicate an association in the minds of government officials between dissenting views and terrorist activities. And as their intended targets point out, they have a chilling effect upon any movement seeking to change the course of American foreign policy.

With the exception of Muslims and Arabs in the United States, the labor movement since 9/11 has felt the greatest brunt of this elite fusion of foreign and domestic fears. In January 2003, Republican leader Tom DeLay, or one of his staffers, sent out a fundraising letter on DeLay's letterhead to thousands of supporters of the National Right to Work Foundation, an antiunion group seeking to overturn labor legislation in the United States. Claiming that the labor movement since 9/11 "presents a *clear-and-present-danger* to the security of the United States at home and the safety of our Armed Forces overseas," the letter denounces "Big Labor Bosses . . . willing to harm free-loving workers, the war effort, *and* the economy to acquire more power!" It asks recipients to donate upward of one thousand dollars so that "the legal ground troops of the National Right to Work Foundation" will "have the ammo they need" to carry out their campaign against unions.[76] Within Congress, DeLay and his conservative allies have worked closely with President Bush to use the threat of terrorism to deny union and civil service rights—including whistleblower protections—to 170,000 federal employees in the newly created Department of Homeland Security. Even though many of these employees are clerical, even though clerical employees in the Defense Department are not denied such rights, and even though it was the lack of basic labor protections within the FBI that helped create a culture of intimidation where individual agents like Coleen Rowley were discouraged from speaking out on vital issues of national security, Homeland Security secretary Tom Ridge has insisted that removing union and other employment protections would make his department as "agile and aggressive as the terrorists themselves." Facing a congressional recess in late summer 2002, Senate Republican leader Trent Lott pushed for immediate passage of the bill, declaring, "What if we leave town, and in August we have some terrorist attack, some disaster, that maybe could have been prevented if we had a way to move people and money and get a focus in an appropriate way? I just think that's unacceptable. This really to me is emergency legislation." The bill finally passed just after the November 2002 midterm election, while a lame-duck Democratic majority still held control of the Senate.[77]

The homeland security bill is just one of many efforts on the part of conservative elites to use the threat of terrorism against the labor movement. Indeed, during the debate on the proposed legislation, White House OMB director Mitchell Daniels, as well as staffers at the conservative Heritage Foundation, declared the homeland security bill a model for restructuring employee relations throughout the federal government, which would radically constrain the labor movement. As early as January 2002, President Bush signed Executive Order 13252, denying union rights to one thousand attorneys in the Department of Justice on the grounds of national security, even though many of these attorneys held positions in the department's Criminal Division, its National Drug Intelligence Center, and other non–terrorism related bureaus. One year later, Admiral James Loy, head of the Transportation Security Administration, denied union and other rights to airport screeners, arguing, like Ridge, that "fighting terrorism demands a flexible workforce that can rapidly respond to threats. That can mean changes in work assignments and other conditions of employment that are not compatible with the duty to bargain with unions."[78] Finally, during the summer of 2002, the Bush administration invoked the threat of national security to intervene in a labor dispute and possible strike between West Coast dockworkers and their employers, to the detriment of the former and benefit of the latter. Before negotiations between the two sides had begun, a coalition of maritime employers and companies like The Gap, Mattel, and Home Depot met secretly with the Bush administration, requesting—and getting—the administration's aid in their dispute. Threatening the unions with everything from a declaration of a national emergency to the use of federal troops, the Bush administration cited testimony from Defense Secretary Donald Rumsfeld justifying its interventions in the name of national security: "The DoD increasingly relies upon commercial items and practices to meet its requirements. Raw materials, medical supplies, replacement parts and components, as well as everyday subsistence needs of our armed forces, are just some of the essential military cargo provided by commercial contractors that typically are not seen as military cargo."[79]

## COLLABORATORS

By conventional understanding, a collaborator is one who assists an enemy, helping groups to which he does not belong threaten groups to which he does belong.[80] But this definition, it seems to me, is too restrictive. It presumes that a group is a discrete whole, that once in it, we can't get out of it or have competing affiliations. Collaborators, however, cannot be so neatly bound. Some do not entirely belong to the group they betray; others, like the

French fascists of Vichy, have a deep affinity for the enemy they aid. Informers are perhaps the most common kind of collaborator, but they are notorious chameleons, making it virtually impossible to pin down their affiliations at all. Knud Wollenberger, an East German dissident who secretly kept the Stasi apprised of his wife's subversive activities, claims that his collaboration was entirely consistent with his membership in the couple's oppositional circle. One way to challenge the government, he explains, was "through open dissidence, and the other way [was] through government channels. I was on the inside and the outside at the same time." Harvey Matusow joined the American Communist Party in 1947, began informing on it in 1950, recanted his testimony in 1954, and then lied about all three phases of his career in his memoir *False Witness*, published in 1955. So promiscuous were Matusow's politics, it is impossible to know what he had been false to, except the truth. The title of another FBI informant's memoir—*I Led Three Lives* (as Communist, informer, and "citizen")—was more apt, suggesting the multiple identities the collaborator regularly assumes.[81]

I don't wish to carry this notion of multiple affiliations too far. Wollenberger could very well be rationalizing a past of which he is ashamed, and Matusow may simply be the hollow man many at the time suspected him to be. Whether we belong to one group or another in some existential sense, in the course of our lives we do incur moral obligations to our comrades and friends, whom we betray when we aid our opponents. But to avoid the question of identity that restrictive definitions of collaboration entail, I will use the definition contained in the word's Latin root *collaborare*: "to work together." By collaborator, I simply mean those men and women who work with elites, and who occupy the lower tiers of power and make political fear a genuinely civic enterprise. Collaborators may be low- or mid-level perpetrators; suppliers, like the warehouse in Jedwabne, Poland, which provided the kerosene local residents used in 1941 to burn a barn containing 1,500 Jews, or Ford and General Motors, which funded a Brazilian security outfit that interrogated and tortured leftists; attendants (cooks, secretaries, and other supporting staff); or spies and informers.[82] Though all are not equally compromised by their deeds, each is guilty of complicity.

The collaborator is an elusive figure. With the exception of *The Persian Letters* and *Eichmann in Jerusalem*, he seldom makes an appearance in the literature of political fear. One of the reasons for his absence, I suspect, is that he confounds our simple categories of elite and victim. Like the elite, the collaborator takes initiative and receives benefits from his collaboration. Like the victim, he may be threatened with punishment or retribution if he does not cooperate. Many collaborators, in fact, are drawn directly from the ranks of the victims. Perhaps then we can distinguish between collaborators of aspiration, inspired by a desire for gain, and collaborators of aversion, inspired by a fear of loss. The first are akin to elites, the second to victims. But even that distinction is too neat. Elites also fear loss, and victims hope for gain, and as the economist's notion of opportunity costs attests, the hope of gain often informs the fear of loss.[83]

Collaborators serve two functions. First, they perform tasks that elites themselves cannot or will not perform. These tasks may be considered beneath the dignity of the elite: cooking, cleaning, or other forms of work. They may require local knowledge—as in the case of informers, who provide information elites cannot access on their own—or specialized skills. We often think of torturers, for example, as thugs from the dregs of society. But torture is a weapon of knowledge, designed to extract information from the victim, often without leaving a physical trace. The torturer must know the body, how far he can go without killing the victim. Who better to assist or direct the torturer than a doctor? Thus, 70 percent of Uruguayan political prisoners under that country's military regime claim that a doctor sat in on their torture sessions.[84] Second, collaborators extend the reach of elites into corners of society that elites lack the manpower to patrol. These collaborators are usually figures of influence within communities targeted by elites. Their status may come from the elite, who elevate them because they are willing to enforce the elite's directives.[85] More often, their authority is indigenous. Figures of trust among the victims, they can be relied upon to persuade the victims not to resist, to compound the fear of disobedience the victims already feel. During its war against leftist guerillas in the late '70s and early '80s, the Salvadoran army worked closely with such indigenous leaders. In 1982, a battalion officer informed Marcos Díaz, owner of the general store in the hamlet of El Mozote, with friends in the military, that the army was planning a major offensive in the region. To ensure their safety, the officer explained, the townspeople should remain in the village. Though many in El Mozote thought such advice unsound, Díaz was the local potentate who knew the army's ways. His voice held sway, the villagers did as they were told, and three days later, some eight hundred of them were dead.[86]

Because their functions are so various, collaborators come in all shapes and sizes. Some travel in or near the orbit of elite power; others are drawn from the lower orders and geographic peripheries. One common, though unappreciated, influence upon their actions is their ambition. While some collaborators hope to stave off threats to their communities and others are true believers,[87] many are careerists, who see in collaboration a path of personal advance. In Brazil, for example, torture was a stepping stone, turning one man into the ambassador to Paraguay and another into a general, while doctors advising the torturers in Uruguay could draw salaries four times as high as those of doctors who did not.[88] Whether the payment is status, power, or money, collaboration promises to elevate men and women, if only slightly, above the fray. Nazi Germany's Reserve Police Battalion 101, for example, was a unit of five hundred "ordinary men," drawn from the lower middle and working classes of Hamburg, who joined the battalion because it got them out of military service on the front. All told, they were responsible for executing 38,000 Polish Jews and deporting some 45,000 others to Treblinka. Why did they do it? Not because of any fear of punishment. No one in the 101 faced penalties—certainly not death—for not carrying out their mission. The unit's commander even informed his men that they could opt out of the killing, which 10 to 15 of them did. Why did the remaining 490 or so stay? According to Christopher Browning, there were different reasons, including anti-Semitism and peer pressure, but a critical one was their desire for advance. Of those who refused to kill Jews, in fact, the most forthright emphasized their lack of career ambitions. One explained that "it was not particularly important to me to be promoted or otherwise to advance. . . . The company chiefs . . . on the other hand were young men and career policemen who wanted to become something." Another said, "Because I was not a career policeman and also did not want to become one . . . it was of no consequence that my police career would not prosper."[89]

Though ambitious collaborators like to believe that they are adepts of realpolitik, walking the hard path of power because it is the wisest course to take, their realism is freighted with ideology. Careerism has its own moralism, serving as an anesthetic against competing moral claims. Particularly in the United States, where ambition is a civic duty and worldly success a prerequisite of citizenship, enlightened anglers of their own interest can easily be convinced that they are doing not only the smart thing, but also the right thing. They happily admit to their careerism because they presume an audience of shared moral sympathy. How else can we understand this comment of director Elia Kazan in response to a colleague's request that he justify his decision to name names? "All right, I earned over $400,000 last year from theater. But Skouras [the head of Twentieth-Century Fox] says I'll never make another movie. You've spent your money, haven't you? It's easy for you. But I've got a stake."[90]

## BYSTANDERS AND VICTIMS

Even with their collaborators, elites have reason to worry that their power will not hold. Most of their potential followers, they suspect, are soft headed and faint hearted, and some might even sympathize with the victims. Were a determined army of victims to muster support among these sympathizers, they could overthrow the elites. To rule effectively, then, elites must reach beyond their collaborators to the rest of the population, persuading victims to act like bystanders and bystanders to act like victims. Though elites by definition comprise a minority of the population, they come to this task with three advantages. First, because they possess power and standing, they can easily mobilize themselves and their collaborators. Where the victims must rouse themselves from quiescence to confrontation, transforming themselves from what they are into what they are not, elites must simply do more of what they already do. Second, because they lack power, victims must generate nearly unanimous support among themselves and significant support among the bystanders. Elites need only make sure that the victims' efforts fail. Finally, as Hobbes argued, power is "like to fame, increasing as it proceeds."[91] Witnessing the advancing pace of elites, victims and bystanders fear them to be more powerful than they are. If that fear persuades victims and bystanders not to challenge elites, elites can move faster, making their power seem greater. Capitulation, in other words, reinforces power, which explains why some victims are as angered by their quiescent comrades as they are by their tormentors. In the words of Solzhenitsyn:

> How we burned in the camps later, thinking: What would things have been like if every Security operative, when he went out at night to make an arrest, had been uncertain whether he would return alive and had to say good-bye to his family? Or if, during periods of mass arrests . . . people had not simply sat there in their lairs, paling with terror at every bang of the downstairs door and at every step on the staircase, but had understood they had nothing left to lose and had boldly set up in the downstairs hall an ambush of half of a dozen people with axes, hammers, pokers, or whatever else at hand? . . .
>
> . . . You aren't gagged. You really can and you really ought to cry out— to cry out that you are being arrested! . . . If many such outcries had been heard all over the city in the course of a day, would not our fellow citizens perhaps have begun to bristle? And would arrests perhaps no longer have been so easy?[92]

Because of this failure to resist, Solzhenitsyn concludes, "We purely and simply *deserved* everything that happened afterward."[93]

Victims thus confront a catch-22. If they challenge elites and are crushed, their defeat benefits elites, and they may find themselves in a worse situation. If they do not mount a challenge, their quiescence also benefits elites, and they may also find themselves in a worse situation. The villagers of El Mozote, for instance, would have been better off had they defied the orders of the army and Díaz, and fled into the mountains or joined the guerillas, who at least offered them protection. The few who fled managed to survive; those who stayed did not.[94] The same logic applies to bystanders, though to a lesser degree. If they act in solidarity with the victims and challenge elites, they may become victims. If they do not, they may become victims anyway, or bystanders who survive but at a great cost to themselves.

Consider the fate of Hollywood's liberals, who tried during the McCarthy years to turn themselves from victims into bystanders, and wound up as both. When HUAC first began investigating Hollywood in 1947, liberals mounted a formidable opposition, accurately sensing that Congress was after not just the Communist Party, but also the satellite of liberal opinion orbiting around it. The liberals ran national broadcasts denouncing the HUAC hearings and led a contingent of celebrities to Washington to speak out in defense of the First Amendment. So initially successful were they that HUAC was forced to cancel its public investigations of Hollywood until 1951.[95] But then HUAC got smart. Rather than take on all of Hollywood at once, the committee and other government officials targeted individuals. HUAC investigators personally visited industry executives, informing them that if they did not take care of their Communist problem, the government would.[96] HUAC and its collaborators also took aim at individual actors. On the floor of the House of Representatives, John Rankin revealed that the real names of Danny Kaye, Melvyn Douglas, and June Havoc—left-liberal actors whose careers were built upon an express denial of their being Jewish—were David Daniel Kamirsky, Melvyn Hesselberg, and June Hovick. Ed Sullivan pulled Humphrey Bogart aside to warn him that "the public is beginning to think you're a Red." Targeted as individuals, these actors began to worry that their politics would hurt their careers, and they soon gave up the cause.[97]

Though the Hollywood liberals survived McCarthyism, Hollywood liberalism fared less well. Not only did the studios fire and refuse to hire Communists, their allies, and anyone refusing to cooperate with HUAC, but they also required suspect employees to renounce all ties to the party and its front groups, testify before HUAC, join an anticommunist organization, condemn Soviet imperialism, and commit never to associate with the party again. It was not enough not to be a Communist, in other words: one had to be an active and aggressive anticommunist. Hollywood liberals also tried to create their own alternative HUAC within the industry. More legally scrupulous and procedurally sound than its government counterpart, their proposed tribunal would operate on the principle that no proven Communist, and no one accused of party membership who refused to deny the accusation or who invoked the Fifth Amendment, should be employed by the industry.[98] And what of the films themselves? Though movies in the thirties and forties hardly offered uniformly brilliant social commentary, Hollywood did manage during these years to produce films like *The Best Years of Our Lives*, *Mr. Smith Goes to Washington*, *Gentlemen's Agreement*, and *The Naked City*, which tackled racism, anti-Semitism, and inequality, injecting a dose of social realism into a genre in which it rarely appeared. But by 1948, according to *Variety*, the studios were dropping "plans for 'message pictures' like hot coals." Twentieth-Century Fox abandoned a script depicting a love relationship between a black nurse and a white doctor. Warner Brothers forced director John Huston to excise one line from *Treasure of Sierra Madre*: "Gold, Mister, is worth what it is because of the human labor that goes into the finding and getting of it." Why the deletion? "It was all on account of the word 'labor,'" Huston recalled. "That word looked dangerous in print, I guess." In 1940, Nunnally Johnson wrote the screenplay for *The Grapes of Wrath*; after the blacklist, he authored *How to Marry a Millionaire* and *How to Be Very, Very Popular*. During these years, Ayn Rand's *Screen Guide for Americans* became required reading for studio heads. Its chapter titles included "Don't Smear the Free Enterprise System," "Don't Smear Success," "Don't Glorify the Collective," and "Don't Smear Industrialists." Above all, Rand warned, "Don't ever use any lines about 'the common man' or 'the little people.' It is not the American idea to be either 'common' or 'little'"[99]

Against the logic of elites and collaborators, then, resisters offer their own counterlogic, combining both rational and moral arguments. Capitulation, they tell victims and bystanders, is not only dishonorable: it is unwise. Silence will not buy you protection: it will only make you vulnerable. The threats we face are not as inevitable as they seem: we have more power, more room for maneuver, than we realize. If you do not resist, you may live, your career may even thrive, but your life and career will not be the ones that inspired you to capitulate in the first place. Jaundiced commentators often overlook these arguments, confusing the resister's counsel with a suicidal death wish, born of ideological fanaticism. What these commentators forget is that resisters understand all too well Hobbes's dictum about power "increasing as it proceeds." Even if unsuccessful, the resisters' challenge suggests that opposition is possible, that power is not as powerful as it seems. In the same way that a soldier charging enemy lines knows that his mad rush to death may expose his enemy's vulnerabilities, contributing to his own survival and the victory of his unit,[100] resisters know that the refusal of fear is a necessary condition of their own success. It is this insight that ties the counterrevolutionary Hobbes, who sought to cultivate a fear of death, to the revolutionary Trotsky, who sought to overcome it: "No matter how important weapons may be," Trotsky told a St. Petersburg jury after the abortive 1905 revolution, "it is not in them, gentlemen the judges, that great power resides. No! Not the ability of masses to kill others, but their great readiness themselves to die, this secures in the last instance the victory of the popular uprising."[101]

# 7 Divisions of Labor

THERE ARE WORDS LIKE *FREEDOM*
SWEET AND WONDERFUL TO SAY.
ON MY HEARTSTRINGS FREEDOM SINGS
ALL DAY EVERYDAY.

THERE ARE WORDS LIKE *LIBERTY*
THAT ALMOST MAKE ME CRY.
IF YOU HAD KNOWN WHAT I KNOW
YOU WOULD KNOW WHY.

—LANGSTON HUGHES

Looking for repressive weapons to arouse political fear, elites and their collaborators often turn to the state, with its laws and trials, punishments and prisons, but that state is not necessarily the one described by Hobbes and his realist successors or by Montesquieu and his liberal successors.[1] It need not be lawless, centralized, or unified, monopolizing the means of coercion. It can be fragmented by the separation of powers and federalism, and constrained by the rule of law, conforming to the most basic strictures of our constitutional faith. Elites and their collaborators also work through pluralist, autonomous institutions of civil society—schools and churches, private associations and the family, civic groups and political organizations, and the workplace—where they find a sizeable armory of repressive weapons. These weapons are seldom as violent or physically coercive as those possessed by the state, though sometimes they are; one thinks of private organizations like the Ku Klux Klan, or the Mafia threatening workers on the waterfront. But often the weapons are nonviolent: firing; blacklisting; denials of promotion and economic opportunity; ostracism; exclusion or expulsion from favored circles of intimates, associates, and friends; and everyday forms of humiliation and degradation. Because the Constitution makes it difficult for the state to wield physical weapons of fear with abandon, elites must turn to these nonviolent weapons of civil society, which are not subject to much constitutional restraint. We best approach the distinction between state and society, then, as a division of labor or joint venture between the public and private sectors: what government officials cannot do well or with efficient ease, private elites do instead, and vice versa.

I focus here on the downsides of the fragmented state and social pluralism. Readers may fairly ask about their upsides: Don't the separation of powers and the rule of law forestall fear? Don't federalism and social pluralism give people opportunities for resistance? They do. I do not discuss their positive effects here because, as I have said before, many scholars have written about them elsewhere. But there is another reason to dwell on their negative effects. All too often in the United States, we assume that political fear arises outside our political system, beyond the Constitution and institutions of civil society. Trying to understand an instance of political fear, we assume that federalism and the separation of powers must have failed, or that the rule of law must have been defeated, as if everything designed to support freedom must stand on one side of the fence and everything designed to arouse fear on the other. When it comes to problems like pollution or poverty, we know that the world is not black and white. But when the issue is fear, and the venue is the United States, we assume that a force for good cannot also be a force for ill. I would like to take a different tack, to see how constituent elements in the American polity can be both instruments of freedom and weapons of fear. Because it suggests that our solutions are also our problems, such an enquiry does not yield easy remedies or simple solutions. Indeed, it only produces paradoxes and incongruities. But such puzzles need not dampen our spirits, for as philosophers discovered long ago, perplexity is often the beginning of wisdom.

## Fragmented State

Inspired to a great degree by Montesquieu, the authors of the United States Constitution believed that a unified, and to a lesser degree, centralized, state posed a threat to freedom. Regardless of who wielded it on whose behalf, government power, indivisible and concentrated, was an invitation to political repression. "The accumulation of all powers . . . in the same hands," wrote James Madison, "is the very definition of tyranny."[2] So the Framers placed in the Constitution three obstacles: the separation of powers, federalism, and the rule of law. They divided the national government into three branches, and the legislative branch into two houses. They created a federalist structure of national and state governments, to which we may add local and county governments. Dividing power between the core and the peripheries, the Framers made sure, through provisions like the Senate and the Electoral College, that the peripheries had a hand in what the core did. The rule of law is not an explicit provision of the Constitution, but its components appear so often throughout—from the enumeration of congressional powers to the due process clauses of the Fifth and Fourteenth Amendments—that we can include it as a constituent element. The rule of law places limits on the arbitrary exercise of legislative or executive power and, in the form of judicial review, enables the judiciary to check the other two branches. Whatever the nationalist aspirations of the Framers, there can be no doubt that the Constitution fragments the state in order to check the repressive ambitions of tyrants old and new.

## THE SEPARATION OF POWERS

In prescribing the separation of powers as a remedy for government tyranny, Madison and the Framers propounded a simple logic: grant independent power to the different branches of government, and each member of that branch will have a personal interest in maintaining that power and will prevent the other branches from carrying out their repressive designs. Though each branch can and does influence the other—the Constitution enjoins not just a separation but also a mingling of powers—the possession of independent power ensures that officials in one branch have, in the words of Madison, "personal motives to resist encroachments" from the others, or to cooperate only with those schemes less malignant to the commonweal.[3] The only two options, then, available to a government of separated powers are stalemate born of attempted repression or cooperation born of benign intent. In the words of the Supreme Court, "if government power is fractionalized, if a given policy can be implemented only by a combination of legislative enactment, judicial application, and executive implementation, no man or group of men will be able to impose its unchecked will."[4]

There is much to recommend this logic, and historical experience demonstrates that it has often held sway.[5] But granting independent power to different branches of government also means that small groups within those branches have significant power at their disposal, which they can use repressively, without consulting other branches of government—indeed, without consulting members of their own branches. These occurrences are not failures of the separation of power; they are directly attributable to it, for as Madison observed, if each branch of government did not possess independent power, how could it check the others or have an investment in checking them? Often overlooked in the grant of independent power, then, is just how coercive that power can be and how small a constituency is required to use it repressively. Tiny outposts of state intimidation, these forms of independent power can pose a considerable threat to dissenters and potential dissenters.

Consider those congressional committees investigating communist infiltration and leftist subversion during the Cold War. Many legislative committees mounted such investigations, but three were particularly important: the House Committee on Un-American Committees (HUAC), the Senate Internal Security Subcommittee, and the Senate Permanent Investigations Subcommittee. Though authorized by legislative majorities, these committees were very much the work of small minorities. Because committee chairs were chosen by seniority, they were seldom controlled by party majorities. Despite procedural constraints, they were free to manage their committees as they saw fit, launching investigations and calling witnesses without informing other committee members. Traditions of senatorial privilege also dictated that party leaders not interfere with individual committees and their chairs. In both houses, committee chairs were able to manipulate congressional rules in order to mount intrusive investigations of the executive branch and civil society.[6]

Congressional committees possess two instruments of coercion, which can be wielded without consent of the other branches of government. Brandishing the weapon of *"prescriptive publicity,"*[7] congressional committees put uncooperative witnesses—as well as their families and friends—under an embarrassing spotlight, exposing them to public obloquy and political stigmas. In 1954, for instance, Sylvia Bernstein, a leftist in Washington and mother of future Watergate journalist Carl Bernstein, was called before HUAC. When her attorney asked HUAC's chair to instruct a newspaper photographer to stop taking pictures of the session, the chair responded, "News photographers have a perfect right, *especially in cases where the witness refuses to give any information,* a perfect right to take their pictures." Publicity, in other words, was a punishment for the uncooperative witness—and a threat to other uncooperative witnesses. The next day, the *Washington Post* ran Bernstein's photograph under the front-page headline "Red Party 'Hard Core' in Capital, Velde Says." Such negative publicity invariably followed the witness to her neighborhood, her friend and family circles, and her workplace, from which she was often fired. Bernstein's daughter was thrown out of nursery school, relatives ceased all communication with the family, and friends of the children were forbidden to associate with them.[8] That hounding, as a 1948 HUAC report intimated, was one of the purposes of its hearings: "to permit American public opinion . . . an . . . opportunity to render a continuing verdict on all of its public officials and to evaluate the merit of many in private life who either openly associate with and assist disloyal groups or covertly operate as members or fellow-travelers of such organizations."[9]

Congressional committees can also threaten uncooperative witnesses with contempt citations or potential charges of perjury. Though Congress cited only 113 witnesses for contempt between 1857 and 1949, it cited 117 between 1950 and 1952.[10] And while contempt citations require the collaboration of the courts in order to yield prison sentences, their mere threat—which Congress wields on its own—can be enough to persuade witnesses to testify and to cease their leftist associations. In 1951, for instance, actor Larry Parks was called before HUAC. Asked to name names, he capitulated, bearing painful witness to the effects of a threatened contempt citation: "Don't present me with the choice," he said, "of either being in contempt of this Committee and going to jail or forcing me to really crawl through the mud to be an informer. For what purpose? I don't think this is a choice at all." Fifty-eight of the subsequent 110 Hollywood witnesses HUAC called that spring made the same choice as Parks.[11]

Madison's argument that the possession of independent power inspires government officials to check each other's repressive policies also overlooks another possible outcome. The investment in the power of one's own branch can inspire officeholders to implement those policies themselves, if for no other reason than to keep intruding meddlers out of their domain. One of the reasons, for example, that Truman implemented EO 9835 was to protect the executive branch from congressional intrusion. In early 1946, congressional Republicans had warned that if they won the midterm election in November, they would conduct, in the words of one Kansas representative, "an immediate and thorough housecleaning" of the executive branch. Fearing that members of Congress wanted "to join in the administration of the loyalty program," Truman decided that the executive branch should police its own employees, thereby keeping congressional investigators at bay.[12] As much as it may inspire a decision to resist other branches, then, the impulse to maintain the autonomy of one's branch can inspire a decision to cooperate with those branches.

## FEDERALISM

Though federalism was more or less the Framers' unhappy brainchild,[13] its conservative proponents often uphold its "counterintuitive" assumption that "freedom," in the words of Justice Kennedy, is "enhanced by the creation of two governments, not one."[14] Since the Civil War, most liberal jurists and writers have been suspicious of federalism, seeing in its celebration of state and local rights a defense of slavery and Jim Crow and opposition to the New Deal. But more recently, some liberals, including the late Justice Brennan, have backed away from their opposition to federalism.[15] Though they remain aware of its covert oppressions, they believe that federalism gives opportunities to state governments to challenge a conservative national government and ordinary citizens a chance to participate in local, and presumably more democratic, forums. Contemporary liberals here borrow from Tocqueville, who claimed, "Local institutions are to liberty what primary schools are to science; they put it within the people's reach; they teach people to appreciate its peaceful enjoyment and accustom them to make use of it. Without local institutions a nation may give itself a free government, but it has not got the spirit of liberty."[16] In the same way that the separation of powers inspires a vested interest in checking the power of ambitious tyrants, federalism is supposed to work against a centralizing state. "Populism and federalism—liberty and localism—work together," writes Akhil Reed Amar. "We the People conquer government power by dividing it between the two rival governments, state and federal."[17]

Though the creation of two or more levels of government is supposed to arouse conflict and check power between the various levels, it also offers more opportunities for repression: not because state and local governments are more tyrannical than the federal government, but because state and local governments often work in tandem with the federal government. Each level replicates what the other levels are already doing, or uses its own particular power to do what the other levels cannot do.[18] Federalism, in other words, enables each level of government to duplicate or supplement the coercion of the other levels, sometimes doubly, even trebly, increasing the burdens born by any one individual. Each level influences the other, with the federal government inspiring in the lower levels the motive and means to act repressively, and vice versa. Federalism also allows local and state elites to customize repression for the sake of preserving regional hierarchies and advancing their geographically specific power.

Consider the duplication of coercive repression during the Cold War. In 1940, the federal government passed the Smith Act, which it used to prosecute the Communist Party leadership in court. In 1947, President Truman implemented Executive Order 9835. In 1950, Congress passed, over Truman's veto, the Internal Security Act, which, among other provisions, mandated that Communist organizations register with the attorney general. In 1954, Congress passed the Communist Control Act, outlawing the Communist Party. Congress also fielded three legislative committees to investigate Communist subversion. Far from challenging these programs, state and local governments mimicked them. An estimated 150 municipalities passed antisubversion ordinances like the Smith Act; eleven states passed registration statutes similar to the 1950 Internal Security Act; eight states passed legislation outlawing the Communist Party. By 1967, forty-five states had an antisedition law on their books. Though the Supreme Court in 1957 would strike down one of these state antisedition laws, it later qualified this position by claiming that states could take action against sedition that threatened them individually. While federalist theory would suggest that Congress would be jealous of any state government threatening to preempt its authority, members of Congress were outraged by the court's 1957 decision. They repeatedly attempted to pass bills stipulating, in the words of one proposed statute, "that no act of Congress shall be construed as indicating an intent on the part of Congress to occupy the field in which such act operates, to the exclusion of all State laws on the same matter." When this legislation was finally amended to apply only to antisubversion laws, it passed the House, though it died in the Senate.[19]

With the exception of antisedition laws, states and local governments most consistently replicated federal programs in the field of public employment. By 1950, thirty-two states barred alleged subversives from working in government, at times turning the most innocuous posts into the front lines of national security. As governor of California, Earl Warren signed the 1950 Levering Act, which made every single state employee a "civil defense worker." New York State defined all of the following as security-sensitive government positions: scientists in the paleontology division of the Department of Education ("they have knowledge concerning the location of caves and their suitability for defense storage purposes"); sanitation workers in New York City ("disease might spread in the event that department did not perform its duty"); and probation workers in the city's Domestic Relations Court. States also had employees take loyalty or test oaths, swearing that they were not, would not be, and had never been, subversive. Some of these oaths, like Oklahoma's, required individuals to swear that they would not advocate "a change in the form of government" not just by force or violence, but also by any "unlawful means." By 1967, thirty-two states required loyalty or test oaths, with an additional five requiring them of public school teachers and university professors. All told, 65 to 75 percent of the nation's state and local employees worked in states requiring such oaths.[20]

Though 9/11 has not yet provoked the states to replicate or go beyond the federal government's Patriot Act, there are stirrings among some state legislators to do just that. In the spring of 2003, for example, an Oregon state senator sponsored a bill defining a terrorist act as "any act that is intended, by at least one of its participants, to disrupt:

(a)  The free and orderly assembly of the inhabitants of the State of Oregon;

(b)  Commerce or the transportation systems of the State of Oregon; or

(c)  The educational or government institutions of the State of Oregon or its inhabitants.

The proposed law prescribed automatic prison sentences of twenty-five years, without possibility of parole, to life.[21] Like Section 802 of the federal Patriot Act, which defines "domestic terrorism" as "acts dangerous to human life that are a violation of the criminal laws" and that "appear to be intended . . . to influence the policy of a government by intimidation or coercion," the Oregon bill defined terrorism not as premeditated, politically inspired violence against civilians, but as peaceful protests that could result in blockage of traffic—and thus of ambulances and emergency vehicles.[22]

Beyond replicating each other, each level of government leverages its more particular powers against dissenters. At the height of the McCarthy years, states like Ohio denied unemployment compensation to those advocating the violent overthrow of the government and required applicants for benefits to file affidavits regarding their beliefs on such matters. California denied honorably discharged veterans who refused to take a loyalty oath property-tax exemptions granted to all other veterans, while the City of Los Angeles denied constitutionally mandated property-tax exemptions to churches refusing to take the oath.[23] In 1969, a government commission found that local police departments used their power not as a neutral force for law and order but as a way to channel conservative political imperatives. Police offers saw "students, other anti-war protestors and blacks as a danger to our political system" and "themselves as the political force by which radicalism, student demonstrations and black power [could] be blocked."[24] More recently, the American Civil Liberties Union in Colorado exposed the Denver police department's maintenance of computer files on 3,200 individuals and 208 organizations, defined by the police as "criminal extremist groups." This database, developed in 1999, included local members of the American Friends Services Committee, Amnesty International, groups organizing for indigenous rights in Chiapas, Catholic nuns, and an eighty-two-year-old great grandmother, all of whom the police believed, according to a *Los Angeles Times* report, "bore watching."[25]

State and local governments can also turn their licensing procedures into instruments of political intimidation. During the Cold War, Texas required pharmacists to take an oath that they did "not believe in" the overthrow of the American government through "illegal or unconstitutional methods." In Washington, D.C., insurance sales representatives were required to answer questions about their membership in the Communist Party and any of the other 197 political organizations proscribed by the attorney general's list. They also had to disclose whether they had refused, for constitutional reasons, to answer questions put to them by a court or other government tribunal. Politically driven licensing procedures often provided occasions of surreal comedy, with local officials costuming themselves as soldiers in a great pageant of national security. Indiana's Athletic Commission, for instance, insisted that professional wrestlers and boxers take loyalty oaths, while New York denied anyone refusing to take an oath permits to fish in the city's reservoirs. Most men and women could forego the right to fish, but what were leftist lawyers in the five states where they were required to take such oaths, or in the nearly twenty states where they were asked questions about their loyalty, to do? Questions could range from "Do you belong to or have you attending the meetings of any group which advocates any theory or 'Ism' which would prevent you from taking the oath wholeheartedly?" to whether applicants thought Communists should be eligible to practice law, to "Did you vote for Henry Wallace in 1948?"[26]

Whether state and local repression are duplicates or substitutes for federal repression, their federalist character makes political fear a denser, more socially repressive enterprise. Struggles in this country over civil rights, labor unions, and social progress have always had a local dimension, and state and local coercion has figured prominently in their suppression. In Houston, real estate magnates used repressive anticommunism to stop anti-zoning legislation; in California, conservative politicians used it to go after sex education in the schools. Throughout the South and the Midwest, government officials and economic elites used anticommunism to fight civil rights. The Alabama Citizens Council declared, "The attempt to abolish segregation in the South is fostered and directed by the Communist Party," and several southern states put this theory into practice. Wielding their power in the name of national security, they outlawed the NAACP, forced it and other civil rights organizations to hand over their membership lists to state investigating committees, and indicted civil rights leaders for sedition.[27] (In the case of the Denver database mentioned earlier, local police also monitored the activities of a local group working against police brutality in the city.)[28] Federalism thus allows local and state elites to customize repressive fear, to use it on behalf of their own peculiar concerns.

Federalism can also make efforts to roll back or resist politically repressive fear more difficult. Not only does federalism force the resisters to fight their battles on multiple fronts, but it also enhances the obscurity and isolation of small towns and specific states. By distributing institutions of state coercion to forgotten nooks and crannies around the country, by circling them with a protective cordon against federal intrusion, federalism shields local and state elites from national publicity and oversight. We often remember the spotlight the national media put on the violent confrontations in Birmingham between civil rights demonstrators and Sheriff Bull Connor's fire hoses and police dogs. But for every Birmingham, there is an obscure hamlet, overlooked state legislative subcommittee, or oblique local ordinance, which garners no publicity, receives no attention. This same criticism could be applied to the federal government: How many reports from a congressional committee can one journalist read? How many administrative regulations can one activist keep track of? The key difference is that centralized government offers a more geographically concentrated, politically coherent target for resistance and opposition: federalism scatters these targets to the wind.

### THE RULE OF LAW

By the rule of law, I refer only to those procedures that limit and regulate the exercise of government power.[29] Political fear, many claim, is aroused by arbitrary, unpredictable government power, subject to no legal constraint. When rulers are free to do as they will, the ruled cannot possibly know which of their actions will or will not incur government sanctions. Such uncertainty, the argument goes, creates political fear in its purest form. Uncertain subjects are not, and cannot be, free because they are perpetually insecure about their lives and liberties.[30] But when rulers are constrained by the rule of law, the argument continues, subjects know the perimeter of legitimate action. They see bright "no trespass" signs and confine themselves to the interior. By generating secure expectations in the population, the rule of law substantially minimizes the fear aroused by unpredictable exercises of power. "Knowing what things [the law] penalizes and knowing that these are within their power to do or not to do," explains John Rawls, "citizens can draw up their plans accordingly. One who com-

plies with the announced rules need never fear an infringement of his liberty."[31] Because the rule of law requires the threat of punishment, it cannot
eliminate all fear. But when the fear of punishment is firmly attached to a
finite set of infractions, its objects are limited, its emotive qualities less intense and paralyzing. By upholding the rule of law, moreover, this fear of
punishment minimizes the immobilizing dread born of lawlessness or arbitrary power.[32] A rule-bound polity may create injustice and unfairness—
imposing uniform duties across the population, as did Jim Crow's rules of
racial segregation, regardless of their deleterious impact upon specific
groups or individuals—but it cannot generate a fear-ridden society.

Taken on its own terms, this account makes some sense. As I will argue,
the McCarthy era was limited by the rule of law, and one finds in the memoirs of and about the time little of the trembling paralysis theorists of the
rule of law seek to avoid. Political options during these years may have
been constricted, but men and women were not uncertain about the limits
of legitimate conduct. The problem with this account is that predictability
can also obtain in societies where no one would doubt that fear governs. By
the time of the Soviet purges, writes Anne Applebaum, it was not easy "to
predict with any certainty" who would be arrested under Stalin, but "it became possible to guess who was *likely* to be arrested." This hardly made
Stalin's persecutions just or reasonable, but it did make them somewhat
foreseeable. Foreigners, for example, were a suspect category in the Soviet
Union, so "most Soviet citizens . . . worked out the pattern, and wanted no
foreign contacts at all." Telling or listening to jokes about Stalin—not to
mention speaking against him—was also suspect, so men and women
learned to stay away from such talk. Though this litany of crimes was remote from any reasonable definition of justice, it was finite.[33] And though
it was arbitrary in the sense that men and women could be punished for
acts that would never be considered crimes under any substantive definition of the rule of law, it was not arbitrary in the sense held to matter most:
it was not irregular.

Repressive regimes may conform to routines, theorists of the rule of law
will respond, but how can one square the rule of law with their titanic violence
and the countries of walking dead they create? The rule of law is supposed not
only to regulate, but also to limit, state power. How can one reconcile its strin-
gent demands with the medieval tortures of a Hitler or Stalin? Here we come
back to the instructive case of McCarthyism. During those years, two hundred
men and women, at most, spent time in jail or a detention center for what we
might call political crimes, usually for no more than one or two years, and the

number of politically driven indictments and convictions lies somewhere in the hundreds.[34] Simply put, the state's violence during the McCarthy era was virtually nil, its levied punishments minimal. And yet repressive fear was rampant.

Where then do the theorists of the rule of law go wrong? In their assumption that the "principal object" of political fear is to frighten men and women "into impotence."[35] No regime, no matter how malignant, can afford to create universal impotence among its subjects. Though some rulers might harbor such fantasies, they still wish to see their subjects bow and scrape before them. They still depend upon a secret police, which must effectively fulfill their duties, possess the most up-to-date instruments of rule, and work with collaborators throughout society. The economy must be maintained, if for no other reason than to support the military against the threat of an invading army. People must be clothed and fed, and social order preserved. Saddam Hussein, explained one army officer after his fall, "could do many things to the people, but while he could kill them, he could not afford to starve them. So yes, he made sure the Ministry of Trade organized things correctly. . . . It helped the regime maintain its legitimacy."[36] Tyrants don't always succeed in this; indeed, some of them can pursue the most harebrained schemes to modernize their economies and societies. But that hardly means that they seek to create an impotent society. What they seek is a politically repressed society, in which men and women perform only those tasks acceptable to the regime or not prohibited by it, and avoid all others.

If we understand the consequence of political fear as suppression rather than impotence, we can see how the wielders of fear can accommodate the rule of law and even benefit from it. If nothing else, the rule of law offers a patina of legitimacy to otherwise repressive acts of power. As Applebaum reports of Stalin's Russia, "Undoubtedly, the conviction that they were acting within the law was part of what motivated those working within the security services, as well as the guards and administrators who later controlled the prisoners' lives in the camps."[37] But again, McCarthyism offers the more instructive example—of how not only the illusion but also the reality of legalism can support repressive fear. Though officials sometimes violated the rule of law, what is most impressive about McCarthyism is just how often they conformed to it. With time, legislators refined the target of their statutes, gradually narrowing the range of actions deemed criminal. Pressed by liberal-minded politicians and writers, they passed successive pieces of legislation that tightened the circle of politically suspect activity and widened the sphere of legitimate activity. Over time, more procedural guarantees were provided to alleged subversives, as well as more elaborate forms of judicial appeal. Courts, moreover, proved increasingly willing to strike down legislation or government acts on procedural grounds, claiming that officials were not acting in accordance with established rules and that individual rights were being threatened. And yet fear flourished.

If we compare the three major pieces of federal antisubversion legislation of the time—the Smith Act, the Internal Security Act, and the Communist Control Act—we see how the rule of law simultaneously inspired a gradual narrowing of the definition of criminal activity and the growth of fear. The Smith Act prohibited advocating or teaching "the duty, necessity, desirability, or propriety of overthrowing or destroying the government of the United States . . . by force or violence" and printing, publishing, selling, or distributing written materials to that effect. So did it criminalize organizing and attempting to organize a group—or being a member of or affiliating with a group—that performed any of these acts, as well as conspiring to advocate, write, or organize groups that advocated, wrote, etc.[38] Yet even this legislation, arguably the broadest and vaguest of the era, put serious constraints on what the government could do. Using it to prosecute the leadership of the Communist Party, Hoover and the FBI had to work a full four years and were forced to amass mountains of evidence—nearly two thousand pages of party documents and testimony—before the Justice Department would even use the Smith Act to launch criminal charges against the party. The first Smith Act trial lasted ten months, one of the longest in American history, offering defendants ample time to rebut the evidence presented against them. Once these leaders were tried and convicted, they used their rights of appeal, all the way up to the Supreme Court. Once the court ruled against them, the government was able to prosecute only 129 of the party's lower-level leaders and members, of whom 96 were convicted. And yet the fear these trials and prosecutions aroused in party members and fellow travelers—coupled with the financial and emotional burden the trials imposed on party leaders—helped to drain its well of support.[39]

The 1950 Internal Security Act mandated that "any Communist-action organization, Communist-front organization, or Communist-infiltrated organization"—the act specified in great detail what each of these terms meant—register with the attorney general. It also created the Subversive Activities Control Board, which, at the request of the attorney general or private individuals, could designate specific persons or groups to be "Communist-action," "Communist-front," or "Communist-infiltrated." The bill was debated extensively in Congress, received a full public hearing, and was vetoed by President

Truman, whose veto was overridden by Congress. Even with all these procedural guarantees, the Internal Security Act was able to tar 197 left-wing groups as Communist and Communist-front organizations, the stigma of which was enough to persuade many individuals to stay away from them.[40]

The Communist Control Act, according to its liberal authors and sponsors, was designed to tighten the noose around the Communist Party and to loosen it around the rest of the progressive Left. It was explicitly aimed at what many liberals, chief among them Hubert Humphrey, thought was the scatter-shot approach of the Internal Security Act. Max Kampelman, one of Humphrey's top advisors, claimed that the bill's purpose was "to protect innocent people from being attacked ruthlessly and recklessly." The Communist Control Act thus made membership in the Communist Party a specifiable crime, which meant that members and suspected members would receive the full range of procedural protections guaranteed to criminal suspects, and identified fourteen acts as evidence of possible membership. Though Humphrey would later admit that the law was "not of one of things I'm proudest of" and Kampelman would acknowledge that it did little to protect individual liberties, most liberals supported it as a significant advance over its predecessors, prompting Michael Harrington to dismiss it as "an abject capitulation by liberalism to illiberalism." The federal government seldom used the bill, though states and localities did invoke it to keep party members off election ballots and to deny unemployment claims to employees.[41]

Equally impressive about each piece of legislation was how the government ensured that individuals and groups targeted by it enjoyed the right of appeal. The initial Smith Act trial, as we have seen, was quite lengthy and thorough, and its convictions were appealed all the way to the Supreme Court. (Interestingly, the two dissenters in that case, Justices Hugo Black and William Douglas, argued against the majority not on the grounds of the rule of law, but on the basis of the First Amendment, suggesting that a robust conception of free speech offers a better defense against repressive legislation than do procedural definitions of the rule of law.) Its successor trials lasted anywhere from three to six months, and were also appealed. In 1957, the Supreme Court finally began overturning some of these lower-level convictions as unconstitutional, even though the individual cases were not markedly different from that decided in the original one. But by then, the damage had been done.[42]

Under the Internal Security Act, the Subversive Activities Control Board was careful not to tar all liberals or progressives as Communist. It established and published detailed internal regulations—some eight to twelve criteria—to guide and constrain its classification powers. The board required the attorney general and the Communist Party to submit almost 15,000 pages of testimony and 507 documents before rendering its decision to register the party. Any individual or group claiming to have been improperly classified by the board had rights of judicial appeal similar to those of suspected criminals, of which the Communist Party made extensive use. The appellate courts struck down two of the board's individual findings about the party because the board lacked sufficient evidence. The Supreme Court remanded the case back to the lower courts on the grounds that the party had not been given adequate opportunity to rebut the testimony of individual witnesses. But when the case finally came back to the Supreme Court—in 1961, after multiple appeals and procedural reversals—the court affirmed the act's registration provision, and the board's decision to register the Communist Party, as constitutional.[43]

The federal and state governments provided equally elaborate checks for their loyalty and security employment programs, resulting in equally long processes of appeal. They also guaranteed individuals a fairly wide range of rights similar to, though not as robust as, those granted to suspected criminals.[44] Likewise did Congress provide procedural protections to committee witnesses. Even HUAC was compelled to establish, among other provisions, that it could initiate investigations only with the approval of a majority of committee members (though "preliminary inquiries" could be conducted by committee staff, if the chair approved). Witnesses had the right to counsel and were "invited" to consult with the committee's counsel or investigators "at any time." Individuals identified as subversives had to be notified by the committee in writing that they had been named—where, when, and by whom. They also had the right to request an appearance before the committee to clear their names, and the committee was required to provide them with a written copy of its procedures.[45]

In each of these cases, government officials and their supporters sought to make sure that innocent persons were not punished, that even the guilty would have the rights of appeal—without stopping to think much about how they defined guilt (communism) and innocence (not just noncommunism but anticommunism) in the first place. They devoted extensive resources to gathering information in order to pass reasonable legislation, issue fair indictments, launch legitimate prosecutions, and reach truthful verdicts. To the extent that they were able, they publicized their decision-making procedures and non-security-sensitive information, making for some level of government transparency. Many cases, even those not of a criminal nature, consumed nearly ten years of the courts' energy. At many points, the courts overturned government and lower court decisions, though usually on procedural grounds and rarely addressing the broader questions of free speech raised by these cases. And yet repression during the McCarthy era flourished, as did political fear. Not the paralyzing fear imagined by theorists of the rule of law, but the repressive fear that makes men and women careful about what they say and do, that makes them draw back from dissident statements and insurgent movements.[46]

Analysts of McCarthyism sometimes claim that repression succeeded because the rule of law failed, while others claim that repression failed because the rule of law succeeded.[47] What neither camp seems willing to entertain is the possibility that repression succeeded, and the rule of law triumphed. Sometimes the first happened in spite of the second, other times—as in the case of the liberal sponsorship of the Communist Control Act, or in the years of appeals that consumed the time, energy, and treasury of the Communist Party—because of it.[48] Ironically, it was one of the Supreme Court's more conservative justices, Felix Frankfurter, who fully understood this relationship. Though he concurred with the majority in the court's main Smith Act case, Frankfurter reminded his colleagues and the nation that "constitutionality does not exact a sense of proportion or the sanity of humor or an absence of fear." True, the federal government and the court had made sure to apply the Smith Act only to the Communist Party. But there was no getting around the fact that "suppressing advocates of overthrow inevitably will also silence critics who do not advocate overthrow but fear that their criticism may be so construed. No matter how clear we may be that the defendants now before us are preparing to overthrow the Government at the propitious moment, it is self-delusion to think that we can punish them for their advocacy without adding to the risks run by loyal citizens who honestly believe in some of the reforms these defendants advance."[49] In the years that followed the *Dennis* decision, and perhaps in our time as well, many reform-minded men and women reacted just as Frankfurter predicted they would, withdrawing from the political fray and from insurgent movements. The rule of law proved too flimsy a buffer against the repressive power hanging over them. Sometimes, it was the repressive power hanging over them.

## Pluralist Society

In September 1954, the Fund for the Republic commissioned a team of researchers and writers, including a young Michael Harrington, to investigate blacklisting in the radio, television, and movie industries. Like a hiker in the woods who picks up a rock and finds a universe underneath, the team uncovered a world of repression in the smallest of places. Perhaps the smallest was *Counterattack*, a four-page weekly newsletter identifying Communists throughout the United States, a source that television and radio networks used to make decisions about hiring and firing. The editors of *Counterattack* had once worked for the FBI but had left after deciding that "the efforts of our government to combat Communist activities have failed to eliminate the effectiveness of this 5th column." Convinced they could do more outside the government, they formed a nonprofit consulting practice, John Quincy Adams Associates, to expose the party and its allies. When the enterprise failed, they established a for-profit company, with private funding from wealthy anticommunists. The firm took off. Its most successful publication was a special report, *Red Channels*, which cited 151 men and women associated with "Communist causes" working in television and radio. Virtually all of these individuals were blacklisted. So frequently was *Red Channels* consulted by network executives, corporate sponsors, and advertising agencies that it was called "the Bible of Madison Avenue."[50]

What connected this rogue outfit of FBI dropouts to New York's striped shirts? A Syracuse grocer by the name of Laurence Johnson. Owner of an upstate supermarket chain, Johnson was a leader in civic affairs and a fervent anticommunist. Whenever specific companies sponsored a radio or television program involving someone cited in *Red Channels*, Johnson threatened to post notices above those companies' products in his stores, informing customers that these companies funded "subversives." He conscripted fellow supermarket owners to do the same, mobilized customers to send letters of complaint, and made personal visits to industry executives. According to the Fund for the Republic, Johnson "not only lends credence to the 'economic' argument for blacklisting; generally speaking, he is the argument." So powerful was the combined force of *Red Channels* and Johnson that one talent agent in the radio industry claimed, "I never hear about the FBI or the Attorney General—all I ever hear about is *Red Channels* and this Johnson of Syracuse and the other characters who have made a business out of this thing."[51]

Repressive fear in America is often like that: the state hovers in the background, civil society looms large. Though its advocates disagree about its definition, civil society generally refers to those social institutions and organizations not explicitly part of the government. These can range from the family and neighborhood groups to the church and the Rotary Club to political parties and labor unions to corporations and the workplace.[52] Most, if not all, of civil society has some connection to the state, but a significant portion of its activity usually transpires outside of government. In theory, that is what makes civil society a source of freedom. Because it lies outside the government, men and women can carry on their activities there without fear of government coercion. To the extent that this activity is political, civil society is supposed to offer opportunities for mobilization through moral suasion, not force. To the extent that the activity is not political, civil society offers a balance to the oppressive demands of politics. If we are involved in churches, synagogues, and mosques, if we spend four nights out of the week at home with our families and the other three nights bowling in leagues, politics cannot claim the whole of our lives. Though Madison never spoke of civil society, it fulfills his dictum that diversity is a source of freedom. "By comprehending in the society so many separate descriptions of citizens," pluralism can "render an unjust combination of a majority of the whole very improbable."[53]

That is the theory. The practice is altogether different. Civil society, even in the most liberal polities, is often either a supplement to state repression or a repressive agent in its own right.[54] Particularly in liberal democracies, where state power is limited, elites have every incentive to use civil society to promote fear. Though this is hardly a hard-and-fast rule, we may surmise that the more liberal a government becomes, the more attractive an instrument of fear civil society will seem. Consider the following statistics. In the Red Scare of 1919–20, the American government put some 10,000 men and women into jails and detention centers and deported about 600.[55] During the McCarthy years, by contrast, liberal limitations upon the state ensured that no more than 200 people spent time behind bars, and only a very few were deported. Yet McCarthyism lasted longer, affected more individuals, inflicted more permanent damage, and was in the long run, a greater influence on American politics. Why? Many factors were at work—not least of which the Cold War—but one of them was the greater involvement of civil society, particularly the workplace, during McCarthyism: though the government directly penalized only a small number of individuals, anywhere from one to two of every five American workers was subject to a loyalty investigation at work.[56]

There is little mystery as to why civil society can serve as a substitute or supplement to state repression. Civil society is not, on the whole, subject to restrictions like the Bill of Rights. So what the state is forbidden to do, private actors in civil society may execute instead. "If there is any fixed star in our constitutional constellation," Justice Jackson famously declared, "it is that no official, high or petty, can prescribe what shall be orthodox in politics, nationalism, religion, or other matters of opinion or force citizens to confess by word or act their faith therein."[57] But what star in our constitutional constellation forbids newspapers like the *New York Times*, which refused during the McCarthy years to hire members of the Communist Party, from prescribing such orthodoxy as a condition of employment? What in the Constitution would stop a publisher from telling poet Langston Hughes that it would not issue his *Famous Negro Music Makers* unless he removed any discussion of Communist singer Paul Robeson? Or stop Little, Brown from refusing to publish best-selling Communist author Howard Fast?[58] The Sixth Amendment guarantees "in all criminal prosecutions" that the accused shall "have the assistance of counsel for his defence." But what in the Constitution would prevent attorney Abe Fortas, who would later serve on the Supreme Court, from refusing to represent a party member during the McCarthy years because, in his words, "We have decided that we don't think we can ever afford to represent anybody that has ever been a Communist"?[59] The Fifth Amendment stipulates that the government cannot compel an individual to incriminate herself, but it does not forbid private employers from firing anyone invoking its protections before congressional committees.[60] To the extent that our Constitution works against an intrusive state, how can it even authorize the government to regulate these private decisions of civil society? What the liberal state granteth, liberal civil society taketh away.

Our current moment has seen a similar, though slightly modified, relationship between the state and civil society. Because immigrants are not entitled to many of the constitutional rights possessed by citizens, the U.S. government has been able to use coercive penalties, like indefinite detentions and deportations, against Arab and Muslim residents that it could not use against American citizens. (Even here, though, the Bush administration has pushed the envelope, deeming some American-born citizens to be enemy combatants lying outside the protection of the Constitution.) While these state measures have received much criticism,[61] scholars and journalists have paid less attention to the repressive weapons of civil society. Vigilante attacks against Muslims and Arabs have declined considerably since the first wave of violence following 9/11, but watchdog groups report a lingering, and consistent, bias against both groups in the workplace. Though usually treated as cases of racial or ethnic discrimination, these instances have a significant chilling effect upon political speech and association, discouraging dissenters within Arab and Muslim communities from saying or doing anything politically suspect that might attract unwanted attention or sanction. According to M. Siddique Sheikh, chair of the Pakistan American Business Association, who has lived in the United States for thirty-two years, workplace discrimination "gives me a very insecure feeling. I feel like I want to hide behind the closet." Other Arab and Muslim citizens and residents claim that they do not even want to come forward to file complaints about discrimination, for fear that speaking up might also earn them unwanted government attention, a fear confirmed by several cases in which filing such complaints has provoked visits from the FBI or other government agencies.[62]

As was true during the Cold War, civil society today serves both as a substitute for the state, exercising repressive instruments prohibited to the government or adding to the penalties it inflicts, and as a supplement to the state, helping government officials do that which they cannot do alone. The media provides the most instructive examples of the former category. Constrained by the First Amendment, the Bush administration has not been able to issue prior restraints or to threaten the media with punitive sanctions like prison or fines for negative coverage. But nothing in the First Amendment has stopped publishers, producers, and editors, as we saw in the last chapter, from censoring themselves. Nor does the First Amendment stop them from threatening sanctions against subordinates who stray from politically correct story lines. Network heads have dressed down high-profile network reporters—like CNN's Christiane Amanpour and NBC's Ashleigh Banfield and Peter Arnett—for making critical comments about either the war in Iraq or their own network's coverage of the war. Though Amanpour was called in only for a "private meeting" with the head of CNN News, Arnett was fired and Banfield was demoted.[63] But underneath these more visible cases of media self-censorship and intimidation are the myriad little stories of low-level staffers, working for local papers or in the backrooms of newspapers and networks. According to one veteran producer at Fox News, the network newsroom "is under the constant control and vigilance of management," and the "pressure to toe a management line . . . ranges from subtle to direct." Among vulnerable "staffers, many of whom are too young to have come up through the ranks of objective journalism, and all of whom are non-union, with no protections regarding what they can be made to do, there is undue motivation to please the big boss."[64] One little-noticed report from late 2001 may shed some light on these coercive internal mechanisms. On October 31 of that year, Ray Glenn, chief copy editor of the *Panama City News Herald* in Florida, issued the following memo to newspaper staffers:

Per Hal's [executive editor Hal Foster] order, DO NOT USE photos on Page 1A showing civilian casualties. Our sister paper in Fort Walton Beach has done so and received hundreds and hundreds of threatening e-mails and the like. Also per Hal's order, DO NOT USE wire stories which lead with civilian casualties from the U.S. war on Afghanistan. They should be mentioned further down in the story. If the story needs rewriting to play down the civilian casualties, DO IT. The only exception is if the U.S. hits an orphanage, school or similar facility and kills scores or hundreds of children.

And then, as if the editor had not made his instructions sufficiently clear, he concluded the memo with the following threat: "Failure to follow any of these or other standing rules could put your job in jeopardy."[65]

In the case of civil society working with the state, we have seen everything from the much publicized Terrorism Information and Prevention System (TIPS) to the collusion between the federal government and corporations monitoring ordinary citizens. According to several reports, the federal government is using TIPS to recruit as many as one in every twenty-four Americans to report on the activities of their fellow citizens, and has retained the Fox-owned *America's Most Wanted* television series to take incoming calls from these informants.[66] Corporations like OfficeMax have agreed to "report suspicious or questionable requests for printing or document reproduction to law enforcement authorities."[67] And though theorists of the state often claim that governments seek to monopolize the means of coercion, the federal government has actively subcontracted those means to the private sector. In late November 2002, the *Wall Street Journal* reported on "the largest intelligence-sharing experiment" the FBI "has ever undertaken with the private sector," in which bureau officials distributed FBI watch lists to banks, travel companies, car rental corporations, and casinos throughout the country. Even though the FBI has admitted that these lists contain the names of innocent people, the lists have been so widely circulated that, according to one bureau chief in the FBI's counterterrorism division, "We have now lost control of that list."[68]

Ironically, the very features of civil society that advocates presume to be its chief virtues—its pluralism, autonomy, and intimacy—often make it conducive to repressive fear. Like the federalist division of power, the pluralism and diversity of civil society create more opportunities for men and women to participate in repression. One report from a New York public relations officer, whose specialty during the McCarthy era was to "clear" blacklisted employees of any suspicion so that they could work in television or radio, captures the connection between a diverse civil society and political repression. I quote it in full, for its very length suggests just how many players, institutions, and interests can be involved in repression. Reading like a parody of Montesquieu, *The Federalist Papers*, and Tocqueville, it invokes checks and balances, procedural justice, and interest group pluralism. It shows that diversity makes repression not less toxic, but more baroque, requiring occasion after occasion of abject display and political submission.

If a man is clean and finds his way to me the first thing I do is examine his record. I look particularly to see if it includes charges that he is a member of the Communist Party. I want to find out if he is "clearable." Once I am convinced that he is not a Communist, or if he has been a Communist, has had a change of heart, I ask him whether he has talked to the FBI. If he hasn't, I tell him the first thing he must do is go to the FBI and tell them everything he knows. I tell him to say to them, "I am a patriotic citizen and I want you to ask me any questions you have in mind."

Then I find out where he is being blacklisted—where it is he can't get work, who in the industry is keeping him from working, and who outside the industry has made him controversial. If, for instance, I find it is the American Legion, I call one of the top Legion officials and tell him this man has come to me for help and says he is innocent. The official may say to me, "Why this guy has 47 listings and I know people who say they don't believe him." But I say, "I'm going to have him make a statement." Then, when the Legion guy gets the statement and has read it, I call and ask him for a note saying he is satisfied by the statement. He will usually say, "I won't put anything in writing but if anyone is interested have him call me."

Somewhere along the line I may find George Sokolsky [a conservative journalist whose columns regularly charged or cleared individuals of being Communists] is involved. I go to him and tell him that the Legion official thinks this boy is all right. If I can convince Sokolsky then I go to Victor Reisel, Fred Woltman [also journalists] or whomever else is involved. When I've gotten four "affidavits" from key people like these, I go to Jack Wren at BBD&O [New York advertising agency Batten, Barton, Durstine and Osborn] and to the "security officer" at CBS.

I wait a few days, then I telephone Wren. He may say to me, "You're crazy. I know 15 things this guy hasn't explained." So I send for the guy.

He comes in here and he moans and wails and beats his head against the wall. "I have searched my memory," he will say. "I have questioned my wife and my agent. There's not a thing they can remember."

I call Wren back and he says, "When your boy is ready to come clean I'll talk to him." In that case we've reached a dead end. My boy has been cleared but he can't get a job. I know cases where victims have sat around eight to ten months after "clearance" before they got work. . . .

Last of all . . . there is the possibility that Wren will pick up the phone and call a casting director or producer and say, "Why don't you give Bill a part in the show?" . . .

A guy who is in trouble, even if he has a good case for himself, will stay dead unless he finds someone like me who can lead him through the jungle of people who have to be satisfied. He has to persuade these people one by one. Usually he finds his way to a lawyer and that comes a cropper, or he finds a public-relations man or press agent who doesn't have the confidence of the "clearance men," and he's only wasting his time.[69]

And this, we should recall, is how the "innocent" are treated.

Diversity in civil society also makes for factional divisions among the very forces that might challenge repression. In *Federalist* 10, Madison argued that social factions should be encouraged as an antidote to government tyranny: the more factions, he argued, the less able they would be to organize the government on their tyrannical behalf.[70] Two centuries later, J. Edgar Hoover brilliantly exploited Madison's prescription in order to foster government repression. During the 1960s, the FBI stoked divisions among civil rights organizations, the student Left, and other progressive organizations. It did not create these divisions—they were already there—but it exacerbated them. In a secret 1967 memo sent to twenty-two field offices throughout the country, the FBI issued the following instructions: "Efforts of the various groups [in the black liberation movement] to consolidate their forces or to recruit new or youthful adherents must be frustrated. No opportunity should be missed to exploit through counterintelligence techniques the organizational and political conflicts of the leadership of the groups and where possible an effort should be made to capitalize upon existing conflicts between competing black nationalist organizations." A year letter, the FBI sent out another memo, instructing its field offices to "prevent the coalition of militant black nationalist groups. In unity there is strength; a truism that is no less valid for its triteness. An effective coalition of black nationalist groups might be the first step toward a real 'Mau Mau' in America, the beginning of a true black revolution." The FBI disrupted efforts by the Black Panthers to form multi-cultural coalitions among Puerto Rican organizations, white urban gangs, and the student movement, encouraging the militant separatism for which the Panthers and other practitioners of identity politics would later be criticized. The FBI also tried to use the women's movement, which it saw as a "divisive and factionalizing factor," as a way "to weaken the revolutionary movement" and the New Left.[71]

In the same way that the desire of officeholders like Truman to maintain the autonomy of their branch of government can lead them to cooperate rather than resist repression, so does a similar desire among elites in civil society inspire a willingness to cooperate with repressive forces. During the Cold War, leaders of civil society often initiated or agreed to implement repressive programs in their own institutions, if for no other reason than to keep the government and private blacklisters at bay. The president of Barnard College announced, "If the colleges take the responsibility to do their own house cleaning, Congress would not feel it has to investigate." One HUAC investigator told the press that he intended to explicitly prey upon this concern when he spoke with Hollywood's studio heads. "I plan to hold a number of meetings with industry heads, and the full resources of the House committee and our investigative staff are at the disposal of those who want to put their house in order before Congress does it for them." Irving Ferman of the ACLU claimed that he worked with the FBI in order to protect his organization from an investigation by HUAC and the American Legion. Likewise the NAACP, which collected files on its entire membership, purging those deemed to be party members, even its founder W. E. B. DuBois, who worked closely with the Communist Party and ultimately joined it late in life.[72]

What also makes civil society useful for repression and fear is that it is a sphere of intimacy and mutual trust. While individuals look upon politicians and state officials with suspicion, civil society is home to our friends and families, priests and rabbis, neighbors and colleagues. Even in the workplace or economy, civil society is populated by men and women we know well: frontline supervisors who live next door or marry our siblings, small business owners with a common touch, wealthy entrepreneurs who only yesterday worked beside us. When these familiars encourage us to capitulate to fear or when they themselves act repressively, we trust that their advice and actions are not impersonal dictates of state but well meaning words and deeds of people who care about us or are like us. This kind of intimacy supposedly holds a community together in the face of a predatory state. But what these analysts overlook is how these concrete links and connections, discussed in the previous chapter, can transform repressive fear from a state-run enterprise into a more personal affair of the heart.

We have already encountered some of the specific mechanisms that individuals and institutions in civil society use to create fear: workplace sanctions, the orchestration of social consensus, the mobilization of civic groups to boycott stigmatized products, the use of teachers and preachers to counsel individuals to submit to fear, and the power of informers.[73] But two other mechanisms—ostracism and rumor mongering—are worth discussing. Ostracism, we are often told, is the democrat's weapon of choice, for in a democracy, the rejection of the crowd is supposed to be the most difficult burden to bear. According to Emerson:

> Yet is the discontent of the multitude more formidable than that of the senate and the college. It is easy enough for a firm man who knows the world to brook the rage of the cultivated classes. Their rage is decorous and prudent, for they are timid as being very vulnerable themselves. But when to their feminine rage the indignation of the people is added, when the ignorant and the poor are roused, when the unintelligent brute force that lies at the bottom of society is made to growl and mow, it needs the habit of magnanimity and religion to treat it godlike as a trifle of no concernment.[74]

Ostracism, in this view, is the work of small-town majorities, of narrow-minded men and women with nothing better to do than poke their noses in other people's affairs. Their chief goal is to reinforce popular tastes and sensibilities, and their target is the lonely genius defended by John Stuart Mill in On Liberty. In actual fact, ostracism is often the work of organized groups and influential elites in civil society. With the help of organizations like the American Legion or publications like Counterattack, elites form broad coalitions to disseminate information about these individuals and specific instructions to target them. These coalitions prey upon not the craven desire of the democratic individual to belong, but the activist's political need for comrades. Isolating the dissenter, they surround her with a stigma, making it difficult for her to mobilize a movement. In the words of Counterattack:

> The way to treat Communists is to ostracize them. How would you act towards men and women who had been convicted of treason? Would you befriend them, invite them, listen to them? Or would you treat them as outcasts?

Total ostracism . . . that's the only effective way. It's the only way to freeze the Communists out. It's the only DEED that will prove you believe what you say about them. And so it's the most convincing propaganda.[75]

As *Counterattack* indicates, ostracism can be a substitute for penalties of state. But it can also supplement those penalties. In 1949, for example, screenwriter Alvah Bessie, out of work and facing mounting bills (he had refused to testify before HUAC and was blacklisted), approached his longtime friend, actor Lee J. Cobb, for a $500 loan. Cobb, who would go on to immortalize the character of Willy Loman in Arthur Miller's *Death of a Salesman*, had a full studio contract at the time, but he also had a radical past as a party member. Cobb was nervous about helping a friend cited for contempt of Congress and on his way to jail. Bessie begged him for the loan, but Cobb refused. He gently escorted Bessie to the door, telling him, "You're a revolutionary, you know. Go *on* being a revolutionary. Go on being an example to me."[76] Such ostracism supplements the penalties of state and civil society, demonstrating how social snubs and stigmas track the acts of repressive elite power rather than those of democratic majorities.

It was Joseph de Maistre, France's preeminent theorist of counterrevolution, who first explained how rumors could crush a revolution and restore the old regime. A cabal of counterrevolutionaries, he wrote in 1797, dispatches couriers to the provinces, falsely announcing that the king has taken back his throne. Then "rumour takes the news and adds a thousand impressive details." Defenders of the revolution are confused, uncertain whether the news is true. The cabal circulates more disinformation, preying upon the revolutionaries' confusion, their distrust of each other and their leaders. While this would seem thin gruel for anything as grand as a counterrevolution, Maistre believed it was all that was required for the old regime to return. With everyone in the revolution suspicious of everyone else, "prudence inhibits audacity." Knowing that their opponents are saddled with indecision, the counterrevolutionaries swoop into the capital and take back the throne. "Citizens!" Maistre proclaimed. "This is how counter-revolutions are made." "Four or five persons," he prophesied, "will give France a king."[77]

It is highly improbable that J. Edgar Hoover ever read Maistre: he didn't have to. Hoover understood, almost intuitively, how rumors circulated within civil society could immobilize movements of radicalism and reform, particularly if those rumors were specially crafted to appeal to the particular values of different groups. Rumors had to be differently tailored to members of the movement, their parents and families, and the move-

ment's liberal allies. "Careful attention" must be "given," explained a 1967
FBI memo, "to insure the targeted group is disrupted, ridiculed, or discredited through the publicity and not merely publicized." Within the civil
rights movement, the FBI circulated rumors, some of them true, of Martin
Luther King's extramarital affairs. When those rumors failed to turn his
followers against him and King was awarded the Nobel Prize, the bureau
made a tape allegedly proving that King had been involved in "orgiastic
trysts" with prostitutes, decrying "the depths of his sexual perversion and
depravity." It threatened to send the tape to the media unless King committed suicide before he received the prize, and it unsuccessfully attempted to
have Benjamin Bradlee, then Washington bureau chief at *Newsweek*, publish its contents. In Oakland, the bureau supplied a steady stream of rumors to the Bay Area press, alerting the media to the fancy apartments
owned by leaders of the Black Panthers, to their alleged venereal disease
and affairs with teenage girls. The bureau sought to sever the links between black radicals in New York and prominent liberals by circulating accusations of black anti-Semitism and anti-Zionism. Among more radical
groups, especially in the counterculture, rumors of sexual promiscuity had
little force. So the bureau relied on something it called "bad-jacketing," in
which student leaders like Tom Hayden or black militants like Stokely
Carmichael were accused of being government informants. "One method"
to circulate rumors about Carmichael, according to a 1968 memo, "would
be to have a carbon copy of an informant report supposedly written by
CARMICHAEL to the CIA carefully deposited in the automobile of a close
Black Nationalist friend. . . . It is hoped that when the informant report is
read it will help promote distrust between CARMICHAEL and the Black
Community. . . . It is hoped that the informants would spread the rumor in
various large Negro communities across the land." And when all else
failed, the FBI could prey upon the homophobia within these movements
and the nation, circulating accusations that individual leaders were involved in same-sex affairs.[78]

# 8   Upstairs, Downstairs

> IN THE GENERAL COURSE OF HUMAN NA-
> TURE, *A POWER OVER A MAN'S SUBSISTENCE*
> *AMOUNTS TO A POWER OVER HIS WILL.*
>
> —ALEXANDER HAMILTON

In the United States, there is arguably no higher virtue than hard work.[1] At other times, in other places, work has been a biblical curse, the mark of the laboring classes, the dividing line between the bourgeoisie and leisured aristocracy. Here, it is the universal instrument of an achieved identity, the symbol of status earned rather than inherited. It seems strange that we in the United States should so fasten work to personal identity, for a deep, if unacknowledged, current in our culture suggests that the workplace has frequently been inhospitable to the individual. Benjamin Franklin, the original self-made man, discovered the self that made the man not through work, as is commonly thought, but through its refusal. Franklin worked at the Boston printing press of his older brother James. Deeming himself the "master" and Ben "his apprentice," the older brother regularly beat the younger, and according to Ben, "demean'd me too much in some he requir'd of me." So Ben decided to "assert my freedom" and look for work elsewhere. But because James made sure no other employer would hire his brother, Ben decided to flee Boston for New York. Fearing that if he "attempted to go openly, means would be used to prevent me," Ben had a ship captain secretly shepherd him out of the city.[2] Thus did the avatar of hard work go into exile—not from the British crown or the elders of the church, but from his employer and the Boston blacklist—and make his first stab at freedom and selfhood.

Though the labor movement and progressive politicians would eventually eliminate some of the workplace autocracy weighing upon Franklin, later complaints attest to its persistence. Two of our most distinctively American political theorists, John Dewey and Robert Dahl, warned near the beginning and the end of the twentieth century that democracy in the United States would never be realized if it was not extended to the workplace.[3] Even Hollywood, the city of dreams, has depicted the workplace as the stuff of nightmares. In *The Apartment*, Billy Wilder's unsettling comedy of 1960, Jack Lemmon plays C. C. Baxter, a go-getter in a modern corporation willing to do anything to make it. But ambition has its price: Baxter must regularly lend his apartment to married company executives so that they can conduct their illicit evening trysts. An abbreviation of carbon copy, Baxter's first name may be an allusion to the proverbial conformist of midcentury social thought. But C. C.'s Spanish homonym—*Sí! Sí!*—suggests an even deeper betrayal of individual freedom: Baxter is a yes man.[4] Eventually, Baxter falls in love with the woman his boss has been carrying on with in his apartment. In the film's final scenes, Baxter confronts his boss and gets the girl. Saying no to his employer, Baxter becomes a full human being.

Like most American stories, Franklin's *Autobiography* and Hollywood movies all have their happy endings. The real American workplace has not seen as many. Even in our postmodern age, the workplace remains a regime of old-world constraint, in which an almost childlike subservience is routinely expected and disobedience is quelled by fear and coercion. At work, employees enjoy few of the rights—privacy, free speech, due process—we take for granted elsewhere. Their personal movements, down to the most basic bodily functions, are patrolled, as are their words and even thoughts. Though the liberal polity has its failings, it is a political paradise compared to the illiberalism reigning inside factory gates and behind office doors. And when workers attempt to form unions in order to bring some modicum of liberalism to the workplace, employers unleash a battery of weapons—some illegal, others not—that would make even the most disabused critic of unlicensed government blanch. So repressive is the contemporary workplace that Human Rights Watch recently sent a team of researchers, led by an Ivy League professor, there to investigate. What did they find? In the last decade alone, according to federal government statistics, nearly 200,000 men and women were punished for exercising their right to form and participate in a union.[5]

If we are to confront Fear, American Style, it is here, in the workplace, that we must begin and end, for it is in the workplace that men and women in the contemporary United States most consistently encounter personal coercion and repressive fear. Though heavy, the personal toll of workplace fear is not the only cause of concern: its political repercussions are equally, if not more, consequential. American elites have consistently found in the workplace a storehouse of repressive weapons, which they are free to use, by law, for the most naked political purposes. This has been true not just during McCarthyism, but throughout American history. In a little-known exchange from his travels in the United States during the 1830s, Tocqueville asked a distinguished Baltimore physician why so many educated Americans professed their belief in religion when they obviously had "numerous doubts on the subject of dogma." The doctor replied that while the clergy had much power in the United States, they did not wield it through the traditional European mechanisms of state but through the making and breaking of private careers:

> If a minister, known for his piety, should declare that in his opinion a certain man was an unbeliever, the man's career would almost certainly be broken. Another example: A doctor is skilful, but has no faith in the Christian religion. However, thanks to his abilities, he obtains a fine practice. No sooner is he introduced into the house than a zealous Christian, a minister or someone else, comes to see the father of the house and says: look out for this man. He will perhaps cure your children, but he will seduce your daughters, or your wife, he is an unbeliever. There, on the other hand, is Mr. So-and-So. As good a doctor as this man, he is at the same time religious. Believe me, trust the health of your family to him. Such counsel is almost always followed.[6]

W. E. B. DuBois, who fully grasped the racist violence that helped defeat Reconstruction in the second half of the nineteenth century, nevertheless insisted that it was fear in the workplace that ultimately undid black political equality after the Civil War. "The decisive influence was the systematic and overwhelming economic pressure. Negroes who wanted work must not dabble in politics. Negroes who wanted to increase their income must not agitate the Negro problem. Positions of influence were only open to those Negroes who were certified as being "safe and sane," and their careers were closely scrutinized and passed upon. From 1880 onward, in order to earn a living, the American Negro was compelled to give up his political power."[7] Likewise during the Vietnam War, when the FBI worked with employers to quell the political activities of their employees.[8]

Though other employers may not use the workplace for such explicitly political purposes, they still treat the workplace as an island refuge amid the stormy seas of democracy. For employees, that means that the bulk of their waking hours are spent not in a liberal democracy, but in the upstairs downstairs world of old Europe. This unfreedom within the workplace also has political ramifications beyond the workplace. If employees in the private sector are afraid of their employers, they are not likely to blow the whistle on employer malfeasance, and citizens and politicians will be deprived of useful information to advance the public good.[9] If employees in the public sector are intimidated by their superiors, or if their superiors retaliate against them for blowing the whistle—as the recent experience of Coleen Rowley, Joseph Wilson, Valerie Plame, and Richard Clarke suggests—they will be reluctant to voice the expert knowledge that might help avert disastrous courses of action pursued by the government.[10] If employers consistently hamper union efforts to organize new workers, workers' bargaining power will be weakened, resulting in the low wages that can dampen consumer demand.[11] A crippled labor movement also means less political education for and political mobilization of workers, and offers a flimsier counterweight to corporate power and the market. So do weakened unions contribute to the contraction of a thriving two-party system into the tepid democracy that so many observers bemoan today.

There is one last political dimension to the workplace we should bear in mind. Political fear entails work. To arouse fear, someone must do something: threaten punishments, mount propaganda, spread rumors, and so on. These activities are neither spontaneous nor episodic: they require the ongoing labor of elites and collaborators. If political fear is to be sustained over time, men and women must be hired and paid, supervised and promoted. Political fear is thus an economic enterprise, and like any such enterprise, it attracts and keeps its employees with the promise of a job and personal advance. At the height of European imperialism, Disraeli wrote, "The East is a career."[12] So has political fear been a career during McCarthyism, Jim Crow, and the union busting of the last half-century. To grasp political fear, then, we must fully understand work and the workplace.

## Autocracy at Work

Fear in the workplace begins and ends in hierarchy, which is the most notable feature of life on the job. Hierarchy is a necessity of any large-scale organization; in the workplace, decisions about production, marketing, and distribution must be made, and democracy is not always the best or most efficient way to make them. But those who preside over the workplace possess a level of power over their subordinates that goes far beyond the requirements of efficiency, productivity, and profit. Studies consistently show, for example, that "employee involvement" programs, in which workers share decision-making power, can increase a firm's productivity by anywhere from 2 to 5 percent per year and can contribute to higher profits. Despite these productivity gains, employers often resist such programs, in part because they do not wish to lose control over their employees. In a survey of management experts in the late 1970s, each respondent agreed or agreed strongly with the following observation: "In many cases control and power are more important to managers than profits or productivity."[13]

What that commitment to hierarchy means for most employees is a regime of constant, pervasive obedience. Among the adult population, only prisoners and soldiers are expected to obey their superiors more often and more unquestioningly. The experience of American employees is thus not likely to be too different from that described by the owner of a yachting crew placement agency: "The No. 1 goal of every yacht crew is to never say no to an owner."[14] Even the highest heights of today's economy can look like the lowest deck of a fancy yacht. In a little noticed report in the *New York Times*, for example, Enron insiders repeatedly complained about the company's culture of submissiveness. One vice president commented, "If you disagreed with anything, if you spoke what you thought was the truth, you didn't fare too well."[15] A website called the "U.S. Campaign Against Workplace Bullying Headquarters" attracts almost half a million hits per year, 30 percent from self-described "professionals" and another 40 percent from people in management positions.[16]

Employees in the United States consistently complain of having to take orders from supervisors and employers more often than seems reasonable and of having less power at work than they would like. (The word "boss," incidentally, derives from the Dutch *baas*, meaning "master.") In the most comprehensive survey to date of American workers, Richard Freeman and Joel Rogers found that almost two-thirds of those polled wished that they had more say on the job. Insufficient power at work was also the leading indicator of job dissatisfaction among these workers, more highly correlated with job dissatisfaction than were other factors like race, gender, or level of education. (In a separate survey from the early 1990s, job satisfaction among workers was inversely proportional to how much supervision they received, with employees reporting lower levels of satisfaction the more often and more closely they were supervised. Aggregate data suggests a similar correlation: from the 1970s through the 1990s, supervisors and managers occupied an increasingly higher percentage of the American workforce, and workers reported decreasingly lower levels of job satisfaction.) Of the workers who sought more power on the job, 56 percent claimed that it was either "not too likely" or "not likely at all" that they would ever get it, "even if [they] tried." The single greatest obstacle, they claimed, was management's refusal to listen to or accommodate their views. In their assessment of management's "willingness to share power or authority," 55 percent of the workers polled gave their supervisors a grade of C or below.[17]

When we consider the organization of the American workplace, we can see why workers complain about management autocracy. In 1996, economist David Gordon reported that, according to the Bureau of Labor Statistics, roughly 19 percent of the entire workforce worked in nonproduction positions, almost always as managers or supervisors. In an even more illuminating survey, 38.9 percent of the workforce claimed that they "supervise the work of other employees or tell other employees what work to do" and 28 percent claimed they had authority to "discipline a subordinate because of poor work or misconduct." In other words, anywhere from one to two of every five American employees keeps watch over—and can discipline—another employee. What is more, the United States sports the highest percentage of managerial and administrative employees of any advanced industrial economy, three times higher than Japan and Germany. Forty percent of American workers report that supervisors check up on them "more than once a day" or "at least once a day," while 32 percent claim that supervisors check up on them "several times a week" or "about once a week." Like Plato's republic, moreover, the American workplace is obsessed with the question of "Who watches the watchers?" Thus, 23 percent of managers and supervisors claim that they themselves are monitored "more than once a day" or "about once a day" by their supervisors, and an additional 40 percent claim that they are monitored "several times a week" or "about once a week."[18] Workplaces relying upon direct supervision of employees are far more likely to produce managers who abuse those working under them.[19]

When a worker applies for a job, she sells, in theory, only her labor and her time, which is all, in theory, her employer buys. In practice, she sells and he buys much more. Even before they are employed, workers are forced to submit to an intimate inspection and supervision. In *Nickel and Dimed*, her bestselling account of working at three different jobs in the service economy, journalist Barbara Ehrenreich describes the drug and personality tests she is forced to take just to get hired. In the bathroom at a Minneapolis Wal-Mart, an "officious woman in blue scrubs" grabs Ehrenreich's hands, squirts a soapy substance onto her palms, and has Ehrenreich wash them in front of her—all to make sure that Ehrenreich does not slip a drug-dissolving agent into her urine. The personality tests that follow are even more invasive. Some questions test Ehrenreich's willingness to obey: Does she believe that "rules have to be followed to the letter at all times"? Others are about the finer points of class politics: Does she think that "management and employees will always be in conflict because they have totally different sets of goals"? Still others press her toward deeper revelations. Is she prone to self-pity? Does she think people talk about her behind her back? "The real function of these tests," Ehrenreich concludes, "is not to convey information to the employer, but to the potential employee, and the information being conveyed is always: You will have no secrets from us."[20]

Once employed, workers can be told not only when to urinate, but when to hold it in. In their 1998 study *Void Where Prohibited*, Marc Linder and Ingrid Nygaard documented how employers often forbid employees from going to the bathroom. At the time of the book's publication, the federal government required employers to provide toilets to their employees, but employees had no corresponding right to use those toilets. Thus, poultry plants would not allow workers to use the bathroom "more than once a week 'on company time.'" In a survey of female public school teachers, 80 percent said that they had to urinate outside official break times, but were forced to hold it in, drinking as little as possible. Four percent urinated into some kind of pad, while 11 percent had their students follow them into the bathroom and wait outside the stall as they urinated. In 1993, the last year for which the Bureau of Labor Statistics collected such data, one-third of medium to large firms in the United States did not provide paid rest breaks for employees to go to the bathroom, and in 1992, more than 50 percent of small firms did not provide such breaks. And though courts throughout the eighties and nineties regularly upheld employer demands that employees urinate on demand—one supervisor in a 1992 drug testing lawsuit was cited as saying, "If you don't piss in the bottle now, you will be terminated for . . . not following a direct order"—they could not find any statutory basis for upholding an employee's right to urinate when necessary.[21] It was not until April 1998 that the federal government required employers to grant employees what it called "timely access" to the bathroom. Six years later, going to the bathroom can still seem to some workers more of a privilege than a right. In the summer of 2002, for example, the media reported that the "potty police" at a Jim Beam distillery in Kentucky kept computer spreadsheets on employee bathroom use, disciplined workers for going outside official break times, and had female employees keep them abreast of their menstrual cycles. Employees in Tucson, Arizona, deemed the 1998 toilet standard "little more than an ineffective piece of paper," with teachers, pharmacists, and call center employees complaining of denied access to the bathroom.[22]

In regulating the movement of their employees, employers often require physical gestures of obedience meant to signal an almost feudal submissiveness. A corporate cleaning company, for instance, advertises its services as follows: "We clean floors the old-fashioned way—*on our hands and knees.*"[23] The white collar world demands different, but no less abject, displays of its employees. Midlevel professionals can be spirited away to mandatory weekend motivational seminars, where consultants tie ropes between two trees, creating a "spider web." Individual employees lie at one end of the web and wait as fellow employees toss them through the web, praying that they will be caught by someone at the other end. According to one participant in these exercises, "This was the most uncomfortable thing for professional men and women. A lot of us felt uncomfortable, embarrassed, reluctant to play the games. But they kept at it. It was almost like it was designed to break you down. I think it was a way of humiliating us."[24]

Why do employees put up with these regimes? Because the law grants to employers considerable power to hire, fire, and punish employees as they see fit, and employees possess few legally enforceable rights to constrain them. In the private, nonunionized sector of the American economy, the combined effect of these legal stipulations is to render employees vulnerable to the demands of their employers, no matter how bizarre they may seem. Unlike European social democracies, the flinty American welfare state links virtually every element of economic well-being to employment, which only adds to the compulsion an employee already faces in the workplace. For most American men and women, living without work is not a good option. So they accept the servility the workplace requires of them.

Consider an employer's legal power to hire, fire, and punish. Employers in the United States often complain that the government significantly restricts that power. Even if we grant employers the most charitable interpretation of their complaints, we can see how much power they still possess. By law, the most protected employees in the United States are unionized or work in the public sector. These two groups can be legally fired or punished only for "just cause," for some failure to perform a duty necessary to the workplace or because the workplace cannot sustain their employment. While these protections do not guarantee workers the right to a job, they do stipulate that workers can be dismissed or disciplined only for reasons related to the needs of the workplace itself. What is significant about "just-cause" protection, however, is not how robust it is, but how small a percentage of the workforce actually enjoys it. In 2003, the public and unionized sectors of the workforce comprised only 23.7 percent of all jobs in the American economy.[25] Every other worker—76.3 percent—is governed by the doctrine of "employment at will," which states that employers and employees have an equal right to terminate an employment relationship whenever either party wishes. This means, in the classic formulation, that employers have the right to hire, fire, and punish for good reasons, bad reasons, or no reason at all. Only Montana has passed legislation abridging this doctrine, stipulating that employees in the state can be fired only for "reasonable job-related grounds."[26] Outside Montana, the absolute, unconstrained right to hire, fire, and punish is the conceptual bedrock of employment law.[27]

Beyond unionized and public employees, the government protects workers against discrimination on account of race, national origin, religion, gender, disability, or age, and against retaliation for filing antidiscrimination complaints or protesting discriminatory treatment. Employees are also protected against retaliation if they inform the government about their employer's violation of specific federal laws, such as the Clean Air Act. In certain states, statutes protect whistle blowing designed to advance the public policy interests of that state. Though the importance of such legislation cannot be underestimated, it should not be overestimated. It generally applies only to workplaces employing more than fifteen people. Federal and state antiretaliation and whistle-blower statutes vary by state and industry. More important, none of these protections mandate that workers can be dismissed only for just cause: they merely stipulate that workers cannot be disciplined or fired for reasons of race, gender, whistle blowing, and so on. It is perfectly legal, in other words, for an employer to punish or fire an employee for entirely arbitrary reasons, so long as race, gender, or any other similar category is not among them.[28]

When we look at the additional protective legislation individual states have passed, we get an even sharper view of how little the government restricts employers' power. Only in ten states, for example, is it illegal to hire, punish, and fire on the basis of sexual orientation; and only in twenty states, on the basis of marital status. Outside these states, in other words, it is legal for private, nonunion employers to hire, fire, and discipline employees on the basis of sexual orientation and marital status. Twelve states have forbidden employers to discriminate on the basis of their employees' political affiliations or political activities outside the workplace. In thirty-eight states, then, it is legal for private, nonunion employers to hire, fire, and discipline on the basis of political belief. Only in a very few states are employees prohibited from discriminating against employees for their lawful conduct, political or otherwise, off the job. Outside of these states, employees can be fired for carrying on extramarital affairs; participating in group sex at home; having children out of wedlock; smoking off the job; wearing, in the case of off-duty male police officers, an earring; and carrying on relationships and friendships with coworkers or employees of a competitor. The courts have upheld each of these decisions.[29]

As an employee in a private, nonunionized workplace, then, I can be fired, disciplined, or not hired for any of the following reasons, without the cushion of unemployment compensation[30]: not smiling at work, smiling too much; not being friendly to my coworkers, being too friendly; demonstrating insufficient initiative, not being a team player; kowtowing to management, being insubordinate; being a leader, being a follower; braiding my hair in corn rows, wearing it straight; wearing long pants, wearing short pants; sporting an earring, refusing to do so; having a beard, shaving it off; fingernails too long, fingernails too short. (Disney World instructs its employees, "Fingernails should not extend more than one-fourth of an inch beyond the fingertips.")[31] In other words, for good reasons, bad reasons, or no reason at all.

What about the rights protecting employees against their employers? In 1988, the American Civil Liberties Union declared, "The time has come to extend the Bill of Rights to the biggest remaining group of forgotten people—America's workers."[32] Fifteen years later, America's workers are still waiting. If we look at just two rights the Constitution guarantees citizens against the government—freedom of speech and the more nebulous right to privacy—we can see how minimal freedom in the workplace truly is. Because the First Amendment applies only to the government, freedom of speech—whether political or not, whether inside or outside the workplace—is highly limited in the private, nonunion sector. In the words of the American Bar Association, "If a private company prevents an employee from speaking out, it probably won't violate the Constitution."[33] If I attend an antiwar rally, write prochoice letters to my congressional representative or senator, wear an antiwar button to work, or talk to my coworkers at lunch about supporting a particular presidential candidate, I can be legally fired or disciplined. Often, speech punished by employers is merely unauthorized. Invoking a novel conception of workplace crime—"time theft" (time spent by an employee doing something on the job other than the job itself)—employers limit the frequency and content of employee speech on the job. As one of Ehrenreich's supervisors explained, if an employee does "anything at all" besides work—including talking—it's "time theft." Th[e m]anagers prowl the aisles, bathrooms, and hallways of the workplace, l[ook]ing for "gossip"— from idle chatter about weekend plans to speaking in [a for]eign language to talking against the boss.[34]

What about the right to privacy on the job? It doesn['t exis]t. Like the First Amendment, the privacy provisions of the Constitutio[n ap]ply only to the government, so private, nonunion employers are free to [viola]te them. It all begins with the body. Workers in the private sector are [rout]inely subject to drug tests, usually performed by urinalysis. Adult men a[nd w]omen can be required to urinate into a cup, often in the immediate pre[senc]e of supervisors or company personnel, and to hand it over to their emp[loyers]. Employers can also test an unwitting employee for drugs by secretly an[alyzi]ng blood or urine samples taken by a company doctor for other purpose[s. Thu]s far, the federal government has issued no restrictions on drug testin[g in th]e private sector. Though seventeen states regulate drug testing by priv[ate em]ployers, none has banned it. Only in a very few states are employers fo[rbidde]n from directly observing employees urinating for a drug test, or from [firing or dis]ciplining a worker for refusing to take it.[35] In at least thirty-s[ix s]tates, then, a private employer can randomly test her employees for d[rugs b]y direct observation or without the latter's knowing it, and can fire o[r disci]pline anyone refusing to comply with such tests.

From the body, an employer's invasions of privacy extend outwa[rd and] inward. On the job, an employee has very little sovereignty over he[r posse]ssions or personal storage areas. Private employers are legally entitle[d—ofte]n without probable cause or reasonable suspicion—to search an emp[loyee's] purse, her pockets, her clothes, her locker, or her car if it is parked o[n com]pany property. In certain states, courts have ruled against employer[s con]ducting strip searches of employees, on the grounds that such searche[s con]stitute a tortious or common-law violation of the right to privacy. But since such decisions are almost never backed up by state statutes, they depend upon lawyers and judges, and the rules of precedent, which vary by state. An employer also can discipline or fire any employee who refuses to be searched or who simply leaves the company's premises. Some employers even engage in searches of employees outside company property. In one case in Michigan, the courts upheld an employer's rights to film an employee at home, with a high-powered lens that could take pictures through the window, in order to verify that she was indeed disabled, as she had claimed.[36]

Moving away from the body, our possessions, and our homes, employers also monitor our thoughts, expressed orally, in writing, or in that modern corporate confessional: the personality test. Though federal law prohibits employers from eavesdropping on personal phone conversations of employees, employers can monitor those phone conversations, without the employee's knowledge, if they themselves are one of the parties on the line. Only Pennsylvania requires both parties to consent to monitoring private phone conversations. Employers are fully entitled by law to monitor all work-related phone conversations. While many industry analysts believe that employers regularly abuse this prerogative by listening into personal conversations under the guise of workplace evaluations, there have been few instances of the government's prosecuting employers for doing so.[37]

But it is in the realm of email and computer technology that employer surveillance thrives. Because Congress and the states have not limited the ability of employers to monitor workplace computer terminals or email traffic, employers are completely entitled by law to check up on anything an employee writes in an email or in a computer file, whether work related or not.[38] Such monitoring is particularly common in the wired workplace, making the high-tech economy the front line of employer surveillance. Companies like Exxon Mobil and Delta have installed on company computers the "Investigator" software program, which can forward, without the employee's knowledge, emails and files—sent or unsent, saved or unsaved—containing "alert" words like "boss" or "union." By 1999, according to the American Management Association, 45 percent of American corporations admitted that they monitored their employees' emails. Sixty-seven percent of companies, in fact, keep tabs on their employees' movements and communications through other electronic means. Small wonder PC Week called contemporary employers "Santa Claus"—not because they are so beneficent but because they "know when you are sleeping, they know when you're awake, they know if you've been bad or good, so. . . . "[39]

All of these invasions of privacy, however, pale in comparison with the personality tests employers regularly administer, either before or after hiring. Though Congress in 1988 banned employers, with certain exceptions, from using polygraph tests, private employers are still legally entitled to ask fairly intrusive questions of their applicants and personnel. In the guise of a "pencil and paper" honesty test or merely a personality questionnaire, employers routinely ask questions of the sort that Ehrenreich was forced to answer—and even worse. In a landmark 1991 case in California, for example, it was revealed that a discount department store chain had subjected 2,500 applicants for the position of security guard to what it called a "psychscreen" test. Each applicant was required to answer 701 questions, including "Do you often think about sex?" "Are you attracted to members of the same sex?" "Do you believe in the Second Coming?" Because California's state constitution has a broad provision for privacy rights—uniquely, it applies to private employers—the court ruled against the company. In no other state would such questions be considered, by statute, illegal. What's more, these questions are a big business. According to a 1999 *New York Times Magazine* article, the personality testing industry contributes $400 million a year to the GNP.[40]

Fear at work arises from this hierarchy of the workplace, and is designed to sustain it. Employers rely upon fear not because they are sadists or abusive personalities but because they believe it is the fuel that powers the contemporary American economy. According to the *Wall Street Journal*, "The workplace is never free of fear, and it shouldn't be. Indeed, fear can be a powerful management tool."[41] What is more, fear is an instrument employers have deliberately chosen to wield. As David Gordon notes, employers in European social democracies rely upon the carrot to motivate workers: higher wages, job security, union protections. Here, employers opt for the stick. Keep wages and benefits low, deny workers job security, watch their every move. And when all else fails, punish. Indeed, as Gordon shows, declining wages and benefits in the United States have gone hand in hand with increasing supervision and monitoring of employees.[42]

American employers often argue that government should offer them incentives. Don't regulate or penalize us, they claim, give us tax breaks, real estate subsidies, and other abatements, for positive inducements are more effective than negative sanctions. When it comes to their employees, however, employers believe the opposite: incentives like job security and higher pay won't work, only threats will. It is as if, in the mind of employers, the American worker belongs to an entirely different species of humanity. According to one study, "American companies tend, fundamentally, to mistrust workers, whether they are salaried employees or blue-collar workers. There is a pervading attitude that, 'if you give them an inch, they'll take a mile,' because they don't really want to work."[43]

Fear in the workplace need not be wholly negative, born solely of the threats of harm that employers wield and carry out. Employers also generate fear by preying upon their employees' positive aspirations for advancement. It is that combination of positive ideal and negative sanction, as we have already seen, that makes fear, especially career-driven fear, such a potent spur to action. And employers understand this. Andrew Grove, the former head of Intel, who was fond of wielding a bat and slamming it on the table during meetings with employees, wrote a book in 1996 titled *Only the Paranoid Survive*. There, he delivered the gospel of the American workplace: "The quality guru W. Edwards Deming advocated stamping out fear in corporations. I have trouble with the simple-mindedness of this dictum. The most important role of managers is to create an environment in which people are passionately dedicated to winning in the marketplace. Fear of competition, fear of bankruptcy, fear of being wrong, and fear of losing can all be powerful motivators. How do we cultivate fear of losing in our employees? We can only do that if we feel it ourselves."[44] Grove is certainly not shy about embracing the negative aspects of this fear.[45] But, as he intimates, the power of threatened sanctions depends upon the aspirations of their intended victim: her desire to win, to succeed, to be right.

## Unions

For many Americans, particularly elite, well-paid professionals, unions are organizations of and for burly, white, sometimes thuggish men. The labor movement, in this view, is the home of the coal miner and the Mafia, black lung and brickbats, fat cigars and bad coffee. Its goals are money and benefits, not justice or rights. Critics of the labor movement concede that at some point in history unions may have been necessary, but in today's global, wired economy, they are relics of the past. This view is mistaken. The contemporary labor movement is increasingly made up of women, immigrants, Latinos, and African Americans, and some of its most important organizing drives are among doctors and nurses, college professors, computer programmers, and other wired workers.[46] Unionizing workers certainly seek money and benefits, but, more important, they wish to break the back of the workplace autocracy I have just described. Union grievance procedures and contracts, stipulations of "just cause" discipline and firing, and those proverbial workplace rules—all are designed to turn the workplace into something like a liberal democracy, with employees enjoying the rights of modern citizens. In pushing the federal government to regulate the workplace, union members seek to put limits on their employers' arbitrary power and personal rule, which can seem so reminiscent of the feudal relationship between lord and serf. Employers view unions and their allies in the government in a similar light: as a third party, interfering with the medieval intimacy between supervisors and supervised. In his memoir, management consultant Marty Levitt, a self-confessed "union buster," recounts how he stoked the opposition to unions among the owners and supervisors of the Cravat Coal Company in

Ohio, which faced a strong organizing campaign from the United Mine Workers Union in 1983:

"Do you have any idea what supervising at Cravat will be like under a union?" I asked the group.

I scanned the faces and focused on a young, blond, gentle-looking man: "You married?" I asked.

"Yes, sir," the man replied, his twang revealing a life in the Appalachians.

I moved in closer. "You love your wife?"

"Yes, sir."

"You sleep with your wife?"

The man blushed. "Uh, yes, sir."

"Well," I continued, "how would you like it if your mother-in-law slept between you and your wife every night?"

The crowd broke out in laughter, and a voice from the back of the room hooted, "Not bad. You should see his mother-in-law." Well, maybe you're lucky, I told the boy, but most of us wouldn't want our mother-in-law in bed with us. That's what it will be like for you if we let the union in; everything you do or say to your employees will have to be cleared through the mother-in-law, the union steward.[47]

Historically, this is what the American labor movement has been about: ending the feudal closeness between employer and employee, introducing a third party, the "mother-in-law" of union and government, to break up the oppressiveness of these otherwise private relationships. Through strikes, boycotts, marches, and sit-ins, unions made America liberal, prying open this medieval "state within a state" to collective bargaining and congressional statute, replacing this ancient hierarchy with something resembling a liberal polity. The capstone of labor's achievement was the 1935 Wagner Act, which finally established for workers the right to organize and join labor unions, free of intimidation and retaliation from their employers. The Wagner Act not only overturned the internal feudalism of the workplace, but also destroyed the remnants of feudalism outside the workplace, in the American polity. Since colonial days, it had been unelected and unaccountable judges, like their counterparts in feudal Britain, who exclusively administered American employment law, itself derived from British common law. Judges repeatedly struck down congressional and state attempts to regulate the workplace, arguing that it was not within the power of the elected branches of government to intrude inside the factory gates. In 1937, when the Supreme Court upheld the Wagner Act, the judiciary finally relinquished political control over the workplace to Congress and the president. From now on, it would be employers and labor unions—backed up by elected politicians—that would establish, together, the rules of governance in the workplace. In other words, the exclusive nexus of power between employers and isolated judges would give way to a more democratic constellation of organized social movements and popularly chosen officeholders.[48]

That, at any rate, was the promise of the Wagner Act. Nearly seventy years after its passage, that promise has been betrayed or remains unfulfilled for a great many American workers, most of whom are not union members and are forced to endure the same autocracy that inspired workers to march and strike throughout the nineteenth and twentieth centuries. Though polls and surveys consistently show that a majority of nonunionized employees in the United States would like to join a union, membership rates in labor unions continue to plummet, and unions lose a majority of elections.[49] How can we explain this disparity? A great many factors could be cited, but by far the most important is the opposition of employers. Not just intellectual opposition, but active, coercive campaigns to stop workers from joining unions. "The intensity of opposition to unionization," writes Theodore St. Antoine, former dean of the University of Michigan School of Law and president of the National Academy of Arbitrators, "which is exhibited by American employers has no parallel in the western industrial world."[50] When Freeman and Rogers asked the managers they surveyed "How would you and your firm respond to worker efforts to unionize?" 53 percent said they would oppose any effort of their employees to unionize, and 32 percent claimed that they themselves would be punished by their superiors were employees in their workplace to vote for a union.[51]

If there remains any doubt that fear is a political instrument of extraordinary tactical value, deployed to quell oppositional movements, the campaigns of antiunion employers should set that doubt to rest. According to the influential 1994 report of the Department of Labor's Dunlop Commission, employers in the late 1980s illegally fired prounion workers in one out of every four union elections. Throughout the 1990s, roughly 20,000 prounion workers—about one in eighteen workers voting in a union election—were disciplined or fired each year. If threats of firing and discipline fail, contemporary employers often threaten, illegally, to shut down the worksite. In 50 percent of organizing campaigns, employers issue such illegal threats, and in the manufacturing sector, the percentage is even higher. Contemporary workers, moreover, are well aware of what might happen to them were they to support a union. According to the Dunlop Commission, 59 percent of workers claim that their support for a union would provoke unfavorable treatment from their employers, and 79 percent say it is "very" or "somewhat" likely that "nonunion workers will get fired if they try to organize a union." Human Rights Watch, which has documented anti-union intimidation of workers—from apple pickers in Washington to shipyard workers in New Orleans to computer programmers at Microsoft—concludes, "Freedom of association is a right under severe, often buckling pressure when workers in the United States try to exercise it."[52]

As is true of Fear, American Style, the fragmented state—the separation of powers, federalism, and the rule of law—and a pluralist civil society augment the coercive power employers already possess and reinforce the fear they already wield during these union campaigns. Let's begin with the rule of law. Though unions aim to bring some measure of law inside the workplace, the rule of law outside the workplace often hampers their efforts. As Levitt puts it, American labor law "can be a union buster's best friend."[53] Labor laws contribute to employer intimidation in four ways. First, even though the Wagner Act is designed to give workers the right to form and participate in unions without fear of intimidation, an amendment passed by Congress in 1947, the so-called employer free speech clause of the Taft-Hartley Act, ensures that employers have the right to communicate their views about unions during election campaigns.[54] Employers, the argument goes, have opinions about unions that the government should not suppress, unless employers express them in an intimidating or threatening manner. But in the context of the workplace, the difference between an employer's expression of opinion and making a threat is fuzzy, to say the least. According to Levitt, antiunion consultants have made a cottage industry of instructing employers in the art of the threatless threat. "A representative of management cannot threaten employees," Levitt would tell employers during union campaigns, "but we're going to show you how you can deliver threats without doing anything unlawful."[55] Supervisors can idly surmise that a prounion vote could prompt the owner of a plant to shut it down and move it to Mexico. An employer can blandly state that a union might make workplace relations more antagonistic, or make labor costs prohibitive and lead to job losses. Framed as objective predictions rather than intimidating threats, such statements are perfectly legal, but they nevertheless communicate to the worker that if she votes union, her employer could take retaliatory action against her and her coworkers. Though judges and lawyers like to parse the distinctions between predictions and threats, those distinctions mean little to workers confronting employers with the power to turn prediction into fact.[56]

Second, the Wagner Act imposes no punitive monetary sanctions upon employers who violate it. If the government rules that an employer has illegally fired a union activist, it can only impose remedial measures: the employer must post a notice in the workplace explaining that his action violated the law and promising never to do it again. He must reinstate the worker and pay her whatever wages she has lost between the time of her firing and the time of her reinstatement—minus whatever wages she has earned elsewhere in the interim, which can mean awarded damages of as little as $1,207 plus $586 in interest.[57] Assuming, in a best-case scenario, that the worker's case does not drag on for years, and that the employer does not fire the worker upon her reinstatement (a 1984 study by Harvard Law School professor Paul Weiler found that 80 percent of reinstated workers are fired within a year of their reinstatement), the cost to the employer of violating the law is minimal. As labor lawyer Thomas Geoghegan writes:

> Breaking the law, i.e., firing people is absurdly cheap. Like jaywalking. The best deal in America, in cold business terms. There is a famous study, somewhere, that says a union on average will increase a company's wage bill by 20 percent. So let us say, at plant X there are 50 workers who make $25,000 a year. A union at this plant would cost an employer, then, about $250,000 *a year*. I don't even mention fringes, pensions, etc. And the penalty for violating the Wagner Act is . . . what, $3,000 a crack? Paid one time only, three or four years from now? An employer who didn't break the law would have to be what economists call an "irrational firm."[58]

Or, as one antimanagement consultant advised his clients in Los Angeles, "The probability is that you will never get caught. If you do . . . the worst thing that can happen to you is that you get a second election and the employer wins ninety-six percent of those."[59]

Third, what little protection to workers American labor law does provide only applies, according to one estimate, to roughly two-thirds of all employees.[60] Through a series of exclusions, Congress and the Supreme Court have gradually narrowed the number of employees who actually enjoy the rights guaranteed by the Wagner Act and its successors. When the Wagner Act was originally passed, its protections did not extend to agricultural and domestic workers. Today, some three million workers, many of them immigrants, labor in the nation's agricultural fields, often under punishing work conditions. Outside a few states that protect their right to organize, these workers have no recourse before the law. Likewise the nearly one million women and men who work in private homes, whether as maids, gardeners, or home health care aides. At least 30 percent of these domestic workers are immigrants, many women. Without union protection, they are easily abused and exploited. In one case, a Bangladeshi woman was allowed out of her employer's East Side apartment in Manhattan only twice during a nine-month period. In another case, an Ethiopian woman was forced to work thirteen hours a day, seven days a week, for eight years—with no time off—for which she received $1,060 in total wages, roughly 3¢ per hour. Such individuals can sue in court, but as immigrants without union protection, they must possess the knowledge and resources to contact the advocates who could help them. Given that American citizens already have a difficult time mustering such resources, it seems unlikely that immigrants would be in a good position to do so.[61]

In addition to these exclusions of the Wagner Act, the Taft-Hartley Act added two more: independent contractors and supervisors. All told, about eleven million workers in the contemporary workforce have been classified as belonging to one of these two categories. Throughout the 1970s, the Supreme Court added managers, employees of religious institutions, and private university professors to this list—roughly eleven million more workers. Employers also can easily manipulate these classifications, calling low-level employees supervisors or managers even though they have virtually no supervisory authority, or calling employees who have worked for them for years "independent private contractors." In addition to these exclusions, public employees in many individual states—no one knows how many, but the number runs into the millions—enjoy no right to organize.[62]

While none of these three failings of American labor law call into question the rule of law itself—indeed, they could easily be rectified by strengthening and expanding labor laws, not abandoning them—the fourth does. A basic element of the rule of law is the right to a trial, or a trial-like hearing, and the right to appeal whatever ruling the trial produces. For employers, the right to a trial and particularly the right to appeal is a bonanza. While each individual complaint brought by an employee or a union winds its way through the courts, the employer is free to continue his course of action or to reap the benefits of his initial illegal action. This process of delay is inherent to any form of the rule of law, but in the context of the workplace, where employees cannot afford to wait for justice and employers have all the time in the world, it can prove lethal. "During all this delay," writes Geoghegan of workplace grievance procedures, "the rule is: 'Management acts, the union grieves.' And grieves and grieves. For two and a half years, the company can have its way."[63] As one worker in south Florida, fired for his union activity in 1994 and not reinstated until 1999, told Human Rights Watch, "It's been four or five years now, and I've got bills to pay. Management has time to do whatever they want."[64] According to the National Labor Relations Board's own statistics, one complaint from a workplace activist penalized during a union election campaign can take easily about five years to make its way through the courts.[65] Even if she ultimately wins her suit, the damage has already been done: in the meantime, her coworkers will have tired, moved on, or given up, convinced that the law and the government—indeed, the union itself—cannot protect them from management coercion. That is the goal of an employer's antiunion campaign, writes Levitt: to "make the union fight drag on long enough" so that "workers would lose faith, lose interest, lose hope."[66]

Several of these weaknesses of American labor law are directly related to the separation of powers, to federalism, or to both. At various points, for instance, Congress has attempted to remedy the flaws of the Wagner Act and its successors. In 1977–78, a liberal coalition finally managed to push through the House of Representatives a reform bill, but it was killed in the Senate by filibuster. The United States Senate is the emblematic institution of the separation of powers and federalism. It was created in order to fragment Congress, thought by the Framers to be the most dangerous branch of government, and to enhance the power of the states at the national level. The filibuster is also often conceived as a relative of the separation of powers, the moment when a lonely senator faces down the tyranny of the majority in order to defend the rights of the minority. But the filibuster has just as often contributed to the tyranny of the minority. The defeat of labor law reform in the late 1970s is just one instance of the negative contributions of the separation of power and federalism. So are some of the previously mentioned exclusions of labor law, which have been put into statutory form for reasons of federalism, which grant states power over portions of the private workforce and the states' public sectors.

Like the Senate, the principle of judicial review is a distinctive element of the separation of powers. But judicial review has always been a favored weapon of employers in their battle against unions, both before the Wagner Act, when judges had tremendous control over the workplace, and since.[67] The Taft-Hartley Act, designed by congressional conservatives to weaken the Wagner Act and to increase the power of employers, explicitly enhanced the authority of the federal courts to review and overturn decisions of the National Labor Relations Board. Today, as in the nineteenth century, it is judges, relying upon their power of judicial review, and not legislators who most contribute to the power of employers. In the words of Human Rights Watch, "many of the features of U.S. labor law and practice that counter international norms" and make unionization difficult "result from court-fashioned doctrine, not just from statutory deficiencies."[68]

And what of the pluralism of civil society? For workers attempting to unionize, it can be lethal. Like the American state, the workplace is highly fragmented and decentralized. Its sheer diversity—of size, geography, and demographic composition—can be a boon to employers. With so many different kinds of workplaces scattered across the country, government regulators, strapped by limited resources, have a difficult time keeping up with all the violations of labor and employment law.[69] The diversity of the workplace also gives employers and their advocates strong arguments against government regulations. Where the market is supposed to be finely tuned to every particular need of the individual consumer, government is depicted as a blunt instrument, imposing one-size-fits-all policies upon a society of intractable differences. In the words of Milton Friedman, "The characteristic feature of action through political channels is that it tends to require or enforce substantial conformity. The great advantage of the market, on the other hand, is that it permits wide diversity."[70] The solution to the problems of the workplace, according to this point of view, is less regulation, more diversity, more pluralism. Only then will workers have the option to quit their jobs for better jobs, allegedly the best mechanism for creating a just workplace.

Diversity, particularly of geography, also makes it difficult for unions to muster public support against employers who break the law. Though employers like General Motors or Microsoft may attract some attention, smaller employers, located in little-known towns, do not. According to Levitt, as an antiunion consultant he traveled to "the most remote outposts: from St. Joseph's Infirmary in Louisville, Kentucky, to the Marvin Window plant in Warroad, Minnesota, to the Fraser Paper Mill in Madawaska, Maine, to the Vollworth Sausage factory in Hancock-Houghton, Michigan." Situated in forgotten tracts of America's vastness, these worksites do not garner national attention, and local media are seldom willing to scrutinize the actions of local employers, upon whom the entire region may be economically dependent. The personal intimacy of these local workplaces—the smaller, the better—is also helpful to employers, who manipulate the personal connections between supervisors and supervised to keep unions out. Levitt, for example, often had line supervisors, who work closely with employees and might even belong to the same family, counsel individual employees to vote against the union. At the Cravat Coal Company, he had foremen approach the coal miners and say, "Hey, I know you need this union, but please don't vote for it. If the union wins, that's the end of me. You and me are like brothers, and I just couldn't go on."[71] In the case of nurses attempting to unionize at a hospital in Milwaukee, according to the National Labor Relations Board, supervisors "personalized the issue and otherwise attempted to brain-wash the nurses."[72]

As union organizers, labor historians, and employers have long recognized, the internal diversity of the workplace—particularly of race—can be a godsend to any owner battling a union. Even before the union arrives, employers often use race to organize the workforce, distributing jobs along racial lines in order to keep workers divided. In its Pulitzer Prize–winning series on race in America, the *New York Times* profiled one slaughterhouse in North Carolina, where "whites, blacks, American Indians and Mexicans . . . all have their separate stations." Supervisors were white, Native Americans cleaned, and blacks and Mexicans competed over who got the dirtiest jobs on the "kill floor." "More than management," the article stated, "the workers see one another as the problem, and they see the competition in skin tones." Whites and Native Americans would amuse themselves with daily arguments about who was worse, blacks or Mexicans. One white man said, "The tacos are worse than the niggers," while the Native Americans standing nearby laughed. In 1997, the United Food and Commercial Workers Union tried to organize the plant. Management fired several black workers and hired Mexican immigrants in their place, on the well grounded assumption that Mexican immigrants, many of them undocumented, would be more vulnerable to management threats. The morning of the election, workers preparing to vote were greeted at the plant by the county sheriff's department, decked out in riot gear, with the epithet "Nigger lover" written across the union's trailer. The union lost the election.[73]

# CONCLUSION: LIBERALISM AGONISTES

> DO NOT ADDICT THEM
> TO THE DRUG OF DANGER—
> THE DREAM OF THE ENEMY
> THAT HAS TO BE CRUSHED, LIKE A HERB,
> BEFORE THEY CAN SMELL FREEDOM.
>
> —AESCHYLUS

Our troubled approach to fear in the United States has much to do with the schizophrenic qualities of American liberalism. Political fear has been both the doing and undoing of American liberalism, but few of our writers seem willing to acknowledge this fact. Drawing on Montesquieu and Tocqueville, American intellectuals possess a liberal diagnosis of political fear and a liberal prescription for its cure. Political fear, they argue, is caused by a centralized, lawless state pulverizing civil society into atomized dust, to which the Constitution is supposed to provide the perfect antidote: separation of powers, federalism, and the rule of law. Though neither the free market nor a pluralist civil society is mentioned in the Constitution, they too are often invoked as prescriptions against fear, reflecting the vision, formulated by Madison, of a complex freedom growing between the cracks of a richly textured society. If political fear does arise in the United States, claim leading writers, it cannot be the result, or even the unanticipated side effect, of these liberal remedies. It must emerge from outside the fragmented state or from some forgotten outpost of civil society.

That is the theory. The practice, as we have seen, is altogether different, for Fear, American Style has been both the fulfillment and the betrayal of liberalism, in ways that few liberals—indeed, few intellectuals of any political stripe—realize. Beyond its commitments to a limited state and a pluralist society, American liberalism is a philosophy that proclaims the inviolability and dignity of the individual and the equality of all men and women. But while freedom and equality may run through our political bedrock, they have been far more volcanic, and far less common, forces than many of liberalism's critics or defenders are willing to admit.[1] Liberal notions of freedom and equality have hurled men and women, sometimes violently, against the ramparts of privilege. Liberal principles enlisted men, black and white, in the slaughter of hundreds of thousands of other men, mostly white, in order to remove chattel slavery from the land. Liberalism has summoned men and women of all colors to march and sometimes give their lives for racial and gender equality, and has inspired men and women to scale the high walls of class authority, to take apart, brick by brick, the edifices of inequality and unfreedom in this country. These struggles for liberalism in the United States have been titanic. But they have also been rare. So rare they bring to mind Gandhi's famous response to the question of what he thought of western civilization: "I think it would be a good idea." What has prevented freedom and equality from becoming a reality in the United States? The politics of fear, and the liberal web of political institutions, laws, ideologies, elites, civic structures, and private associations that support that politics. Underwritten by our constitutional arrangements, political fear is a friend of American liberalism; undermining our great national efforts on behalf of freedom and equality, it is its foe. And it is our liberal commitment to a limited state and a pluralist civil society that prevents us from seeing both sides of this ambivalent relationship.

While liberal mechanisms and contrivances have been mobilized on behalf of fear, what has fear done for liberalism? It has often curtailed it, or at least significantly stemmed liberalism's advancing tide. Whether in the contemporary workplace or during the Cold War or today's war on terrorism, fear has undermined liberal commitments to freedom and equality, empowering some of the most revanchist, conservative forces in American life. From white racists during Jim Crow, who used fear to keep civil rights out of the South, to congressional conservatives and J. Edgar Hoover during the McCarthy years, to union busters over the last fifty to one hundred years.

If we seek to counter political fear in the United States, if we hope to make freedom and equality practices rather than promises, we must confront this assemblage of liberal institutions and practices that fragment the state and civil society and promote fear. We must cease our worship of these icons, cultivating a more skeptical appreciation of their deficits and limitations, and seek more robust protections against fear elsewhere. We must be less nervous about popular movements, which seek to make freedom and equality a reality, and more sympathetic to the aggressive, national state policies that support them. For in the United States, it is these movements, even when inspired by seemingly utopian ideologies, and a centralized, unified, national state, that have been the most important and driving forces behind freedom and equality.

More important, we must remember that fear is not, and cannot be, a foundation of moral and political argument. We must look instead to principles of freedom and equality as the ground of our politics. Throughout the thirties and forties, and during the sixties and seventies, American liberals spoke a language of crusading confrontation, envisioning freedom and equality in the toppling of old regimes—of class, race, and gender. They found their various, often conflicting, but always combative arguments in the dissonant voices of philosophers like John Rawls and Ronald Dworkin. But as the movements for social progress inevitably failed to achieve their full results, self-doubt and second-guessing among liberals set in. Aided by the rise of a conservative counterrevolution and the collapse of communism—which should have liberated progressives from the burden of defending an indefensible regime, but which instead only confirmed their doubts about social democracy—this mood of dwindled possibility found succor and putative realism in fear. Liberals became careful not to imagine or to ask for too much, grew wary of confrontation with the dominant forms of domestic power, and gave up all doctrinal certitude except the certitude that allegedly comes from the experience of fear. Contemporary liberals still make arguments, but not in the emancipatory spirit of Rawls and Dworkin. They speak not for, but against; they do not aspire to the *summum bonum*, but seek to fend off the *summum malum*. Contemporary liberals are no less prone to crusades than their radical predecessors were. In their willingness to combat genocide and other evils throughout the world, they have demonstrated the same energy that a previous generation applied to the evils of domestic racism and inequality. But today's liberals look to these evils in a way their predecessors did not, deriving confidence and purpose, a deep sense of foundation, from evil itself, from cruelty and the terrible fear it arouses.

To combat Fear, American Style, we must return to the egalitarian and libertarian principles of Rawls and Dworkin, and to the emancipatory strains of American liberalism more generally. Though I do not defend or explain these principles here, their proponents have already supplied us with sufficiently robust and politically salient, if not always consistent, arguments on their behalf. Dissatisfaction with these principles reflects less, I suspect, their internal weaknesses than a waning faith in their viability, in the difficult and strenuous tasks of social reconstruction they impose upon us all. In an age of Cold War triumphalism and now terrorism—in which the state can be praised as only a minimal solution to the problems of anarchy and disorder, and the market displaces politics as the sphere of human betterment—it is far easier to believe in cruelty and fear than in freedom and equality. But it is freedom and equality that inspire us to oppose political fear, and it is freedom and equality that underwrite our struggle against it. Fear, in other words, does not come first. Fear is an obstacle and a stumbling block, but it is not, and cannot be, a foundation for politics. The struggle against Fear, American Style cannot and will not spring from a transpolitical, humanitarian horror at the experience of fear itself; indeed, anyone looking for the atrocities of a Bosnia or Rwanda in the American workplace will be sorely disappointed. But for those who believe in freedom and equality as foundational principles, the struggle against Fear, American Style is imperative, for it is that fear which today makes the greatest mockery of those principles, in the United States and increasingly throughout the world.

# NOTES

## INTRODUCTION

1. Genesis 1–3.
2. David Brooks, "The Age of Conflict," *The Weekly Standard* (November 5, 2001); Don DeLillo, "In the Ruins of the Future," *Harper's* (December 2001), p. 33; Frank Rich, "The Day Before Tuesday," *New York Times* (September 15, 2001), p. A23; David Brooks, "Facing Up to Our Fears," *Newsweek* (October 22, 2001); George Packer, "Recapturing the Flag," *New York Times Magazine* (September 30, 2001), pp. 15–16.
3. *The Complete Essays of Montaigne*, trans. Donald M. Frame (Stanford: Stanford University Press, 1943), p. 53; Henry Sidgwick, *The Elements of Politics* (London: Macmillan, 1891), p. 41; Max Horkheimer and Theodor Adorno, *Dialectic of Enlightenment*, trans. John Cumming (New York: Continuum, 1986), p. 3; Franz Neumann, "Anxiety and Politics," in *The Democratic and Authoritarian State: Essays in Political and Legal Theory*, ed. Herbert Marcuse (New York: Free Press, 1957); Judith N. Shklar, "The Liberalism of Fear," in *Liberalism and the Moral Life*, ed. Nancy L. Rosenblum (Cambridge: Harvard University Press, 1989), p. 29; Franklin D. Roosevelt, "First Inaugural Address," in *Inaugural Addresses of the Presidents of the United States* (Washington, D.C.: U.S. Government Printing Office, 1961), p. 235; Aung San Suu Kyi, *Freedom from Fear* (New York: Penguin, 1991), pp. 180–85; Eric Foner, *The Story of American Freedom* (New York: Norton, 1998), pp. 221–27.
4. John Locke, *An Essay Concerning Human Understanding*, ed. Alexander Campbell Fraser (New York: Dover, 1959), 2.20.6,10; 2.21.34, pp. 304–5, 334; Edmund Burke, *A Philosophical Enquiry into the Origin of Our Ideas of the Sublime and the Beautiful*, ed. Adam Phillips (New York: Oxford University Press, 1990), pp. 32, 36, 123, 135–36.
5. Abraham Lincoln, "Address to the Young Men's Lyceum," in *The Portable Lincoln*, ed. Andrew Delbanco (New York: Penguin, 1992), pp. 17–26.
6. Thomas L. Friedman, "9/11 Lesson Plan," *New York Times* (September 4, 2002), p. A21.

7. Serge Schemann, "What Would 'Victory' Mean?" *New York Times* (September 16, 2001), *Week in Review*, p. 1; Thomas L. Friedman, "Smoking or non-Smoking?" *New York Times* (September 14, 2001), p. A27; Barbara Crossette, "Feverish Protests Against the West Trace Grievances Ancient and Modern," *New York Times* (October 22, 2001), p. B4; Lamin Sanneh, "Faith and the Secular State," *New York Times* (September 23, 2001), Section 4, p. 17; Ethan Bronner, "21st-Century Jihad," *New York Times* (November 18, 2001), Book Review, p. 15; Ronald Steel, "The Weak at War With the Strong," *New York Times* (September 14, 2001), p. A27; John Burns, "America Inspires Longing and Loathing in Muslim World," *New York Times* (September 16, 2001), p. A4; Fouad Ajami, "Out of Egypt," *New York Times Magazine* (October 7, 2001), p. 19; Edward Rothstein, "Explaining the Flaws in the Notion of the 'Root Causes' of Terror," *New York Times* (November 17, 2001), p. A17; Elaine Sciolino, "Who Hates the U.S.? Who Loves It?" *New York Times* (September 23, 2001), Week in Review, p. 1

8. Neil MacFarquhar, "A Portrait of the Terrorist: From Shy Child to Single-Minded Killer," *New York Times* (October 10, 2001), p. B9.

9. Corey Robin, "Close-Case Studies," *New York Times Magazine* (December 16, 2001), pp. 23–24. Also see Bruce Fudge, "The Two Faces of Islamic Studies," *Boston Globe* (December 15, 2002), p. C4.

10. Aristotle, *Nicomachean Ethics* 1115a6–1115b, trans. Martin Ostwald (New York: Macmillan, 1962), pp. 68–70.

11. Augustine, *City of God*, trans. John O'Meara (New York: Penguin, 1972), 14.6, 9, pp. 555, 561, 565.

12. Deuteronomy 3:22; 6:2, 13–15, 24; 7:18–21; 10:17, 20.

13. Plato, *The Republic* 386a–88a, trans. Allan Bloom (New York: Basic, 1968), pp. 63–65.

14. There are exceptions. In contemporary philosophy and the social sciences, Martha Nussbaum, Ronald de Sousa, Mary Douglas, Barry Glassner, and Cass Sunstein have offered accounts of fear, from which I have learned much, that depart, implicitly or explicitly, from the conceptions I trace here. See Martha Nussbaum, *The Therapy of Desire: Theory and Practice in Hellenistic Ethics* (Princeton: Princeton University Press, 1994), pp. 83–89, 91–94, 103–4, 192–328, 261–62; Ronald de Sousa, *The Rationality of Emotion* (Cambridge: MIT Press, 1987); Mary Douglas, *Purity and Danger: An Analysis of Concepts of Pollution and Taboo* (New York: Routledge, 1966); Mary Douglas and Aaron Wildavsky, *Risk and Culture: An Essay on the Selection of Technological and Environmental Dangers* (Berkeley: University of California Press, 1982); Barry Glassner, *The Culture of Fear: Why Americans Are Afraid of the Wrong Things* (New York: Basic, 1999); Cass R. Sunstein, *Risk and Reason: Safety, Law, and the Environment* (New York: Cambridge University Press, 2002).

15. Raymond Aron, *Main Currents in Sociological Thought I: Montesquieu, Comte, Marx, Tocqueville, the Sociologists of the Revolution of 1848*, trans. Richard Howard and Helen Weaver (Garden City, N.Y.: Doubleday, 1968), pp. 20–21.

16. Judith N. Shklar, *Montesquieu* (New York: Oxford University Press, 1987), p. 84.

17. Michael Sandel, *Democracy's Discontent: America in Search of a Public Philosophy* (Cambridge: Harvard University Press, 1996), pp. 3–4; Jean Bethke Elshtain, *Democracy on Trial* (New York: Basic, 1995), p. 37.

18. Cited in Jean-Claude Lamberti, *Tocqueville and the Two Democracies*, trans. Arthur Goldhammer (Cambridge: Harvard University Press, 1989), p. 229; Alexis de Tocqueville, *Democracy in America*, trans. George Lawrence, ed. J. P. Mayer (New York: Harper and Row, 1969), p. 702.

19. Hannah Arendt, *The Origins of Totalitarianism* (New York: Harcourt Brace Jovanovich, 1951, 1973), p. 442.

20. Shklar, "The Liberalism of Fear," p. 29.

21. Michael Ignatieff, *The Warrior's Honor: Ethnic War and the Modern Conscience* (New York: Henry Holt, 1997), pp. 18–19. Also see Judith Shklar, *Ordinary Vices* (Cambridge: Cambridge University Press, 1984), pp. 1–44, 226–49; Richard Rorty, *Contingency, Irony, and Solidarity* (Cambridge: Cambridge University Press, 1989), pp. 192–98; Anthony Giddens, *Beyond Left and Right: The Future of Radical Politics* (Stanford: Stanford University Press, 1994), p. 20; Ira Katznelson, *Liberalism's Crooked Circle: Letters to Adam Michnik* (Princeton: Princeton University Press, 1996); Avishai Margalit, *The Decent Society*, trans. Naomi Goldman (Cambridge: Harvard University Press, 1996); John Gray, *Two Faces of Liberalism* (New York: New Press, 2000); Jacob Levy, *The Multiculturalism of Fear* (New York: Oxford University Press, 2000).

22. Charles Taylor, *Sources of the Self: The Making of the Modern Identity* (Cambridge: Harvard University Press, 1989).

23. Irving Howe, "The Self in Literature," in *A Critic's Notebook*, ed. Nicholas Howe (San Diego: Harcourt Brace, 1994), p. 264.

24. Hobbes, *Leviathan*, ed. Richard Tuck (New York: Cambridge University Press, 1991), p. 9.

25. Locke, 2.21.34, p. 334; Burke, pp. 30, 122.

26. Sheldon S. Wolin, *Politics and Vision: Continuity and Innovation in Western Political Thought* (Boston: Little, Brown, 1960), p. 243.

27. Tocqueville, p. 444.

28. Tocqueville, p. 702.

29. *Inaugural Addresses of the Presidents*, p. 235; Frank Freidel, *Franklin D. Roosevelt: A Rendezvous with Destiny* (Boston: Little, Brown, 1990), pp. 360–61; James MacGregor Burns, *Roosevelt 1882–1940: The Lion and the Fox* (New York: Harcourt Brace Jovanovich, 1956, 1985), p. 162.

30. Arthur M. Schlesinger, Jr., *The Vital Center: The Politics of Freedom* (New York: DaCapo Press, 1949, 1988), pp. 1–7, 51–53, 244.

31. Shklar, "The Liberalism of Fear," pp. 21, 30.

32. See *The Radical Right*, ed. Daniel Bell (Garden City, N.Y.: Anchor Books, 1965); Richard Hofstadter, *The Paranoid Style of American Politics and Other Essays* (Chicago: University of Chicago Press, 1965).

33. Leslie Fiedler, "McCarthy," *Encounter* 3 (July 1954): 13.

34. The lower and higher estimates are from, respectively, Ralph S. Brown, Jr., *Loyalty and Security: Employment Tests in the United States* (New Haven: Yale University Press, 1958), p. 181; Griffin Fariello, *Red Scare: Memories of the American Inquisition* (New York: Avon, 1996), p. 43.

35. LexisNexis search. Also see Bob Woodward and Dan Eggen, "FBI and CIA Suspect Domestic Extremists," *Washington Post* (October 27, 2001), p. A1; William J. Broad,

"Terror Anthrax Resembles Type Made by U.S.," *New York Times* (December 3, 2001), p. A1; William J. Broad and David Johnston, "U.S. Inquiry Tried, but Failed, to Link Iraq to Anthrax Attack," *New York Times* (December 22, 2001), p. A1; Eric Lipton and Kirk Johnson, "Tracking Bioterror's Tangled Course," *New York Times* (December 26, 2001), p. A1; Nicholas D. Kristof, "Anthrax? The F.B.I Yawns," *New York Times* (July 2, 2002), p. A21; Iver Peterson, "Anthrax Cleanup to Close Mail Center a Year More," *New York Times* (April 11, 2003), p. D1.

36. LexisNexis search. Also see Eric Lichtblau and Judith Miller, "Indictment Ties U.S. Professor to Terror Group," *New York Times* (February 21, 2003), p. A1.

37. LexisNexis search. Also see Rex Hutting, "US Companies Quietly Caught Trading With the Enemy," *CBS MarketWatch* (April 15, 2003).

38. Martin Luther King, Jr., "Letter from Birmingham City Jail," in *A Testament of Hope: The Essential Writings and Speeches of Martin Luther King, Jr.*, ed. James M. Washington (New York: Harper Collins, 1986), pp. 292–93. Also see James Baldwin, "In Search of a Majority," in *Nobody Knows My Name* (New York: Vintage, 1960), pp. 127–37.

39. In his memoirs, journalist Carl Bernstein, of Watergate fame, recalls the fear aroused in him, the young child of Communist parents, by the execution of the Rosenbergs. "To a child the connection was unavoidable: if [the Rosenbergs] could be executed, what was to prevent the execution of one's own parents, particularly one's own mother? The Rosenbergs had been married on June 18, 1939, the same day as my mother and father." The political message of the Rosenbergs' execution was not lost on him either: "The Rosenbergs too were *progressive* people—and they were going to die for it; they were going to fry." Carl Bernstein, *Loyalties* (New York: Simon and Schuster, 1989), p. 101.

40. *NAACP v. Button*, 371 U.S. 415 (1963).

41. King, "The Strength to Love," in *A Testament of Hope*, pp. 513–14.

42. George Bailey, "Manager's Journal: Fear Is Nothing to Be Afraid of," *Wall Street Journal* (January 27, 1997), p. A22.

43. Cited in Jill Andresky Fraser, *White-Collar Sweatshop: The Deterioration of Work and Its Rewards in Corporate America* (New York: Norton, 2001), p. 155.

44. Marc Linder and Ingrid Nygaard, *Void Where Prohibited: Rest Breaks and the Right to Urinate on Company Time* (Ithaca: Cornell University Press, 1998), p. 49; Corey Robin, "Lavatory and Liberty: The Secret History of the Bathroom Break," *Boston Globe* (September 29, 2002), p. D1.

45. Richard B. Freeman and Joel Rogers, *What Workers Want* (Ithaca: Cornell University Press, 1999), p. 127.

46. Fraser, pp. 87–88, 152.

47. Fraser, pp. 191–95.

48. Christopher Hitchens, "Images in a Rearview Mirror," *The Nation* (December 3, 2001), p. 9. Lest he be misunderstood, Hitchens insists that his enthusiasm is not for a war of the purely moral or political—that is, metaphorical—variety. He praises the U.S. war in Afghanistan, particularly the American military's use there of cluster bombs, which explode in a shower of lethal bomblets: "Those steel pellets will go straight through somebody and out the other side and through somebody else. And if they're bearing a Koran over their heart, it'll go straight through that, too. So they won't be able to say, 'Ah, I was bearing a Koran over my heart and guess what, the

missile stopped halfway through.' No way, 'cause it'll go straight through that as well." And lest his December 3 statement be misconstrued as too much enthusiasm in response to the war's initial victories, Hitchens chose to repeat it, almost verbatim, just three days shy of the one-year anniversary of September 11. See Hitchens, "It's a Good Time for War," *Boston Globe* (September 8, 2002); Adam Shatz, "The Left and 9/11," *The Nation* (September 23, 2002). For praise of Hitchens as the "conscience of the left" and the "Orwell for our time," see Judith Shulevitz, "What Would Orwell Do?" *New York Times Book Review* (September 8, 2002), p. 31; Ron Rosenbaum, "The Men Who Would Be Orwell," *New York Observer* (January 14, 2002), pp. 1, 5.

49. Zbigniew Herbert, "The Monster of Mr. Cogito," in *Report from the Besieged City and Other Poems*, trans. John Carpenter and Bogdana Carpenter (New York: Ecco Press, 1986), pp. 39–40.

## PART 1: HISTORY OF AN IDEA

1. Edmund Burke, *A Philosophical Enquiry into the Origin of Our Ideas of the Sublime and the Beautiful*, ed. Adam Phillips (New York: Oxford University Press, 1990), p. 123.

2. Raymond Aron, *Main Currents in Sociological Thought* I: *Montesquieu, Comte, Marx, Tocqueville, the Sociologists of the Revolution of 1848*, trans. Richard Howard and Helen Weaver (Garden City, N.Y.: Doubleday, 1968), pp. 20–21.

## 1: FEAR

1. A. P. Martinich, *Hobbes: A Biography* (New York: Cambridge University Press, 1999), pp. 1–2; *Aubrey's Brief Lives*, ed. Oliver Lawson Dick (New York: Penguin, 1949), p. 227.

2. Thucydides, *The Peloponnesian War*, trans. Richard Crawley (New York: Modern Library, 1982), p. 44; Machiavelli, *The Prince*, in *The Portable Machiavelli*, ed. Peter Bondanella and Mark Musa (New York: Penguin, 1979), p. 131.

3. Thomas Hobbes, *De Cive*, in *Man and Citizen*, ed. Bernard Gert (Indianapolis: Hackett, 1991), 1.2, p. 113.

4. Thomas Hobbes, *The Elements of Law: Natural & Politic*, ed. Ferdinand Tönnies (London: Frank Cass, 1969), 2.10.8, p. 188.

5. "They are, therefore, so long in the state of war, as by reason of the diversity of the present appetites, they mete good and evil by diverse measures." *De Cive*, 3.31, p. 150.

6. Charles Carlton, "The Impact of the Fighting," in *The Impact of the English Civil War*, ed. John Morrill (London: Collins & Brown, 1991), p. 20.

7. Hobbes, *Behemoth, or the Long Parliament*, ed. Ferdinand Tönnies (Chicago: University of Chicago Press, 1990), p. 23.

8. In addition to the Renaissance skepticism discussed here, Hobbes was influenced by the scientific revolutions of Galileo, Bacon, and Mersenne; the natural rights philosophy of Grotius and Selden; and the rhetorical and humanist conventions of the Renaissance. See Tom Sorrell, *Hobbes* (London: Routledge, 1986); J. W. N. Watkins, *Hobbes's System of Ideas*, 2nd ed. (London: Hutchinson, 1973); M. M. Goldsmith, *Hobbes's Science of Politics* (New York: Columbia University Press, 1966); Richard Tuck, *Hobbes* (New York: Oxford University Press, 1989); Tuck, *Philosophy and Government 1572–1651* (Cambridge: Cambridge University Press, 1993); Tuck, "Hobbes's moral philosophy," in *The Cambridge Companion to Hobbes*, ed. Tom Sorrell (Cam-

bridge: Cambridge University Press, 1996), pp. 175–207; Leo Strauss, *The Political Philosophy of Hobbes: Its Basis and Its Genesis* (Chicago: University of Chicago Press, 1952); Quentin Skinner, *Reason and Rhetoric in the Philosophy of Hobbes* (Cambridge: Cambridge University Press, 1996); David Johnston, *The Rhetoric of Leviathan: Thomas Hobbes and the Politics of Cultural Transformation* (Princeton: Princeton University Press, 1986).

9. I am indebted here to Tuck, *Hobbes*, pp. 5–11, 19–23, 51–76; Tuck, *Philosophy and Government*, ch. 7; Tuck, "Hobbes's moral philosophy," pp. 175–207. Also see Michael Oakeshott, "Introduction to *Leviathan*," in *Rationalism in Politics and Other Essays* (Indianapolis: Liberty Press, 1991), pp. 230–31, 242–43, 245–46; Richard Flathman, *Thomas Hobbes: Skepticism, Individuality, and Chastened Politics* (Newbury Park, Calif.: SAGE, 1993). For a spirited rejoinder, see Skinner, *Reason and Rhetoric*, pp. 8–9.

10. *Elements of Law*, 1.7.3, p. 29. Also see *De Homine*, in *Man and Citizen*, 11.4, p. 47; *Leviathan*, ed. Richard Tuck (New York: Cambridge University Press, 1991), ch. 6, p. 39.

11. *Leviathan*, ch. 6, p. 39.

12. *Elements of Law*, 1.10.3, p. 49; *Leviathan*, ch. 6, pp. 40–41.

13. "Of the voluntary acts of every man, the object is some Good to himselfe." *Leviathan*, ch. 14, p. 93. We could interpret this statement in one of two ways. First, that when we act, we act for the sake of bringing some good to ourselves. Second, that when we act, we act for the sake of some good that we believe is good. The first is a statement of philosophical egoism, which claims that we act for the sake of that which benefits us. The second is a statement of moral skepticism, which claims that whatever I deem to be good, the point is that *I* deem it to be good, that it is good in my eyes as opposed to yours. Though I prefer the latter interpretation, here I am merely arguing that Hobbes claims all human action is motivated by the belief that the action will bring about some good, however the actor understands that term. For Hobbes on egoism, see Gregory S. Kavka, *Hobbesian Moral and Political Theory* (Princeton: Princeton University Press, 1986), pp. 44–51; Bernard Gert, "Introduction," in *Man and Citizen*, pp. 3–32.

14. Even in the case of salvation, Hobbes's stipulation might still apply, for the point about human goods in the Hobbesian account is not only that we seek to *enjoy* them, but that we *seek* to enjoy them. We wish not only to secure the good of eternal salvation, but also to pursue, and continue pursuing, that good. To do so, we must be alive. See *Leviathan*, ch. 11, p. 70.

15. *De Homine*, 11.6, pp. 48–49. Hobbes scholars have long debated whether Hobbes conceived the fear of death and the pursuit of self-preservation as an empirical description of human behavior or as a moral injunction men are obliged to follow. I do not believe either position approximates Hobbes's. For examples of the first account, see Richard Peters, *Hobbes* (Baltimore: Penguin, 1956), pp. 143–44, 160; Watkins, pp. 50–51, 80–84; David Gauthier, *The Logic of Leviathan: The Moral and Political Theory of Thomas Hobbes* (Oxford: Oxford University Press, 1969), p. 7; Jean Hamptom, *Hobbes and the Social Contract Tradition* (Cambridge: Cambridge University Press, 1986), pp. 14–17, 34–35. (Peters is ambivalent on this question, at times suggesting that the principle of self-preservation is not a physiological drive but a logical postulate of human action. See pp. 144, 154.) For representatives of the sec-

ond position, see A. E. Taylor, "The Ethical Doctrine of Hobbes," *Philosophy* 13 (1938): 406–24; Howard Warrender, *The Political Philosophy of Hobbes: His Theory of Obligation* (Oxford: Clarendon Press, 1957); Michael Oakeshott, "The Moral Life in the Writing of Thomas Hobbes," in *Rationalism in Politics*, pp. 295–300. My own view is drawn from the following accounts, which generally argue that the dichotomy between empirical description and moral injunction is falsely posed in Hobbes's work and that Hobbes understood the pursuit of self-preservation as a logical premise of human action and rational agency. See Stuart M. Brown, Jr., "Hobbes: The Taylor Thesis," *Philosophical Review* 69 (1959): 303–23; Kavka, pp. 80–82, 329–31, 428–29; Sorrell, pp. 96–109; Tuck, *Hobbes*, pp. 58–63.

16. "Not every man in passion," but "all men by reason," call life good and death evil. *Elements*, 1.17.14, p. 94.

17. *De Homine*, 12.1, p. 55; *Leviathan*, ch. 27, p. 206.

18. *Elements*, 1.9.6, p. 39; *De Cive*, 3.12, 6.13, pp. 142, 183; *Leviathan*, ch. 15, p. 107.

19. *Elements*, p. xv. In *Leviathan*, Hobbes offers a slightly different estimate of the relation between passion and reason, though not one that fundamentally contradicts the account I have set out here. There, he claims that man's ability to get himself out of the state of nature depends "partly in the Passions, partly in his Reason." *Leviathan*, ch. 13, p. 90.

20. *Elements*, 1.7.2, p. 29. Elsewhere in *Elements*, he claims that the two passions governing deliberation and conduct are actually appetite and fear. See 1.12.1, p. 61.

21. *De Homine*, 12.1, p. 55. Only later, in *Leviathan*, does Hobbes entertain the notion that some appetites, like hope, can focus the individual upon his long-term good and persuade him to seek peace and submit to sovereign power. "The Passions that encline men to Peace," he writes in *Leviathan*, "are Feare of Death; Desire of such things as are necessary to commodious living; and a Hope by their Industry to obtain them." Not long after this statement, however, Hobbes declares that it is fear, the apprehension of evil in the future, that truly motivates an individual not only to seek peace, but to maintain it. "The Passion to be reckoned upon, is Fear." Still later, he writes, "Of all Passions, that which enclineth men least to break the Lawes, is Fear. Nay, (excepting some generous natures,) it is the onely thing, (when there is apparence of profit, or pleasure by breaking the Lawes,) that makes them keep them." *Leviathan*, chs. 13, 14, 27, pp. 90, 99, 206.

22. *Elements*, 1.7.2, pp. 28–29.

23. *Leviathan*, chs. 6, 11, pp. 42, 75.

24. *De Cive*, 1.2, p. 113. In *Elements*, he defines fear as "some conception of evil to happen unto us by such actions" that we consider, that "withholdeth us from proceeding." In Leviathan, fear is defined as an "*Aversion*, with opinion of *Hurt* from the object." *Elements*, 1.12.1, p. 61; *Leviathan*, ch. 6, p. 41.

25. *Leviathan*, ch. 4, p. 31.

26. Further evidence of the low repute of fear among the revolutionaries can be seen in Milton's defense of his behavior during the Civil War. John Milton, *The Second Defense of the People of England*, in *Complete Poems and Major Prose*, ed. Merritt Y. Hughes (New York: Macmillan, 1957), pp. 818–19; Michael Walzer, *The Revolution of the Saints: A Study in the Origins of Radical Politics* (Cambridge: Harvard University Press, 1965), pp. 21, 270, 279.

27. *Behemoth*, p. 114.
28. *Behemoth*, p. 45.
29. Cf. Albert O. Hirschman, *The Passions and the Interests: Political Arguments for Capitalism Before Its Triumph* (Princeton: Princeton University Press, 1977).
30. Milton, p. 819; *Puritanism and Liberty*, 3rd ed., ed. A. S. P. Woodhouse (London: J.M. Dent & Sons, 1986), p. 53. Milton was by no means a democrat; scholars have long noted the elitist inflections of his and his comrades' republican sensibilities. But with his strong anticlericalism and hatred of servility, Milton undoubtedly subscribed to the more generous enthusiasms of this democratic moment. See Christopher Hill, *Society and Puritanism in Pre-Revolutionary England* (London: Penguin, 1964), pp. 45–46; Tuck, *Philosophy and Government*, pp. 252–53. On the new vocabulary of the English Revolution and its contributions to later democratic thinking, see Christopher Hill, *The World Turned Upside Down: Radical Ideas During the English Revolution* (New York: Penguin, 1975), pp. 378–84; *Divine Right and Democracy: An Anthology of Political Writing in Stuart England*, ed. David Wootton (New York: Penguin, 1986), pp. 38–58; J. G. A. Pocock, *The Machiavellian Moment: Florentine Political Thought and the Atlantic Republican Tradition* (Princeton: Princeton University Press, 1975), pp. 462–505; Tuck, *Philosophy and Government*, pp. 222–23. The best account of the Puritans as forerunners of modern revolutionaries remains Walzer, *Revolution of the Saints*.
31. Machiavelli, *The Prince*, p. 131.
32. *Behemoth*, p. 59. Also see *Leviathan*, ch. 30, p. 232.
33. *Behemoth*, p. 3; *De Cive*, 5.5, p. 169. This argument runs counter to that of many scholars who claim that Hobbes held an atomistic view of society, that his all-powerful Leviathan ruled over isolated human subjects shorn of any social ties or mediating institutions. Hobbes, I would argue, believed that most men and women were ensconced in local institutions of deference and hierarchy. The problem for him was not the anarchic or antisocial tendencies of individuals but their willingness to "follow their immediate leaders; which are either the preachers, or the most potent gentlemen that dwell amongst them," even in defiance of the sovereign's laws. While Hobbes believed there was no pre-political *moral obligation* binding individuals either to each other or to sovereign authority, he was quite sensitive to the institutional context of human action and to the everyday influence of elites over popular behavior. He feared that "the Popularity of a potent Subject" was a "a dangerous Disease." The authority of elites could be easily mobilized against the sovereign, as it was during the Civil War. But no sovereign, not even Leviathan, could eliminate these popular forms of authority. The only solution was for the sovereign to "have very good caution" of these elites' "fidelity," to ensure that they used their authority to argue for the sovereign's necessity and legitimacy. Behemoth, p. 39; *Leviathan*, ch. 29, p. 229. Also see *De Cive*, I.2, p. 110; *Behemoth*, pp. 23, 27–28, 54; *Leviathan*, ch. 29, p. 224. For interpretations of Hobbes as atomist, see C. B. Macpherson, *The Political Theory of Possessive Individualism: Hobbes to Locke* (Oxford: Oxford University Press, 1962), pp. 22, 38–42, 49–61; Leo Strauss, *Natural Right and History* (Chicago: University of Chicago Press, 1973), p. 110; Steven Lukes, *Individualism* (Oxford: Basil Blackwell, 1973), p. 110; Thomas Nagel, "Hobbes's Concept of Obligation," *Philosophical Review* 68 (1959), pp. 68–83; Alasdair MacIntyre, *After Virtue: A Study in Moral Theory*, 2nd ed.

(Notre Dame, Ind.: University of Notre Dame Press, 1981, 1984), pp. 60–61, 195–96; Michael Sandel, *Liberalism and the Limits of Justice* (New York: Cambridge University Press, 1982), p. 175; Sheldon S. Wolin, *Politics and Vision: Continuity and Innovation in Western Political Thought* (Boston: Little, Brown, 1960), pp. 239–41; Oakeshott, "Introduction to *Leviathan*," pp. 280–83; Watkins, pp. 28–54; Peters, chs. 2, 8; Gauthier, pp. 1–9; Hampton, pp. 6–11. For excellent critiques of this view, see Deborah Baumgold, *Hobbes's Political Theory* (Cambridge: Cambridge University Press, 1988); and Baumgold, "Hobbes's Political Sensibility: The Menace of Political Ambition," in *Thomas Hobbes and Political Theory*, ed. Mary G. Dietz (Lawrence: University Press of Kansas, 1990), pp. 74–90.

34. *Behemoth*, p. 59.

35. *Behemoth*, pp. 40, 56, 58. Also see *Behemoth* pp. 2–3, 40–43; *Leviathan*, "A Review, and Conclusion," p. 491.

36. Wolin, p. 266.

37. *Behemoth*, pp. 23, 27, 30, 32.

38. "For if we look on men full grown, and consider how brittle the frame of our human body is, which perishing, all its strength, vigour, and wisdom itself perisheth with it. . . ." *De Cive*, 1.3, p. 114.

39. To simplify a complex argument, negative liberty is the absence of external, usually physical constraints; positive liberty is a condition of autonomous, rational self-direction, in which we are freed of our socially constructed, crippling desires (honor and glory might be examples, in the Hobbesian analysis, of such desires). Hobbes never used either term, though one can find elements of both principles in his work. Quentin Skinner argues, persuasively, that Hobbesian fear is consistent with what we think of negative liberty. As Skinner points out, Hobbes believes that deliberation is merely the oscillation between two passions: appetite and fear. The will—that is, the decision to do what we do—is, in the Hobbesian account, the last passion we experience before we act. If that passion is fear, it is the determinant of our will. When we act in accordance with fear, we act in accordance with what we have willed. So long as no external impediments stop us from acting upon or against our will, we are free. For that reason, fear and negative liberty are consistent. Skinner, however, presumes that only negative liberty is reconcilable with fear, or at least that that is what Hobbes claims. While Hobbes certainly defines liberty in negative terms, there is much in his account to suggest that fear also lies at the heart of what we think of as positive liberty. See Quentin Skinner, "Hobbes's Antiliberal Theory of Liberty," in *Liberalism without Illusions: Essays on Liberal Theory and the Political Vision of Judith N. Shklar*, ed. Bernard Yack (Chicago: University of Chicago Press, 1996), pp. 159–60; also see Sorrell, *Hobbes*, pp. 92–25.

40. *Elements*, 1.9.1, pp. 36–37; *Leviathan*, ch. 10, p. 63.

41. *Leviathan*, ch. 10, p. 62.

42. *Elements*, 1.9.1, pp. 36–37; *Leviathan*, ch. 10, p. 63.

43. *De Cive*, 1.2, p. 113.

44. *Elements*, 1.14.4, p. 71; *Leviathan*, ch. 8, p. 54.

45. *Leviathan*, ch. 11, p. 72.

46. "But without Stedinesse, and Direction to some End, a great Fancy is one kind of Madnesse." *Leviathan*, ch. 8, p. 51.

47. *De Homine*, 12.4, p. 57.

48. *De Cive*, 1.2, p. 113.

49. Franz Neumann, "Anxiety and Politics," in *The Democratic and Authoritarian State: Essays in Political and Legal Theory*, ed. Herbert Marcuse (New York: Free Press, 1970), p. 270. Also see Max Horkheimer and Theodor Adorno, *Dialectic of the Enlightenment* (London: Verso, 1979), p. 3; Henry Sidgwick, *The Elements of Politics* (London: Macmillan, 1891), p. 41.

50. Tzvetan Todorov, *Facing the Extreme: Moral Life in the Concentration Camps*, trans. Arthur Denner and Abigail Pollack (London: Weidenfeld & Nicolson, 1999), pp. 9–10.

51. See Barry Glassner, *The Culture of Fear* (New York: Basic, 1999); Mary Douglas, *Purity and Danger: An Analysis of Concepts of Pollution and Taboo* (New York: Routledge, 1966); Mary Douglas and Aaron Wildavsky, *Risk and Culture: An Essay on the Selection of Technological and Environmental Dangers* (Berkeley: University of California Press, 1982); Cass R. Sunstein, *Risk and Reason: Safety, Law, and the Environment* (New York: Cambridge University Press, 2002).

52. John Gaventa, *Power and Powerlessness: Quiescence and Rebellion in an Appalachian Valley* (Urbana: University of Illinois Press, 1980).

53. *Leviathan*, ch. 6, pp. 39, 41.

54. *Leviathan*, ch. 13, p. 89.

55. *Leviathan*, ch. 3, p. 22.

56. *Leviathan*, ch. 8, p. 53; also see ch. 27, p. 207.

57. *Leviathan*, ch. 27, p. 207.

58. *Leviathan*, ch. 18, p. 129.

59. *De Cive*, p. 100. Also see *De Cive*, 1.3, pp. 113–14; *Leviathan*, chs. 13, 14, pp. 86–89, 91, 96.

60. Alan Ryan aptly compares the state of nature to nuclear deterrence, in which all parties are bound by "the logic of the situation" to fear each other and treat each other as hostile enemies. Alan Ryan, "Hobbes's political philosophy," in *Cambridge Companion to Hobbes*, p. 220.

61. In the state of nature, fear is "perpetual in its own nature; because . . . it cannot be ended in victory." *De Cive*, 1.3, p. 118.

62. *Leviathan*, ch. 13, p. 89.

63. *Leviathan*, ch. 14, p. 91.

64. *Leviathan*, chs. 14, 21, pp. 93, 151.

65. *Leviathan*, ch. 14, p. 92.

66. *Leviathan*, chs. 21, 28, pp. 151–52, 214.

67. Wolin, p. 281–85; Michael Walzer, *Obligations: Essays on Disobedience, War, and Citizenship* (Cambridge: Harvard University Press, 1970), pp. 80–87.

68. The only crime warranting arbitrary, open-ended punishment is treason. *Leviathan*, chs. 26, 27, 28, pp. 187, 190, 209, 214–16, 219.

69. *Leviathan*, ch. 28, p. 215.

70. *Leviathan*, ch. 28, p. 215.

71. *De Cive*, 2.19, p. 131.

72. *De Cive*, 6.13, p. 183.

73. *Leviathan*, ch. 13, p. 89.

74. *Leviathan*, ch. 11, p. 71.

75. *Leviathan*, ch. 46, p. 459.

76. I borrow the terms "party of movement" and "party of order" from historian Arno Mayer, who derived them from John Stuart Mill and Harvard president Lawrence Lowell. See Arno J. Mayer, *Political Origins of the New Diplomacy* (New York: Vintage, 1970, 1959), p. 4. Also see Noberto Bobbio, *Left and Right: The Significance of a Political Distinction*, trans. Allan Cameron (Chicago: University of Chicago Press, 1996).

77. Maximilien Robespierre, "Report on the Principles of Political Morality," in *The Old Regime and the French Revolution*, ed. Keith Michael Baker (Chicago: University of Chicago Press, 1987), p. 375.

78. Todorov, pp. 3–70. Also see, in a different vein, Alan Ryan's remarks on R.H. Tawney in his "Socialism for the Nineties," *Dissent* (Fall 1990), p. 440.

79. For excellent accounts of counterrevolutionary theory and practice, see Isaiah Berlin, "Joseph de Maistre and the Origins of Fascism," in *The Crooked Timber of Humanity: Chapters in the History of Ideas*, ed. Henry Hardy (New York: Vintage, 1992), pp. 91–174; Fritz Stern, *The Politics of Cultural Despair: A Study in the Rise of Germanic Ideology* (Garden City, N.Y.: Anchor Books, 1961); Arno Mayer, *The Furies: Violence and Terror in the French and Russian Revolutions* (Princeton: Princeton University Press, 2000); Greg Grandin, *The Last Colonial Massacre: Latin America in the Cold War* (Chicago: University of Chicago Press, 2004); Tina Rosenberg, *Children of Cain: Violence and the Violent in Latin America* (New York: Penguin, 1991), pp. 77–142, 331–87.

80. Rosenberg, *Children of Cain*, p. 13.

81. Aubrey, *Brief Lives*, p. 236; Martinich, p. 91; G. A. J. Rogers, "Hobbes's Hidden Influence," in *Perspectives on Thomas Hobbes*, ed. G. A. J. Rogers and Alan Ryan (Oxford: Clarendon, 1988), pp. 196–97; Skinner, *Reason and Rhetoric*, p. 225; *Leviathan*, ch. 46, pp. 471–72. Also see Tuck, *Hobbes*, pp. 13–16; Watkins, pp. 28–41; and Strauss, *The Political Philosophy of Hobbes*, pp. 151–52.

82. Bertolt Brecht, *Galileo* (New York: Grove Press, 1966), pp. 99, 110.

83. Brecht, pp. 122–24.

84. Brecht, pp. 61–64.

85. Brecht, p. 123.

## 2: TERROR

1. Thomas Hobbes, *Behemoth, or the Long Parliament*, ed. Ferdinand Tönnies (Chicago: University of Chicago Press, 1990), p. v.

2. Pierre Goubert, *Louis XIV and Twenty Million Frenchmen*, trans. Anne Carter (New York: Vintage, 1966, 1970), pp. 57, 63–70, 87–89, 92–97; Alfred Cobban, *A History of Modern France. Volume One: The Old Regime and the French Revolution, 1715–1799*, 3rd ed. (New York: Penguin, 1963), pp. 9, 11–12; Montesquieu, *The Persian Letters*, trans. and ed. Robert Loy (New York: Meridian, 1961), letter 37, p. 95.

3. Robert Shackleton, *Montesquieu: A Critical Biography* (London: Oxford University Press, 1961), pp. 3–5, 13–18, 85–89, 202, 226–28; Judith N. Shklar, *Montesquieu* (New York: Oxford University Press, 1987), pp. 1–5, 18–19, 69, 74–75, 79–81; Nannerl Keohane, *Philosophy and the State in France: The Renaissance to the Enlightenment* (Princeton: Princeton University Press, 1980), pp. 403–7; Franz Neumann, "Mon-

tesquieu," in *The Democratic and Authoritarian State: Essays in Political and Legal Theory*, ed. Herbert Marcuse (New York: Free Press, 1957), pp. 111–12; Melvin Richter, *The Political Theory of Montesquieu* (Cambridge: Cambridge University Press, 1977), pp. 31–32, 45–46; Melvin Richter, "Despotism," in *Dictionary of the History of Ideas*, vol. 2, ed. Philip P. Wiener (New York: Charles Scribner's Sons, 1973), pp. 7–9; Raymond Aron, *Main Currents in Sociological Thought I: Montesquieu, Comte, Marx, Tocqueville, the Sociologists of the Revolution of 1848*, trans. Richard Howard and Helen Weaver (Garden City, N.Y.: Doubleday, 1968), p. 26; R. Koebner, "Despot and Despotism: Vicissitudes of a Political Term," *Journal of the Warburg and Courtland Institutes* 14 (1951): 293–302; Orest Ranum, "Personality and Politics in the *Persian Letters*," *Political Science Quarterly* 84 (December 1969): 609–12, 617–22; Franco Venturi, "Oriental Despotism," *Journal of the History of Ideas* 24 (January–March 1963): 134–36; David Young, "Montesquieu's View of Despotism and His Use of Travel Literature," *Review of Politics* 40 (July 1978): 404–5.

4. Montesquieu, *The Spirit of the Laws*, ed. Anne M. Cohler et al. (New York: Cambridge University Press, 1989), 1.2, pp. 6–7.

5. Voltaire, *L'A, B, C*, in *Philosophical Dictionary*, vol. 2, trans. Peter Gay (New York: Basic, 1962), p. 508.

6. Scholars who have paid attention to *The Persian Letters* have mistakenly assumed either that its account of despotic terror is identical to that of *The Spirit of the Laws*, or that it is a youthful corollary to his later work. See Roger Boesche, "Fearing Monarchs and Merchants: Montesquieu's Two Theories of Despotism," *Western Political Quarterly* 43 (December 1990): 742; Mark Hulliung, *Montesquieu and the Old Regime* (Berkeley: University of California Press, 1976), p. 138; Pauline Kra, "The Invisible Chain of the Lettres Persanes," *Studies on Voltaire and the Eighteenth Century* 23 (1963): 11; Tzvetan Todorov, *On Human Diversity: Nationalism, Racism, and Exoticism in French Thought*, trans. Catherine Porter (Cambridge: Harvard University Press, 1993), p. 353; Neumann, p. 102; Richter, "Despotism," p. 9; Richter, *The Political Theory of Montesquieu*, p. 45; Shackleton, *Montesquieu*, p. 45; Shklar, *Montesquieu*, p. 67. For a critique of these accounts and a fuller analysis of how *The Persian Letters* challenges *The Spirit of the Laws*, see Corey Robin, "Reflections on Fear: Montesquieu in Retrieval," *American Political Science Review* 94 (June 2000): 347–60.

7. *Persian Letters*, letters 1, 8, 17, 105–6, 115, pp. 47, 54, 68–69, 195–99, 210–12; Shklar, *Montesquieu*, pp. 26–27, 30.

8. Hulliung, p. 123; Shklar, *Montesquieu*, pp. 31, 34; Todorov, pp. 355–56.

9. Isaiah Berlin, "Montesquieu," in *Against the Current: Essays in the History of Ideas*, ed. Henry Hardy (London: Hogarth Press, 1990), pp. 130–61; Sheldon Wolin, "Montesquieu and Publius: The Crisis of Reason and The Federalist Papers," in *The Presence of the Past: Essays on the State and the Constitution* (Baltimore: Johns Hopkins University Press, 1989), pp. 100–19; Shklar, *Montesquieu*, pp. 107, 124.

10. *Persian Letters*, letters 2, 20, pp. 47–48, 73–74.

11. *Persian Letters*, letter 9, p. 55; also see letter 64 and appendix 2, pp. 134–37, 285–88.

12. *Persian Letters*, letters 15, 41–42, pp. 67, 100–101.

13. *Persian Letters*, letters 4, 9, pp. 50, 55–58.

14. Montesquieu's text also suggests a connection between the gazing eye of the pornographer and totalitarian domination, a relationship that has haunted critics,

feminist and nonfeminist alike, throughout the twentieth century. Cf. George Steiner, "Night Words," in *George Steiner: A Reader* (New York: Oxford University, 1984), pp. 305–14; Roger Shattuck, *Forbidden Knowledge: From Prometheus to Pornography* (New York: St. Martin's Press, 1996), pp. 206–7.

15. *Persian Letters*, letter 3, p. 49.

16. *Persian Letters*, letter 62, pp. 132–33. According to a recent *New York Times Magazine* report, a similar phenomenon occurs in today's international sex-trafficking rings, where older, trusted women are used as "principals" to inculcate fear and submission among younger female captives. Peter Landesman, "The Girls Next Door," *New York Times Magazine* (January 25, 2004), p. 37.

17. Cobban, pp. 19–27, 51.

18. Cobban, pp. 19–27, 51.

19. Shklar, *Montesquieu*, pp. 21–22.

20. Melvin Richter, "Montesquieu's Comparative Analysis of Europe and Asia: Intended and Unintended Consequences," in *L'Europe de Montesquieu* (Napoli: Linguori Editore, 1995), pp. 331, 335–37.

21. *Spirit*, 11.6, p. 157. On the differences between the liberalism of Montesquieu and Locke, see Pierre Manent, *An Intellectual History of Liberalism*, trans. Rebecca Balinski (Princeton: Princeton University Press, 1995), pp. 53–64.

22. Although Montesquieu did define terror in his personal journals. See Shklar, *Montesquieu*, p. 84.

23. Peter Gay, *The Enlightenment: An Interpretation*, vol. 2, *The Science of Freedom* (New York: W. W. Norton, 1969), pp. 320–22; Thomas Pangle, *Montesquieu's Philosophy of Liberalism* (Chicago: University of Chicago Press, 1973), pp. 11–21; Berlin, pp. 137–38; Richter, *The Political Theory of Montesquieu*, pp. 32–35; Shklar, *Montesquieu*, p. 30; Wolin, pp. 102–4.

24. *Spirit*, 5.14, 6.1, pp. 60, 74.

25. *Spirit*, 3.10, 4.5, pp. 29, 35.

26. *Spirit*, 3.8–10, 4.3, 5.13–14, 6.1, 19.27, pp. 27–29, 35, 59–60, 74, 332.

27. *Spirit*, 3.8, 10, 5.14, 6.1, 9, pp. 27, 29–30, 63, 74, 82.

28. Michael Sandel, *Liberalism and the Limits of Justice* (New York: Cambridge University Press, 1982), pp. 55, 19, 177.

29. *Spirit*, 3.9–10, 4.3, pp. 28–29, 34–35.

30. Immanuel Kant, *On the Common Saying: 'This May be True in Theory, but it does not Apply in Practice'*, in *Political Writings*, ed. Hans Reiss, trans. H. B. Nisbet, 2nd ed. (New York: Cambridge University Press, 1970), p. 73; *Foundations of the Metaphysics of Morals*, trans. Lewis White Beck (Indianapolis: Bobbs-Merrill, 1959), pp. 43, 71.

31. *Spirit*, 5.12, 14–15, pp. 58–59, 61, 64.

32. *Spirit*, 2.5, 3.10, V.12, 14, pp. 20, 29, 59.

33. Cf. Plato, *The Republic*, trans. Allan Bloom (New York: Basic Books, 1968), 562a–64a, pp. 240–42; Aristotle, *The Politics*, trans. Ernest Barker (New York: Oxford University Press, 1962), 1279b, 1295a, pp. 114–15, 178–79; John Locke, *The Second Treatise*, in *Two Treatises of Government*, ed. Peter Laslett (New York: Cambridge University Press, 1988), § 199, pp. 398–99.

34. *Spirit*, 2.5, 3.8–10, 4.3, 5.1, 14, pp. 20, 27–30, 34–35, 57, 59. It should be noted that Montesquieu's attitude toward religion was ambivalent. While he did believe that re-

ligion would provide a counter to despotism, he also occasionally suggested that religion, which he called "fear added to fear," might be a critical aid to the despot's power. See *Spirit*, 4.3, 5.14, pp. 34, 61.

35. *Spirit*, 2.4–5, 3.8–9, 5.1, 16, pp. 17–20, 27–28, 57, 66.
36. *Spirit*, 2.4, 6.1, 21, pp. 18, 72–73, 95.
37. *Spirit*, 2.5, 3.9, 5.16, pp. 20, 28, 65.
38. Thomas Hobbes, *Leviathan*, ed. Richard Tuck (New York: Cambridge University Press, 1991), p. 9.
39. Cited in Shklar, *Montesquieu*, p. 115.
40. *Spirit*, 5.14, 8.17, pp. 59–60, 125.
41. *Spirit*, 5.14, 19.12, 14, pp. 60, 314–15.
42. Hannah Arendt, "On the Nature of Totalitarianism: An Essay in Understanding," in *Essays in Understanding 1930–1954*, ed. Jerome Kohn (New York: Harcourt Brace, 1994), p. 329; also see pp. 315–16.
43. Sigmund Freud, *Beyond the Pleasure Principle* (New York: Liveright Publishing Corporation, 1950), pp. 49–50.
44. *Spirit*, 2.5, 3.10, 5.14, pp. 20, 30, 59–60, 63.
45. *Spirit*, 3.9, p. 28.
46. Michel de Montaigne, *The Complete Essays*, trans. Donald M. Frame (Stanford: Stanford University Press, 1957), pp. 52–53; Georg Wilhelm Friedrich Hegel, *Lectures on the Philosophy of World History*, trans. H. B. Nisbet (Cambridge: Cambridge University Press, 1975), p. 190.
47. For discussions of Montesquieu on Asia, see Ali Behdad, "The Eroticized Orient: Images of the Harem in Montesquieu and his Precursors," *Stanford French Review* 12 (Fall/Winter 1989), pp. 109–26; Robert Shackleton, "Asia as Seen by the French Enlightenment," in *Essays on Montesquieu and the Enlightenment*, ed. David Gilson and Martin Smith (Oxford: Voltaire Foundation, 1988), p. 239; Richter, "Despotism," pp. 12–13; Richter, "Montesquieu's Comparative Analysis of Europe and Asia," pp. 329–48; Venturi, pp. 137–39; David Young, "Montesquieu's View of Despotism," pp. 392–405. On Montesquieu's cosmopolitanism, see Norman Hampson, *Will and Circumstance: Montesquieu, Rousseau and the French Revolution* (London: Gerald Duckworth, 1983), pp. 4, 11; Shklar, *Montesquieu*, p. 30; Todorov, *On Human Diversity*, pp. 353–99.
48. Denis Diderot, *Observations sur le Nakaz*, in *Political Writings*, ed. John Hope Mason and Robert Wokler (New York: Cambridge University Press, 1992), p. 90; Robespierre, "Report on the Principles of Political Morality," in *The Old Regime and the French Revolution*, ed. Keith Michael Baker (Chicago: University of Chicago Press, 1987), p. 375; Saint-Just and de Staël cited in Richter, "Despotism," p. 14; Hegel, p. 190.
49. Elaine Scarry, *The Body in Pain: The Making and Unmaking of the World* (New York: Oxford University Press, 1985), pp. 3–59; Michael Taussig, *The Nervous System* (New York: Routledge, 1992), pp. 1, 6, 16, 20, 26, 33; Tina Rosenberg, *Children of Cain: Violence and the Violent in Latin America* (New York: Penguin, 1991); Amy Wilentz, *The Rainy Season* (New York: Simon and Schuster), 1989.
50. Cf. Jean Bethke Elshtain, *Democracy on Trial* (New York: Basic, 1995), pp. 38–39, 42–43, 45–52; John Gray, *Post-Liberalism: Studies in Political Thought* (London: Routledge, 1993), p. 158; Charles Taylor, "Invoking Civil Society," in *Philosophical Argu-*

*ments* (Cambridge: Harvard University Press, 1995), pp. 204–5, 214, 222; Charles Taylor, "Liberal Politics and the Public Sphere," in *New Communitarian Thinking: Persons, Virtues, Institutions, and Communities,* ed. Amitai Etzioni (Charlottesville: University Press of Virginia, 1995), pp. 185, 211; *Civil Society and the State: New European Perspectives,* ed. John Keane (London: Verso, 1988); Ernest Gellner, *Conditions of Liberty: Civil Society and its Revival* (New York: Penguin, 1994); *Freedom of Association,* ed. Amy Guttman (Princeton: Princeton University Press, 1998); *The Essential Civil Society Reader: The Classic Essays,* ed Don E. Eberly (Lanham: Rowman & Littlefield, 2000).

51. James Madison, Alexander Hamilton, and John Jay, *The Federalist Papers* (New York: Penguin, 1987), No. 47, p. 303; Daniel T. Rodgers, *Contested Truths: Keywords in American Politics Since Independence* (New York: Basic, 1987), p. 57; Shklar, *Montesquieu,* p. 121; Jack N. Rakove, *Original Meanings: Politics and Ideas in the Making of the Constitution* (New York: Vintage, 1996).

52. Edmund Burke, *A Philosophical Enquiry into the Origins of our Ideas of the Sublime and Beautiful* (New York: Oxford University Press, 1990), p. 54.

## 3: ANXIETY

1. These opening three paragraphs are indebted to Georg Lukács, *The Historical Novel,* trans. Hannah and Stanley Mitchell (Boston: Beacon Press, 1962), pp. 23–25; George Steiner, *In Bluebeard's Castle: Some Notes Towards the Redefinition of Culture* (New Haven: Yale University Press, 1971), pp. 11–13; François Furet, *Interpreting the French Revolution,* trans. Elborg Forster (Cambridge: Cambridge University Press, 1981), pp. 23–25, 43–46.

2. Steiner, p. 12.

3. Thomas Paine, *The Rights of Man,* in *The Thomas Paine Reader,* ed. Michael Foot and Isaac Kramnick (New York: Penguin, 1987), p. 259; William Wordsworth, *The Prelude,* in *The Poetical Works of Wordsworth* (Boston: Houghton Mifflin, 1982), 9.166–67, p. 189.

4. *The Recollections of Alexis de Tocqueville,* trans. Alexander Teixeira de Mattos (New York: Columbia University Press, 1949), p. 40.

5. Cf. Simon Schama, *Citizens: A Chronicle of the French Revolution* (New York: Alfred A. Knopf, 1989); Lynn Hunt, *Politics, Culture and Class in the French Revolution* (Berkeley: University of California Press, 1984).

6. Tocqueville and Michelet cited in Roger Boesche, *The Strange Liberalism of Alexis de Tocqueville* (Ithaca: Cornell University Press, 1987), pp. 59, 65.

7. J. S. Mill, *On Liberty,* ed. Stefan Collini (New York: Cambridge University Press, 1989), p. 62.

8. Cited in Jean-Claude Lamberti, *Tocqueville and the Two Democracies,* trans. Arthur Goldhammer (Cambridge: Harvard University Press, 1989), p. 229.

9. Cited in Lamberti, p. 220. My account of the shifts from volume one to volume two corresponds to one pole in a long-running debate about whether *Democracy in America* is two different books sharing the same title, or a unified whole. For representatives of the "two democracies" thesis, with which I agree, see Seymour Drescher, "Tocqueville's Two *Democraties," Journal of the History of Ideas* 25 (April/June 1964): 201–16; Arthur Schlesinger, "Individualism and Apathy in Tocqueville's Democracy," in *Reconsidering Tocqueville's Democracy in America,* ed. Abraham S. Eisenstadt

(New Brunswick: Rutgers University Press, 1988), p. 101; Richard Sennett, "What Tocqueville Feared," in *On the Making of Americans: Essays in Honor of David Riesman*, ed. Herbert J. Gans et al. (Philadelphia: University of Pennsylvania Press, 1979), pp. 105–6, André Jardin, *Tocqueville: A Biography*, trans. Lydia Davis with Robert Hemenway (New York: Farrar Straus Giroux, 1988), p. 251. For more nuanced, but tempered, support for Drescher's argument, see Larry Siedentop, *Tocqueville* (New York: Oxford University Press, 1994), pp. 69–70; Lamberti, pp. 141–43, 228–29, 236–39. James Schleifer rejects much of the Drescher thesis, but even he points to real divisions between the first and second volumes. See Schleifer, *The Making of Tocqueville's Democracy in America* (Chapel Hill: University of North Carolina Press, 1980), pp. 154–55, 176, 207, 285.

10. For excellent discussions of Tocqueville's relationship to the "new liberalism," see George Armstrong Kelly, *The Humane Comedy: Constant, Tocqueville, and French Liberalism* (New York: Cambridge University Press, 1991); Larry Siedentop, "Two Liberal Traditions," in *The Idea of Freedom: Essays in Honour of Isaiah Berlin*, ed. Alan Ryan (Oxford: Oxford University Press, 1979), pp. 153–74; and Siedentop, *Tocqueville*.

11. Guizot cited in E. J. Hobsbawm, *The Age of Revolution 1789–1848* (New York: New American Library, 1962), p. 148; Tocqueville, *Selected Letters on Politics and Society*, ed. Roger Boesche, trans. James Toupin and Roger Boesche (Berkeley: University of California Press, 1985), pp. 127, 153, 284.

12. For a useful discussion of the relationship between Tocqueville's political defeats and his increasing fatalism, see François Furet, "The Conceptual System of 'Democracy in America,'" in *In the Workshop of History*, trans. Jonathan Mandelbaum (Chicago: University of Chicago Press, 1986), pp. 169, 171. Also see Lamberti, pp. 123, 126–30; Schleifer, p. 29.

13. *Letters*, p. 294.

14. Lamberti, p. 220.

15. Jardin, pp. 1–9, 37–91.

16. Daniel Rodgers, "Of Prophets and Prophecy," in Eisenstadt, pp. 198–99, 205.

17. *Democracy*, p. 255.

18. *Democracy*, pp. 72, 373, 494. Also see *Democracy*, p. 56; Schleifer, pp. 197, 201.

19. Hobbes, *Leviathan*, ed. Richard Tuck (New York: Cambridge University Press, 1989), ch. 16, p. 114.

20. *Democracy*, pp. 119–20, 246–47.

21. *The Federalist Papers*, ed. Isaac Kramnick (New York: Penguin, 1987), No. 22, p. 184.

22. *Democracy*, pp. 155, 171, 173; Schleifer, pp. 145, 197.

23. *Democracy*, pp. 255–56.

24. *Democracy*, p. 256.

25. See Rodgers, "Of Prophets and Prophecy," p. 199; Furet, "The Conceptual System of 'Democracy in America,'" p. 185.

26. *Democracy*, pp. 262–76.

27. *Democracy*, pp. 257, 313, 16. Also see Raymond Aron, *Main Currents of Sociological Thought I: Montesquieu, Comte, Tocqueville, and the Sociologists of the Revolution of 1848*, trans. Richard Howard and Helen Weaver (Garden City: Anchor Books, 1968), p. 274; Pierre Manent, *Tocqueville and the Nature of Democracy*, trans. John Waggoner (Lanham: Rowman & Littlefield, 1996), p. 20; Kelly, p. 65.

28. *Democracy*, p. 313.

29. *Democracy*, pp. 254, 256, 577.

30. *Democracy*, pp. 254–55, 313. Also see Tocqueville, "France Before the Revolution," in *Memoir, Letters, and Remains* (Boston: Ticknor and Fields, 1862), pp. 244–48.

31. *Democracy*, pp. 50–51, 58–59; Schleifer, p. 46.

32. *Democracy*, pp. 431, 435, 641.

33. *Democracy*, p. 435. Also see Manent, pp. 38–42.

34. *Democracy*, p. 643. Emphasis added. Also see *Democracy*, p. 436.

35. *Democracy*, p. 655.

36. *Democracy*, pp. 198, 243–47.

37. *Democracy*, p. 507.

38. *Democracy*, pp. 507–8, 510, 444–45.

39. *Democracy*, pp. 444, 701.

40. *Democracy*, pp. 444, 702.

41. Cited in Lamberti, p. 151.

42. Arthur M. Schlesinger, Jr., *The Vital Center: The Politics of Freedom* (New York: Da Capo, 1959, 1988), pp. 247, 250.

43. *Democracy*, pp. 503–6, 509–10, 520, 539, 576–77.

44. Like many contemporary communitarians and proponents of civil society and social capital, Tocqueville praised associations that helped build local infrastructure and that served as a substitute for the power of the central administrative state, but was quite critical of associations that took a more political or radical turn. Indeed, Tocqueville often supported the suppression of political associations he feared were radical or dangerous. Tocqueville, *Journey to America*, trans. George Lawrence, ed. J. P. Mayer (Garden City, N.Y.: Anchor Books, 1971), pp. 38–39, 219–20, 222–24; Lamberti, pp. 80, 210; Manent, pp. 34–35; Boesche, pp. 179–80.

45. *Democracy*, pp. 511, 515–16, 52–24. There is no doubt that Tocqueville understood the centralized state as the adjutant of egalitarianism and revolution, and localism and decentralization as remnants of aristocratic politics, or "the aristocratic temperament," as he wrote to John Stuart Mill (Schleifer, p. 158). Thus, resistance to centralization and further equality, which Tocqueville thought was critical to the project of resisting anxiety, would have to be conducted with the same aristocratic tools that resisted the march of revolution and democracy. See Lamberti, pp. 210, 214, 228–29; Schleifer, pp. 157–59; Siedentop, *Tocqueville*, pp. 25, 64.

46. For an excellent account of Tocqueville's romanticism, see Boesche, *The Strange Liberalism of Alexis de Tocqueville*. Also see the scattered, but suggestive, comments in Furet, "The Conceptual System of 'Democracy in America,'" pp. 169, 171, 186.

47. Although romanticism had extensive appeal throughout Europe, I refer here primarily to its literary embodiments in France and Germany. For various accounts of the relationship between revolution and romanticism, from which I have learned much, see Steiner, *In Bluebeard's Castle*; Isaiah Berlin, *The Roots of Romanticism* (Princeton: Princeton University Press, 1999); and Lionel Trilling, *Sincerity and Authenticity* (Cambridge: Harvard University Press, 1971).

48. *Letters*, pp. 147–49, 153, 157; Boesche, p. 62.

49. *Letters*, pp. 67, 134–36, 160, 187; *Remains*, pp. 270–76; Siedentop, *Tocqueville*, pp. 22–24, 29–31, 45–46; Kelly, pp. 1–69; Lamberti, pp. 51–53, 126–35, 208.

50. Boesche, pp. 40, 62; *Letters*, pp. 143, 146, 158; Tocqueville, *The Old Regime and the French Revolution*, trans. Stuart Gilbert (New York: Anchor Books, 1983), pp. x–xi; *Recollections*, p. 90.

51. *Old Regime*, p. xii; *Letters*, pp. 154, 184; *Recollections*, pp. 54–55.

52. Melvin Richter, "The Uses of Theory: Tocqueville's Adaptation of Montesquieu," in *Essays in Theory and History: An Approach to the Social Sciences* (Cambridge: Harvard University Press, 1970), p. 78; Lamberti, pp. 55, 58.

53. *Letters*, pp. 105, 153, 181; Schleifer, p. 256. Also see Tocqueville, *Journey to America*, pp. 155, 163–64.

54. Lending added credence to the argument that Tocqueville's commitments were distinctively modern and romantic rather than republican or humanist, Chateaubriand comments that "the Ancient scarcely knew this secret anxiety, the bitterness of strangled passions, all fermenting together. A large political life, games in the gymnasium or on the field of Mars, the business of the Forum—public business—filled their time and left no place for the ennui of the heart." (Cited in Berlin, *The Roots of Romanticism*, p. 132.) There are two other reasons why Tocqueville's vision of public life should not be viewed through the lens of civic republicanism. First, he saw liberty and action as goads to progress, an idea that runs counter to the cyclical conceptions of time found in the civic republican tradition. (On Tocqueville's vision of progress and development, see *Journey to America*, p. 155; Lamberti, pp. 42, 54, 58, 153–54.) Second, he was extremely sensitive to what he believed were the tyrannical, anti-individualist tendencies of the civic republican tradition. He was far too concerned about the privacy and freedom of individuals to endorse a full-blown conception of public or positive liberty. (See *Remains*, p. 263; Lamberti, pp. 187–88; and Schleifer, p. 256.)

55. *Recollections*, p. 7; *Letters*, p. 247; Boesche, p. 65; Siedentop, *Tocqueville*, p. 14.

56. For an excellent discussion of Tocqueville's views on imperialism, see Jennifer Pitts's introduction in Tocqueville, *Writings on Empire and Slavery*, ed. and trans. Jennifer Pitts (Baltimore: Johns Hopkins University Press, 2001), pp. ix–xviii.

57. To this point, Mill, no stranger to the argument that Europe was threatened by softened mores and flabby spirits or to arguments defending imperialism, responded that the French—and perhaps Tocqueville himself—were acting like "sulky schoolboys." After this exchange, the society of mutual admiration between Tocqueville and Mill dissipated. *Letters*, pp. 141–42, 150–51; Boesche, p. 65; Jardin, pp. 309–14, 348–49.

58. *Recollections*, p. 246; Jardin, pp. 407–26.

59. *Recollections*, p. 99.

60. *Recollections*, p. 87.

61. *Recollections*, pp. 91, 116.

62. Edmund Burke, *A Philosophical Enquiry into the Origins of our Ideas of the Sublime and Beautiful* (New York: Oxford University Press, 1990), pp. 45–46. Also see Machiavelli, *The Prince*, in *The Portable Machiavelli*, ed. and trans. Peter Bondanella and Mark Musa (New York: Penguin, 1979), pp. 92–93.

63. Cited in Hannah Arendt, *The Origins of Totalitarianism* (New York: Harcourt Brace Jovanovich, 1951, 1973), p. 69.

64. Tocqueville, "France Before the Consulate," in *Memoirs, Letters, and Remains*, pp. 262–63.

## 4: TOTAL TERROR

1. As a much younger man, Trotsky was also dubbed the "Benjamin" of the Bolshe-viks. Isaac Deutscher, *The Prophet Armed. Trotsky: 1879–1921* (New York: Oxford University Press, 1954), pp. 64, 71; Stephen F. Cohen, *Bukharin and the Bolshevik Revolution: A Political Biography, 1888–1938* (New York: Oxford University Press, 1971, 1980), pp. 13, 152; J. Arch Getty and Oleg V. Naumov, *The Road to Terror: Stalin and the Self-Destruction of the Bolsheviks, 1932–1939* (New Haven: Yale University Press, 1999), p. 40.

2. Getty and Naumov, pp. 559, 588; Cohen, pp. 270–381; Genesis 22:12.

3. Cohen, p. 152.

4. Søren Kierkegaard, *Fear and Trembling: A Dialectical Lyric*, in *A Kierkegaard Anthology*, ed. Robert Bretall (Princeton: Princeton University Press, 1946), pp. 131–34.

5. Arthur M. Schlesinger, Jr., *The Vital Center* (New York: Da Capo, 1949, 1988), pp. 104–5; Leslie Fiedler, "Afterthoughts on the Rosenbergs," *An End to Innocence* (New York: Stein and Day, 1971), pp. 42, 45. Also see Richard Rorty, *Contingency, Irony, and Solidarity* (New York: Cambridge University Press, 1989), p. 179; François Furet, *The Passing of an Illusion: The Idea of Communism in the Twentieth Century*, trans. Deborah Furet (Chicago: University of Chicago Press, 1999), pp. 116–24; Richard Rorty, *Achieving Our Country: Leftist Thought in Twentieth-Century America* (Cambridge: Harvard University Press, 1998), p. 118.

6. Getty and Naumov, pp. 40, 48–49, 369–70, 392–99, 411, 417–19, 526; Cohen, pp. 375–80; *The Great Purge Trial*, ed. Robert C. Tucker and Stephen F. Cohen (New York: Grosset and Dunlap, 1965), pp. xlii–xlviii; Robert Conquest, *The Great Terror: Stalin's Purge of the Thirties* (London: Macmillan, 1968), pp. 142, 301.

7. *The God That Failed*, ed. Richard Crossman (New York: Bantam, 1949), p. 163.

8. Fiedler, p. 26.

9. Hannah Arendt, *The Origins of Totalitarianism* (New York: Harcourt Brace Jovanovich, 1951, 1973), p. 458. Also see Hannah Arendt, "Social Science Techniques and the Study of Concentration Camps," in *Essays in Understanding 1930–1954* (New York: Harcourt Brace, 1994), p. 243.

10. See Abbott Gleason, *Totalitarianism: The Inner History of the Cold War* (New York: Oxford University Press, 1995); Stephen J. Whitfield, *Into the Dark: Hannah Arendt and Totalitarianism* (Philadelphia: Temple University Press, 1980), pp. 8–24; Jeffrey C. Isaac, *Arendt, Camus, and Modern Rebellion* (New Haven: Yale University Press, 1992), pp. 37–45.

11. Margaret Canavon, *Hannah Arendt: A Reinterpretation of Her Political Thought* (New York: Cambridge University Press, 1992), pp. 17–23, 28–29; Seyla Benhabib, *The Reluctant Modernism of Hannah Arendt* (Thousand Oaks, Calif.: SAGE, 1996), pp. 63–65; Dana R. Villa, *Politics, Philosophy, Terror: Essays on the Thought of Hannah Arendt* (Princeton: Princeton University Press, 1999), pp. 180–81; Elisabeth Young-Bruehl, *Hannah Arendt: For Love of the World* (New Haven: Yale University Press, 1982), pp. 200–3.

12. "An Exchange of Letters between Gershom Scholem and Hannah Arendt," in *The Jew as Pariah: Jewish Identity and Politics in the Modern Age*, ed. Ron H. Feldman (New York: Grove Press, 1978), p. 246.

13. Canavon, *Hannah Arendt*, p. 86; *Within Four Walls: The Correspondence between*

*Hannah Arendt and Heinrich Blücher, 1936–1968*, ed. Lotte Kohler (New York: Harcourt, 2000), p. 80; Hanna Fenichel Pitkin, *The Attack of the Blob: Hannah Arendt's Concept of the Social* (Chicago: University of Chicago Press, 1998), p. 116. While Heidegger's influence on Arendt is by now well known—indeed, it recently has become the topic of racy academic gossip (the two were lovers for several years)—her debt to Montesquieu and Tocqueville has yet to be fully itemized. For some suggestive comments on these influences, see Canavon, *Hannah Arendt*, pp. 60, 67, 117, 120, 159–60, 186–91, 214, 273; Benhabib, pp. 68–71; and Pitkin, *The Attack of the Blob*. On Heidegger and Arendt, see Elżbieta Ettinger, *Hannah Arendt/Martin Heidegger* (New Haven: Yale University Press, 1995); Richard Wolin, *Heidegger's Children: Hannah Arendt, Karl Löwith, Hans Jonas, and Herbert Marcuse* (Princeton: Princeton University Press, 2001), pp. 31–69; Villa, pp. 61–86; Benhabib, pp. 51–56, 102–22; and Villa, *Arendt and Heidegger: The Fate of the Political* (Princeton: Princeton University Press, 1996), pp. 230–40.

14. I confess to be unpersuaded by the claim of one of Arendt's most able interpreters—indeed, by the occasional testimony of Arendt herself—that *Eichmann in Jerusalem* was simply an account of one man, on trial for specific crimes, rather than a reconsideration of the Holocaust and of totalitarianism as a whole. As Arendt and her interlocutors made clear in their correspondence, she and they understood all too well how Eichmann revised some of the main tenets of Origins. See Villa, *Philosophy, Politics, and Terror*, p. 44; Arendt, *Eichmann in Jerusalem* (New York: Penguin, 1963, 1964), pp. 280, 285; Young-Bruehl, p. 367; Hannah Arendt and Karl Jaspers, *Correspondence 1926–1969*, ed. Lotte Kohler and Hans Saner (New York: Harcourt Brace Jovanovich, 1992), pp. 525, 542; *Between Friends: The Correspondence of Hannah Arendt and Mary McCarthy 1949–1975*, ed. Carol Brightman (New York: Harcourt Brace, 1995), pp. 147–48, 160–61; "An Exchange of Letters between Gershom Scholem and Hannah Arendt," in *The Jew as Pariah*, pp. 240–51.

15. For various reports on the Eichmann controversy, see Young-Bruehl, pp. 347–78; *Between Friends*, pp. 146–54, 160–62, 166–67; *Correspondence*, pp. 510–11, 515–16, 521–33, 535–36, 539–43, 545–47, 562, 564, 566, 581–82, 593.

16. Mary McCarthy, "The Hue and Cry," *Partisan Review* (January–February 1964).

17. My entire discussion here is drawn from the last third of *The Origins of Totalitarianism*, the section titled "Totalitarianism." I have limited myself to this section for two reasons. First, unlike the first two sections of the book, "Totalitarianism" was the only section where Arendt addressed the phenomenon of totalitarianism itself. It is her most sustained enquiry into the problem of total terror, and therefore of most interest and significance to us here. Second, this was the section of the book that received the most notice and attention throughout the Cold War: it was certainly the most influential.

18. *Origins*, p. 308.

19. *Origins*, pp. 438, 458–59; "Social Science Techniques and the Study of Concentration Camps," in *Essays in Understanding*, p. 243; Villa, *Philosophy, Politics, and Terror*, pp. 16–17.

20. "Dedication to Karl Jaspers," in *Essays in Understanding*, p. 215.

21. *Origins*, pp. 306, 311, 314–15, 348.

22. *Origins*, pp. 311, 314. Also see Arendt, "A Reply to Eric Voegelin," in *Essays in Under-*

standing, p. 406; Margaret Canovan, "The People, the Masses, and the Mobilization of Power: The Paradox of Hannah Arendt's 'Populism,'" *Social Research* 69 (Summer 2002): 404–11.

23. *Origins*, p. 317; more generally, pp. 313–18.

24. *Origins*, p. 315. Though Arendt generally disapproved of psychological explanations of politics, she often entertained them in the context of totalitarianism and its mass origins. For a useful discussion of Arendt's "moral psychology," see George Kateb, *Hannah Arendt: Politics, Conscience, Evil* (Totowa, N.J.: Rowman & Allanheld, 1983), pp. 53–55.

25. *Origins*, pp. 317, 323–34, 465, 478.

26. *Origins*, pp. 318–19, 460.

27. *Origins*, p. 316. Though in her personal letters and other works, Arendt occasionally drifted toward the Tocquevillian equation of equality and anomie. Cf. *Between Friends*, pp. 167, 293.

28. Few of Arendt's contemporaries and admirers heeded this caveat. They argued that it was democracy and equality that created the conditions of totalitarianism. As one representative text put it, "The plain fact is that most of the requisites of mass democracy are requisites of totalitarianism." Cited in Benjamin R. Barber, "Conceptual Foundations of Totalitarianism," in Carl J. Friedrich, Michael Curtis, and Benjamin R. Barber, *Totalitarianism in Perspective: Three Views* (New York: Praeger, 1969), pp. 18–19. Also see *Totalitarianism*, ed. Carl J. Friedrich (New York: Grosset and Dunlap, 1954), pp. 17, 57.

29. *Origins*, p. 475. Also see p. 459.

30. *Origins*, p. 475.

31. *Origins*, pp. 476–77.

32. *Origins*, pp. 476, 478, 315.

33. *Origins*, p. 398.

34. *Origins*, pp. 305, 348, 355–56, 361–63, 412. Also see "On the Nature of Totalitarianism: An Essay in Understanding," in *Essays in Understanding*, p. 356.

35. *Origins*, pp. 362–70.

36. *Origins*, pp. 307, 314, 349–50.

37. *Origins*, p. 356.

38. *Origins*, pp. 469–70, 477, 353.

39. *Origins*, pp. 472–43.

40. *Origins*, p. 353.

41. *Origins*, pp. xxxiii, 438, 441, 456–7.

42. *Origins*, pp. 433, 443, 468.

43. "Social Science Techniques" and "On the Nature of Totalitarianism," in *Essays in Understanding*, pp. 236, 357.

44. *Origins*, p. 455. Also see Canavon, *Hannah Arendt*, pp. 34–35.

45. *Origins*, p. 316. At times, though, Arendt did suggest that terror was propelled by nature itself. See Arendt, *On Revolution* (New York: Penguin, 1963, 1965), pp. 112–14.

46. *Origins*, pp. 305, 325, 374–75, 395–401, 403–49, 413, 459.

47. *Origins*, p. 459. Also see "Social Science Techniques," in *Essays in Understanding*, p. 239.

48. *Origins*, pp. xxxiii–xiv, 344, 393, 412, 440, 464. Also see "Mankind and Terror," in *Essays in Understanding*, p. 298.

49. *Origins*, pp. 412, 454, 465–66.

50. *Origins*, 468.

51. "On the Nature of Totalitarianism," in *Essays in Understanding*, p. 357.

52. It is Arendt's emphasis in *Origins* on the impersonality of totalitarianism that makes me skeptical of Richard Bernstein's argument that *Eichmann in Jerusalem* is not a repudiation of *Origins*. According to Bernstein, those who claim that *Eichmann* is a departure from *Origins* believe, mistakenly, that in *Origins*, Arendt viewed the Nazis as possessed by a "Satanic greatness," that they were monsters or demons akin to Shakespeare's grand villains. As he correctly points out, and as I have argued here, that is not what Arendt argued in *Origins*. There, she argued that that were no monsters—no doers of deeds—under totalitarianism. But as I argue here, Arendt revised this theory in *Eichmann*, claiming that while there were no monsters under totalitarianism, there were doers of deeds. In *Eichmann*, total terror was the work of specific actors pursuing specific ends. Superfluousness no longer referred to the impersonality of the entire totalitarian regime, to the loss of self and agency under terror. Superfluousness now meant the eradication of whole groups. See Richard Bernstein, "From Radical Evil to the Banality of Evil: From Superfluousness to Thoughtlessness," in *Hannah Arendt and the Jewish Question* (Cambridge: MIT Press, 1996), pp. 137–53. For an excellent discussion of these issues, see Villa, *Politics, Philosophy, Terror*, pp. 39–60.

53. *Origins*, p. 478. Also see *Origins*, p. v; "On the Nature of Totalitarianism" and "The Eggs Speak Up," in *Essays in Understanding*, pp. 279–80, 328; Young-Bruehl, p. 201.

54. *Origins*, p. 478. Also see Canavon, *Hannah Arendt*, p. 2.

55. "The Image of Hell," in *Essays in Understanding*, p. 199; *Origins*, p. 441.

56. *Origins*, p. 442. Also see Canavon, *Hannah Arendt*, p. 199; *Correspondence*, p. 105; Young-Bruehl, p. 211.

57. *Origins*, pp. 327, 459–60, 478.

58. *Origins*, p. 459.

59. *Correspondence*, p. 165. As Arendt wrote in several places: "The manipulators of this system believe in their own superfluousness as much as in that of all others." "The unreality which surrounds the hellish experiment, which is so strongly felt by the inmates themselves and makes the guards, but also the prisoners, forget that murder is being committed when somebody or many are killed, . . . ." "No one except for the leader in power at the moment is immune from terror." "The ideal type of the totalitarian functionary is the one who functions no matter what, who has no life outside his function." "The totalitarian dictator, in sharp distinction from the tyrant, does not believe that he is a free agent with the power to execute his arbitrary will, but, instead, the execution of laws higher than himself. The Hegelian definition of Freedom as insight into and conforming to 'necessity' has here found a new and terrifying realization." *Origins*, p. 459; "Social Science Techniques," "Mankind and Terror," and "On the Nature of Totalitarianism," in *Essays in Understanding*, pp. 241, 303, 305, 346.

60. Young-Bruehl, p. 371.

61. For Arendt's own account of the differences between the two works, see *Between Friends*, pp. 147–48; "An Exchange of Letters between Gershom Scholem and Hannah Arendt," in *The Jew as Pariah*, pp. 240–51.

62. For useful discussions of the planning and writing of *Origins*, see Canavon, *Hannah Arendt*, pp. 17–20, 28–55; Young-Bruehl, pp. 157–58, 184–88, 199–211; Roy Tsao, "The Three Phases of Arendt's Theory of Totalitarianism," *Social Research* 69 (Summer 2002): 579–619.

63. "Approaches to the 'German Problem,'" in *Essays in Understanding*, pp. 112–17. Also see "Power Politics Triumphs," in *Essays in Understanding*, p. 156; *Correspondence*, pp. 66, 611; Canavon, *Hannah Arendt*, p. 65.

64. "Preface: The Gap Between Past and Future," in *Between Past and Future: Eight Exercises in Political Thought* (New York: Vintage, 1961, 1968), p. 4.

65. "Approaches to the 'German Problem,'" in *Essays in Understanding*, pp. 117–20. Also see "Power Politics Triumphs," in *Essays in Understanding*, pp. 156–57; *Correspondence*, p. 23.

66. *Correspondence*, pp. 210–12; also see p. 111, 231; *Between Friends*, p. 5.

67. Young-Bruehl, p. 203; Canavon, *Hannah Arendt*, p. 19; Tsao, pp. 587–612.

68. Canavon, *Hannah Arendt*, pp. 65–66; *Correspondence*, pp. 29, 98, 111, 150–51; *Within Four Walls*, p. 100.

69. "French Existentialism," in *Essays in Understanding*, p. 188.

70. For Arendt's reflections on the relationship between political defeat and philosophy more generally, see *Correspondence*, p. 685; *Between Friends*, pp. 343–44.

71. "Preface," in *Between Past and Future*, p. 5.

72. *Origins*, p. vii.

73. "Preface," in *Between Past and Future*, p. 4.

74. "A fighting revolution requires economics (Marx); a victorious revolution requires engineers (Russia); a defeated revolution calls for psychology." Paul Lazarsfeld, "An Episode in the History of Social Research: A Memoir," in *The Intellectual Migration: Europe and America, 1930–1960*, ed. Donald Fleming and Bernard Bailyn (Cambridge: Harvard University Press, 1969), p. 272. I am indebted to Allen Hunter for this reference.

75. "'What Remains? The Language Remains': A Conversation with Günter Gaus," in *Essays in Understanding*, pp. 10–11.

76. Young-Bruehl, pp. 360–61.

77. *Eichmann*, p. 153.

78. George Winstanley, "A New-Yeers Gift for the Parliament and Armie," in *Divine Right and Democracy: An Anthology of Political Writing in Stuart England*, ed. David Wootton (New York: Penguin, 1986), p. 321; Jean-Jacques Rousseau, *Discourse on the Origin and Foundation of Inequality Among Men*, in *Rousseau's Political Writings*, ed. Alan Ritter and Julia Conaway Bondanella (New York: Penguin, 1988), p. 52.

79. For classic statements of this argument, see Montesquieu, *The Spirit of the Laws*, ed. Anne Choler et al. (New York: Cambridge University Press, 1989), 2.4, 5.11, 6.1, 8.6, 11.1–6, pp. 18, 57–58, 72–73, 116–17, 154–66; *The Federalist Papers*, ed. Isaac Kramnick (New York: Penguin, 1987), Nos. 10 and 51, pp. 122–28, 319–22; Robert A. Dahl, *Who Governs? Democracy and Power in an American City* (New Haven: Yale University Press, 1961), pp. 63–86, 89–103; Milton Friedman, *Capitalism and Freedom* (Chicago: University of Chicago Press, 1962, 1982), pp. 7–36.

80. When Arendt did mention jobholding in *Origins*, it was only to say that it didn't matter: few Nazis had any "genuine interest in specific jobs." Though she admitted that

Himmler understood that "most people are neither bohemians, fanatics, adventurers, sex maniacs, crackpots, nor social failures, but first and foremost job holders and good family men," she concluded that he recognized that deep within the jobholder was a desire "to sacrifice everything." *Origins*, pp. 339, 409, 459, 475. Also see "Organized Guilt and Universal Responsibility," in *Essays in Understanding*, pp. 128–29. For hints of Arendt's evolving view of the political significance of jobholding (as opposed to her more philosophical explorations in *The Human Condition* of the distinctions between work and labor), see *Correspondence*, pp. 212, 223; "Franz Kafka," in *Essays in Understanding*, p. 75.

81. *Eichmann*, pp. 65, 75–76.
82. *Eichmann*, p. 126.
83. *Eichmann*, pp. 287, 45.
84. *Eichmann*, pp. 29, 31–33, 52, 61–62, 81–82, 113, 126, 234.
85. *Eichmann*, pp. 31–32.
86. *Eichmann*, pp. 111, 134.
87. *Between Friends*, p. 275.
88. *Eichmann*, p. 286. Also see *Between Friends*, p. 160.
89. *Eichmann*, p. 75.
90. *Eichmann*, p. 93.
91. *Eichmann*, p. 42.
92. *Eichmann*, p. 105.
93. *Eichmann*, pp. 29, 46, 47, 238.
94. *Eichmann*, p. 238.
95. *Eichmann*, p. 33.
96. *Eichmann*, p. 105.
97. *Eichmann*, p. 93.
98. *Eichmann*, pp. 93, 105, 135–38, 143–50.
99. *Eichmann*, p. 276.
100. *Eichmann*, pp. 85–86, 277.
101. *Eichmann*, p. 126.
102. *Eichmann*, p. 126.
103. *Eichmann*, pp. 269, 277, 279. I thus take issue with Canavon, Villa, and Bernstein, who conflate Arendt's treatment in *Origins* of the superfluousness of individuals with her treatment in *Eichmann* of the superfluousness of peoples. In *Origins*, superfluousness meant the individual's loss of significance; in *Eichmann*, superfluousness meant the obsolescence of a discrete people. See Canavon, *Hannah Arendt*, p. 24; Villa, *Politics, Philosophy, Terror*, pp. 13–14, 19–20; Bernstein, pp. 143–45. I also take issue with those critics who claim that Arendt showed a greater appreciation of the assault upon the Jewish people in *Origins* than she did in *Eichmann*. If anything, *Origins* was far less concerned with these crimes as crimes against the Jews.
104. Cited in Young-Bruehl, p. 356.
105. *Eichmann*, pp. 120, 124, 165, 171–73, 279. Also see *Correspondence*, p. 485.
106. *Eichmann*, pp. 11–12, 124–25.
107. *Correspondence*, p. 417.
108. *Eichmann*, p. 125.
109. *Eichmann*, pp. 10–11, 39, 117, 131–33, 154, 186–88.

110. See Yehuda Bauer, *Rethinking the Holocaust* (New Haven: Yale University Press, 2001), pp. 119–66.

111. "An Exchange of Letters between Gershom Scholem and Hannah Arendt," in *The Jew as Pariah*, pp. 250–51.

112. "Franz Kafka," in *Essays in Understanding*, p. 78; *Correspondence*, p. 62.

113. *Between Friends*, p. 166; also see *Correspondence*, p. 479; "'What Remains? The Language Remains,'" in *Essays in Understanding*, p. 16.

114. Daniel Goldhagen, *Hitler's Willing Executioners: Ordinary Germans and the Holocaust* (New York: Knopf, 1996), pp. 580–81; Christopher Browning, *Ordinary Men: Reserve Police Battalion 10 and the Final Solution in Poland* (New York: HarperCollins, 1992, 1998), pp. 159–89. Also see William Sheridan Allen, *The Nazi Seizure of Power: The Experience of a Single German Town 1922–1945* (New York: Franklin Watts, 1954, 1984).

115. Bauer, p. 105.

116. Saul Friedländer, *Nazi Germany and the Jews*, Volume 1: *The Years of Persecution* (New York: HarperCollins, 1997), pp. 73–112; Jeffrey Herf, *Reactionary Modernism: Technology, Culture and Politics in Weimar and the Third Reich* (New York: Cambridge University Press, 1984).

117. Tzvetan Todorov, *Facing the Extreme: Moral Life in the Concentration Camps* (New York: Metropolitan Books, 1996).

118. Getty and Naumov, pp. 6, 14.

119. Lewis Siegelbaum and Andrei Sokolov, *Stalinism as a Way of Life: A Narrative in Documents* (New Haven: Yale University Press, 2000), p. 8; Sheila Fitzpatrick, *Everyday Stalinism: Ordinary Life in Extraordinary Times: Soviet Russia in the 1930s* (New York: Oxford University Press, 1999), pp. 175–78.

120. Elena Zubkova, *Russia After the War: Hopes, Illusions, and Disappointments, 1945–1957* (Armonk: M. E. Sharpe, 1998), pp. 161–63.

121. Fitzpatrick, p. 208.

122. Richard Bernstein, "The Origins of Totalitarianism: Not History, but Politics," *Social Research* (Summer 2002), pp. 382, 391; Villa, *Politics, Philosophy, Terror*, pp. 13–14, 37–38, though see his thoughtful qualifications on pp. 52–60; Tsao, pp. 611–12.

123. See, among others, Robert D. Putnam, *Bowling Alone: The Collapse and Revival of American Community* (New York: Simon and Schuster, 200); Michael Walzer, *On Toleration* (New Haven: Yale University Press, 1997), pp. 91, 98–101; Michael Sandel, *Democracy's Discontent: America in Search of a Public Philosophy* (Cambridge: Harvard University Press, 1996), pp. 3–4; Amitai Etzioni, *The New Golden Rule* (New York: Basic Books, 1996), p. 27; Benjamin Barber, *Jihad vs. McWorld: How Globalism and Tribalism Are Reshaping the World* (New York: Ballantine, 1995, 1996); Benjamin Barber, *Strong Democracy: Participatory Politics for a New Age* (Berkeley: University of California Press, 1984), pp. 109–14.

124. Isaac, pp. 60–64; Irving Howe, "Totalitarianism Reconsidered: Yesterday's Theories, Today's Realities," *Dissent* (Winter 1991), p. 67. For a more careful statement, see Kateb, p. 54.

125. *Intimacy and Terror: Soviet Diaries of the 1930s*, ed. Véronique Garros, Natalia Korenevskaya, and Thomas Lahusen (New York: New Press, 1995); Sheila Fitzpatrick, *Stalin's Peasants: Resistance and Survival in the Russian Village After Collectivization* (New York: Oxford University Press, 1994); Jan T. Gross, *Neighbors: The Destruction of*

the Jewish Community in Jedwabne, Poland (Princeton: Princeton University Press, 2001); Tina Rosenberg, The Haunted Land: Facing Europe's Ghosts After Communism (New York: Vintage, 1995); Patricia Politzer, Fear in Chile: Lives Under Pinochet (New York: New Press, 1989, 2001); Lawrence Wechsler, A Miracle, A Universe: Settling Accounts with Torturers (Chicago: University of Chicago Press, 1990, 1998); Tina Rosenberg, Children of Cain: Violence and the Violent in Latin America (New York: Penguin, 1991), pp. 77–142, 333–87; Mark Danner, The Massacre at El Mozote: A Parable of the Cold War (New York: Vintage, 1993); Daniel Wilkinson, Silence on the Mountain: Stories of Terror, Betrayal, and Forgetting in Guatemala (Boston: Houghton Mifflin, 2002).

126. Kristin Ross, May Day and Its Afterlives (Chicago: University of Chicago Press, 2002), pp. 150–51; Todd Gitlin and Sean Wilentz, "To Those Who Supported the Nader Campaign," Dissent (Spring 2001), pp. 93–96.

## 5: REMAINS OF THE DAY

1. Alexis de Tocqueville, "France Before the Consulate," in Memoirs, Letters, and Remains of Alexis de Tocqueville (Boston: Ticknor and Fields, 1862), pp. 262–63; Coriolanus, IV.v.236–40. Also see Georg Wilhelm Friedrich Hegel, Philosophy of Right, trans. T. M. Knox (New York: Oxford University Press, 1952, 1967), § 324, p. 210; Ralph Waldo Emerson, "Heroism," in Essays: First and Second Series (New York: Vintage, 1990), pp. 143–44.

2. Julian Bond, "The Future of the Democratic Party," New York Free Press (October 31, 1968), reprinted in The New Left: A Documentary History, ed. Massimo Teodori (Indianapolis: Bobbs-Merrill, 1969), p. 445; Rubin cited in John Patrick Diggins, The Rise and Fall of the American Left (New York: Norton, 1973, 1992), p. 261.

3. Paul Berman, A Tale of Two Utopias: The Political Journey of the Generation of 1968 (New York: Norton, 1996), pp. 84–85; Ron Rosenbaum, "Goodbye, All That: How Left Idiocies Drove Me to Flee," New York Observer (December 14, 2002), p. 1. Also see Richard Rorty, Achieving Our Country: Leftist Thought in Twentieth-Century America (Cambridge: Harvard University Press, 1998); Michael Kazin, "A Patriotic Left," Dissent (Fall 2002): 41–44; Todd Gitlin, "Liberalism's Patriotic Vision," New York Times (September 5, 2002), p. A23.

4. Corey Robin, "The Ex-Cons: Right-Wing Thinkers Go Left!" Lingua Franca (February 2001): 32–33.

5. Francis Fukuyama, The End of History and the Last Man (New York: HarperCollins, 1992, 2002), 304–5, 311–12.

6. Michael Walzer, On Toleration (New Haven: Yale University Press, 1997), p. 100; Amitai Etzioni, "Old Chestnuts and New Spurs," in New Communitarian Thinking: Persons, Virtues, Institutions, and Communities, ed. Amitai Etzioni (Charlottesville: University Press of Virginia, 1995), p. 19; Jean Bethke Elshtain, Democracy on Trial (New York: Basic Books, 1995), p. 15; Jennifer Block, "Roe v. Wade, then v. now," Village Voice (January 15–21, 2003), p. 59; Elshtain, "The Communitarian Individual," in New Communitarian Thinking, p. 106. Also see William A. Galston, Liberal Purposes: Goods, Virtues, and Diversity in the Liberal State (New York: Cambridge University Press, 1991), pp. 6, 13–15; Charles Taylor, The Ethics of Authenticity (Cambridge: Harvard University Press, 1991), p. 76; Robert D. Putnam, Bowling Alone: The Collapse and Revival of American Community (New York: Simon and

Schuster, 2000), pp. 36, 74, 258; Michael J. Sandel, *Democracy's Discontent: America in Search of a Public Philosophy* (Cambridge: Harvard University Press, 1996), pp. 47–54, 278–94.

7. One of the few critics to recognize the liberal dimensions of the liberalism of anxiety is Nancy L. Rosenblum, in her "Pluralism and Self-Defense," in *Liberalism and the Moral Life*, ed. Nancy Rosenblum (Cambridge: Harvard University Press, 1989), pp. 207–8, 214–15, 218–19.

8. Etzioni, "Old Chestnuts and New Spurs," pp. 17–18, 23, 25; Sandel, *Democracy's Discontent*, pp. 319–21; Walzer, "The Communitarian Critique of Liberalism," in *New Communitarian Thinking*, pp. 52–53; Will Kymlicka, *Liberalism, Community, and Culture* (Oxford: Clarendon, 1989); Galston, *Liberal Purposes*.

9. One can see the links between the romantic individualist ethos of the 1960s and the contemporary liberalism of anxiety most clearly in the abiding concerns and career of Charles Taylor, who began as a romantic New Leftist and ended up as a communitarian. See Taylor, *Hegel* (Cambridge: Cambridge University Press, 1975); Taylor, *Hegel and Modern Society* (Cambridge: Cambridge University Press, 1979); Taylor, "The Politics of Recognition," in *Multiculturalism: Examining the Politics of Recognition*, ed. Amy Guttman (Princeton: Princeton University Press, 1994), pp. 25–73; Taylor, *The Ethics of Authenticity*. For an excellent discussion of the romantic individualist dimensions of communitarianism, see Rosenblum, "Pluralism and Self-Defense," pp. 214–15, 218–19.

10. Etzioni, "Old Chestnuts and New Spurs," p. 22; Kymlicka, *Multicultural Citizenship: A Liberal Theory of Minority Rights* (Oxford: Clarendon Press, 1995), p. 83; Walzer, "The Communitarian Critique of Liberalism," p. 60.

11. Yael Tamir, *Liberal Nationalism* (Princeton: Princeton University Press, 1993), pp. 7–8, 13–34; William M. Sullivan, "Institutions as the Infrastructure of Democracy," in *New Communitarian Thinking*, pp. 171–72, 174–75, 180; Taylor, *The Ethics of Authenticity*, pp. 33–39.

12. As Brian Barry has noted, the family often appears in these arguments as a model of social life. Brian Barry, *Culture and Equality: An Egalitarian Critique of Multiculturalism* (Cambridge: Harvard University Press, 2001), pp. 14–15.

13. Walzer, *On Toleration*, p. 91; Walzer, "The Communitarian Critique of Liberalism," p. 69; Galston, "Civic Education and the Liberal State," in *Liberalism and the Moral Life*, p. 101. Also see Taylor, *The Ethics of Authenticity*, pp. 37–41, 57; Richard Rorty, *Achieving Our Country*, pp. 24–25.

14. Kymlicka, *Liberalism, Community, and Culture*, pp. 61–62. Also see Etzioni, "Old Chestnuts and New Spurs," p. 22; Sandel, *Democray's Discontent*, pp. 308–15, 322–23; Benjamin Barber, *Strong Democracy: Participatory Politics for a New Age* (Berkeley: University of California Press, 1984), pp. 109–14.

15. Walzer, "The Communitarian Critique of Liberalism," p. 60; Walzer, *On Toleration*, p. 104. Also see Putnam, *Bowling Alone*, p. 114; Charles Taylor, "Liberal Politics and the Public Sphere," in *New Communitarian Thinking*, p. 211; Sandel, *Democracy's Discontent*, p. 3; Etzioni, "Old Chestnuts and New Spurs," p. 16; Sullivan, p. 173; Taylor, *The Ethics of Authenticity*, pp. 9–10, 112–19.

16. Cf. Seymour Martin Lipset, *Political Man: The Social Bases of Politics* (Garden City, N.Y.: Anchor, 1960), p. 24; Richard Hofstadter, *The Progressive Historians: Turner,*

Beard, Parrington (New York: Vintage, 1968), p. 444; John Higham, "The Cult of the 'American Consensus': Homogenizing Our History," Commentary 27 (February 1959): p. 94; John Higham with Leonard Krieger and Felix Gilbert, History: The Development of Historical Studies in the United States (Englewood Cliffs: Prentice-Hall, 1965), pp. 221–22; Richard Pells, The Liberal Mind in a Conservative Age: American Intellectuals in the 1940s and 1950s (New York: Harper & Row, 1985), pp. 149, 187, 239; George H. Nash, The Conservative Intellectual Movement in America Since 1945 (New York: Basic Books, 1976), pp. 63–64.

17. David Riesman, "The Intellectuals and the Discontent Classes: Some Further Reflections," and Talcott Parson, "Social Strains in America: A Postscript," in The Radical Right, ed. Daniel Bell (Garden City, N.Y.: Anchor, 1965, 1955), pp. 83, 88, 143, 237. Also see David Riesman, The Lonely Crowd: A Study of the Changing American Character (Garden City, N.Y.: Anchor, 1950, 1953); Edward Shils, The Torment of Secrecy: The Background and Consequences of American Security Policies (Chicago: Elephant Paperbacks, 1956, 1996); William Kornhauser, The Politics of Mass Society (Glencoe, Ill.: The Free Press, 1959).

18. Lionel Trilling, The Liberal Imagination (Garden City, N.Y.: Anchor, 1950), p. 5. Also see Louis Hartz, The Liberal Tradition in America (New York: Harcourt Brace Jovanovich, 1955); Richard Hofstadter, The American Political Tradition (New York: Vintage, 1973), pp. xxxvii–xxxviii; Robert Dahl, Who Governs? Democracy and Power in an American City (New Haven: Yale University Press, 1961), p. 317.

19. Martin Luther King, "The Strength to Love" and "Why We Can't Wait," in A Testament of Hope: The Essential Writings and Speeches of Martin Luther King, Jr., ed. James M. Washington (New York: HarperCollins, 1986), pp. 513–14, 528; The Autobiography of Malcolm X (New York: Grove, 1964), p. 253; Remembering Jim Crow: African Americans Tell About Life in the Segregated South, ed. William H. Chafe et al. (New York: The New Press, 2001), pp. 1–55, 268–303.

20. Putnam, Bowling Alone, pp. 82, 258–9; Walzer, On Toleration, pp. 100, 102; Taylor, Ethics of Authenticity, pp. 2–3, 10.

21. David Miller, On Nationality (New York: Oxford University Press, 1995), p. 1. As political theorist Nancy Fraser has argued, debates over identity—or recognition, as she puts it—need not preclude issues of distribution and social inequality. Indeed, as Iris Marion Young and Mahmoud Mamdani have shown, identity and difference are often the instruments of distributive inequities—whether in Western Europe and North America, or in the relationship between European colonizers and their local agents in the colonized world. But in most debates over identity, these subtler counsels are ignored. See Fraser, Justice Interruptus: Critical Reflections on the 'Postsocialist Condition' (New York: Routledge, 1997), pp. 11–39, 121–49; Iris Marion Young, Justice and the Politics of Difference (Princeton: Princeton University Press, 1990); Mahmoud Mamdani, Citizen and Subject: Contemporary Africa and the Legacy of Late Colonialism (Princeton: Princeton University Press, 1996); Mamdani, When Victims Become Killers: Colonialism, Nativism, and the Genocide in Rwanda (Princeton: Princeton University Press, 2001).

22. Seyla Benhabib, "The Democratic Moment and the Problem of Difference," in Democracy and Difference: Contesting the Boundaries of the Political, ed. Seyla Benhabib (Princeton: Princeton University Press, 1996), pp. 3–4; Samuel Huntington,

*The Clash of Civilizations and the Remaking of World Order* (New York: Simon and Schuster, 1996), p. 21.

23. Catharine MacKinnon, "Not by Law Alone: From a Debate with Phyllis Schlafly," *Feminism Unmodified: Discourses on Life and Law* (Cambridge: Harvard University Press, 1987), p. 22.

24. King, "The Strength to Love," p. 514; James Baldwin, "In Search of a Majority," *Nobody Knows My Name* (New York: Vintage, 1960), pp. 127–37.

25. Benhabib, p. 3.

26. During the 1950s, Richard Hofstadter argued that an "insecurity over one's identity and sense of belonging" in the United States gave "our personal status problems . . . an unusual intensity," and David Riesman and Nathan Glazer claimed that "fluidity of boundaries threatens" people's "self-assurance." Hofstadter, "The Pseudo-Conservative Revolt," and Riesman and Glazer, "The Intellectuals and the Discontented Classes," in *The Radical Right*, pp. 83, 88, 111.

27. Though even when political actors argue about issues that do not necessarily involve questions of identity—for instance, the recent debates about globalization and the imposition of market regimes throughout the world—political theorists have chosen to interpret these conflicts as debates over identity. See Benjamin Barber, *Jihad v. McWorld* (New York: Ballantine, 1996); John Gray, *False Dawn: The Decline of Global Capitalism* (New York: The New Press, 1997), pp. 2–3, 13, 26, 57–60; James Tully, *Strange Multiplicity: Constitutionalism in an Age of Diversity* (Cambridge: Cambridge University Press, 1995), p. 2.

28. Huntington, p. 21; Taylor, "The Politics of Recognition," in *Philosophical Arguments* (Cambridge: Harvard University Press, 1995), pp. 225, 228; Miller, p. 11. Emphasis added.

29. Etzioni, "Old Chestnuts and New Spurs," pp. 26–27; Elshtain, "The Communitarian Individual," p. 108; Taylor, "Liberal Politics and the Public Sphere," p. 185.

30. Taylor, "Cross Purposes: The Liberal-Communitarian Debate," in *Philosophical Arguments*, p. 189.

31. Taylor, "Cross Purposes," pp. 190–91.

32. Walzer, "The Communitarian Critique of Liberalism," pp. 65–66; also see Putnam, *Bowling Alone*, pp. 80–92.

33. George W. Bush, "The National Security Strategy of the United States of America" (September 17, 2002) (http://www.whitehouse.gov/nsc/nssal.html) <last accessed on March 30, 2004>.

34. Cheney cited in Donald Kagan and Frederick W. Kagan, *While America Sleeps: Self-Delusion, Military Weakness, and the Threat to Peace Today* (New York: St. Martin's Press, 2000), p. 294; Condoleezza Rice, "Promoting the National Interest" *Foreign Affairs* (June 2000): 45; Joseph S. Nye, Jr., *The Paradox of American Power: Why the World's Only Superpower Can't Go It Alone* (New York: Oxford University Press, 2002), p. 139.

35. Don DeLillo, *Underworld* (New York: Scribner, 1997), p. 170. Also see Thomas Friedman, *The Lexus and the Olive Tree* (New York: Farrar Straus Giroux, 1999), pp. 10–11; Mark Edmunson, *Nightmare on Elm Street: Angels, Sadomasochism, and the Culture of the Gothic* (Cambridge: Harvard University Press, 1997), p. 66; Huntington, pp. 125–30; Todd Gitlin, *The Twilight of Common Dreams: Why America Is Wracked by*

*Culture Wars* (New York: Metropolitan Books, 1995), pp. 2–3, 61–66. Ironically, at the height of the Cold War, American intellectuals invoked similar categories to make the opposite argument. It was precisely the enigmas of the Soviet Union, they argued, that made Americans so nervous about their identity. Where the overt aggression of the Nazis provoked a bracing moral crusade and simple strategy of unconditional surrender, the baroque movements of the Soviets required a strategy of extraordinary subtlety called "containment." Such protean tactics made Americans apprehensive, unsure of themselves and their purpose in the world. Needless to say, there was more than a bit of nostalgia—and fuzzy thinking—hovering about the end of the Cold War. How else to explain an interpretation treating American anxiety as a response, first, to an enemy's elusiveness, and, then, to the loss of that enemy's conspicuous intelligibility? See Talcott Parsons, "Social Strains in America," pp. 209, 211, 217–18; Nora Sayre, *Running Time: Films of the Cold War* (New York: Dial Press, 1982), pp. 25–26, 198–201; Andrew Ross, *No Respect: Intellectuals and Popular Culture* (New York: Routledge, 1989), pp. 46–47.

36. Kagan and Kagan, pp. 1–2, 4; Robert D. Kaplan, *The Coming Anarchy: Shattering the Dreams of the Post Cold War* (New York: Vintage, 2000), pp. 23–24.

37. Judith N. Shklar, *Ordinary Vices* (Cambridge: Harvard University Press, 1984), p. 4.

38. Shklar "The Liberalism of Fear," in *Liberalism and the Moral Life*, ed. Nancy Rosenblum, pp. 21, 27, 32, 36.

39. Shklar, "Liberalism of Fear," p. 30.

40. Shklar, *Ordinary Vices*, pp. 6, 9.

41. Shklar, *Ordinary Vices*, pp. 5, 9, 237; Shklar, "Liberalism of Fear," pp. 29–30. Also see Elaine Scarry, *The Body in Pain: The Making and Unmaking of the World* (New York: Oxford University Press, 1985), pp. 13–14.

42. Avishai Margalit, *The Decent Society*, trans. Naomi Goldblum (Cambridge: Harvard University Press, 1996), p. 5.

43. Richard Rorty, *Contingency, Irony, Solidarity* (New York: Cambridge University Press, 1989), pp. 192, 198.

44. Michael Ignatieff, *The Warrior's Honor: Ethnic War and the Modern Conscience* (New York: Henry Holt, 1997), pp. 18–19.

45. David Rieff, *Slaughterhouse: Bosnia and the Failure of the West* (New York: Simon and Schuster, 1995, 1996); Anthony Lewis, "War Crimes," *The New Republic* (March 20, 1995). Though see Rieff's second thoughts in *A Bed for the Night: Humanitarianism in Crisis* (New York: Simon and Schuster, 2002).

46. Celestine Bohlen, "On a Mission to Shine a Spotlight on Genocide," *New York Times* (February 5, 2003), p. E1.

47. Philip Gourevitch, *We Wish to Inform You that Tomorrow We Will Be Killed with Our Families* (London: Picador, 1998), pp. 6–7, 19.

48. Gourevitch, pp. 16, 19, 33. Emphasis added.

49. Shklar, *Ordinary Vices*, p. 17.

50. Shklar, *Ordinary Vices*, p. 37.

51. Shklar, *Montesquieu* (New York: Oxford University Press, 1987), p. 84.

52. Shklar, *Ordinary Vices*, p. 8.

53. Shklar, *Ordinary Vices*, pp. 23–25, 30–31.

54. Shklar, *Ordinary Vices*, pp. 26–29; Shklar, "Liberalism of Fear," pp. 27, 29.

55. Shklar, *Ordinary Vices*, pp. 28–29; also see Shklar, "Liberalism of Fear," p. 28.

56. Shklar, *Ordinary Vices*, p. 242.

57. Shklar, *Ordinary Vices*, pp. 43, 237–38; Shklar, "Liberalism of Fear," pp. 26–28, 30.

58. Shklar, "Liberalism of Fear," p. 21.

59. Ignatieff, p. 6.

60. Huntington, pp. 67, 76, 97–98, 101, 116, 125. Also see Kaplan, pp. 26–27, 35; Barber, *Jihad v. McWorld*, pp. 155–68, 205–16; Gray, pp. 35–38, 57–60.

61. Ignatieff, p. 36.

62. Ignatieff, pp. 38–45, 50, 53–54.

63. Ignatieff, pp. 46–48; Gourevitch, p. 47.

64. Gourevitch, pp. 17, 47–62; Ignatieff, pp. 38–45, 50, 53.

65. Ignatieff, pp. 48–61.

66. Kaplan, p. 47.

67. Ignatieff, p. 95.

68. Ignatieff, p. 95.

69. Alfred Cobban, *A History of Modern France*, Volume 1: 1715–1999 (New York: Penguin, 1957), p. 190.

70. Rexford Tugwell, *The Stricken Land* (New York: Doubleday, 1947); Tugwell, *The Place of Planning in Society* (San Juan: Puerto Rico Planning Board, 1956); Charles Goodsell, *Administration of a Revolution: Executive Reform in Puerto Rico under Governor Tugwell, 1941–1946* (Cambridge: Harvard University Press, 1965). I am grateful to Alyosha Goldstein for pointing to me to Tugwell's, case as well as to these cites.

71. Kaplan, p. 108.

72. Kaplan, p. 143.

73. Kaplan, p. 147.

74. Kaplan, p. 154.

75. Christopher Hitchens, "The Ends of War," *The Nation* (December 17, 2001), p. 9. Also see Edward Rothstein, "Cherished Ideas Refracted in History's Lens," *New York Times* (September 7, 2002), p. B11; Christopher Hitchens, "Stranger in a Strange Land," *The Atlantic Monthly* (December 2001), pp. 32–33; Richard A. Posner, "Strong Fiber After All," *The Atlantic Monthly* (January 2002), p. 22; Michael Kelly, "With a Serious and Large Intent," *Washington Post* (October 10, 2001), p. A23.

76. Putnam, *Bowling Alone*, p. 402. Emphasis in original.

77. See Todd Gitlin, "America's Left Caught Between a Flag and a Hard Place," *San Jose Mercury News* (November 2, 2001); Michael Kelly, "Pacifist Claptrap," *Washington Post* (September 26, 2001), p. A25; Michael Kelly, "The Left's Great Divide," *Washington Post* (November 7, 2001), p. A29; Christopher Hitchens, "Against Rationalization," *The Nation* (October 8, 2001), p. 8; Hitchens, "Blaming bin Laden First," *The Nation* (October 22, 2001), p. 9; Michael Walzer, "Can There Be a Decent Left?" *Dissent* (Spring 2002).

78. David Brooks, "Facing Up to Our Fears," *Newsweek* (October 22, 2001), p. 62; Maureen Dowd, "From Botox to Botulism," *New York Times* (September 26, 2001), p. A19; Francis Fukuyama, "Francis Fukuyama says Tuesday's Attack marks the end of 'America's Exceptionalism'," *Financial Times* (September 15, 2001), p. 1; Libby cited in Nicholas Lemann, "The Next World Order," *The New Yorker* (April 1, 2002), p. 48; Bush cited in "In Bush's Words: 'We Will Do What is Necessary' in the Fight

Against Terror," *New York Times* (September 8, 2003), p. A10; DeLay cited in Alain Gresh, "Waves of chaos," *Le Monde Diplomatique* (September 2003). Also see Frank Rich, "The Day Before Tuesday," *New York Times* (September 15, 2001), p. A23; Maureen Dowd, "All That Glistens," *New York Times* (October 13, 2001), p. A23.

79. Brooks, "Facing Up to Our Fears"; Brooks, "The Age of Conflict," *The Weekly Standard* (November 5, 2001), p. 19.

80. Brooks, "Facing Up to Our Fears."

81. On 9/11, trust in government, and the welfare state, see Jacob Weisberg, "Feds Up," *New York Times Magazine* (October 21, 2001), pp. 21–22; Robert Putnam, "Bowling Together," *The American Prospect* (February 11, 2002), p. 20; Bernard Weinraub, "The Moods They Are a'Changing in Films," *New York Times* (October 10, 2001), p. E1; Nina Bernstein, "On Pier 94, a Welfare State That Works, and Possible Models for the Future," *New York Times* (September 6, 2001), p. B8; Michael Kazin, "The Nation: After the Attacks, Which Side is the Left On?" *New York Times* (October 7, 2001), Sec. 4, p. 4; Katrina vanden Heuvel and Joel Rogers, "What's Left? A New Life for Progressivism," *Los Angeles Times* (November 25, 2001), p. M2; Michael Kelly, "A Renaissance of Liberalism," *The Atlantic Monthly* (January 2002), pp. 18–19. On 9/11 and the culture wars, see Posner, "Strong Fiber After All," pp. 22–23; Rick Lyman, "At Least for the Moment, a Cooling of the Culture Wars," *New York Times* (November 13, 2001), p. E1; Maureen Dowd, "Hunks and Brutes," *New York Times* (November 28, 2001), p. A25; Richard Posner, "Reflections on an America Transformed," *New York Times* (September 8, 2002), Week in Review, p. 15. On 9/11, bipartisanship, and the new presidency, see "George Bush, G.O.P. Moderate," *New York Times* (September 29, 2001), p. A18; Maureen Dowd, "Autumn of Fears," *New York Times* (November 23, 2001), Week in Review, p. 17; Richard L. Berke, "Bush 'Is My Commander,' Gore Declares in Call for Unity," *New York Times* (September 30, 2001), p. A29; Frank Bruni, "For President, a Mission and a Role in History," *New York Times* (September 21, 2001), p. A1; "Politics Is Adjourned," *New York Times* (September 20, 2001), p. A30; Adam Clymer, "Disaster Forges a Spirit of Cooperation in a Usually Contentious Congress," *New York Times* (September 20, 2001), p. B3. For a general statement of these various themes, see "In for the Long Haul," *New York Times* (September 16, 2001), Week in Review, p. 10.

82. Judy Keen, "Same President, Different Man in Oval Office," *USA Today* (October 29, 2001), p. 6A.

83. Andrew Sullivan, "High Impact: The Dumb Idea of September 11," *New York Times Magazine* (December 9, 2001), p. 25; George Packer, "Recapturing the Flag," *New York Times Magazine* (September 30, 2001), pp. 15–16.

84. Christopher Hitchens, "It's a Good Time for War," *Boston Globe* (September 8, 2002). Emphasis in original.

85. Thomas L. Friedman, "9/11 Lesson Plan," *New York Times* (September 4, 2002), p. A21; Thomas L. Friedman, "Smoking or non-Smoking?" *New York Times* (September 14, 2001), p. A27.

86. Serge Schemann, "What Would 'Victory' Mean?" *New York Times* (September 16, 2001), Week in Review, p. 1; Friedman, "Smoking or non-Smoking?" p. A27; Barbara Crossette, "Feverish Protests Against the West Trace Grievances Ancient and Modern," *New York Times* (October 22, 2001), p. B4.

87. Ronald Steel, "The Weak at War with the Strong," *New York Times* (September 14, 2001), p. A27; John Burns, "America Inspires Longing and Loathing in Muslim World," *New York Times* (September 16, 2001), p. A4; Fouad Ajami, "Out of Egypt," *New York Times Magazine* (October 7, 2001), p. 19.

88. George Packer, "The Liberal Quandary Over Iraq," *New York Times Magazine* (December 8, 2002), p. 107.

89. Francis Fukuyama, "Beyond Our Shores," *Wall Street Journal* (December 24, 2002), p. A10.

90. Fukuyama, "Beyond Our Shores," p. A10.

91. Thomas Paine, *Common Sense*, in *The Thomas Paine Reader*, ed. Michael Foot and Isaac Kramnick (New York: Penguin, 1987), p. 65.

## PART 2: FEAR, AMERICAN STYLE

1. C. Wright Mills, *White Collar: The American Middle Classes* (New York: Oxford University Press, 1951), p. 8; Christopher Lasch, *The Culture of Narcissism: American Life in an Age of Diminished Expectations* (New York: Norton, 1979), p. 218. Also see Sheldon S. Wolin, "What Revolutionary Action Means Today," *Democracy* 2 (Fall 1982): 17.

2. Hobbes, *Leviathan*, ed. Richard Tuck (New York: Cambridge University Press, 1991), ch. 21, p. 153.

3. Martin Luther King, "Letter from Birmingham City Jail," in *A Testament of Hope: The Essential Writings and Speeches of Martin Luther King, Jr.*, ed. James Melvin Washington (New York: HarperCollins, 1986), p. 295.

4. H. L. A. Hart, *The Concept of Law*, 2nd ed. (Oxford: Clarendon Press, 1961, 1994), p. vii.

5. Abraham Lincoln, "Second Inaugural Address," in *The Portable Abraham Lincoln*, ed. Andrew Delbanco (New York: Penguin, 1992), pp. 320–21.

6. Michael Walzer, "On Negative Politics," in *Liberalism without Illusions: Essays on Liberal Theory and the Political Vision of Judith N. Shklar*, ed. Bernard Yack (Chicago: University of Chicago Press, 1996), pp. 19, 24.

## 6: SENTIMENTAL EDUCATIONS

1. Victor Navasky, *Naming Names* (New York: Penguin, 1980, 1991), pp. 258–64, 281–82; Larry Ceplair and Steven Englund, *The Inquisition in Hollywood: Politics in the Film Community, 1930–1960* (Garden City, N.Y.: Anchor Press, 1980), pp. 248, 328–31, 445.

2. See Thomas I. Emerson, David Haber, and Norman Dorsen, *Political and Civil Rights in the United States* (Boston: Little, Brown, 1967), vol. I, pp. 158–59; Robert Griffith, *The Politics of Fear: Joseph R. McCarthy and the Senate*, 2nd ed. (Amherst: University of Massachusetts Press, 1987), pp. 117–21; Alonzo Hamby, *Beyond the New Deal: Harry S. Truman and American Liberalism* (New York: Columbia University Press, 1973), pp. 411–14; Mary Sperling McAuliffe, *Crisis on the Left: Cold War Politics and American Liberals, 1947–1954* (Amherst: University of Massachusetts Press, 1978), pp. 79–80.

3. By McCarthyism, I do not mean the actions of the Senator from Wisconsin, but the repressive measures in the public and private sector, directed at the Communist Party but affecting much of left-liberal America, that began in 1947 and lasted until the late 1950s.

4. Navasky, pp. 259–64, 305.

5. This perhaps is the kind of fear that Augustine had in mind when he wrote, "That fear which is 'pure, enduring for ever' . . . is not the fear that frightens someone away from an evil which may befall him, but the fear that keeps him in a good which cannot be lost." Augustine also writes, "The phrase 'fear that is pure' signifies without doubt the act of will which makes it inevitable that we shall refuse to sin and that we shall be on our guard against sin, not with the anxiety of weakness, in fear of sinning, but with a tranquillity [sic] based on love." Augustine, *City of God*, trans. John O'Meara (New York: Penguin, 1972), 14.9, p. 565.

6. Navasky, p. 260.

7. For similar examples from the blacklist, see Stefan Kanfer, *A Journal of the Plague Years: A Devastating Chronicle of the Era of the Blacklist* (New York: Atheneum, 1973), p. 198; Navasky, p. xvii.

8. Project for Excellence in Journalism, "Return to Normalcy? How the Media Have Covered the War on Terrorism" (January 8, 2002) (http://www.journalism.org/resources/research/reports/normalcy) <last accessed on March 30, 2004>; Howard Kurtz, "Into the Punditry Vacuum, Fresh Wind," *Washington Post* (January 28, 2002), p. C1.

9. Jim Rutenberg and Bill Carter, "Network Coverage a Target of Fire from Conservatives," *New York Times* (November 7, 2001), p. B2.

10. Alessandra Stanley, "Opponents of the War Are Scarce on Television," *New York Times* (November 9, 2001), p. B4; Howard Kurtz, "CNN Chief Orders 'Balance' in War News," *Washington Post* (October 31, 2001), p. C1.

11. Rutenberg and Carter, "Network Coverage a Target of Fire," p. B2.

12. By separating the rational from the moral, I do not wish to suggest that the rational is not moral, or that the moral is not rational. I merely wish to draw attention to the considerations of interest and moral belief that underlie political fear.

13. Michael Kinsley, "Listening to Our Inner Ashcrofts," *Washington Post* (January 4, 2002), p. A27.

14. Matthew Engel, "US Media Cowed by Patriotic Fever, says CBS Star," *The Guardian* (May 17, 2002), p. 4.

15. Tina Rosenberg, *The Haunted Land: Facing Europe's Ghosts After Communism* (New York: Vintage, 1995), p. 49.

16. Navasky, pp. 201–2.

17. Navasky, p. 262.

18. Robert Conquest, *The Great Terror: Stalin's Purge of the Thirties* (London: Macmillan, 1968), pp. 142, 301; Anne Applebaum, *Gulag: A History* (New York: Doubleday, 2003), p. 139; Sheila Fitzpatrick, *Everyday Stalinism: Ordinary Life in Extraordinary Times* (New York: Oxford University Press, 1999), p. 25; Stephen F. Cohen, *Bukharin and the Bolshevik Revolution: A Political Biography, 1888–1938* (New York: Oxford University Press, 1971, 1980), p. 375; J. Arch Getty and Oleg V. Naumov, *The Road to Terror: Stalin and the Self-Destruction of the Bolsheviks, 1932–1939* (New Haven: Yale University Press, 1999), pp. 418, 526; Adam Hochschild, *The Unquiet Ghost: Russians Remember Stalin* (New York: Viking, 1994), pp. 13, 21–22; Rosenberg, *The Haunted Land*, pp. 28–29.

19. Tzvetan Todorov, *Facing the Extreme: Moral Life in the Concentration Camps* (London: Weidenfeld & Nicolson, 1999), pp. 8, 22.

20. Fitzpatrick, p. 25. Also see Rosenberg, *The Haunted Land*, pp. xi–xiii; Todorov, pp. 18–19, 33.

21. *Crito* 45d, in *The Trial and Death of Socrates*, trans. G. M. A. Grube (Indianapolis: Hackett, 1975), p. 46.

22. Ellen Schrecker, *No Ivory Tower: McCarthyism in the Universities* (New York: Oxford University Press, 1986), p. 196; David Caute, *The Great Fear: The Anti-Communist Purge Under Truman and Eisenhower* (New York: Simon and Schuster, 1978), p. 554; Ceplair and Englund, p. 378; Navasky, p. 178.

23. "Force is a physical power," writes Rousseau. "I do not see how its effects could produce morality. To yield to force is an act of necessity, not of will; it is at best an act of prudence. In what sense can it be a moral duty?" Extending this distinction between force and morality, Bertrand Russell argues that in cases of rule by "cooperation," one person submits to another out of a moral respect for the legitimacy of that person's power; in rule by "naked power," however, the powerful "wins from [the powerless] only submission through fear." Distinguishing between coercive orders and authoritative commands, H. L. A. Hart writes, "To command is characteristically to exercise authority over men, not power to inflict harm, and thought it may be combined with threats of harm a command is primarily an appeal not to fear but to respect for authority." In her account of Montesquieu's theory of terror, Judith Shklar writes that terror is a "physiological reaction" to violence, "where our physical and moral impulses meet and struggle, and where the former triumph." More recently, Charles Taylor contrasts despotism, in which obedience is "externally imposed by fear," with the "patriotic identification" of free citizens, which is "self-imposed" and "inwardly generated." Jean-Jacques Rousseau, *The Social Contract*, trans. Maurice Cranston (New York: Penguin, 1968), 1.3, p. 52; Bertrand Russell, "The Forms of Power," in *Power*, ed. Steven Lukes (New York: New York University Press, 1986), p. 22; H. L. A. Hart, *The Concept of Law*, 2nd ed. (Oxford: Clarendon Press, 1961, 1964), pp. 19–20; Judith Shklar, *Montesquieu* (New York: Oxford University Press, 1987), p. 84; Charles Taylor, "Cross-Purposes: The Liberal-Communitarian Debate," in *Philosophical Arguments* (Cambridge: Harvard University Press, 1995), pp. 192–93. Though see Shklar's more nuanced account in her earlier work *Legalism: Law, Morals, and Political Trials* (Cambridge: Harvard University Press, 1964, 1986), pp. 43–47.

24. Joseph Brodsky, "Nadezhda Mandelstam (1899–1980): An Obituary," in Nadezhda Mandelstam, *Hope Against Hope*, trans. Max Hayward (New York: Modern Library, 1970, 1999), p. x.

25. Tina Rosenberg, *Children of Cain: Violence and the Violent in Latin America* (New York: Penguin, 1991), p. 94.

26. Hochschild, p. 39. Also see William Ian Miller, *The Mystery of Courage* (Cambridge: Harvard University Press, 2000), pp. 207–8.

27. Sterling Hayden, *Wanderer* (New York: Knopf, 1963), pp. 265–72, 282–333, 344–50, 382–91; Navasky, pp. 75, 100–101; Ceplair and Englund, 372, 447.

28. Hayden, p. 371–72; Ceplair and Englund, pp. 386–89.

29. Hayden, p. 297.

30. Navasky, p. 83; Ceplair and Englund, p. 259.

31. Ceplair and Englund, p. 285; Kanfer, p. 86; Navasky, p. 145.

32. Hayden, pp. 370–71, 374, 378, 386.

33. Elizabeth Llorente, "Fear Inhibits U.S. Arabs, Muslims," *Bergen Record* (March 25, 2003), p. A13.

34. In today's international sex-trafficking circles, trusted older women are used as "principals," as they were in Usbek's harem in *The Persian Letters*, to inculcate submission and fear among younger female captives. Peter Landesman, "The Girls Next Door," *New York Times Magazine* (January 25, 2004), p. 37.

35. Thomas Hobbes, *Leviathan*, ed. Richard Tuck (New York: Cambridge University Press, 1991), ch. 27, p. 206; Michael Walzer, *Obligations* (Cambridge: Harvard University Press, 1970), p. 78.

36. Todorov, pp. 34–36.

37. Aristotle, *Nicomachean Ethics* 1115a6–1117b21, trans. Martin Ostwald (New York: Macmillan, 1972), pp. 68–77. Also see Plato, *Apology* 28d, 29a, in *The Trial and Death of Socrates*, pp. 31–32; Miller, pp. 47–65.

38. *Remembering Jim Crow: African Americans Tell About Life in the Segregated South*, ed. William H. Chafe et al. (New York: The New Press, 2001), pp. 288–92.

39. Mandelstam, p. 42. Also see Privo Levi, *Survival in Auschwitz*, trans. Stuart Woolf (New York: Simon and Schuster, 1958), p. 19; Yehuda Bauer, *Rethinking the Holocaust* (New Haven: Yale University Press, 2001), pp. 26–27, 119–66; Christopher R. Browning, *Ordinary Men: Reserve Police Battalion 101 and the Final Solution in Poland* (New York: HarperCollins, 1992, 1998), pp. 136–37; Todorov, pp. 14, 25.

40. *Crito* 47e, p. 48.

41. Obviously this rule does not apply to racist regimes or policies that target people for who they are rather than for what they do, think, say, or might do, think, or say.

42. Lawrence Weschsler, *A Miracle, A Universe: Settling Accounts with Torturers* (Chicago: University of Chicago Press, 1990, 1998), pp. 88–89.

43. Mandelstam, p. 25.

44. Mark Danner, *The Massacre at El Mozote: A Parable of the Cold War* (New York: Vintage, 1993), p. 26.

45. For competing figures, see David Firestone and Christopher Drew, "Al Qaeda Link Seen in Only a Handful of 1,200 Detainees," *New York Times* (November 29, 2001), p. A1; Andrew Gumbel, "The Disappeared," *The Independent* (February 26, 2002), p. 1; David Cole, *Enemy Aliens* (New York: The New Press, 2003).

46. See Ann Davis, Maureen Tkacik, and Andrea Petersen, "Nation of Tipsters Answers FBI's Call," *Wall Street Journal* (November 21, 2001), p. A1; David Rosenbaum, "Competing Principles Leave Some Professionals Debating Responsibility to Government," *New York Times* (November 23, 2001), p. B7; Jodi Wilgoren, "Michigan 'Invites' Men from Mideast to Be Interviewed," *New York Times* (November 27, 2001), p. A1; Matthew Rothschild, "If You Don't Want American Flag Stamps, Watch Out!" *The Progressive* (December 8, 2001) (http://www.progressive.org/webex/wxmc120801.html) <last accessed on March 30, 2004>; Matthew Rothschild, "Don't Criticize Bush at Your Gym," *The Progressive* (December 19, 2001) (http://www.progressive.org/webex/wxmc1219a01.html) <last accessed on March 30, 2004>; Robert F. Worth, "Gay Muslims Face a Growing Challenge Reconciling Their Two Identities," *New York Times* (January 13, 2002), p. 30; Chisun Lee, "Manhunt Puts Middle Easterners at Mercy of Ordinary Americans," *Village Voice* (Janu-

ary 29, 2002), p. 45; Nat Hentoff, "J. Edgar Hoover Lives!" *Village Voice* (February 19, 2002), p. 37; Nat Hentoff, "Eyeing What You Read," *Village Voice* (February 26, 2002), p. 25; Nat Hentoff, "Big John Wants Your Reading List," *Village Voice* (March 5, 2002), p. 27; Matthew Rothschild, "Red Squad Hits Denver," *The Progressive* (March 14, 2002) (http://www.progressive.org/webex/wxmc031402.html) <last accessed on March 30, 2004>; Matthew Rothschild, "An Olympic Experience," *The Progressive* (March 27, 2002) (http://www.progressive.org/webex/wxmc032702.html) <last accessed on March 30, 2004>.

47. Llorente, "Fear Inhibits U.S. Arabs, Muslims," p. A13. Also see Jacques Steinberg, "U.S. Has Covered 200 Campuses to Check Up on Mideast Students," *New York Times* (November 12, 2001), p. A1; Jodi Wilgoren, "Prosecutors Begin to Interview 5,000, but Basic Questions Remain," *New York Times* (November 15, 2001), p. B7; Danny Hakim, "Inquiries Put Mideast Men in Spotlight," *New York Times* (November 16, 2001), p. B10; Greg Winter, "F.B.I. Visits Provoke Waves of Worry in Middle Eastern Men," *New York Times* (November 16, 2001), p. B1; Greg Winter, "Some Mideast Immigrants, Shaken, Ponder Leaving U.S.," *New York Times* (November 23, 2001), p. B1; Susan Sachs, "U.S. Begins Crackdown on Muslims Who Defy Orders to Leave Country," *New York Times* (April 2, 2002), p. A13; Chisun Lee, "NY Immigrants Underground," *Village Voice* (May 28, 2002), p. 25; Robert E. Pierre, "Fear and Anxiety Permeate Arab Enclave Near Detroit," *Washington Post* (August 4, 2002), p. A3; Eric Lichtblau, "F.B.I. Tells Offices to Count Local Muslims and Mosques," *New York Times* (January 28, 2003), p. A13.

48. James Sterngold, "Muslims in San Diego Waver on Bail Pledge," *New York Times* (December 9, 2001), p. B6.

49. *Remembering Jim Crow*, pp. 5–7.

50. Salim Muwakkil, "Should Homegrown Terrorism Be Targeted?" *Chicago Tribune* (December 24, 2001), p. 15; Kris Axtman, "The Terror Threat at Home, Often Overlooked," *Christian Science Monitor* (December 29, 2003), p.2; Scott Gold, "Case Yields Chilling Signs of Domestic Terror Plot," *Los Angeles Times* (January 7, 2004), p. A1.

51. Curt Gentry, *J. Edgar Hoover: The Man and the Secrets* (New York: Norton, 1991), pp. 322–25; Ellen Schrecker, *Many Are the Crimes: McCarthyism in America* (Boston: Little Brown, 1998), pp. 205–6, 213–14.

52. *Memoirs of Harry S. Truman 1946–1952: Years of Trial and Hope* (New York: Da Capo, 1956), p. 273; David McCullough, *Truman* (New York: Simon & Schuster, 1992), p. 523; Gentry, p. 319; Alonzo L. Hamby, *Man of the People: A Life of Harry S. Truman* (New York: Oxford University Press, 1995), pp. 427–29.

53. *Free Government in the Making*, ed. Alpheus Thomas Mason and Gordon E. Baker (New York: Oxford University Press, 1985), 4th ed., pp. 119–21.

54. *Lawrence v. Texas*, 123 U.S. 2472 (2003) (Scalia, dissenting).

55. "An Homily Against Disobedience and Wylful Rebellion (1570)," in *Divine Right and Democracy: An Anthology of Political Writings in Stuart England*, ed. David Wootton (New York: Penguin, 1986), p. 95.

56. Georg Lukács, *The Historical Novel*, trans. Hannah and Stanley Mitchell (Boston: Beacon Press, 1962), pp. 23–25; George Steiner, *In Bluebeard's Castle: Some Notes Towards the Redefinition of Culture* (New Haven: Yale University Press, 1971), pp. 11–13.

57. Ruth Rosen, "When Women Spied on Women," *The Nation* (September 4/11,

2000), pp 18–25; Richard Gid Powers, *Secrecy and Power: The Life of J. Edgar Hoover* (New York: The Free Press, 1987), pp. 6, 9–10, 109–10; Ronald Lora, "A View From the Right: Conservative Intellectuals, the Cold War, and McCarthy," in *The Specter: Original Essays on the Cold War and the Origins of McCarthyism*, ed. Robert Griffith and Athan Theoharis (New York: New Viewpoints, 1974), p. 46; *The COINTELPRO Papers: Documents from the FBI's Secret Wars Against Dissent in the United States*, ed. Ward Churchill and Jim Vander Wall (Cambridge: South End Press, 1990, 2002), pp. 93, 96–97, 100, 183; William W. Keller, *The Liberals and J. Edgar Hoover: Rise and Fall of a Domestic Intelligence State* (Princeton: Princeton University Press, 1989), pp. 92–110; Schrecker, *Many Are the Crimes*, p. 145.

58. Earl Latham, *The Communist Conspiracy in Washington: From the New Deal to Mc-Carthy* (Cambridge: Harvard University Press, 1966), p. 136; James T. Patterson, *Congressional Conservatism and the New Deal: The Growth of the Conservative Coalition in Congress, 1933–1939* (Lexington: University of Kentucky Press, 1967), p. 29.

59. Nora Sayre, *Running Time: Films of the Cold War* (New York: Dial Press, 1982), p. 11; Schrecker, *Many Are the Crimes*, p. 282; Schrecker, *No Ivory Tower*, p. 101.

60. Schrecker, *Many Are the Crimes*, pp. 390–91.

61. Rosenberg, *Children of Cain*, p. 109.

62. Rosenberg, *Children of Cain*, p. 110.

63. Weschler, pp. 59, 63–65, 121.

64. Kenneth O'Reilly, *Hoover and the Un-Americans: The FBI, HUAC, and the Red Menace* (Philadelphia: Temple University Press, 1983), pp. 76–82, 168; J. Edgar Hoover, *Masters of Deceit: The Story of Communism in America and How to Fight It* (New York: Pocket Books, 1958), p. 294; Powers, p. 284. Also see Richard M. Fried, *Nightmare in Red: The McCarthy Era in Perspective* (New York: Oxford University Press, 1990), pp. 97–99; Athan Theoharis, "The Rhetoric of Politics: Foreign Policy, Internal Security, and Domestic Politics in the Truman Administration, 1945-1950," in *Politics and Policies of the Truman Administration*, ed. Barton J. Bernstein (Chicago: Quadrangle Books, 1970), pp. 196–241; Richard M. Freeland, *The Truman Doctrine and the Origins of McCarthyism* (New York: New York University Press, 1985).

65. Churchill and Vander Wall, p. 96.

66. Mandelstam, p. 33.

67. *The Smith Act* and *Dennis v. United States*, in Emerson, Haber, and Dorsen, pp. 98–120; Ellen Schrecker, *The Age of McCarthyism: A Brief History with Documents*, 2nd ed. (Boston: Bedford, 2002), p. 49.

68. Marc Schultz, "Careful: The FB-Eye May Be Watching," *Creative Loafing* (July 17, 2003).

69. "Americans for Victory Over Terrorism," *New York Times* (March 16, 2002), p. A7; Michelle Goldberg, "Osama University?" *Salon* (November 6, 2003); Michael Dobbs, "Middle East Studies Under Scrutiny in U.S." *Washington Post* (January 13, 2004), p. A1.

70. Peter Beinart, "Sidelines," *The New Republic* (September 24, 2001), p. 8.

71. James Harding, "The Anti-Globalisation Movement," *Financial Times* (October 10, 2001), p. 8.

72. Robert Zoellick, "Countering Terror with Trade," *Washington Post* (September 20, 2001); Paul Krugman, "The Hitchhiker Syndrome," *New York Times* (September

30, 2001), p. 13; E. J. Dionne, "Trade and Terror," *Washington Post* (October 2, 2001), p. A25; Gregory Palast, "The Fast Track Trade Jihad," *The Guardian* (October 14, 2001); Eric Laursen, "Terrorism and Free Trade," *Village Voice* (November 5, 2001); Joseph Kahn, "House Supports Trade Authority Sought by Bush," *New York Times* (December 7, 2001), p. A1; Lisa Climan, "On a Fast Track to 'Free Trade' Hell," *Dollars and Sense* (January–February 2002); Richard W. Stevenson, "House and Senate Reach Initial Deal on Trade Powers for Bush," *New York Times* (July 26, 2002), p. A6.

73. See John Elliston, "A Durham Student Activist Gets a Visit from the Secret Service," *Independent Online* (November 21, 2001) (http://www.indyweek.com/durham/2001-11-21/triangles.html) <last accessed on March 30, 2004>; Rothschild, "If You Don't Want American Flag Stamps, Watch Out!"; Rothschild, "Don't Criticize Bush at Your Gym?"; Robert F. Worth, "Gay Muslims Face a Growing Challenge Reconciling their Two Identities," *New York Times* (January 13, 2002), p. 30; Lee, "Manhunt Puts Middle Easterners at Mercy of Ordinary Americans"; Hentoff, "J. Edgar Hoover Lives!"; "Santa Fe Police Detain Library Patron over Chat-Room Visit" (February 24, 2003) (http://www.ala.org/alonline/currentnews/newsarchive/2003/february2003/santafepolice.html) <last accessed on March 30, 2004>; Hentoff, "Eyeing What You Read," *Village Voice* (February 26, 2002), p. 25; Hentoff, "Big John Wants Your Reading List"; Rothschild, "An Olympic Experience."

74. Matthew Rothschild, "More Anti-War Activists Snagged by 'No Fly' List," *The Progressive* (October 16, 2002) (http://ww.progressive.org/webex/wxmc101602.html) <last accessed on March 30, 2004>; David Lindorff, "Grounded," *Salon* (November 15, 2002); Andrew Gumbel, "US Anti-War Activists Hit by Secret Airport Ban," *The Independent* (August 3, 2003), p. 19.

75. Eric Lichtblau, "F.B.I. Scrutinizes Antiwar Rallies," *New York Times* (November 23, 2003). Also see David Johnston and Don Van Natta Jr., "Ashcroft Weighs Easing F.B.I. Limits for Surveillance," *New York Times* (December 1, 2001), p. A1; Adam Liptak, "Changing the Standard," *New York Times* (May 31, 2002), p. A1.

76. Letter from Tom DeLay to supporters of National Right to Work Foundation (January 8, 2003) (http://www.iaff.org/across/news/archive2003/media2003/022003del.pdf) <last accessed on March 30, 2004>.

77. Nathan Newman, "'Homeland Security' as Union Busting," *Progressive Populist* 8 (July 15, 2002) (http://www.populist.com/02.13.html) <last accessed on March 30, 2004>; Steven Greenhouse, "Labor Issue May Stall Security Bill," *New York Times* (July 28, 2002), p. A22; David Firestone, "For Homeland Security Bill, a Brakeman," *New York Times* (July 31, 2002), p. A14; Elizabeth Becker, "Administration Insists on Control Over New Agency's Labor Rules," *New York Times* (August 1, 2002), p. A20.

78. Newman, "'Homeland Security' as Union Busting;" David Bacon, "Screened Out," *The Nation* (May 12, 2003), p. 19.

79. Nancy Cleeland, "White House Signals It Will Move to Forestall West Coast Port Strike," *Los Angeles Times* (August 5, 2002), p. 1; David Bacon, "Unions Fear 'War on Terror' Will Overcome Right to Strike," *Inter Press Service* (August 10, 2002) (http://www.commondreams.org/headlines02/081002.htm) <last accessed on March 30, 2004>; David Bacon, "In the Name of National Security" *The American*

*Prospect* (October 21, 2002), p. 15; Rick Fantasia and Kim Voss, "Bush Administration's Low-Intensity War Against Labour," *Le Monde Diplomatique* (June 2003).

80. The word "collaboration" first took on this negative connotation—as opposed to the more neutral notion of two parties working together—with the Nazi invasion of France, whereupon it was used to refer to natives of occupied countries who colluded with the Germans. Jan Gross, *Neighbors: The Destruction of the Jewish Community in Jedwabne, Poland* (Princeton: Princeton University Press, 2001), pp. 5, 205–6.

81. Rosenberg, *The Haunted Land*, p. xiii; Herbert A. Philbrick, *I Led Three Lives: Citizen, 'Communist,' Counterspy* (New York: Grosset & Dunlap, 1952); Schrecker, *Many Are the Crimes*, pp. 310–13, 344–49.

82. Gross, pp. 97–100; Wechsler, p. 44.

83. See Mandelstam, p. 42; Levi, p. 19.

84. Weschler, p. 126.

85. Levi, p. 33.

86. Danner, pp. 17, 20, 23, 50, 59.

87. See Bauer, pp. 77–82; Navasky, pp. 3–69; Gross, pp. 37–40, 60–62, 65, 91, 123–25; Browning, pp. 162, 177, 180, 196–200, 202.

88. Weschler, pp. 76, 127.

89. Browning, pp. 1–2, 55–77, 169–70; Bauer, p. 37.

90. Kanfer, p. 173. Even if Kazan had refused to testify and been penalized by Hollywood, he undoubtedly could have had a thriving career as a Broadway director—a point he affirmed before his death. Bernard Weinraub, "Book Reveals Kazan's Thoughts on Naming Names," *New York Times* (March 4, 1999), p. E1.

91. Hobbes, *Leviathan*, ch. 10, p. 62.

92. Aleksandr I. Solzhenitsyn, *The Gulag Archipelago: 1918–1956*, trans. Thomas P. Whitney (New York: Westview Press, 1973), pp. 13–15.

93. Solzhenitsyn, p. 13.

94. Danner, pp. 20, 33.

95. Ceplair and Englund, pp. 275–77, 281–82, 288; Navasky, p. 80; Kanfer, p. 72.

96. Ceplair and Englund, pp. 257–60, 329, 337.

97. Ceplair and Englund, pp. 289–91; Kanfer, p. 86.

98. Navasky, pp. 92, 122–26.

99. Navasky, pp. 337–38; Ceplair and Englund, pp. 254, 292, 299–324, 340; Sayre, pp. 32–33, 48, 50; Kanfer, pp. 82, 87.

100. Miller, p. 21.

101. Isaac Deutscher, *The Prophet Armed. Trotsky: 1879–1921* (New York: Oxford University Press, 1954), pp. 166–67. Also see Todorov, p. 6.

## 7: DIVISIONS OF LABOR

1. For realist examples, see Max Weber, "Politics as a Vocation," in *From Max Weber: Essays in Sociology*, ed. H. H. Gerth and C. Wright Mills (New York: Oxford University Press, 1948), pp. 78–80; Theda Skocpol, *States and Social Revolutions: A Comparative Analysis of France, Russia, and China* (New York: Cambridge University Press, 1979), pp. 22, 29–30; Skocpol, "Bringing the State Back In: Strategies of Analysis in Current Research," in *Bringing the State Back In*, ed. Peter B. Evans, Dietrich

Rueschmeyer, and Theda Skocpol (New York: Cambridge University Press, 1985), p. 9; Gianfranco Poggi, *The State: Its Nature, Development and Prospects* (Stanford: Stanford University Press, 1990), pp. 5, 8, 9, 13, 19–23. For liberal examples, see John Locke, *Two Treatises of Government* (Cambridge: Cambridge University Press, 1988); Montesquieu, *The Spirit of the Laws* (Cambridge: Cambridge University Press, 1989); *The Federalist Papers* (New York: Bantam, 1982); Friedrich Hayek, *The Constitution of Liberty* (Chicago: University of Chicago Press, 1960), pp. 21, 137, 142, 185; John Rawls, *A Theory of Justice* (Cambridge: Harvard University Press, 1971), pp. 58, 239–41; Judith Shklar, "The Liberalism of Fear," in *Liberalism and the Moral Life*, ed. Nancy L. Rosenblum (Cambridge: Harvard University Press, 1989), pp. 21–38; Bruce Ackerman, *We the People I: Foundations* (Cambridge: Harvard University Press, 1991), pp. 254–57; John Gray, *Post-Liberalism: Studies in Political Thought* (London: Routledge, 1993), p. 158; Akhil Reed Amar, *The Bill of Rights: Creation and Reconstruction* (New Haven: Yale University Press, 1998), pp. 6–7, 123.

2. *Federalist* 47, p. 303. On Montesquieu's influence, see Bernard Bailyn, *The Ideological Origins of the American Revolution* (Cambridge: Harvard University Press, 1967), pp. 272–301; Gordon S. Wood, *The Creation of the American Republic 1776–1787* (New York: Norton, 1969), pp. 150–61, 446–53, 547–53, 602–6; Jack N. Rakove, *Original Meanings: Politics and Ideas in the Making of the Constitution* (New York: Vintage, 1996), pp. 245–87.

3. *Federalist* 10, 51; pp. 122–28, 319–20.

4. *United States v. Brown*, 381 U.S. 437, 443 (1965). Also see Laurence H. Tribe, *American Constitutional Law*, vol. 1 (New York: Foundation Press, 2000), 3rd ed., p. 122; Hayek, p. 185.

5. Cf. Telford Taylor, *Grand Inquest: The Story of Congressional Investigations* (New York: Simon and Schuster, 1955); David R. Mayhew, *Divided We Govern: Party Control, Lawmaking, and Investigations, 1946–1990* (New Haven: Yale University Press, 1991).

6. Walter Goodman, *The Committee: The Extraordinary Career of the House Committee on Un-American Activities* (Baltimore: Penguin, 1968), pp. 168–69; Robert Griffith, *The Politics of Fear: Joseph R. McCarthy and the Senate*, 2nd ed. (Amherst: University of Massachusetts Press, 1987), pp. 58, 89, 104–13, 206–7, 210–12, 303–4. Also see David W. Rohde, *Parties and Leaders in the Postreform House* (Chicago: University of Chicago Press, 1991), pp. 4–5; Nelson W. Polsby, "The Institutionalization of the House of Representatives," *American Political Science Review* 62 (1968): 144–68.

7. Earl Latham, *The Communist Conspiracy in Washington: From the New Deal to McCarthy* (Cambridge: Harvard University Press, 1966), p. 381.

8. Carl Bernstein, *Loyalties: A Son's Memoir* (New York: Simon and Schuster, 1989), pp. 33, 105–6, 113, 115–16, 118–21. Emphasis added.

9. Latham, p. 381.

10. David Caute, *The Great Fear: The Anti-Communist Purge Under Truman and Eisenhower* (New York: Simon and Schuster, 1978), p. 96.

11. *Thirty Years of Treason: Excerpts from Hearings Before the House Committee on Un-American Activities, 1938–1968*, ed. Eric Bentley (New York: Viking, 1971), p. 333; Ellen Schrecker, *Many Are the Crimes: McCarthyism in America* (Boston: Little, Brown, 1998), p. 329.

12. Alan D. Harper, *The Politics of Loyalty: The White House and the Communist Issue,*

*1946–1952* (Westport: Greenwood, 1969), pp. 23–25; *Memoirs of Harry S. Truman 1946–1952: Years of Trial and Hope* (New York: Da Capo, 1956), p. 281; Richard M. Freeland, *The Truman Doctrine and the Origins of McCarthyism* (New York: New York University Press, 1985), pp. 120–21; Griffith, pp. 40–43, 90–93; Latham; pp. 364–65; Caute, pp. 25–29; Schrecker, *Many Are the Crimes*, pp. 209ff.

13. Federalism, it should be recalled, was a compromise forced upon the Framers. Madison was a nationalist, who conceived of a strong national government as a check against tyrannical states and localities. So was Hamilton, who thought of the national government as an instrument of a continental empire. Inspired by his nationalism, Madison had initially proposed a scheme that ran just shy of "abolishing the states altogether." But loyalty to the states being what it was, his nationalism had to give way. Rakove, p. 169.

14. *United States v. Lopez*, (514U.S.549) (1995) (Kennedy, concurring). Also see Milton Friedman, *Capitalism and Freedom* (Chicago: University of Chicago Press, 1962, 2002), p. 3; Hayek, pp. 183–86.

15. William J. Brennan, Jr., "State Constitutions and the Protection of Individual Rights," *Harvard Law Review* 90 (1977): 489; William J. Brennan, Jr., "The Bill of Rights and the States: The Revival of State Constitutions as Guardians of Individual Rights," *New York University Law Review* 61 (1986): 535–53; Bruce Ackerman, "The Political Case for Constitutional Courts," in *Liberalism without Illusions: Essays on Liberal Theory and the Political Vision of Judith N. Shklar*, ed. Bernard Yack (Chicago: University of Chicago Press, 1996), pp. 212–13, 215–16; Ackerman, *We the People*, pp. 254–57; George Kateb, *The Inner Ocean: Individualism and Democratic Culture* (Ithaca: Cornell University Press, 1992), pp. 42, 70. For excellent critiques, see Edward L. Rubin and Malcolm Feeley, "Federalism: Some Notes on a National Neurosis," *UCLA Law Review* 41 (1994): 903; John D. Donahue, *Disunited States* (New York: Basic Books, 1997).

16. Alexis de Tocqueville, *Democracy in America*, trans. George Lawrence, ed. J. P. Mayer (New York: Harper and Row, 1969), pp. 62–63.

17. Amar, p. 123.

18. This is not to be confused with Hayek's contention that federalism requires both levels of government to work together in order to act coercively. Hayek, p. 185.

19. Thomas I. Emerson, David Haber, and Norman Dorsen, *Political and Civil Rights in the United States*, vol. 1 (Boston: Little, Brown, 1967), pp. 99, 192, 194–205; Caute, pp. 70–74, 568–69.

20. Caute, pp. 339, 341–42; Ralph S. Brown, Jr., *Loyalty and Security: Employment Tests in the United States* (New Haven: Yale University Press, 1958), pp. 92–93, 96–97, 106–7, 169, 178, 181; Emerson, Haber, and Dorsen, pp. 322–39, 348–49.

21. http://www.pub.das.state.or.us/LEG_BILLs/PDFS/SB742.pdf <last accessed on March 30, 2004>.

22. Lee Douglas, "Oregon Law Would Jail War Protesters as Terrorists," Reuters News Service (April 2, 2003); Nancy Chang, *Silencing Political Dissent: How Post–September 11 Anti-Terrorism Measures Threaten Our Civil Liberties* (New York: Seven Stories Press, 2002), pp. 44–45.

23. Emerson, Haber, and Dorsen, pp. 252, 265.

24. *The COINTELPRO Papers: Documents from the FBI's Secret Wars Against Dissent in*

*the United States,* eds. Ward Churchill and Jim Vander Wall (Cambridge: South End Press, 1990, 2002), p. 217.

25. "Red Squad Hits Denver," *The Progressive* (March 14, 2002) (http://www.progressive. org/webex/wxmc031402.html) <last accessed on March 30, 2004>; Tom Gorman, "'Spy Files Anger Many in Denver," *Los Angeles Times* (September 24, 2002). For other contemporary examples, see Ian Demsky, "TBI Took Names at MTSU Peace Rally," *The Tennessean* (March 6, 2003), p. 1A; Ian Demsky, "Taking Names Was Mistake, TBI Says," *The Tennessean* (March 7, 2003), p. 1A; Matthew Rothschild, "Cop Makes Midnight Raid of Teacher's Classroom," *The Progressive* (May 10, 2003) (http://www.progressive.org/mcwatch03/mc051003.html) <last accessed on March 30, 2004>; Eric Lichtblau, "F.B.I. Scrutinizes Antiwar Rallies," *New York Times* (November 23, 2003), p. A1.

26. Emerson, Haber, and Dorsen, pp. 247–49, 269; Brown, pp. 110–12.

27. Richard M. Fried, *Nightmare in Red: The McCarthy Era in Perspective* (New York: Oxford University Press, 1990), pp. 105, 159; Emerson, Haber, and Dorsen, p. 212; Schrecker, *Many Are the Crimes*, pp. 391–94.

28. Rothschild, "Red Squad Hits Denver."

29. For some scholars, reducing the rule of law to the "law of rules"—that is, to mere procedures—misses the aspirations of the law: its commitment to robust individual rights, its moral vision of fairness and equity. The rule of law, these scholars claim, contains substantial principles of justice, a higher law if you will. By restricting myself to the procedural, I do not mean to suggest that the rule of law excludes these substantive claims. Indeed, I am quite sympathetic to interpretations that highlight them, and agree that the strictly procedural often contains, at least implicitly, substantive principles of justice. I only focus here on the procedural because it is law's procedures, according to many writers, that preclude or make difficult rule by fear. For procedural interpretations, see Antonin Scalia, "The Rule of Law as a Law of Rules," 56 *University of Chicago Law Review* 1175 (1989); Joseph Raz, *The Authority of Law* (New York: Oxford University Press), p. 210. For more substantive interpretations, see John Rawls, *A Theory of Justice* (Cambridge: Harvard University Press, 1971), p. 58; Judith Shklar, *Legalism: Law, Morals, and Political Trials* (Cambridge: Harvard University Press), pp. 39–47; 120–21; Ronald Dworkin, *A Matter of Principle* (Cambridge: Harvard University Press, 1985), pp. 9–28.

30. "Freedom of Men under Government," writes Locke, entails among other things "not to be subject to the inconstant, uncertain, unknown, Arbitrary Will of another Man." According to Rawls, if laws are "vague and imprecise, what we are at liberty to do is likewise vague and imprecise. The boundaries of our liberties are uncertain. And to the extent that this is so, liberty is restricted by a reasonable fear of its exercise." Hayek claims that "the coercion which a government must still use . . . is reduced to a minimum and made as innocuous as possible by restraining it through known general rules, so that in most instances the individual need never be coerced unless he has placed himself in a position where he knows he will be coerced. Even where coercion is not avoidable, it is deprived of its most harmful effects by being confined to limited and foreseeable duties, or at least made independent of the arbitrary will of another person." When "there is a general and drastic deterioration in legality," argues Fuller, "the principal object of government seems to be, not that of

giving the citizen rules by which to shape his conduct, but to frighten him into impotence." What the rule of law seeks to prevent, writes Shklar, is fear "created by arbitrary, unexpected, unnecessary, and unlicensed acts of force." Locke, 2.22, p. 284; Rawls, p. 239; Hayek, p. 21; Lon Fuller, *The Morality of Law* (New Haven: Yale University Press, 1964), p. 40; Shklar, "The Liberalism of Fear," p. 29.

31. Rawls, p. 241. Also see Hayek, pp. 21, 142.

32. Rawls, pp. 240–41; Shklar, "The Liberalism of Fear," p. 29; Hayek, pp. 21, 137, 142.

33. Anne Applebaum, *Gulag: A History* (New York: Doubleday, 2003), pp. 121–26.

34. Schrecker, *Many Are the Crimes*, pp. 361, 532.

35. Fuller, p. 40.

36. David Rieff, "Were Sanctions Right?" *New York Times Magazine* (July 27, 2003), p. 44.

37. Applebaum, p. 122.

38. Emerson, Haber, and Dorsen, pp. 98–99.

39. Schrecker, *Many Are the Crimes*, pp. 190–200; Emerson, Haber, and Dorsen, p. 121. Also see Michael R. Belknap, *Cold War Political Justice: The Smith Act, the Communist Party, and American Civil Liberties* (Westport: Greenwood Press, 1977); Peter L. Steinberg, *The Great "Red Menace": United States Prosecutuion of American Communists, 1947–1952* (Westport: Greenwood Press, 1984).

40. Emerson, Haber, and Dorsen, pp. 147–53, 182, 185; Ellen Schrecker, "McCarthyism and the Decline of American Communism, 1945–1960," in *New Studies in the Politics and Culture of U.S. Communism*, ed. Michael E. Brown, et al. (New York: Monthly Review Press, 1993), 123–40. For a list of the 197 organizations cited on the attorney general's list, see Ellen Schrecker, *The Age of McCarthyism: A Brief History with Documents*, 2nd ed. (Boston: Bedford, 2002), pp. 190–96.

41. Emerson, Haber, and Dorsen, pp. 186–90; Mary Sperling McAuliffe, *Crisis on the Left: Cold War American Politics and American Liberalism, 1947–1954* (Amherst: University of Massachusetts Press, 1978), pp. 132–44; William W. Keller, *The Liberals and J. Edgar Hoover: Rise and Fall of a Domestic Intelligence State* (Princeton: Princeton University Press, 1989), pp. 65–67.

42. Emerson, Haber, and Dorsen, pp. 115–47.

43. Emerson, Haber, and Dorsen, pp. 147–78.

44. Emerson, Haber, and Dorsen, pp. 281–350; Schrecker, *The Age of McCarthyism*, pp. 171–87; Schrecker, *Many Are the Crimes*, pp. 266–358.

45. Emerson, Haber, and Dorsen, pp. 419–23.

46. For an exhaustive inventory of fear under McCarthyism, see Shrecker, *Many Are the Crimes*, pp. 359–415.

47. For the latter claim, see Stanley I. Kutler, *The American Inquisition: Justice and Injustice in the Cold War* (New York: Hill and Wang, 1982).

48. For examples from the 1960s, see Churchill and Vander Wall, pp. 143, 183–84.

49. *Dennis et al. v. United States*, 341 U.S. 494 (1951) (Frankfurter, concurring).

50. John Cogley, *Report on Blacklisting: Volume 2: Radio–Television* (Fund for the Republic, 1956), pp. 1–4.

51. Cogley, pp. 100–101, 171.

52. Some theorists define civil society as a "third way" between or beyond the state and the market. Given the intimate involvement of civil society in the market—from the Catholic Church's real estate holdings to labor unions to civic associations like the

Chamber of Commerce; virtually all of these organizations, it should be pointed out, are also employers—I see no basis for this definition. If we equate civil society solely with voluntary, noneconomic associations, with minimal to no involvement in the market, we would have to exclude universities, professional associations, religious institutions, political parties, social movements, the family, and many other organizations, leaving us with little more than the PTA, the Rotary Club, and the Jaycees.

53. *Federalist* 51, p. 321.

54. Contemporary advocates of civil society are not blind to its oppressive dimensions, but they conceive of these oppressions along a distinctive axis. In Robert Putnam's formulation, what distinguishes positive and negative "social capital" is whether it "bridges" or "bonds." Bonding organizations connect us to people like us, bridging organizations to people who are different. While bonding organizations have their benign or useful qualities, the specter of exclusion, intolerance, and hatred of outsiders always hangs over them. We cannot eliminate bonding organizations, nor would we wish to. But we must make sure, to the extent that we can, that they educate citizens in the values of tolerance and mutual accommodation, not narrow group identities and exclusion. For theorists of civil society, in other words, trouble in civil society tracks issues of identity and membership, who is included and excluded, not repression and fear. Robert D. Putnam, *Bowling Alone: The Collapse and Revival of American Community* (New York: Simon and Schuster, 2000), pp. 22–24, 350–63. Also see Amy Gutmann, "Freedom of Association: An Introductory Essay," in *Freedom of Association* (Princeton: Princeton University Press, 1998), pp. 3–32.

55. William Preston, Jr., *Aliens and Dissenters: Federal Suppression of Radicals, 1903–1933* (New York: Harper and Row, 1963), p. 221; Robert K. Murray, *Red Scare: A Study in National Hysteria, 1919–1920* (New York: McGraw-Hill, 1955), p. 251; Robert Justin Goldstein, *Political Repression in Modern America: From 1870 to the Present* (Cambridge: Schenkman, 1978), pp. 156, 160.

56. Brown, p. 181; Griffin Fariello, *Red Scare: Memories of the American Inquisition* (New York: Avon, 1995), p. 43.

57. *West Virginia State Board of Education v. Barnette* (319 U.S. 624).

58. Brown, pp. 147, 149; Schrecker, *Many Are the Crimes*, p. 397.

59. Schrecker, *Many Are the Crimes*, p. 304. Also see Brown, pp. 109–16; Kutler, pp. 152–82; Jerold S. Auerbach, *Unequal Justice: Lawyers and Social Change in Modern America* (New York: Oxford University Press, 1976), pp. 231–62.

60. Brown, pp. 130, 136, 146–48.

61. Nancy Chang, *Silencing Political Dissent: How Post–September 11 Anti-Terrorism Measures Threaten Our Civil Liberties* (New York: Seven Stories Press, 2002); Nat Hentoff, *The War on the Bill of Rights and the Gathering Resistance* (New York: Seven Stories Press, 2003); David Cole, *Enemy Aliens* (New York: The New Press, 2003).

62. Mary Beth Sheridan, "Backlash Changes Form, Not Function," *Washington Post* (March 4, 2002), p. B1. Also see Jacob H. Fries, "Complaints of Anti-Arab Bias Crimes Dip, but Concerns Linger," *New York Times* (October 22, 2001), p. B8; "Hearing for Pakistani Student," *New York Times* (November 15, 2001), p. B6; Susan Sachs, "For Many American Muslims, Complaints of Quiet but Persistent Bias," *New York Times* (April 25, 2002), p. A16; "Bias Incidents Against Muslims Are Soaring, Islamic Council Says," *New York Times* (May 1, 2002), p. A22; Hillary Russ,

"Credit Card Companies Close Muslim Accounts," *City Limits* (April 15, 2003); Susan Saulny, "Muslim Workers Claim Bias at the Plaza," *New York Times* (October 1, 2003), p. B3; American-Arab Anti-Discrimination Committee, "Hotel Employee Removed by Secret Service Before Bush Fundraiser on the Basis of Name Mohamed," Press Release (December 5, 2003).

63. Howard Kurtz, "Peter Arnett, Back in the Minefield," *Washington Post* (March 31, 2003), p. C1; Doug Ireland, "Honesty: The Worst Policy," *Tom Paine* (March 31, 2003); David Bauder, "NBC Severs Ties with Journalist Arnett," Associated Press (March 31, 2003); Matt Moline, "MSNBC's Banfield: Media Filtered Realities of War," *Topeka Capital-Journal* (April 25, 2003); Andrew Grossman, "NBC News Correspondent Ashleigh Banfield Has Ripped Television News Networks," *Hollywood Reporter* (April 28, 2003); "NBC's Banfield Chided Over Criticism," *Hollywood Reporter* (April 29, 2003); Jim Rutenberg, "From Cable Star to Face in the Crowd," *New York Times* (May 5, 2003), p. C1; "Amanpour: CNN Practices Self-Censorship," *USA Today* (September 4, 2003); "CNN Gives Christiane 'Private' Dress Down," *New York Post* (September 16, 2003), p. 83.

64. "Ex–Fox News Staffer on the Memo," (October 31, 2003) (http://www.poynter.org/forum/?id=thememo) <last accessed on March 30, 2004>; Tim Rutten, "Miles From 'Fair and Balanced,'" *Los Angeles Times* (November 1, 2002), p. E1. For other examples, see Matthew Rothschild, "Another Prize-Winning Journalist Fired," *The Progressive* (March 9, 2002) (http://www.progressive.org/webex/wxmc030902.html) <last accessed on March 30, 2004>; David Kirkpatrick, "Mr. Murdoch's War," *New York Times* (April 7, 2003), p. C1; Andrew Buncombe, "US Cartoonists Under Pressure to Follow the Patriotic Line," *The Independent* (June 23, 2002), p. 16; Paul Farhi, "For Broadcast Media, Patriotism Pays," *Washington Post* (March 28, 2003), p. C1; Janine Jackson, Peter Hart, and Rachel Cohen, "FAIR's Third Annual 'Fear & Favor' Report, 2002: How Power Shapes the News," in *Censored 2004: The Top 25 Censored Stories*, ed. Peter Phillips and Project Censored (New York: Seven Stories Press, 2004), pp. 283–96.

65. For the memo's full text, see http://www.poynter.org/medianews/memos.htm <last accessed on December 15, 2003>. Also see Rothschild, "Another Prize-Winning Journalist Fired"; Buncombe, "US Cartoonists Under Pressure," p. 16.

66. Bill Berkowitz, "AmeriSnitch," *The Progressive* (May 2002) (http://www.progressive.org/May%202002/berko502.html) <last accessed on March 30, 2004>; Ritt Goldstein, "US Planning to Recruit One in 24 Americans as Citizen Spies," *Sydney Morning Herald* (July 15, 2002) (http://www.smh.com.au/articles/2002/07/14/1026185141232.html) <last accessed on March 30, 2004>; David Lindorff, "When Neighbors Attack," *Salon* (August 6, 2002).

67. Matthew Rothschild, "OfficeMax Rats Out Its Customers," *The Progressive* (March 13, 2002) (http://www.progressive.org/webex/wxmc031302.html) <last accessed on March 30, 2004>; Phillip Swann, "Is Your Television Watching You?" *Television-Week* (March 03, 2003) (http://www.tvweek.com/technology/030303isyourtv.html) <last accessed on March 30, 2004>; Erik Baard, "Buying Trouble," *Village Voice* (July 24, 2002), p. 34.

68. Ann Davis, "FBI Listed People Wanted for Questioning, but Out-of-Date Versions Dog the Innocent," *Wall Street Journal* (November 19, 2002), p. A1. Also see Na-

tional Crime Prevention and Privacy Compact Council, "Notice of Intent to Publish a Rule Permitting the Privatization of Noncriminal Justice History Record Check Functions," (February 19, 2003).

69. Cogley, pp. 89–91.

70. *Federalist* 10, p. 127.

71. Churchill and Vander Wall, pp. 92–93, 110–11, 139; also see pp. 103, 114, 120, 125; Ruth Rosen, "When Women Spied on Women," *The Nation* (September 4/11, 2000), p. 20.

72. Caute, p. 405; Ceplair and Englund, p. 260; O'Reilly, p. 172–73, 185; Schrecker, *Many Are the Crimes*, p. 375.

73. On informers in the United States, see Schrecker, *Many Are the Crimes*, pp. 107, 228; O'Reilly, pp. 83–88, 173–87; Sayre, p. 13; Rosen, pp 18–25.

74. Ralph Waldo Emerson, "Self-Reliance," in *Essays: First and Second Series* (New York: Vintage, 1990), pp. 34–35.

75. Cogley, p. 12.

76. Alvah Bessie, *Inquisition in Eden* (New York: Macmillan, 1965), pp. 243–45.

77. Joseph de Maistre, *Considerations on France*, ed. Richard A. Lebrun (New York: Cambridge University Press, 1974, 1994), pp. 77–79.

78. Churchill and Vander Wall, pp. 92–93, 97, 110–101, 118–19, 125–26, 133, 135–37, 146, 159, 181–83, 185–86.

## 8: UPSTAIRS, DOWNSTAIRS

1. Alexis de Tocqueville, *Democracy in America*, trans. George Lawrence, ed. J. P. Mayer (New York: Harper and Row, 1969), p. 550; Frederick Douglass, *Narrative of the Life of Frederick Douglass* (Mineola: Dover, 1995), p. 68; Ralph Waldo Emerson, "Self-Reliance," in *Essays: First and Second Series* (New York: Vintage, 1990), pp. 33–34; Walt Whitman, "I Hear America Singing," in *Walt Whitman: The Complete Poems*, ed. Francis Murphy (New York: Penguin, 1975), p. 47; Judith N. Shklar, *American Citizenship: The Question of Inclusion* (Cambridge: Harvard University Press, 1991), pp. 63–101; Daniel T. Rodgers, *The Work Ethic in Industrial America 1850–1920* (Chicago: University of Chicago Press, 1974, 1978).

2. Benjamin Franklin, *The Autobiography of Benjamin Franklin* (Mineola: Dover, 1996), pp. 15–16.

3. John Dewey, *The Public and Its Problems* (Athens: Ohio University Press, 1927, 1954), pp. 134, 143, 147; Robert A. Dahl, *Democracy and Its Critics* (New Haven: Yale University Press, 1991).

4. I am grateful to Nancy Grey for this insight.

5. *Unfair Advantage: Workers' Freedom of Association in the United States Under International Human Rights Standards* (New York: Human Rights Watch, 2000), p. 73.

6. George Wilson Pierson, *Tocqueville in America* (Baltimore: Johns Hopkins University Press, 1996, 1938), p. 500.

7. W. E. B. DuBois, *Black Reconstruction in America* (New York: Free Press, 1999), p. 693.

8. *The COINTELPRO Papers: Documents From the FBI's Secret Wars Against Dissent in the United States*, ed. Ward Churchill and Jim Vander Wall (Cambridge: South End Press, 1990, 2002), pp. 184, 198–201.

9. See Richard B. Freeman and Joel Rogers, *What Workers Want* (Ithaca: Cornell University Press, 1999), pp. 122–27; "Whistle-Blowers Being Punished, A Survey Shows," *New York Times* (September 3, 2002), p. A14; Matthew Barakat, "Whistle-Blower Priest in Trouble with Diocese," Associated Press Wire Service (December 2, 2002).

10. Paul Magnusson, "Toting the Casualties of War," *Business Week Online* (February 6, 2003) (http://www.businessweek.com/bwdaily/dnflash/feb2003/nf2003026_0167_db052.htm) <last accessed on March 30, 2004>; William J. Broad, "U.S. Civilian Experts Say Bureaucracy and Infighting Jeopardize Search for Weapons," *New York Times* (April 16, 2003), p. B2; Greg Gordon, "Minneapolis FBI Agent Told She Will Be Fired for Hurting Bureau's Image," *Star Tribune* (May 1, 2003), p. 7B.

11. Lawrence Mishel, Jared Bernstein, and Heather Boushey, *The State of Working America* (Ithaca: Cornell University Press, 2003), pp. 189–96.

12. Cited in Edward W. Said, *Orientalism* (New York: Vintage, 1978, 1994), p. xiii.

13. Freeman and Rogers, pp. 103–7, 213–14; David M. Gordon, *Fat and Mean: The Corporate Squeeze of Working Americans and the Myth of Managerial Downsizing* (New York: Free Press, 1996), p. 75.

14. Warren St. John, "Upstairs, Downstairs on the High Seas," *New York Times* (August 3, 2003), Sec. 9, p. 2.

15. John Schwartz, "As Enron Purged Its Rank, Dissent Was Swept Away," *New York Times* (February 4, 2002), p. C1.

16. Jill Andresky Fraser, *White-Collar Sweatshop: The Deterioration of Work and Its Rewards in Corporate America* (New York: Norton, 2001), pp. 32–33.

17. Freeman and Rogers, pp. 40–47, 60–62; Gordon, pp. 110–14.

18. Gordon, pp. 35, 38–39, 44, 71–72; also see Freeman and Rogers, p. 10.

19. Randy Hodson, *Dignity at Work* (New York: Cambridge University Press, 2001), pp. 74, 87, 93–97, 147–48.

20. Barbara Ehrenreich, *Nickel and Dimed: On (Not) Getting By in Boom-Time America* (New York: Metropolitan, 2001), pp. 24, 59, 122, 126–27.

21. Marc Linder and Ingrid Nygaard, *Void Where Prohibited: Rest Breaks and the Right to Urinate on Company Time* (Ithaca: Cornell University Press, 1998), pp. 2–3, 8, 44, 55–56, 174.

22. Marc Linder, *Void Where Prohibited Revisited: The Trickle-Down Effect of OSHA's At-Will Bathroom-Break Regulation* (Iowa City: Fǎpìhuà Press, 2003), pp. 7, 139–85, 197–277, 301–40; Corey Robin, "Lavatory and Liberty: The Secret History of the Bathroom Break," Boston Globe (September 29, 2002), p. D1.

23. Ehrenreich, p. 83.

24. Fraser, pp. 194–95, 197.

25. My calculation of the unionized sector of the workforce reflects not the actual number of union members in the United States but the total number of workers covered by a union or employee association contract. In 2003, that number was 17,448,000 workers, or 14.3 percent of the workforce. (The actual number of union members in 2003 was 15,776,000 or 12.9 percent of the workforce.) The overall number of public employees in the United States in 2003 was 19,710,000, or 16.1 percent of the workforce. Of these public employees, 8,185,000, or 41.5 percent of the total, were covered by a union contract. To avoid counting these unionized, public employees twice, I

subtracted the 8,185,000 from the overall total of public employees. See United States Department of Labor Bureau of Labor Statistics, *Union Members in 2003* (news release) (January 21, 2004) http://www.bls.gov/news.release/pdf/union2.pdf) <<last accessed on March 30, 2004>>.

26. Wayne N. Outten, Robert J. Rabin, and Lisa R. Lipman, *The Rights of Employees and Union Members* (Carbondale: Southern Illinois University Press, 1994), pp. 10–39; Freeman and Rogers, p. 216; *The American Bar Association Guide to Workplace Law* (New York: Three Rivers Press, 1997), pp. 31, 6–65, 78–79.

27. Though a few state courts have abridged this doctrine in individual cases, their decisions are spotty and rarely accumulate the force of precedent. See Outten et al., pp. 26–28; *American Bar Association Guide*, pp. 66–67, 84–85.

28. Outten et al., pp. 20, 24–26, 29–30, 526–27, 544–57; *American Bar Association Guide*, pp. 80–82, 91.

29. Outten et al., p. 10, 500–504; *American Bar Association Guide*, pp. 31, 64–65, 78–79.

30. On the rules of unemployment compensation, see *American Bar Association Guide*, pp. 93–96; Outten et al., pp. 144–45.

31. Robin Leidner, *Fast Food, Fast Talk: Service Work and the Routinization of Everyday Life* (Berkeley: University of California Press, 1993), p. 9.

32. Cited in Outten et al, p. 505.

33. *American Bar Association Guide*, p. 131.

34. Ehrenreich, pp. 144, 156, 186–87.

35. Outten et al., pp. 483–87; *American Bar Association Guide*, pp. 35–36.

36. Outten et al., pp. 493–95, 504; *American Bar Association Guide*, p. 64; Ehrenreich, p. 24.

37. Outten et al., pp. 492–93; Fraser, p. 89.

38. Outten et al., pp. 495–96.

39. Fraser, pp. 87–89.

40. Outten et al., pp. 11–16, 479–82; Ehrenreich, p. 58.

41. George Bailey, "Manager's Journal: Fear Is Nothing to Be Afraid Of," *Wall Street Journal* (January 27, 1997), p. A22. Also see Gordon, pp. 111, 115; Ehrenreich, pp. 38, 41; Freeman and Rogers, p. 127.

42. Gordon, pp. 61–75.

43. Cited in Gordon, p. 66.

44. Fraser, p. 155.

45. Fraser, p. 156.

46. *Your Father's Union Movement: Inside the AFL-CIO*, ed. Jo-Ann Mort (New York: Verso, 1998).

47. Marty Jay Levitt with Terry Conroy, *Confessions of a Union Buster* (New York: Crown, 1993), pp. 16–17.

48. Karen Orren, *Belated Feudalism: Labor, the Law, and Liberal Development* (New York: Cambridge University Press, 1991).

49. Freeman and Rogers, pp. 68–69, 81–89; Kate Bronfenbrenner and Tom Juravich, "It Takes More Than House Calls: Organizing to Win with a Comprehensive Union-Building Strategy," in *Organizing to Win: New Research on Union Strategies*, ed. Kate Bronfenbrenner et al. (Ithaca: Cornell University Press, 1998), pp. 20, 27.

50. Cited in *Unfair Advantage*, p. 71.

51. Freeman and Rogers, pp. 62, 88, 211.

52. *Unfair Advantage*, pp. 7–8, 71–74. Also see Freeman and Rogers, p. 62; Kate Bronfenbrenner, "The Effects of Plant Closing or the Threat of Plant Closing on the Right of Workers to Organize," report submitted to the Labor Secretariat of the North American Commission for Labor Cooperation (September 1996).

53. Levitt, p. 13.

54. *National Labor Relations Act*, Section 8(c).

55. Levitt, p. 17.

56. *Unfair Advantage*, pp. 21–22.

57. *Unfair Advantage*, pp. 9–10, 84; also see pp. 67–68.

58. Thomas Geoghegan, *Which Side Are You On? Trying to Be for Labor When It's Flat on Its Back* (New York: Penguin, 1991), pp. 253, 255.

59. Robert Michael Smith, *From Blackjacks to Briefcases: A History of Commercialized Strikebreaking and Unionbusting in the United States* (Athens: Ohio University Press, 2003), p. 109.

60. Nelson Lichtenstein, personal communication, March 30, 2004.

61. *Unfair Advantage*, pp. 171–78.

62. *Unfair Advantage*, pp. 181–90.

63. Geoghegan, p. 165.

64. *Unfair Advantage*, p. 84.

65. *Unfair Advantage*, pp. 63–69. Also see Geoghegan, pp. 254–55.

66. Levitt, pp. 59, 13. Also see Smith, *From Blackjacks to Briefcases*, p. 114.

67. See Orren, *Belated Feudalism*, and William E. Forbath, *Law and the Shaping of the American Labor Movement* (Cambridge: Harvard University Press, 1991).

68. *Unfair Advantage*, p. 17; Robert A. Gorman, *Basic Text on Labor Law: Unionization and Collective Bargaining* (St. Paul, Minn.: West, 1976), pp. 5, 10–14.

69. Linder, *Void Where Prohibited Revisited*, pp. 7, 139–85, 197–277, 301–40; Freeman and Rogers, p. 127.

70. Milton Friedman, *Capitalism and Freedom* (Chicago: University of Chicago Press, 1962, 2002), p. 15. Also see pp. 4, 23.

71. Levitt, pp. 10, 24, 55.

72. Smith, *From Blackjacks to Briefcases*, p. 113.

73. Charlie LeDuff, "At a Slaughterhouse, Some Things Never Die," *New York Times* (June 16, 2000), p. A1.

## CONCLUSION: LIBERALISM AGONISTES

1. There are three notable exceptions to this claim, and I am indebted to each of them: Rogers M. Smith, *Civic Ideals: Conflicting Visions of Citizenship in U.S. History* (New Haven: Yale University Press, 1997); Karen Orren, *Belated Feudalism: Labor, the Law, and Liberal Development* (New York: Cambridge University Press, 1991); and, in a different, though no less instructive, vein, Arno J. Mayer, *The Persistence of the Old Regime: Europe to the Great War* (New York: Pantheon, 1981).

# INDEX